Light of Reason, Light of Faith

Other Books of Interest from St. Augustine's Press

Dietrich von Hildebrand, *The Heart: An Analysis of Human and Divine Affectivity*

Peter Kreeft, *Ethics for Beginners: "Big Ideas" from 32 Great Minds*

Peter Kreeft, *If Einstein Had Been a Surfer*

Peter Kreeft, *A Socratic Introduction to Plato's Republic*

Peter Kreeft, *Socrates' Children: The 100 Greatest Philosophers*

Peter Kreeft, *The Platonic Tradition*

Peter Kreeft, *The Philosophy of Jesus*

Peter Kreeft, *Socratic Logic (3rd Edition)*

Marvin R. O'Connell, *Telling Stories that Matter: Memoirs and Essays*

Rémi Brague, *Moderately Modern*

Josef Pieper, *Exercises in the Elements: Essays–Speeches–Notes*

Josef Pieper, *A Journey to Point Omega: Autobiography from 1964*

John von Heyking, *Comprehensive Judgment and Absolute Selflessness: Winston Churchill on Politics as Friendship*

Joseph Bottum, *The Decline of the Novel*

D. Q. McInerny, *Being Ethical*

Roger Scruton, *An Intelligent Person's Guide to Modern Culture*

Roger Scruton, *The Meaning of Conservatism: Revised 3rd Edition*

Roger Scruton, *The Politics of Culture and Other Essays*

Roger Scruton, *On Hunting*

Leon J. Podles, *Losing the Good Portion: Why Men Are Alienated from Christianity*

Allen Mendenhall, *Shouting Softly: Lines on Law, Literature, and Culture*

René Girard, *A Theater of Envy: William Shakespeare*

Marion Montgomery, *With Walker Percy at the Tupperware Party*

Charles R. Embry and Glenn Hughes, editors, *The Timelessness of Proust: Reflections on In Search of Lost Time*

Light of Reason, Light of Faith
Joseph Ratzinger and the German Enlightenment

MAURICE ASHLEY AGBAW-EBAI

ST. AUGUSTINE'S PRESS
South Bend, Indiana

Manufactured in the United States of America.

1 2 3 4 5 6 26 25 24 23 22 21

Library of Congress Control Number: 2021931113

∞ The paper used in this publication meets the minimum requirements of the American National Standard for Information Sciences – Permanence of Paper for Printed Materials, ANSI Z39.48-1984.

St. Augustine's Press
www.staugustine.net

To

Joseph Ratzinger/Benedict XVI

Vergelt's Gott, Geliebter Heiliger Vater

Contents

Foreword

On the occasion of the conferral of the prestigious *Ratzinger Prize* 2019 to the first African theologian, Father Paul Bere from Burkino Faso—along with the Canadian philosopher Charles Taylor—Pope Francis paid tribute to the theological accomplishments of his predecessor, Pope Emeritus Benedict XVI, a theological *oeuvre* unprecedented among popes. "He is a seeker of truth, who wanted to keep faith alive also in the present time," the Pope stated. "His aim was to maintain a living faith in spite of changing times and situations," said the head of the Church at the presentation of the *Ratzinger Prize* in a festive ceremony in the Vatican. The faithful, as Benedict XVI underscored time and again, should be able to bear witness to their faith in a language understood by contemporaries, Francis continued. "The theologian and shepherd" Joseph Ratzinger had never locked himself into an abstract culture of mere models of thought. Rather, he had been an example for "a search for truth in which reason and faith, intelligence and spirituality, are constantly connected."[1]

Pope Benedict XVI, as professor of theology, archbishop of Munich, prefect of the Congregation for the Doctrine of the Faith and finally as supreme pontiff, inaugurated what over the long term may be described as "the Christocentric shift." His classics *Introduction to Christianity* and the *Jesus of Nazareth* trilogy initiated an epochal personalist approach to our faith. The Counter-Reformation had placed the Church's juridical nature into prominent focus, Neo-Scholasticism had emphasized the intelligibility of our faith, and transcendental Thomism (K. Rahner) had thematized her philosophical compatibility. Theology, much like faith in general, thrives

1 *Domradio*, November 9, 2019. Cf. https://www.domradio.de/themen/benedikt-xvi/2019-11-09/bewahrer-eines-lebendigen-glaubens-franziskus-wuerdigt-benedikt-xvi-als-theologe-und-hirten, accessed 6/17/2020.

from a living, personal relationship with Jesus Christ. Jesus Christ is *the* singular *universale concretum* to which all people and peoples as well as cultures can relate and, in fact, in whom they discover their deepest personal meaning and supreme dignity in life. It seems not unrealistic to assume this turn of this discipline to the second person of the Blessed Trinity, to Jesus Christ, will define much of 21st century theology.

It belongs to the idiom of members of the German-speaking *Bildungsbürgertum* (cultured, professional segment of society) to reflect in their thinking and actions the message of Gotthold Ephraim Lessing's (1729–81) celebrated "ring parable" in his dramatic poem *Nathan the Wise* (1779). Not one of the three rings of Nathan represents the true religion. The play defines the quintessential attitude of *Aufklärung* and henceforth the public ethos of the average German up to the present: tolerance is the civilized order of the day as God does not reveal Himself to us mortals. Thereby Lessing succeeded in popularizing the rejection of any positive divine revelation as taught by Immanuel Kant (1724–1804) and Georg Friedrich Wilhelm Hegel (1770–1831)—the preeminent *Aufklärungsdenker.* Countless Christian thinkers have attempted to reconcile Enlightenment and the Christian statement: from Friedrich Schleiermacher (1768–1834), via Adolf von Harnack (1851–1930) to Karl Rahner (1904–84).

Influenced by Augustine and Bonaventure, Ratzinger knows of human reason's inherent movement toward faith. On numerous occasions he addressed this issue head-on: in his inaugural lecture at Bonn University (1959), in *Introduction to Christianity* (1968), at the 60th anniversary of the allied landing in Normandy (2004), in his much-discussed exchange with the German philosopher Jürgen Habermas (2004) at the Bavarian Academy in Munich, and again 2008 in the Collège des Bernardins in Paris. Preoccupation with *Aufklärung* is an underlying, constantly recurring *sostenuto* and leitmotif in Ratzinger's thinking.

Nevertheless, the term is not treated by secondary literature on Ratzinger. Embarrassingly, it is not listed as an entry in the anthology of important terms in Ratzinger's theology *Ratzinger/Benedikt XVI, Kleines ABC des Glaubens*.[2]

2 Robert Zollitsch, Institut Papst Benedikt XVI, eds., *Joseph Ratzinger/Benedikt XVI, Kleines ABC des Glaubens, Ein Lesebuch von Abba bis Zweifel* (Freiburg i. Br., Herder, 2014).

Father Agbaw-Ebai's precious study *Joseph Ratzinger and the German Enlightenment* fills this *lacuna*, this sorely missing link. He seems a felicitous representative of a coming generation of African theologians. After Christianity had been shaped in the first centuries, also by North African theologians such as Tertullian, Cyprian, Athanasius, and Augustine, the sudden spreading of Islam over North Africa in the seventh and eighth centuries prevented Christianity from growing south of the Sahara. The only exception is the venerable, alas quite isolated, Christian culture of Ethiopia in the east. Now seems a *kairotic* moment for sub-Saharan African theology to develop her particular idiom and uplifting contributions to the global Church. This comes at a time when both Europe and North America appear to lack an energizing vision.

There is no gainsaying, colonialism was a terrible scourge and its effects cannot be easily overcome. Our redeemer Jesus Christ offered his life magnanimously for all of humankind, large or minor sinners. Perhaps Christianity grows in sub-Saharan Africa precisely because Africans are not embittered about the past and do not harbor rancor, but seek the Holy Spirit working throughout the long history of our Catholic Church. The Catholic Church—this is my firm impression—flourishes whenever her members meditate on the pierced heart of the Crucified Lord.

Father Agbaw-Ebai's original and thorough study *Light of Reason and Light of Faith Joseph Ratzinger and the German Enlightenment*, is a significant contribution to this epochal process. It fills a gap Ratzinger scholars of all continents felt. It is an investigation every serious Ratzinger expert should read. Highly recommended!

Munich, June 19th, 2020 on the Feast of the Sacred Heart

Father Emery de Gaál, Ph. D.
Chairman and Professor of Dogmatic Theology
University of Saint Mary of the Lake
Mundelein Seminary, Chicago, IL

Acknowledgments

If it takes a village to raise a child, so it is with becoming a theologian: we stand on the shoulders of others. My first expression of thanks is to Benedict XVI, whose life continues to offer me the decisive orientation for seeking the Face of Jesus Christ. Gratitude likewise goes to Profs. Brian Dunkle, S.J.; Margaret Guider, O.S.F; Emery de Gaál; and Romanus Cessario, O.P., for their painstaking improvements of the manuscript of this work. Many thanks to Prof. Mary Ann Glendon, Prof. Tracey Rowland, Prof. Paulinus Odozor, C.S.Sp, Prof. Peter Kreeft, and Dr. George Weigel for their helpful recommendations and support.

Appreciativeness also goes to Boston College School of Theology and Ministry, Brighton, MA, and the Institut Papst Benedikt XVI, Regensburg, for providing me with the academic environment thanks to which my thinking regarding this question of Ratzinger and the *Aufklärung* matured. I am grateful as well to Bishop Francis T. Lysinge, Emeritus Bishop of Mamfe Diocese, Cameroon, and Archbishop Andrew F. Nkea, Metropolitan Archbishop of Bamenda, Cameroon, and Apostolic Administrator of Mamfe Diocese, for allowing me to spend so much time in the classroom and in libraries in pursuit of what Ratzinger terms the "pastorality of truth." I wholeheartedly thank Bishop Arthur Kennedy and Bishop Mark O'Connell of the Archdiocese of Boston, for their support and encouragements. Fr. James P. Burns, IVD, has remained an inspirational mentor, and I will forever be in his debt. My thankfulness also goes to my brother priests of Mamfe Diocese, Cameroon, for their love, friendship, and support.

I am indebted to my classmates at St. Thomas Aquinas Major Seminary, Bambui, Cameroon, and Hekima University College, Nairobi, Kenya. Thank you for enriching my life in so many ways. My gratefulness likewise goes to the parishioners of St. Ignatius, Newton, MA; St. Joseph's, Medford, MA; St. Mary's, Georgetown/Rowley, MA; and St. Anne's, Salem, MA. You have taught me that the true enlightenment is Christian faith, hope, and love. To my priest friends in Boston, especially from Eastern Nigeria and East Africa, I say thank you for your companionship. And thank you to the members of the Cameroon Catholic Community of Boston. To my priest friends of the Archdiocese of Boston, I will eternally be in your debt for your generosity and supportive presence. Any scholar needs an echo chamber to try out his or her thoughts. I am grateful to my students at Woods, Boston College, for our critical and engaging class interactions. I am indebted to Virginia M. Greeley of Boston College and James P. Gilbert for the layout of this work. My enduring appreciation goes to Bruce Fingerhut and Catherine Godfrey at St. Augustine's Press, South Bend, IN, for accepting this work for publication.

Studying Ratzinger over the years, I have always been struck by Ratzinger's attentiveness to modern philosophical thought. In other words, Ratzinger's theological reflections mirror a profound engagement with the world of pure reason. I believe it was no sheer coincidence that Ratzinger's 1959 Inaugural Lecture at the University of Bonn reflected this attentiveness to the philosophical world: "The God of Faith and the God of Philosophers: A Contribution to the Problem of Natural Theology." With this Lecture, the Mozart of Theology made the case that human rationality, reason qua reason, cannot exclude truth, the object of the human intellect, from encountering human beings as a person in Jesus of Nazareth, the *universale concretum et personale*, the divine-human *Logos*. This is what this book intends to demonstrate, that is, that the Bavarian theologian is one profoundly rooted in philosophical thought to the extent that by engaging Augustine, Aquinas, Bonaventure, Pascal, Buber, Newman, and others, on the one hand, and Kant, Hegel, Nietzsche, Heidegger, Wittgenstein, and other thinkers who embody that spirit of the *Aufklärung*, on the other hand—that is, thinkers of merely the rational and the logical, Ratzinger helps reason to discover its limits and, precisely by doing so, breaks the barriers and limitations of the Kantian *mere reason*, opening up reason to the broader vistas and enrichments of faith.

Toward the end of his *City of God*, the great Bishop of Hippo had this to say: "From all who think that I have said too little or too much, I beg pardon; and those who are satisfied I ask, not to thank me, but to join me in rejoicing and in thanking God. Amen." (Book XXII, XXX). Every Ratzingerian is, in a sense, a crypto Augustinian, and hence, I make these sentiments of Augustine mine.

Maurice Ashley Agbaw-Ebai
Boston College

Introduction

0.1 Ratzinger, the *Aufklärung* and *Logos* Christo-Ecclesiology

The eighteenth-century Enlightenment movement that swept across much of Europe, notably France, England, and Germany, came to mean different things to different peoples, embodying different strands and currents of thought.[1] Even with the national and cultural specificities, the common element that cut across national boundaries was the appeal to reason as the point of departure in interpreting individual and communal behavior. The *Aufklärung*, that is, the German strand of the Enlightenment, was particularly acute in its interaction and, more pointedly, its challenge of traditional Christian orthodoxy and doctrines. As Alister McGrath points out, "the ultimate foundation of the theology of the *Aufklärung* may be regarded as the doctrine that the natural faculty of human reason is qualitatively similar to (although quantitatively weaker than) the divine reason."[2] McGrath further describes the *Aufklärung* as a *Weltanschauung*, rather than a system of doctrines or methods, a world-view best characterized as moralist, naturalist, and rationalist.[3] At the center of the *Aufklärung*, therefore, was a human-centered perception of reality. The focus was therefore much more immanent than transcendent.

Given this obvious interest in Christian thought on the part of the *Aufklärung*, it is quite predictable that Joseph Ratzinger/Benedict XVI[4] became concerned with the perspectives and positions of the *Aufklärer*. To Ratzinger, the *Aufklärung* marked an enduring criticism of revealed faith, a critique that the Church must continue to engage and respond to, for it touched on the fundamental relationship between faith and reason, between the God of Abraham, Isaac and Jacob and the God of the philosophers. Given the primacy that *logos* or reason has in the Christian imagination, every age must seek anew how to respond to the challenge that comes not only with the tendency of severing the relationship between faith and reason, but, more importantly, with speaking about the faith in a way that is meaningful, reasonable, and accessible. To Benedict, therefore, the criticisms meted against Christianity by the *Aufklärung* are not dated, but continue to be relevant, especially given the pervasive influence of the *Aufklärung* in the post-*Aufklärung* culture, as seen in the anonymous Kantians, Hegelians, Feuerbachians, and Nietzscheans, even in the pews. The mode of thinking that followed the *Aufklärung* has resulted in a situation in which faith is viewed as extrinsic to what is truly human. Ratzinger explains:

> Accordingly, faith would always have to live from borrowed cultures, which remain in the end somehow external and capable of being cast off. Above all, one borrowed cultural form would not speak to someone who lives in another culture. Universality would thereby finally become fictitious. Such thinking is at root Manichean. Culture is debased, becoming a mere exchangeable shell. Faith is reduced to disincarnated spirit ultimately void of reality. To be sure, such a view is typical of the post-Enlightenment mentality. Culture is reduced to mere form; religion, to inexpressible mere feeling or pure thought.[5]

Unmistakably for Ratzinger, the interpretation of faith that came with the *Aufklärung* led to a disintegration of the harmony of faith and culture. And Ratzinger believes that in every age, but more so, especially living in the worldview shaped by the Enlightenment with its radical challenge to the Christian faith, the believer must be able to give an answer to the question of the reason for Christian hope (1 Pt 3:15), doing so reasonably, for as Benedict declared in Regensburg, the person who desires to bring another to faith must do so with good articulation and sound reason.[6] And such is the case because the experience of faith is a sourcc of rational discernment and apprehension as well. In other words, faith is a source of knowledge in its own right.

However, the critique of faith by the *Aufklärung* has lost nothing of its airiness and attraction, two centuries later. And to Ratzinger, this continues to explain, in large part, the unprecedented indifference or hostility toward Christianity, especially in large sectors of the developed world. It would seem that the Christianity that emerged after the *Aufklärung* appears to be, in Ratzinger's own interpretive analysis of Kierkegaard's famous story of the blazing circus, a Christian Church that modern men and women, especially in the large sectors of the Western world, increasingly view as a clown, dressed in fancy costumes.[7] The more the Church seeks to speak about Christ to contemporary men and women and the more theologians put forth one theological insight after another, the more both the Church and theologians are laughed at, for at the end of the day, a clown is always a clown, with fanciful costumes.[8] This interpretation shows a mind unwilling to simply yield to a defeatist vision of the Church and the world.

In the preface to the 1968 edition to *Introduction to Christianity*, Ratzinger again displays his unflattering sense about the state of faith and practice in the life of the contemporary Church. Employing the story of Clever Hans' the lump of gold, Ratzinger calls attention to his conviction that an uncritical accommodation of the Church with the Zeitgeist will end up leaving the Church with the lamentable whetstone, fit only to be thrown away.[9] And to Ratzinger, much of this disinterest or indifference toward all things religious, toward the faith, is in large part an offshoot of the severing of the relationship between faith and reason that came with the *Aufklärung*, which sought to grant an unbridled autonomy to reason, as seen in the thinking of some of its exponents, for example, Kant and Hegel.

After all, there is no denying the fact that the *Aufklärung* as a cultural and philosophical movement sought the exclusion of revealed religion to be replaced, at best, with rational faith, and at worst, with full-blown atheism that declared the death of God. This process of the deconstruction of religious faith was supposed to liberate human beings from fear and install them as masters over nature and their own destiny.[10] How did large sectors of the Western world become engulfed in this systematic rejection or indifference to Catholicism? One could advance many reasons: material prosperity; science; the clerical abuse scandal and the cover up by the upper hierarchy; religious illiteracy; breakdown of culture and family life; the dominance of the entertainment industry with its foremost messages of *eros*, wealth, power and violence that are often antithetical to the Christian message; and many others.[11] While a complex set of factors could as well account for these issues, a this-worldly focus by the *Aufklärung* is certainly a contributory factor.

But what does Ratzinger seek, in the face of this eschewing of religious dogma and revealed truths of faith as challenged by *Aufklärung* philosophical *Weltanschauung*? A dialogue. In other words, Ratzinger is not interested in rolling back the objectively good gains of the *Aufklärung*, such as the value of human rationality in moral discernment, or an attention to the historical dimension of truth claims. Ratzinger graciously accepts the gains of the *Aufklärung*. In his conversation with Jürgen Habermas, Ratzinger takes seriously the opinion put forward on the question as to whether the process of European secularization is an aberration in need of course correction.[12] Ratzinger does not think so. To Ratzinger, what is urgent is to open up spaces of conversation and dialogue so that together the currents of secular rationality and faith might mutually enrich each other. This calls for a deeper insight into the philosophical and theological currents that have shaped contemporary secular societies vis-à-vis the life of the Christian faith in Western Europe and other sectors of the Western world. To Ratzinger, it is legitimate to pose the question of whether "the modern philosophies inspired by the Enlightenment, taken as a whole, can be considered the last word of that reason which is common to all men?"[13] Ratzinger clearly does not think so. To him, modern philosophies born of the Enlightenment "are characterized by their positivist—and therefore anti-metaphysical—character, so that ultimately there is no place for God in them. They are based on a self-limitation of the positive reason that is adequate in the technological sphere but entails a mutilation of man if it is generalized."[14] Positivism mutilates the human person because it reduces the human being to the techno-person, to the mere scientific, the demonstrable, thereby overlooking the profundity of being beyond mere calculability and demonstrability. While Ratzinger does not deny the elements of truth that could be found in positivistic philosophy, he is convinced that these elements of truth are not neutral and universally objective. Ratzinger writes:

> These (that is, the truth elements of positivistic philosophy) are based on a self-limitation of reason that is typical of one determined cultural situation, that of the modern West, and, as such, certainly cannot be considered the last word of reason. Although they seem totally rational, they are not in fact the voice of reason. They, too, have their cultural ties, since they are linked to the situation of the West today. This is why they are not that philosophy which one day could enjoy validity throughout the whole world.[15]

To Ratzinger, therefore, the *Aufklärung*'s positivistic understanding of reason failed to grasp the wider picture of not only reason but of the human being as well, for it reduced the human being to a bi-product of reason, understood as a faculty of cognition, devoid from the wider concept of being, the ground of things. And Ratzinger sees this reductionism as rooted in the technological and productive mindset of the West in which wonder and mystery no longer occupy much space. What dominates is doability: that which is knowable must be doable, and reason is reasonable to the extent that it is doable. The next logical step, therefore, was to subject God and the necessity of God for the human being to this principle of the doable and the provable. At this point, modern philosophy, Ratzinger maintains, transformed philosophy into a hard science, a fateful turn of things for philosophy, and thereby for reason. Ratzinger writes:

> For all the contradictions by which it seems to have been hopelessly fragmented, philosophical thought today is guided by a common basic tendency: by the attempt to turn philosophy into an exact science, to practice it *more geometrico*, as Spinoza put it. This endeavor becomes all the more fateful for philosophy the more the exact natural sciences develop and express themselves in a method, for in the same measure does the distance between the scientific quality of philosophy and that of the natural sciences increase. The universality, the generality, the communicability and demonstrability of the constantly advancing natural sciences, which never cease to

> increase their common treasure of assured knowledge, confront philosophy, which, despite all efforts, has been utterly torn in shreds and whose practitioners understand one another less and less, with scarcely two heads to be found among them who agree.[16]

Clearly, the evidence points to Ratzinger's claim of the fragmentation of philosophical thought, with irreconcilable schools of thought. And whatever interpretation one might give to the thesis and antithetical texture of philosophy today, it is not hard to see that beneath the various positions of thought lies a radical subjectivism that makes any possibility of agreement illusory. Therefore, the desire to turn philosophy into an exact science, at least from the Ratzingerian point of view, leaves philosophy in a much more weakened position, unable to speak uniformly to the human search for meaning in the light of the breath of truth. Ratzinger writes:

> This (i.e., the fragmentation and positivization of philosophy) damages the prestige of philosophy, and it is always making fresh starts, but these now seek, by rigorous limitations of scope and clear definition of method, to make philosophy "positive" in the sense of the natural science, which is limited to what is given and amenable to verification. The history of philosophy since Kant tells of a continuous succession of such attempts. Kant himself tried to take a decisive step in this direction by debunking metaphysics as "precritical" philosophy, by pushing the "thing in itself," that is, the essential depth of the real, out onto the edge of philosophy, to become that which is unknowable by man. To put it very roughly, he reduced philosophy to the analysis of the conditions of the possibility of human knowledge, to the elucidation of the laws of human consciousness.[17]

Granted what Ratzinger says here, it might be helpful to note that Kant's original problem in the *Critique* was *a priori* representation, that is, how it might be possible that *non-empirical representation* can refer or apply to empirical objects. In two subsequent works Kant is compelled to shift his emphasis. That is, instead of reference, his chief manifestation now becomes a certain type of knowledge, from semantics to epistemological facts. But the two problems—*a priori* representation and *a priori* knowledge—were always intertwined in early modern philosophy. Kant calls this synthetic *a priori* knowledge. Modern philosophy calls this analytic knowledge. Kant realized with dismay that the reviewers had failed to grasp his doctrine. Kant switched his emphasis from reference to *a priori* knowledge as the key problem.

With his Transcendental Idealism, Kant sought to resolve the dilemma between Humean skepticism and Lockean empiricism, regarding not only the possibility of knowing, but the establishment of true and certain knowledge. Kant's intention was to demonstrate his own critical stance toward what he considered to be the pretensions of traditional metaphysics embodied by the school of Christian Wolff (1679–1754). Kant considered both the skeptical position of David Hume (1711–1776) and the empirical position of John Locke (1632–1704), which both ground knowledge solely in ideas acquired in the course of individual experience, as dogmatism and dangerous to reason, even though both skepticism and empiricism had equally tried to override dogmatism. Kant proposes the solution of synthetic *a priori* knowledge, that is, knowledge not contingent on experience, as the explanation for the true and necessary knowledge, because *a posteriori* knowledge, that is, knowledge derived from any particular experience, could not justify a claim to universal and necessarily valid knowledge. Because the focus shifts to knowledge, the emphasis shifts to concepts, which is not knowledge, but an ingredient for it. The evidence for synthetic *a priori* knowledge is in the mind, and not in the world. And yet, it is objective evidence, not arbitrary fancy. This is because for Kant, such evidence is in everyone's mind, simply as human beings. This reduction of philosophy to the analysis of the conditions of human knowledge, and hence, human consciousness, becomes for Kant the fulcrum of philosophy. This development made an impact, for good or for ill, for as Ratzinger points out:

> Ever since then, (namely, Kant's *Critiques*), this verdict has determined the fate of philosophy, the scope of which has

> progressively diminished, even though men like Fichte, Hegel and Schelling did try once again to break through into the realm of total reality, more boldly and pretentiously than ever before, taking their stand upon absolute reason and seeking to comprehend the reason of being as a whole. But it was this very attempt to grasp being as reason that led in Feuerbach and Marx to its transformation into the opposite: to the denial of a reason permeating all things, to the absolutization of matter, allied in Marx to the affirmation that there is no such thing as enduring truth, which would depend upon the former spiritual definition of things. Reality, then, is change, and man's task is to intervene in this process of change and himself create truth. From being the measure of man, truth now became his creature.[18]

In other words, once philosophy becomes reducible to mere consciousness and the possibility of knowledge, then the objectivity of truth that is independent to the individual (truth that is antecedent to the subjective individual) is left on a shaky foundation, paving the way for action, for truth easily becomes identifiable with workability. And the desire for action brings matter to the fore, for it is the human being that must fashion matter into his or her own image and likeness. And Marxism embodies this materialistic utilization of philosophy.

At this point, as Ratzinger points out, "philosophy then became a function of the party—party philosophy."[19] But even at this point, there remains in philosophy an inner restlessness, and it could not give up on its desire to inquire about the whole of reality and not just about the possibility of human consciousness or knowledge. And as Ratzinger observes, "the sobering result of all of these attempts was simply that, a century and a half later after Kant's *Critique of Pure Reason*, philosophy still had not become an exact science but, rather, found itself more fragmented and more helpless than ever."[20] In other words, the battle for the direction of modern philosophy attests to the impossibility of reducing philosophy to the exact sciences, as helpful as the notion and practice of exactness in the sciences might be. And if Kant et al. could not achieve this transformation of philosophy into an exact science, Ratzinger sees in Wittgenstein a final attempt to do so:

> The name Wittgenstein stands for the program whose aim is to turn philosophy once and for all into an exact science by causing it to renounce completely all attempts to solve unanswerable questions about reality and to confine itself to the analysis of human language. Even the attempt to elucidate consciousness seems, according to this program, to be too ambitious; that which is immediately accessible is merely the expression of consciousness in language, and it is the structures of language that are elucidated. This is a feasible task and one that yields much valuable knowledge. But it does not fulfill the function of philosophy, for man has to go on living and fill his life with a meaning that extends beyond the bounds of arbitrary theorizing and is to be found in responsibility toward reality.[21]

Certainly, the Viennese philosopher tended to identify philosophy with logic and mathematics, precisely because of the attraction of the exactness of the logical and the mathematical. And this logic of analytic philosophy showed itself in the logical positivism and ideal language philosophy of Wittgenstein's *Tractatus*. It is a logic of the machine, the mathematical and the quantitative, computer logic, very different from the syllogistic logic of Aristotle, or the dialogical logic of Socrates. As Peter Kreeft points out, the philosophical logic of Wittgenstein "is a logic for the hard sciences but not for the humanities [...]. The question is whether logic should match the world (as the old logic tried to do) or whether 'the world' must match the new logic."[22] Interpretations vary. For Ratzinger, as seen above, the logical system of language philosophy in Wittgenstein is a continuation of the pattern of reduction of philosophy to the exclusive domain of the rational. For Kreeft, there is a silver lining beneath Wittgensteinianism, namely, that at the center is neither a new philosophy nor its picture theory of language, but the trans-logical ethics, the mystical.[23] The question whether logic or ethics is the meaning of life for Wittgenstein therefore remains an open one. At this point, however, philosophy is capitulated toward logical clarifications of thoughts, marked by an exactitude discernible in the hard sciences, which inevitably seeks to transform philosophy into such a science, at least, from the Ratzingerian reading of things. At this point, Ratzinger makes this evaluation:

> Something of very great import is revealed by all of this: the moment that philosophy finally submits to the canon of the exact sciences and tries to fit into the last available space in the system of modern thought, this completion of the system leads to absurdity. Where exact thinking is the rule, we are left with the *homme absurde*, who protests (as has happened): "A life that does not know that it has no meaning makes little sense." A man who can no longer transcend the limits either of his consciousness or of his speech fundamentally can no longer speak of anything at all. The language of formulae, of the technical calculus, is the only thing that is left for him. Much as that might be, if man possesses some reason for these formulae, how appallingly little it is if there is nothing more besides. To make positivity an absolute, as Comte prophesied would happen, makes not only inquiry about God, but inquiry about man and reality in general quite impossible. In the process, this turns existence itself into a luxury positivism cannot afford.[24]

Following Ratzinger's argument, the positivism and exactness of modern philosophy has rendered it incapable of speaking to and addressing the concerns of life beyond or outside the logical. Human experiences cannot be restricted to the rationally classifiable, as useful as logical systematization might be. And if language is employed to articulate this scientific exactness of logical thought, such a speech inevitably becomes restricted by the mathematical outlook of things. In effect, rather than communicating the expansiveness of reality, language itself becomes reality. And just as thought had become fixated on the mathematical, language as well is eventually tied to the mathematical and the positivistic. In this sense, language becomes a *play* of words and numbers, for which the wider world owes language conformity, and not the other way around. As Ratzinger points out:

> The triumphantly sober sentence with which Wittgenstein concludes his *Tractatus logico-philosophicus*: "What we

> cannot speak about we must consign to silence" is only apparently logical. The *logos*, the intellect of man, reaches farther than formal logic. Man simply has to speak about the inexpressible if he would speak about himself. He must reflect precisely on the incalculable if his thinking is to touch the sphere of the truly human.[25]

Summarily, Ratzinger is making the case for the type of rationality as exhibited in formal logic—in the case of Wittgenstein—and that rationality typical of the *Aufklärung* in general, in which *logos* was reducible to the rational and thereby misses out on the non-formal dimension of reality, the supra-logical. By closing itself to the supra-logical, *Aufklärung* rationality, its gains notwithstanding, tended to shut itself from the religious in that the religious had to conform to formal logic, a position that inevitably eclipsed the sense of the genuinely mystical that comes about in the encounter with the wholly Other. For Ratzinger, the next step of this process is shutting the door to the core of human experience, to that which accounts for the human reality, for, following Augustine, the meaning of human life finds its fullest and most comprehensive understanding and articulation in God. In a word, the human being is more than rational consciousness, and the inability to transcend that limits the horizon of what it means to be human in the grand scheme of reality, sensible and non-sensible. Thus, philosophy must transcend strict empirical thinking and give up on the desire to conform to the exactness of the hard sciences like physics and chemistry. As Ratzinger puts it, "for good or for ill, we will have to accept the fact that human thought runs in several channels [...]. Philosophy will have to seek its continuity and its universality in something other than an ever-growing heap of commonly accepted formulae." In other words, philosophy possesses a universality and continuity of its own that is not typical of the exact sciences. Added to this universality and continuousness is the timelessness of philosophy, as Ratzinger argues:

> The works of Plato, of Augustine, of Thomas Aquinas, of Pascal, and of Hegel are as topical today as when they were written [...]. What does this signify? That philosophical

> thought must first rediscover itself in a changed situation; that in a certain respect it will always have something to do with "faith," that is, with the attempt to reflect, to purify, and to universalize spiritual fundamental judgments in responsible thought.[26]

This text gives us a clue into Ratzinger's philosophical hermeneutics. His engagement with philosophical thought is meant not only to safeguard the freedom of philosophy to be philosophy, to be itself without being transformed into the exact sciences, but more importantly, to offer philosophy a broader outlook by safeguarding faith's space in philosophical reflection. With the *Aufklärung*'s exactness, there emerged, from the Ratzingerian perspective, a philosophical homelessness of faith, which plunged not only faith but likewise thought into a crisis.

Therefore, engaging the philosophical movement of the *Aufklärung* became for Ratzinger an urgent pastoral necessity, leading to a lively interest in the debate or dialogue between faith and reason. To Ratzinger, if the Church had to make new inroads into the lives of post-World War II and today, contemporary secularized Germans and Europeans at large, it must take seriously the claims and charges of the *Aufklärung*, especially regarding its certainties on science, religion and philosophy, often interpreted in a manner that renders religious faith absurd and irrational. To Ratzinger, while one must not allow oneself to be affected by what he calls "the superficial obligatory optimism of certain trends," one must not only recognize the positive elements of the *Aufklärung* and contemporary culture, but must continue to bring the insights of faith, revealed faith, to bear on the present in order to open the path to the future.[27] Hence, this present work seeks to be a modest contribution to this Ratzingerian overarching goal, namely, to open the present to the future with the healing touch of faith. This is the rationale underpinning this work, which seeks to tell the story of *Aufklärung* as the hermeneutical context of understanding the Christological ecclesiology of Joseph Ratzinger.

This task of opening avenues of rational engagements with the modes of thought of the *Aufklärung* is all the more urgent and necessary for the Christian faith, not just because it is the expedient thing to do, but for another more profound reason: Christianity, as Ratzinger has repeatedly pointed out, is a religion of the *Logos*, a *Logos* that at the fullness of time (Gal 4:4) entered history. When John characterizes Jesus as *Logos*, he is implying two things, says Ratzinger: Firstly, that the idea of rationality is implicit in Christianity as it is essential in Greek philosophy; and secondly, that this *Logos*, reason, is in this specific context, word, *verbum*.[28] In this sense, rationality or the appeal to reason is something that was very early on assimilated from Greek philosophy into Christian thought, in the very initial stages of Christianity's development. John's appropriation of *logos* of Greek philosophy marks an early stage of Christian inculturation. From this perspective, the *Aufklärung's* concern for reason and history are already very much present in Christian self-understanding, centuries before the formal beginnings of the *Aufklärung* in the eighteenth century.

Hence, when Ratzinger takes on the *Aufklärung*, in a sense, he is making a return to the sources of the Christian self-understanding that took roots in the context of Greek philosophy. Ratzinger's approach is, therefore, that of a circular movement between faith and reason, faith and history, theology and philosophy, seeking always to keep both in a dialogical equilibrium. To listen to Ratzinger:

> Philosophy, too, ought not to shut itself within its own material, within what it has itself thought up. Just as it has to pay heed to empirical perceptions that emerge within the various scientific disciplines, so also it ought to regard holy traditions of religions and especially the message of the Bible as the source of perception and let itself be made more fertile by this [...] When philosophy completely blanks out this dialogue with the thought of faith, it ends—as Jaspers once expressed it—in a "seriousness that is becoming empty." In the end, it finds itself forced to renounce the question of truth, that is, it is forced to give up itself. For a philosophy that no longer asks who we are, what we are here for, whether there is a God and an eternal life, has abdicated its role as a philosophy.[29]

For Ratzinger, therefore, severing the link between philosophy and theology constitutes a disservice to philosophy, for by eschewing the ultimate questions of human inquiry, it ends up leaving out the most relevant and significant questions about human existence. This is the sense in which we can understand Ratzinger when he says that "to believe as a Christian means understanding our existence as a response to the Word, the *Logos*, that upholds and maintains all things. It means affirming that the meaning we do not make but can only receive is already granted to us, so that we have only to take it and entrust ourselves to it."[30] In a word, reason and faith ought to be placed in a dialogical relationship, with a mutual enrichment of both.

To foster this rapport between faith and the *Aufklärung*, Ratzinger therefore finds a ready tool in the Johannine appropriation of the Greek concept of *logos*. By taking up the Greek philosophical concept of *logos* as a central theological metaphor to bridge the gap between the *Aufklärung* and Christian faith, Ratzinger enters the history of a long philosophical tradition dating back to Heraclitus (535–475 BC), the philosopher of *logos*,[31] and to Justin the Martyr (100–165 AD). Chronologically, in Heraclitus, one encounters *logos* in a primitive and mainly materialistic way. In Justin Martyr, we read an enthusiastic crediting of Heraclitus, Socrates, and Plato with *logos* in his "First Apology." Justin calls them "Christians" because of it.[32] What Plato had felt, Justin found in Christ. In the *Enneads*, Plotinus subordinates *logos* to "an essentially immaterial being," that is, to the "One."[33] The One is beyond all being, immaterial, utterly different from all. From Heraclitus through Plotinus, and from Irenaeus, Justin, Origen and taken up by Ratzinger, therefore, the concept of *logos* has continued to play a useful role in both philosophical and theological discourses. In all these sources, *logos* find multiple layers of meaning that are relevant to our investigation of Ratzinger's appropriation of this Hellenistic concept, within the context of its Heraclitan philosophical foundations, which is certainly Johannine for the Christian tradition. This historical trajectory will be further elucidated in chapter three, in the consideration of Christ/*Logos* in its multiple appropriations as Ratzinger's response to the *Aufklärung*. For Ratzinger, this Greek concept of *logos* and the choice for philosophy over pagan beliefs by the early church meant "the definitive demythologization of the world and of religion."[34] *Eo ipso*, the choice of *logos* over pagan mythology by the early Church is a choice for truth over cultural myths, illusions, and contradictions. *Logos* is therefore a grounding in the faith, in terms of its application in the Ratzingerian *Weltanschauung*.

In Ratzinger, one discerns a five-fold understanding or appropriation[35] of the concept of *logos* that could be useful in creating a space of interaction and engagement with the *Aufklärung*.[36] In the first place, the *Logos* as the Creative Reason of God is central to Ratzinger's theology of creation. At creation, for example, it is the Creative *Logos* that brings about the cosmos, so much so that Ratzinger maintains that the only proper hermeneutical framework for interpreting creation theology is via the lens of Christology, granted that following the principle of allegory this Creative *Logos* becomes the Christ of God at the fullness of time (Gal 4:4).[37] Ratzinger writes: "Creation is born of the *Logos* and indelibly bears the mark of the creative Reason which orders and directs it; with joy-filled certainty the psalms sing: 'By the word of the Lord the heavens were made, and all their host by the breath of his mouth' (Ps 33:6)."[38] In this sense, where the *Aufklärung* saw reason as autonomous and closed in on itself, Ratzinger will see reason as a reflection of the creative reason of God, and that human reason is not diminished when it opens up to the rationality of faith. For Ratzinger, creation is the decisive enlightenment of history, for it establishes history as truth and love.[39] As will be seen in the later part of this thesis, Ratzinger makes the case that reason as understood by the *Aufklärung* thinkers is not an autonomous entity devoid of any bearings with God. Rather, Judeo-Christian faith rescued matter from the irrationality of pagan myths and indeed elevated matter, which is the material cause of science, to the noble heights of rationality.

Going further, we have the second Ratzingerian appropriation of *logos* as Son, Jesus of Nazareth, who, as Son of God, brings God's revelation, at the fullness of time (Gal. 4:4), to a new and definitive phase.[40] If in former times God has spoken through the prophets, in these latter days, God has spoken through the Son, Jesus of Nazareth. A major conviction of the *Aufklärung* is its understanding of revelation and its insistence on this historically-conditioned nature of revelation. The Sonship of Jesus is not seen by the *Aufklärung* to be unique and exclusive, but at best, exemplary. If such is the state of things, then the figure and teachings of Jesus lose their obligatory character. How can we interpret the gains of the Christological councils with the gains of the *Aufklärung* in a way that Christ can still speak to contemporary men and women because Christ marks the definitive intervention of God into human history? This is the question Ratzinger takes up in his engagements with the *Aufklärung*, as will be shown further on in the work.

The third layer of meaning of *logos* as appropriated by Ratzinger is that of *Logos* as a Person (*Prosopon*), Jesus Christ, whose life and death constitutes the defining moment of the emergence of the new people of God, the Church. Ratzinger argues that faith in the *Logos*, the meaningfulness of being, corresponds perfectly with a tendency in human reason. There is therefore, a staggering alliance of *Logos* and *sarx*, of meaning and a single historical figure, in the man Jesus of Nazareth.[41] In this text, Ratzinger brings together two layers of meaning from the one concept of *Logos*, that is, human reason and human flesh, because *logos*, reason, has become flesh, and thanks to this incarnation of *Logos*, we can hear *Logos* speak.[42] Certainly, there is no disputing the fact that the *Aufklärung* in particular, and the Enlightenment in general, marked a major achievement in terms of underscoring the significance of the dignity of every human being. But with the advance of science and technology, what does it mean today to say someone is a person? Given an ever-increasing utilitarian mindset, what does it mean to say that a person's dignity is intrinsic and inalienable and cannot be disposed of?

The fourth facet of Ratzinger's theology of the *Logos* is that of *Logos* as unity of love, that is, embodying *philia*, *eros* and *agape*. If the *Aufklärung* tended to make the charge that Christianity had destroyed or poisoned *eros*, as one reads in Nietzsche, Ratzinger argues against Nietzsche that in Christ Christianity has a more compelling and humane vision of love.[43] The *Logos* that one has encountered as Creative Reason, as Word, and as Person, is beyond and above all God's Eternal Son, the self-gift of the Father to the world, Love, because, following Augustine, the Father is the Lover, the Son, the Beloved, and the Holy Spirit, the bond between the Father and the Son.[44] And Augustine, in his exegesis on Wisdom 11:20, interprets the Father as the measure without measure; the Son as the number without number; and the Spirit as the weight without weight.[45] This Immanent Trinitarian reality of love finds its fullest expression in the Economic Trinity encountered in the Incarnation of God's Son and the Mission of the Holy Spirit. There is little wonder, then, that Ratzinger began his papacy with the encyclical "God is Love," for this to him constitutes the crux of Christian revelation. *Logos* as love therefore presents a critical space for engagement between the *Aufklärung* and Christian faith, for at its most essential level, Christianity is a religion that understands itself as love.

Finally, we find in Ratzinger, the understanding of *Logos* as the Spoken and Written Word, through which we are able to discern what God has called us to become as believers: "We proclaim to you the eternal life which was with the Father and which was made manifest to us—that which we have seen and heard we proclaim also to you, so that you may have fellowship with us; and our fellowship is with the Father and with his Son Jesus Christ" (1 Jn 1:2–3). The appeal to the senses is very evident: hearing, seeing, and touching. In effect, the fact of the historical entering of the *Logos* into the limits of time and space are known, thanks to the presence of the receiving community called Church, that received and continues to receive the spoken Word of the *Logos*. The critique of the Church by *Aufklärung* is well documented and legendary. In Nietzsche, for example, following "the death of God," the churches will become the sepulchers of God.[46] While not taking the defensive against the *Aufklärung*'s biting criticisms, especially of the institutional Church as seen in Nietzsche and Hegel for example, Ratzinger argues that in spite of all her noticeable failures, the Church is the locus where the Word is not only preserved but proclaimed and encountered. This is a reason why one must continue to be a Christian in and with the Church, because the Church is the locus of encounter with the message of Christ. And this exchange between the *Aufklärung*'s critics of the Church and the Church itself could be viewed anew through the spectrum of *Logos* as the Word, spoken and written, that is preserved and transmitted as a message of hope for contemporary men and women.

In precis, these five usages of *Logos* will therefore provide avenues by which Ratzinger will engage the *Aufklärung*. While they are clearly not exhaustive regarding the connecting concerns between *Aufklärung* and Christian dogmatics, this fivefold interpretation of *Logos* allows Ratzinger to engage key *Aufklärung* figures such as Kant, Nietzsche,

Hegel, and Habermas, to cite a few. As will be seen in the evolution of this work, underlining these appropriations is the figure of Christ, the *Logos* of God, and it is from Christ that Ratzinger is able to draw the applications of *logos* as Son, Person, Word, Unity of Love, and Reason, in his genuine attempts to engage the *Aufklärung*. It is thanks to this method of proceeding that we will be able to enter into the ecclesiological and Christological positions of Ratzinger vis-à-vis the *Aufklärung*, to the extent that the *Aufklärer* did engage the dogmatic claims regarding the Church and the person of Jesus of Nazareth.

0.2 Book Structure

This book is divided into six chapters. Chapter one studies Ratzinger in terms of this historical outline of his life. It studies the philosophical and theological formation of Ratzinger that prepared him for the eventual encounter with the major figures of the *Aufklärung*. There are three things that stand out in this chapter: Firstly, the theological interpretation that Ratzinger gives regarding the circumstances of his birth on April 16, 1927; Secondly, the ecclesiological convictions that emerge from Ratzinger's engagement with Augustine of Hippo, in which the Church, studied from the perspective of the people and house of God, has love or caritas as her animating force. And finally, the question of the figure of Christ vis-à-vis the life of the Church, in terms of both the historical revelation in Jesus of Nazareth and what that means for and in the continuous life of the Church in its past, present, and eschatological mission as apprehended by Bonaventure from the perspective of the Franciscan tradition. What this chapter succeeds in doing is laying the groundwork in terms of the ecclesiological and Christological positions that Ratzinger adopts, from which he will engage the expansive reality called the *Aufklärung*.

Chapter two opens up with a treatment of the broad insights of what characterized the eighteenth-century *Aufklärung* movement. It makes the argument that when the *Aufklärer* define the *Aufklärung* from the perspective of Reason, *sapere aude*—dare to use your reason—what is meant here is not just the faculty of rationality that easily comes to mind when the word "reason" is used. As the German-Jewish historian of philosophy Ernst Cassirer points out, "reason" for the *Aufklärer* connotes all of reality, that is, nature, science, history, politics, economics, and much more:

> Perhaps no other century is so completely permeated by the idea of intellectual progress as that of the Enlightenment. But we mistake the essence of this conception if we understand it merely in a quantitative sense as an extension of knowledge indefinitely [...]. All the various energies of the mind are, rather, held together in a common center of force. Variety and diversity of shapes are simply the full unfolding of an essentially homogeneous formative power. When the eighteenth century wants to characterize this power in a single word, it calls it "reason." "Reason" becomes the unifying and central point of this century, expressing all that it longs and strives for, and all that it achieves.[47]

Clearly, not only did the eighteenth century understanding of reason go beyond the mere cognitive, mere rationality, but this century had a much broader understanding of reason. Reason was perceived to be cross-cultural and all encompassing, of all cultures, all thinking subjects and nations. Reason was the ground of all reality. It was the word that meant everything to all people. And as Cassirer points out, "from the changeability of religious creeds, of moral maxims and convictions, of theoretical opinions and judgments, a firm and lasting element can be extracted which is permanent in itself, and which in this identity and permanence expresses the real essence of reason."[48] Owing to this all-encompassing understanding of reason, therefore, the concept of reason that is front and center in philosophy serves as the ground on which Ratzinger can enter into dialogue with the claims and positions of the *Aufklärung*, and hence serves to bridge the ever-widening gap between the God of faith and the God of philosophers.

Chapter two likewise offers a comprehensive insight into the meaning and implications of the *Aufklärung*, from the perspective of the 1959 Inaugural Lecture of Ratzinger, titled "The God of Faith and the God of the Philosophers." By adopting this lecture as the framework of this chapter, we are able to do two things: Firstly, confront the philosophical prism of Ratzinger in what has certainly remained his most forthright and profound philosophical literature thus far; and secondly, this framework of the inaugural lecture offers us the spectrum on which we might delve deeper into the distinguishing marks of the *Aufklärung* in general as a pan-European and German movement, but also the specific character of the *Katholische Aufklärung*.

What stands out from these philosophical considerations is that one is able to discern a very broad understanding of the *Aufklärung*, thanks to which one can make the case for the plural appropriations of the concept of *Logos* or Reason that will define chapters four and five. Yet prior to this, chapter three offers a historical trajectory of the philosophical and theological understanding of the concept of *Logos*. The advantage this chapter brings to the conversation is that it situates the appropriations of the concept of *logos* by Ratzinger in a historical and theological framework that makes Ratzinger's own appropriations stand out in sharper focus. This chapter offers a panoramic history of the evolution of the concept of logos in Greek philosophy particularly with Heraclitus and follows its logical development in the Fathers especially Justin Martyr, Origen, and Irenaeus. This connection from Greek philosophy and Patristic literature thus sets the background against which one can read the further developments of *Logos* theology in Ratzinger.

Chapter four therefore builds on this broad understanding of reason, taking the Greek concept of *logos* as its point of departure. Because *logos* in its multiplicity has what it takes to act as a ground for all, as the concept of reason did with the *Aufklärung*'s understanding of reason as encompassing all of natural reality, Ratzinger is able to appropriate *logos* as Creative Reason, Son, and Person. These three theological metaphors serve the purpose of a Christological reading of the concept of *logos* from a Ratzingerian perspective.

Chapter five further studies Ratzinger's theological appropriation of *Logos* as Love and *Logos* as Word. As Love, the Incarnate *Logos* is the example par excellence of oblative, sacrificial love that is not an antithesis to eros, which is the deepest and most consuming expression of human love. On the contrary, *Logos* as love provides the human possibility of reconciling *agape* and *eros*. And the fruit of this is the life of the Christian faith in the community called Church, whose identity and mission is that of love. Next, as Word, *Logos* not only makes God's revelation known, but in calling all to the worship of God, brings about the centrality of liturgical worship whose *fons et culmen* is the *oratio rationabilis*, the Eucharistic prayer. From these two theological understanding of the concept of the *Logos*, therefore, is discernable Ratzinger's doctrine of the Church, that is, Ratzinger's Ecclesiology, seen through the lenses of the *Aufklärung*.

Chapter six draws out the theological and philosophical implications of this interchange between faith and reason, philosophy and theology, and the relevance for today's Church. In this chapter, it emerges that the hope that the Church can offer thanks to the historical revelation of Christ, accessed via faith and reason, might be helpful in overcoming the fragmentary seductions of the post-*Aufklärung* contemporary world. Ratzinger presents the figure of Christ as the Church's response to the *Aufklärung*, with the conviction that even for today's secularized contemporary men and women, a second look at the figure and message of Christ could still offer hope and meaning to today's scientific, naturalistic, moralistic, technological, and media-influenced men and women. And since Ratzinger is not without his critics, this chapter likewise pays attention to the central criticism leveled against Ratzinger in the light of the *Aufklärung*, which is essentially the charge that Ratzinger appears unwilling to subscribe to the gains made by the pure reason of the *Aufklärung*.

A Conclusion that ties everything to Ratzinger's philosophical hermeneutics to faith brings the work to a close.

Notes — Introduction

1 Alister E. McGrath, *The Making of Modern German Christology: From the Enlightenment to Pannenberg* (New York: Basil Blackwell Inc. 1953), 9.

2 McGrath, *The Making of Modern German Christology*, 11.

3 McGrath, *The Making of Modern German Christology*, 13.

4 Throughout this work, I will use the names Ratzinger or Benedict XVI interchangeably. However, as a general rule, I will use Ratzinger in texts penned before his election as Pope, and Benedict XVI in writings generally penned during and after his pontificate.

5 Joseph Ratzinger, "Christ, Faith and the Challenge of Cultures", 2. accessed July 21, 2020, at http://www.vatican.va/roman_curia/congregations/cfaith/incontri/rc_con_cfaith_19930303_hong-kong-ratzinger_en.html

6 Benedict XVI, *The Regensburg Lecture* (South Bend, IN: St. Augustine's Press, 2007), #13.

7 Søren Kierkegaard, *Either/Or*, Part 1, ed. and trans. Howard V. Hong and Edna H. Hong, (Princeton, NJ: Princeton University Press, 1982), 30. Ratzinger cites this Kierkegaardian parable in the introduction to his *Introduction to Christianity*. It might be helpful to note that Ratzinger resonates to some degree with Søren Kierkegaard, on reflections related to truth, sacrifice, love, and Christendom versus Christianity. Profoundly influenced by Luther, however, Kierkegaard makes for some incompatibility. Yet the irony is the power and influence of Augustine on Luther as well as the other Reformers, as well as the influence of Augustine on Bonaventure's writings, specifically his theology of history, which Ratzinger takes up in his *Habilitation*.

8 Joseph Ratzinger, *Introduction to Christianity* (San Francisco: Ignatius Press, 2004), 39.

9 Ratzinger, *Introduction to Christianity*, 31.

10 Max Horkheimer and Theodor W. Adorno, *Dialectic of Enlightenment: Philosophical Fragments* (Stanford, CA: Stanford University Press, 2002), 1.

11 Charles Taylor, *A Secular World* (Cambridge, MA: Harvard University Press, 2007), 1–14.

12 Jürgen Habermas and Joseph Ratzinger, *The Dialectic of Secularization: On Reason and Religion* (San Francisco: Ignatius Press, 2006), 75.

13 Joseph Ratzinger, *Christianity and the Crisis of Cultures*, trans. Brian McNeil (San Francisco: Ignatius Press, 2006), 40.

14 Ratzinger, *Christianity and the Crisis of Cultures*, 40.

15 Ratzinger, *Christianity and the Crisis of Cultures*, 41.

16 Joseph Ratzinger, *Faith and the Future* (San Francisco: Ignatius Press, 2006), 75–76.

17 Ratzinger, *Faith and the Future*, 76.

18 Ratzinger, *Faith and the Future*, 77.

19 Ratzinger, *Faith and the Future*, 77.

20 Ratzinger, *Faith and the Future*, 78.

21 Ratzinger, *Faith and the Future*, 78–79.

22 Peter Kreeft, *Socrates' Children The 100 Greatest Philosophers Volume IV: Contemporary Philosophers* (South Bend, IN: St. Augustine's Press, 2019), 209–211.

23 Kreeft, *Socrates' Children*, 212.

24 Ratzinger, *Faith and the Future*, 79–80.

25 Ratzinger, *Faith and the Future*, 81.

26 Ratzinger, *Faith and the Future*, 82–83.

27 Joseph Ratzinger, *A Turning Point for Europe?* (San Francisco: Ignatius Press, 1994), 23.
28 Ratzinger, *Introduction to Christianity*, 189.
29 Joseph Ratzinger, *Truth and Tolerance* (San Francisco: Ignatius Press, 2004), 208–209.
30 Ratzinger, *Introduction to Christianity*, 73.
31 Eva Brann, *The Logos of Heraclitus* (Philadelphia, PA: Paul Dry Books Inc. 2011), 9.
32 Justin, Martyr, *First Apology*, I, 46, in Johannes Quasten, *Patrology* Vol. I. (Westminster, MD: Christian Classics Inc. 1993), 209.
33 Plotinus, *Enneads*, trans. A. H. Armstrong (Cambridge, MA: Harvard University Press, 1989), I, 6, 7.
34 Ratzinger, *Introduction to Christianity*, 138.
35 Throughout this work, the word "appropriation" when used regarding the five-fold meaning of concept of *Logos*, designates the manner in which Ratzinger uses the term, or more precisely, the usage of the term as discernable in the writings of Ratzinger. "Appropriation" does not refer in any way to the Trinitarian implications of the term as found, for example, in Book VI of Augustine's *De Trinitate*.
36 Christopher Collins, *The Word Made Love: The Dialogical Theology of Joseph Ratzinger* (Collegeville, MN.: Liturgical Press, 2013), 82.
37 Joseph Ratzinger, *"In the Beginning ..." A Catholic Understanding of the Story of Creation and the Fall* (Grand Rapids, MI: Eerdmans Publishing Co., 1986), 17–19.
38 Benedict XVI, Post-Synodal Apostolic Exhortation *Verbum Domini*, on the Word of God in the Life and Mission of the Church (Vatican City: Libreria Editrice Vaticana, 2010), 8.
39 Ratzinger, *"In the Beginning ...,"* 14.
40 Second Vatican Council, Dogmatic Constitution on Divine Revelation *Dei Verbum*, 4.
41 Ratzinger, *Introduction to Christianity*, 193.
42 Ratzinger, *Introduction to Christianity*, 346.
43 Benedict XVI, Encyclical Letter on Christian Love *Deus Caritas Est* (December 25, 2005), 3, accessed, December 15, 2018 at www.vatican.va.
44 Augustine, *De Trinitate*, trans. Edmund Hill, O.P. (New York: New City Press, 2012), VIII, 10.14.
45 Augustine, *De Trinitate*, XI, 10.17–11.18.
46 Friedrich Nietzsche, *The Gay Science*, trans. Walter Kaufmann (New York: Vintage Books, 1974), 125.
47 Ernst Cassirer, *The Philosophy of the Enlightenment* (Princeton, NJ: Princeton University Press, 2009), 5.
48 Cassirer, *Enlightenment*, 6.

Chapter One
Joseph Ratzinger: The Life and Intellectual Formation of a Theologian

Much has been written about the life of Joseph Ratzinger, and very fine literature exists that sheds light on the childhood and historical development of Joseph Ratzinger.[1] The goal of this chapter, therefore, is not to repeat their insights, but to allow the historical data to help in setting the stage for Ratzinger's engagement with the specific questions that largely followed the spirit of the *Aufklärung*. Hence, this biographical section will be selective and relevant to the question of how Ratzinger built, over time, the convictions that shaped his theological philosophy of the centrality and necessity of a rapprochement of the dialectics of faith and reason, mindful of reason as the defining Enlightenment maxim, and how, with the aid of the Greek concept of the *logos*, a bridge is built between faith and reason that serves both parties of philosophy and theology.

1.1 Biographical Framework

The consensus amongst Ratzingerian scholars tends to view Ratzinger's life in three stages or phases, that is, the early, middle and later Ratzinger.[2] Mary McCaughey spells out this demarcation thus: "Details of Ratzinger's life are usually divided into three main stages: firstly, his early years growing up in Bavaria and his studies as a seminarian; secondly, the period after ordination and his post-graduate studies up to the Second Vatican Council and thirdly, his work in an official capacity for the Church up to his appointment as the successor of St. Peter, shepherd of the universal Catholic Church."[3] Certainly, this broad division of Ratzinger's life into three phases pays attention to the major changes in his life. They also take cognizance of the theological themes and pursuits he undertook vis-à-vis his historical context. For example, with the collapse of the Berlin Wall in 1989, Ratzinger saw a momentous new era, for he suddenly realized the new field for evangelization in previously atheistic communist countries. The collapse of the Berlin Wall, to Ratzinger, provided an opportunity for Christianity to test itself out once more, as the great absent One, in the lives of many in the post-Soviet republics. And yet, in his own judgment, Christianity failed to meet the challenge of the spiritual void of the hour:

> The year 1989 brought the surprising collapse of the socialist regimes in Europe, which left behind a sorry legacy of ruined land and ruined souls. Anyone who expected that the hour had come again for the Christian message was disappointed. Although the number of believing Christians throughout the world is not small, Christianity failed at that historical moment to make itself heard as an epoch-making alternative.[4]

Given this legacy of spiritual vacuity left behind by Marxism, atheism therefore became an urgent pastoral concern for Ratzinger, as he faced the East. Even in the West, secularism had taken on a new militancy that was beginning to interpret the separation of Church and State as the exclusion of the Church from the public life of the State.

Two aspects of Ratzinger's childhood life bear special significance, owing to the emphasis that Ratzinger himself places on them, viz., the significance of his birth on Holy Saturday which, in other words, is the beginning of the life of faith, and the reality of growing up under the shadow of National Socialism in Germany. In these two events lie an admixture of the Christ, Person, Son, Word, and Unity of Love in the mystery of Holy Saturday, and the consequences of reason detached from faith, in National Socialism. These themes will be taken up in more detail in the subsequent chapters.

It all began on April 16, 1927, when the family of Joseph and Maria Ratzinger welcomed their new baby, Joseph Aloysius Ratzinger, into this world. It was Holy Saturday. Ratzinger, the adult theologian, offers a rich symbolic meaning:

> I was born on Holy Saturday, April 16, 1927, in Marktl am Inn. The fact that my day of birth was the last day of Holy Week and the eve of Easter has always been noted in our family history. This was connected with the fact that I was baptized immediately on the morning of the day I was born with the water that had just been blessed. (At that time the solemn Easter Vigil was celebrated on the morning of Holy Saturday.) To be the first person baptized with the new water was seen as a significant act of Providence. I have always been filled with thanksgiving for having had my life immersed in this way in the Easter mystery, since this could only be a sign of blessing. To be sure, it was not Easter Sunday but Holy Saturday, but, the more I reflect on it, the more this seems to be fitting for the nature of our human life; we are still awaiting Easter; we are not yet standing in the full light but walking toward it full of trust.[5]

One senses the existential realism of Ratzinger in these lines: Life is such that we never completely have it all, but must learn to live with the incomplete, with the brokenness of human nature, for it is only in the full light of eschaton, of the Easter of the culmination of history when the Risen Lord offers all back to the Father, that the longing of the human heart will be fulfilled. The present time, the time of Holy Saturday, is to be lived with the reality of the present, for the future is yet to be.

In his *Last Testament*, Benedict XVI still finds great significance that he was born on Holy Saturday. He says: "Both as a theologian and also in temporal events, which sometimes seemed very Holy Saturday-esque, it has been increasingly impressed upon me. I have also tried to understand it ever more deeply—actually as a title, something considered as a program for my life."[6] When Peter Seewald responds to these words of Benedict XVI by saying to the latter that "your words concerning this are very deep and touching," Benedict XVI replies: "Because it is not just something I thought up, but something bound up with the beginning of my existence, with the ground of my being, which I have not only thought my way into, but lived into as well."[7] It is certainly telling that Ratzinger sees his life as programmatic on the mysteries of Holy Saturday, for this says two things about Ratzinger: In the first place, prior to Holy Saturday, there is the Cross of Good Friday, on which Christ paid the ultimate price for fidelity to his saving mission. The day ends with an apparent failure on the part of Christ. He is unable to save himself from the powerful of the world, a helpless victim to human vengeance of the penned-up charges of blasphemy before the Jewish religious hierarchy, and treason before the Roman political authorities. That is the story antecedent to Holy Saturday.

But that is not the end of the story, for there is Easter Sunday, on which the apparent failure of Good Friday is given a decisive turn-around that reverses everything and sets the record straight regarding what is truly successful, victorious and powerful: "We suffer on account of God's patience. And yet, we need his patience. God, who became a lamb, tells us that the world is saved by the Crucified One, not by those who crucified him. The world is redeemed by the patience of God. It is destroyed by the impatience of man."[8] And that is what Holy Saturday embodies, the saving patience of God.

Ratzinger's theological fascination about the circumstances is again mirrored in his recollections and interpretation of his baptism on the same Holy Saturday:

> Since I was born on a Holy Saturday, this day has had a special meaning for me from the beginning. In my early years it was important to me mainly that this was my baptismal day and that I was, as my parents emphasized with particular pride, the first to be baptized in the newly blessed Easter water. Being born on Holy Saturday brought home to me the privilege of a Baptism that was quite noticeably joined to the Christian *pasch*, that is, that let Baptism's inner origin and foundation for life appear particularly clearly. The tidings of my birthday were thus joined in a special way to the liturgy of the Church; my life from its beginning seemed oriented to this strange coincidence of light and darkness, of pain and hope, of the hiddenness and presence of God.[9]

Certainly, the overarching reading of his baptism on Holy Saturday is based on the theme of hope, which Ratzinger sees in the symbol of the Easter candle that illumines the darkness of the night. There is a passage from death to the Resurrection, and that, to Ratzinger, is precisely what happens to the newly baptized.[10] In a sense, the silence of Holy Saturday is filled with the mystery of hope. But this light is not without challenges, not without forces that are bent on blowing it out: "Again and again there are anticipations of hope—lightning strokes in which suddenly the victory of God seems to break through," writes Ratzinger, "but also again and again darknesses that take everything back and confront us again, relentlessly, with the absence of God."[11] Life is thus a drama between these two poles, these two forces seeking dominance over the human soul.

To Ratzinger, the strange power of the powerlessness of Christian life and witness that suffers on account of God's abandonment, which is precisely God's patience, offers the world the opportunity to be saved. God's patience as well offers the world the opportunity to enter into friendship with Christ, which is life's goal. In addition, the circumstances of his birth and Ratzinger's interpretation of it reflects the sense of provisional nature of all things temporal vis-à-vis God. In other words, it is in the nature of faith not to idolize the present of this world, but to remain permanently on a mission oriented toward God. The purpose of life is to live for and toward God, not allowing oneself to be captured or enslaved by the present moment, attractive and seductive as the present might be. This is the life of faith, of the believer who follows Jesus of Nazareth.

For Ratzinger, the locus of the cultivation and flourishing of this life of faith that began with his birth on Holy Saturday was not only the deeply religious atmosphere of his biological home, but, over and above all, the home of the Church community in which he encountered the mysteries of the faith in the liturgical celebrations. He ruminates:

> Then I got a *Schott*[12] for Sundays, which contained the complete liturgy for Sundays and feast days. Finally, I received the complete missal for everyday of the year. Every new step into the liturgy was a great event for me. Each new book I was given was something precious to me, and I could not dream of

> anything more beautiful. It was a riveting adventure to move by degrees into the mysterious world of the liturgy, which was being enacted before us and for us there on the altar. It was becoming more and more clear to me that here I was encountering a reality that no one had simply thought up, a reality that no official authority or great individual had created. The mysterious fabric of texts and actions had grown from the faith of the Church over the centuries. It bore the whole weight of history within itself, and yet, at the same time, it was much more than the product of human history [...]. The inexhaustible reality of the Catholic liturgy has accompanied me through all phases of life, and so I shall have to speak of it time and again.[13]

Ratzinger's faith journey that began with his birth and baptism on Holy Saturday was clearly nurtured by two factors, viz., the religious life at home, and the liturgical life of his parish community, and these two are somewhat related. By giving the young boy the missals of the Church sequentially, the elder Joseph Ratzinger was clearly introducing and nurturing in his son the knowledge and love of the sacred rites. Given this religious piety of the Ratzingers, perhaps, one could say that instead of the Ratzingers keeping Easter and by extension, the whole liturgical life of the Church, rather the liturgical life of the Church played a vital role in keeping the Ratzingers together, with the center being the mysteries of the faith celebrated in the life of the Church. At this point, one might raise the question: What might be some of the theological insights that Ratzinger arrives at from his reflection on the circumstances of his birth?

Firstly, there is the question about the death of God. Quoting Nietzsche, perhaps oddly approvingly, Ratzinger writes:

> Talk of God's death haunts our time more and more. First, for Jean Paul (Sartre), it was only like a nightmare [...]. With Nietzsche, it was deadly seriousness coming to expression in a shrill cry of dread: "God is dead! God remains dead! And we have killed him!" In the meantime, another fifty years later, people speak with almost academic composure about it and begin to inaugurate a "theology after the death of God,"

> looking about to see how to proceed and to encourage man to prepare himself to jump in to take God's place.[14]

Holy Saturday, therefore, captures the sentiments of the "death of God" for many in the contemporary world. To some, the noun "God" is meaningless, an empty concept that conveys or signifies nothing. For others, owing to one reason or the other, and in most cases, the reality of evil and the effect this has had on the emotive level, to believe in the existence of a benevolent God is an existential impossibility. The conviction that God is dead in either the former or the latter scenario is hence an act of the will for many contemporary men and women. It is not really that they cannot reason through the existence of God, but that they have willed God's non-existence, even if they are unsure about what world emerges from a world in which God no longer exists, that is, where God no longer has any signification.

Secondly, Holy Saturday, besides symbolizing the death of God and all that comes with the decision for rational and emotive atheism, likewise embodies not just the death of God, but likewise the hiddenness of God. It is a day which speaks of the fact of God's obscurity:

> For this is Holy Saturday, the day of the hiddenness of God. It is the day of that frightful paradox that we express in the Creed with the words "descended into hell," descended into the mystery of death. On Good Friday we could at least look at the Pierced One. But Holy Saturday is empty, the heavy stone of the new tomb covers the deceased, everything is over, faith seems definitively unmasked as fanaticism. No God has saved this Jesus who called himself his son. One can rest assured. Those sober ones, who may at times have secretly vacillated in their conviction that there is nothing else, they were right all along.[15]

Holy Saturday speaks, therefore, to the question of spiritual darkness in our world. While the previous reading of Holy Saturday sought to speak to the concerns of decided atheism, this second interpretation seeks to engage the frustration of those that genuinely give faith in God a chance, but continuously feel a powerlessness to their human concerns and struggles, on the part of God. In other words, Holy Saturday captures the sentiments of those for whom, even with the best of intentions, God has become the great Absent One. While for atheism the difficulty lies with faith in God, the religious challenge that comes with the hiddenness of God is much more at the level of an unfulfilled longing bordering on despair, since the "failure" of God to save his Son from death leaves both believer and onlooker with no guarantees that this God who is unable to save his Son is capable of doing anything for anyone.

A third theological insight that Ratzinger draws from Holy Saturday in the light of his natural and supernatural birth has to do with the symbolism of the burial of God and its universal and social implications, which fits into the context of the death of God and the hiddenness of God. Ratzinger writes:

> Holy Saturday, day of the burial of God—is that not in an uncanny way our day? Does our century not begin to become one large Holy Saturday, a day of God's absence, a day when an icy emptiness grows even in the hearts of the disciples so that they prepare for the way home with shame and fear and on their Emmaus journey, gloomy and disturbed, sink into hopelessness, failing to notice that the one thought to be dead is in their midst? God is dead, and we killed him. Did we actually notice that this statement was taken almost word for word from the language of Christian tradition, that we have often enough stammered something similar in our Stations of the Cross prayers without being aware of the terrifying earnest and uncanny reality of what we are saying? We have killed him by rejecting him in the shell of antiquated modes of thinking, by banishing him to a piety void of reality, which becomes more and more a devotional slogan or archaeological curiosity. We have killed him through the ambiguity of our lives that obscured him.[16]

It is perhaps astonishing to see Ratzinger "agreeing" with the Nietzschean characteristic maxim regarding God, though the Ratzingerian interpretation is more nuanced and complex. But what stands out in Ratzinger's perspective is that the questionability of the life of faith and love by Christians is creating a situation of a religious desertification. This is the sense in which contemporary world has become one large Holy Saturday. Thus, Holy Saturday, the day of Ratzinger's birth, becomes a potent symbol for a world making choices that exclude God. Holy Saturday is symbolic of the loss of the sense of hope in the world. And for Ratzinger, this sense of hopelessness is not a spectacle for a despairing nihilism, but rather, a pragmatic program for the pastor. The sense of insecurity, helplessness, and emptiness that is symbolized by Holy Saturday offers an urgent invitation to ecclesial mission. Benedict says:

> For the Fathers of the Church, the parable of the lost sheep, which the shepherd seeks in the desert, was an image of the mystery of Christ and the Church. The human race—each one of us—is the sheep lost in the desert which no longer knows the way [...]. The pastor must be inspired by Christ's holy zeal: for him it is not a matter of indifference that so many people are living in the desert. And there are so many kinds of desert. There is the desert of poverty, the desert of hunger and thirst, the desert of abandonment, of loneliness, of destroyed love. There is the desert of God's darkness, the emptiness of souls no longer aware of their dignity or the goal of human life. The external deserts in the world are growing, because the internal deserts have become so vast. Therefore, the earth's treasures no longer serve to build God's garden for all to live in, but they have been made to serve the powers of exploitation and destruction. The Church as a whole and all her Pastors, like Christ, must set out to lead people out of the desert, toward the place of life, toward friendship with the Son of God, toward the One who gives life, and life in abundance.[17]

On this note, therefore, rather than assuming a despairing tone, Ratzinger turns the lemon into lemonade, seeing, in spite of the sense of hopelessness that comes with the absence of God, an opportunity for Christian hope. And even after stating that today large swaths of society no longer seem to accept the content of the Christian faith and the values inspired by it owing to a crisis of faith, Benedict is still convinced, as he states in the *Motu Proprio Porta Fidei*, that "the people of today can still experience the need to go to the Well, like the Samaritan woman, in order to hear Jesus, who invites us to believe in him and to draw upon the source of living water welling up within him" (cf. Jn 4:14).[18] Consequently, the absence of God who offers hope and meaning to human life all the more renders urgent the mission of the Church as the bearer of hope, in spite of the obvious shadows eclipsing what ought to be the evangelical radiance of the Church and her mission in the contemporary world.

Finally, Ratzinger reads Holy Saturday, the day of his birth, as the expression of God's solidarity with humanity in the experience of the crushing reality of death, and the experience of the silent tomb:

> The darkness of God of this day, of this century, which is becoming more and more a Holy Saturday, addresses our conscience—it has something to do with us too. But despite everything it also has something consoling about it. For God's dying in Jesus Christ is at the same time an expression of his radical solidarity with us. The darkest mystery of faith is simultaneously the brightest sign of a hope that is without limits. And one thing further: only through the failure of Good Friday, only through the deathly stillness of Holy Saturday could the disciples be led to grasp who Jesus really was and what his proclamation truly meant. God had to die for them, so that he could truly live in them. Their image that they had formed of God, into which they tried to force him, had to be destroyed so that they could see him who always remains the infinitely greater. We need the darkness of God, the silence of God, in order to experience the abyss of his greatness and that of our nothingness, which would open if he were not.[19]

To Ratzinger, therefore, Holy Saturday embodies the twin realities of pain and hope. In Christ, God experiences the full dregs of the cup of death and the descent into Hades, and even more so, for death does not constitute the end point of the narrative. This experience of death by Divinity is the highest point of solidarity with humanity, for, if God in Christ never experienced death, then one could argue that God does not understand the full depth of humanity. Isn't it the germ of Christianity that the Christian God suffers, that the Christian God knows pain from the inside? This is certainly not an anthropocentrism of God, but rather a *kenosis* of Divinity, a self-emptying that can only come about thanks to God's freedom and love.

And yet in a world increasingly shaped by the temporal mentality, the irony is not lost on the believer that the sleep of Christ on Holy Saturday captures the sentiments in some of a God who sleeps while the issues pertaining to God appear to be sinking in a boat. Ratzinger voices this iconic situation: "God sleeps while his affairs are about to sink—is that not the experience of our own lives? Do the Church and the faith not appear like a little sinking ship that uselessly struggles against wind and waves while God is absent?"[20] And from the depths of current crises and challenges of the faith in today's world, Ratzinger utters a heartfelt prayer to the Lord:

> Wake up—don't you see that we are sinking? Wake up, don't let the darkness of Holy Saturday last forever, let a gleam of Easter fall in our day too. Go with us when we walk despondently to Emmaus so that our hearts may be enkindled by Your nearness. You who, in hiddenness, guided Israel's path, until finally you were a man among men, don't leave us in darkness; don't let Your word be drowned in the prattle of these days. Lord help us, for without You we would perish. Amen.[21]

It is certainly symbolic that Ratzinger turns to prayer, in encapsulating his theological insights regarding his birth on Holy Saturday. It reflects the spiritual heart of Ratzinger, for whom theology opens the soul to the impracticability of human self-sufficiency, thereby preparing the soul for an opening to the transcendent, to the Divine experience of encountering the God of Jesus Christ.

Nevertheless, even as a child with the happy family atmosphere at home and the joys of childhood such as the family's celebration of Easter, Christmas, and other Bavarian cultural delights, Ratzinger was already exposed to the ugliness of political absolutism in terms of the coming to power of National Socialism in Germany.[22] Standing in threatening opposition to the life of family and faith of the Ratzingers and all of Germany was the growing ideology of National Socialism. Despite claims that Joseph Ratzinger was a pro-forma member of the "Hitler Youth," it is important to state here that there was not an iota of affection for Nazism in the Ratzinger family, both in the parents and their children and extended relations. Like every seminarian, Ratzinger was registered into the "Hitler Youth" by the seminary authorities who had registered all the seminarians in order to save the seminary from the Nazis who wielded power in Germany at the time. Ratzinger is convinced that being a Christian is irreconcilable with the Nazi ideology. Talking about the Nazis, Benedict recounts:

> It was really clear to us that a clergyman must be against the Nazis. Our father was so against them you cannot imagine that anyone in the family would have supported them. Aunt Theres, one of my father's sisters, was particularly fierce against the Nazis. She had a house with several siblings in Osterhofen, with some ground on which the railway ran. When a train with Nazi top brass shot past on the train, she showed them the long nose (Pope makes a gesture, laughing). They were enraged, but there was nothing they could do from a speeding train.[23]

Ratzinger's brother, Msgr. Georg Ratzinger, offers a corroborative account of the family's anti-Nazi sentiments: "Father spoke with us very little about politics at that time, for he knew the proverb: 'Children and fools speak the truth.' [...] At any rate, our parents made no secret of the fact that they were anti-Nazi and despised Hitler wholeheartedly."[24] This first-hand experience of Nazism will create in Ratzinger a very measured sense of expectation regarding politics. It would not be out of place to conclude that Nazism formed in Ratzinger a very suspicious view of the closeness between the Church and the political State. He consistently argues for the autonomy of each, to the extent that any usurpation of the role of the other becomes counterproductive to both, and therefore unhelpful to broader society.

1.2 The Question of the State of the Church in the Perception of the Young Ratzinger

To Ratzinger, the principle of the separation of Church and State—a sacred principle in secular democracies who see themselves as heirs of the *Aufklärung*—is foundational in the de-sacralization of Caesar that the Christian Church took up following the teaching of Christ. Nevertheless, this in no way implies the exclusion of the life of faith in the public discussion and discernment of the State, for freedom of religion does not imply freedom from religion, and neither should it be understood as restricted to freedom of worship.

In the introduction to this thesis, it became evident that Ratzinger as early as the 1960s was already sensing that the world, understood in terms of the wider society, was already moving away from the life of faith as proposed by the Church. And not only was he perceiving the erosion of the life of the Church in many of the baptized, he was likewise noticing that even the figure of Christ, which ought to shape the Church's faith and Christian spirituality, was likewise being eviscerated by patterns of thought shaped by secular currents of the *Aufklärung*. Reflecting on this eclipse of the Christological foundations of the Church, whose absence had a clear corrosive effect on the faith of many in post-war Germany and Western Europe, Ratzinger declares:

> Herein (ecclesiology) lies the cause of a good part of the misunderstanding or real errors which endanger theology and common Catholic opinion alike. My impression is that the authentically Catholic meaning of the reality "Church" is tacitly disappearing, without being expressly rejected. Many no longer believe that what is at issue is a reality willed by the Lord himself. Even with some theologians, the Church appears to be human construction, an instrument created by us and one which we ourselves can freely reorganize according

> to the requirements of the moment. In other words, in many ways a conception of Church is spreading in Catholic thought, and even in Catholic theology, that cannot even be called Protestant in a "classic" sense. Many current ecclesiological ideas, rather, refer to the model of certain North American "free churches," in which in the past believers took refuge from the oppressive model of the "State Church" produced by the Reformation. Those refugees, no longer believing in an institutional Church willed by Christ, and wanting at the same time to escape the State Church, created their *own* church, an organization structured according to their needs.[25]

It certainly comes across as highly significant that Ratzinger will zero in on ecclesiology as the fulcrum of contention in the theological landscape of Catholicism. In effect, what Ratzinger perceives as the crisis of spiritual and religious desertification is at bottom a crisis of the meaning, place, and mission of the Church. He is eager to maintain the supernatural or transcendental dimension of the origins of the Church because the supernatural life is what the Church is all about and what the Church has to offer the world. Ratzinger states:

> If the Church, instead, is viewed as a human construction, the product of our own efforts, even the contents of the faith end up assuming an arbitrary character: the faith, in fact, no longer has an authentic, guaranteed instrument through which to express itself. Thus, without a view of the mystery of the Church that is also supernatural and not only sociological, Christology itself loses its reference to the divine in favor of a purely human structure, and ultimately it amounts to a purely human project: The Gospel becomes the Jesus-project, the social-liberation project or other merely historical, immanent projects that can still seem religious in appearance, but which are atheistic in substance.[26]

These remarks criticize the tendencies to want at times to square the Church not only with the Zeitgeist, but to invest in and place accents on the institutional and administrative dimension of the Church, seen in an array of conferences, structures, organizational plans and ever new bureaucracies that, while sapping much of the human resources of the Church, does not leave in its wake a concomitant evangelical fruitfulness. Ratzinger would surely have in mind the astonishingly large bureaucratic character of the modern German Church, whose chancelleries are loaded with staff, while the pews grow empty with minimal sacramental life. Ratzinger counsels, "In general, the Church should keep the administrative arrangements she makes for herself as minimal as possible. She should not overinstitutionalize herself; rather, she should ever remain open to the unforeseen and unplanned call of the Lord."[27] If such is the case, it is necessary that initiatives of institutionalization remain open to the divine path already evident in the Church. Like Augustine, Ratzinger is conscious that the city of the world that is very much present in the Church will not forever define the life and the future of the Church. In the final analysis, the city of God, which is the life of faith, hope and love of believers, triumphs over the shadow of worldliness that disfigures the face of the Church. This reclaiming of the beauty of the Church does not preclude her purifying trials.

However, for Ratzinger, the greatest challenge facing the Church today is what he has repeatedly and forcefully pointed out on several occasions as the crisis of faith. It therefore came as no surprise to many observers of Ratzinger that as Pope, Benedict declared 2012–2013 a "Year of Faith," with the *motu proprio* "Porta Fidei." Ratzinger paints the challenging picture of faith today in the life of the Church thus:

> We must acknowledge, however, that faith is seriously weakened and threatened within the Church. Even we in the Church have lost courage. We feel it to be arrogance or triumphalism to assume that the Christian faith tells us the truth. We have picked up the idea that all religions are the products of history, some developing this way and others that, and that every person is as he is because of the accident of birth. Such a view reduces religion from the level of truth to the level of habit. It becomes an empty flux of inherited traditions which no longer have any significance. But this view eliminates a

> crucial affirmation from the Christian faith, namely, Christ's "I am the Truth"—and hence the Way, hence also the Life.[28]

Ratzinger's diagnosis runs thus: Firstly, the current Church is undergoing a crisis of faith. It is difficult to argue against this premise, if one were to call to mind not only the decline in religious practice especially in the large sectors of the Western world, but also the emptying of the pews, with the ever-increasing numbers of people becoming indifferent to religion. Secondly, this crisis of faith is due in large part to the abandonment of the conviction that contemporary men and women can know the truth. We seem to have become radical agnostics and skeptics. Thirdly, the crisis of truth which has elicited the crisis of faith is a consequence of the abandonment of the centrality of the person of Jesus Christ in the history of the world.

Following the recent emphasis on religious pluralism, Ratzinger fears the uniqueness of Jesus risks being diluted, and Christianity, interpreted as a product of the Western culture, a kind of relic that might not have much to say to present concerns and challenges facing not only contemporary Europe, but the world at large. In Ratzinger's diagnosis, the tendency on the part of some in the Church, specifically in theology, to give up on objective truth and on Jesus, is resulting in a lack of courage on the part of the Church to bring others into friendship with Christ, which, to Ratzinger, is the purpose of being a Christian. From this analysis, therefore, faith, truth, Jesus, and courage are the four marks that brings the current diagnosis of the state of the Church into bold relief, from the Ratzingerian reading of things. Along this line of thinking, Ratzinger observes:

> In our generation the Christian faith finds itself in a much deeper crisis than at any other time in the past. The problem of whether it is still possible in this century to live an honorable life by this faith and to have confidence in it in time and in eternity is met not only by those who find themselves on the fringe of the Church, but every single one of us. In this situation it is no solution to shut our eyes in fear in the face of pressing problems, or to pass over them. If faith is to

> survive this age, then it must be lived, and above all, lived in this age. And this is possible only if a manifestation of faith is shown to have value for the present day, by growing to knowledge and fulfillment.[29]

I think three key words stand out from this text, viz., manifestation, knowledge, and fulfillment. In other words, if faith is to survive today, believers or those who have received the gift of faith must be willing to live out the faith today. Such a willingness cannot be something that is postponed or set aside until other more pressing needs are met or considered. Put differently, the only testimony to faith is a life of faith itself, lived in the present, in the here and now. And to Ratzinger, this sense of manifestation of the faith is not a pompous proclamation, but, in the spirit of the logic of the Gospel, a manifestation that is a hidden sign, an obscure God hidden in the ordinary day to day events, such as was the case with the proclamation of the angels to the shepherds: "And here is a sign for you: you will find a baby wrapped in swaddling clothes and lying in a manger" (Lk 2:12).

In other words, says Ratzinger, "the sign for the shepherds is that they will find *no* sign, but only God in the form of a child; and despite this concealment they must still believe in God's nearness. The sign demands of them that they learn to discover God in the unknown nature of his concealment."[30] In effect, given the secular age in which the Church is called to proclaim God today, Ratzinger, in his understanding of what it means for the Christian to live out the faith today, that is, Christian manifestation, opts for a sense of Christian witness that seeks to reveal the life of God in the ordinariness of life. To witness, therefore, invites the believer to cultivate the capacity to discern God in surprising places and act as a lens thanks to which men and women could find God today, God in "strange" and unexpected places.

For this to happen, the second concept that we identified above, namely, knowledge, enters the picture. Knowledge here must be understood as a deeper formation in the theoretical principles of faith. Though essential, knowledge should not encapsulate the entire story of Christian witness. Hence, when Ratzinger talks about growing in knowledge in the text cited above, it must be understood as a growth that is organically related to the praxis of faith, growing from not just the theoretical principles, but from the allowance of a synthesis of theory and practice. In this sense, Christianity emerges as an experience that is not gnostic, some secret knowledge, but as a growth in a friendship with Christ that comes about thanks to spending time with Christ and getting to know Christ more intimately.

And it is from this friendship that the third key term follows, fulfillment. When talking about Christian fulfillment, or the fulfillment that comes from being a Christian, Ratzinger's sophistication as a theologian comes into bold display. He appears reluctant to concede to theories that seek to convey the message that belonging to the Church solves all problems. Even if Ratzinger appreciates the attempt to explain history as divided between the era before and after Christ, signifying sin and redemption respectively, Ratzinger makes the case that even the period after Christ is existentially experienced as before Christ.[31] In other words, while there was an historical advent, the realities of our personal lives, the realities of the Church and the realities of the world undeniably point to the fact that we continue to live in advent. In this sense, can I be completely fulfilled in this life, or do I have to wait for another life to experience the complete joy of knowing Christ? Does history, especially in its modern form, attest to a post-redemptive era that should follow the Christ-event? And shouldn't we be living in a better time in terms of human fulfillment because of the Incarnation? Isn't a better and more fulfilling life what the Old Testament oracles pointed to as a sign of the Messianic era? These questions and more ring urgent in the light of certain biblical prophecies and oracles, such as this from the prophet Isaiah:

> The wolf shall dwell with the Lamb,
> and the leopard shall lie with the kid,
> and the calf and lion and the fatling together,
> and a little child shall lead them.
> The cow and the bear shall feed;
> their young shall lie down together;
> and the lion shall eat straw like the ox.
> The sucking child shall play over the hole of the asp,
> and the weaned child shall put his hand on the adder's den.
> They shall not hurt or destroy in all my holy mountain;

for the earth shall be full of the knowledge of the Lord
as the waters cover the sea
(Is 11:6–9, Revised Standard Version, Catholic Edition).

Ratzinger concedes that the images contained in this text are metaphorical expressions that while they convey the image of peace, are certainly not intended to be concretely actualized in the world of today.[32] But as Ratzinger points out, these images have a deeper significance, for they point to peace as the sign of the redeemed, that is, the redeemed are men and women of peace who no longer act from malicious or vicious intentions, thanks to the fact that the earth is full of the knowledge of the Lord, as the waters cover the sea.[33] But Ratzinger the pragmatist is still not content with this interpretation. Looking around him, Ratzinger further queries:

> But what has happened to this vision in the Church among us who call ourselves redeemed? We all know that it has not been fulfilled, that the world has been and is still more than ever a world of strife and unrest, a world which lives on war between men, a world stamped with the mark of evil, of enmity and egoism; a world which is not covered with the knowledge of God—as the earth is by the sea—but which lives separated from him, surrounded by darkness.[34]

Such a pragmatic assessment might come across as pessimistic, but it is difficult to deny the fact of what Ratzinger states here, for in the final analysis, the question of fulfillment derived from the life of following Christ is about the practicability of the Christian message. In other words, if the Church is to make inroads into the hearts of contemporary men and women, the latter must find the message of the Church useful, or one would say, in a language of the digital age, "user-friendly," to the effect that I can feel the power of the message of the Church in my life. Along this line of thinking, Ratzinger makes a challenging diagnosis, worth citing at length here:

> I believe that the real temptation of today's Christian does not consist in the theoretical problems of whether or not God

> exists, or of whether he is three persons in one; nor in whether Christ is simultaneously God and man. Rather, what troubles and tempts us today is the impracticability of Christianity; after two thousand years of Christian history we do not see that there has come about any new state of affairs in the world—a world which is filled with the same fears, doubts, and hopes as before. In our private lives, too, we notice the weakness of the Christian truth in comparison with all the other forces which oppress us. And if, after living a Christian life in the midst of struggle and temptation, we take a look at the final result, we are once again filled with the feeling that the truth has slipped through our fingers, that we have lost it and are left with nothing but the weak flame of our good will as a last resort. At this point, in these moments of depression, when we look back over the path we have taken, a question springs to mind: What is the point of all this dogma, of religion, and of the Church if at the end we still find ourselves engulfed in our wretchedness?[35]

In effect, to be a Christian demands an honest assessment and acknowledgement that the world and one's own subjective life are often far from the message proclaimed by Christianity. Any talk of fulfillment will be superficial if it does not take cognizance that even with the best of intentions, the reality of Christian living is that we continuously miss the mark. How often do we feel left to our own strengths and efforts? In this consciousness that we do not fully experience the promises of Christianity lies the discrepancy between hope and fulfillment. To Ratzinger, the message of Christian hope is vital in helping the Christian today find meaning in Christian spirituality:

> Christian theology, which was soon confronted with the discrepancy between hope and fulfillment, made the kingdom of God a heavenly kingdom situated in the hereafter; it changed the salvation of mankind into the salvation of the soul; which also takes place in the next world, after death. But this is no answer. For the greatness of the teaching lies in the fact that our Lord is not only speaking about the

> hereafter or about the soul, but is challenging the body, the whole man in his very person and as part of history and society; the wonderful thing is that he has promised his kingdom to the man who actually lives, bodily, in society.[36]

In effect, by confronting head-on the challenge of another-worldly Christianity, Ratzinger is saving Christianity from the charge of being considered an opium that disillusions people against challenges of the present. If many have abandoned and are abandoning Christianity in large sectors of the Western world, while other reasons abound as I pointed out earlier in the introduction, it cannot be denied that the feeling that Christianity is not fulfilling, not meeting individual needs, constitutes a great concern for many. This is especially the case in the affluent and scientific communities. Wealth and science appear more fulfilling than the Christian message, which apparently promises much but ends up delivering little, at least, in the here and now of this world.

But such a view of Christianity, as attractive as it might be to some, misses an essential aspect of the good news of Jesus Christ, which is that in my daily search for meaning and fulfillment, I am not alone. In Christ, grace is offered me such that I am not only counting on my own efforts.[37] Even if in all our illnesses, weaknesses, loneliness, distress, anxieties, we continue to be under the power and constant presence and power of death, the Christian, if living true to Christianity, is always with Christ. This to me, is how Ratzinger understands Christian fulfillment: it is not that I cease having anxieties; not that I cease carrying that yoke of sin, of brokenness and even death, but that even with all these, and more, such as the joy which the Lord also gives, I am never alone, but always with Christ. Christian fulfillment is not to live without life's burdens and hopelessness, but to live with those burdens because God in Christ has entered my human situation, can understand it, and has not left me alone; even when I suffer, he suffers with me, on the ultimate path to redemption of that suffering and the whole cosmos. Along these lines, Benedict recently commented:

> Let's place ourselves in front of the incredible amount of evil, violence, falsehood, hatred, cruelty and arrogance that infect

> and destroy the whole world. This mass of evil cannot simply be declared non-existent, not even by God. It must be cleansed, reworked and overcome. Ancient Israel was convinced that the daily sacrifice for sins and above all the great liturgy of the Day of Atonement (*Yom Kippur*) were necessary as a counterweight to the mass of evil in the world and that only through such rebalancing the world could, as it were, remain bearable. Once the sacrifices in the temple disappeared, it had to be asked what could be opposed to the higher powers of evil, how to find somehow a counterweight. The Christians knew that the temple destroyed was replaced by the Resurrected body of the crucified Lord and in his radical and incommensurable love was created a counterweight to the immeasurable presence of evil. Indeed, they knew that the offerings presented up until then could only be conceived of as a gesture of longing for a genuine counterweight. They also knew that in front of the excessive power of evil only an infinite love was enough, only an infinite atonement. They knew that the crucified and risen Christ is a power that can counter the power of evil and save the world. And on this basis, they could even understand the meaning of their own sufferings as inserted into the suffering love of Christ and included as part of the redemptive power of such love.[38]

In the final analysis, Christian fulfillment lies not in the denial of the reality of evil and brokenness in this world, but in the faith that evil, irrespective of its volume and ubiquitous presence, is restricted by the power of good that entered in the world in the life, death, Resurrection, and ascension of Christ, and the sending of the Holy Spirit. And this life of Christ is lived in the community of the Church, a people called from the nations, "a story God himself has created,"[39] to quote Ratzinger.

1.3 Ratzinger's Philosophical Formation

Studies in philosophy and theology have long been a prerequisite for men preparing for ordained ministry in the Catholic Church. After the war, Joseph and his elder brother Georg, enrolled in seminary studies for the priesthood for the Archdiocese of Munich and Freising. How did the young Ratzinger view this intellectual phase of his preparation for the Catholic priesthood? In his own words:

> We were forward-looking. We wanted to renew theology from the ground up, and thereby form the Church in newness and vitality. In this respect we were lucky that we lived in a time in which both the youth and liturgical movements had opened up new horizons, new paths. Here we wanted to press forward with the Church, so that, in precisely this way, she should be young again.[40]

From the onset, therefore, Ratzinger had what might be considered an ecclesial sense of his academic formation in the seminary and at the University of Munich. Studies were not to be an end in themselves but a means to helping the Church speak meaningfully and profoundly to the concerns of contemporary men and women.

This pastoral orientation of studies in no way diminished the fervor with which Ratzinger engaged the world of philosophy and theology, for as he himself says, "I was fascinated by academic theology. I found it wonderful to enter into the great world of the history of faith; broad horizons of thought and faith opened up before me, and I was learning to ponder the primordial questions of human existence, the questions of my own life."[41] In his memoirs, *Milestones*, Ratzinger writes concerning the orientation of himself and his seminary peers that "we wanted not only to do theology in the narrower sense but to listen to the voices of man today."[42] This portrays Ratzinger as someone for whom studies do not entail belonging to another planet. Rather, the theologian is one who, while delving into sacred science, does so in a spirit of carrying the baggage of the challenges, difficulties, joys and hopes of the world. This gives a very contextualizing manner of doing theology, one that reflects Ratzinger's attentiveness to the socio-political and economic issues of the day. What constituted, in broad terms, the academic structure and contents of Ratzinger's intellectual formation in philosophy and theology? Who were the authors he engaged that shaped his thinking and listening to, in his own words, "the voices of man today"? Ratzinger gives us a broad and comprehensive picture of his philosophical and theological formative landscape:

> We also followed closely the recent developments in the natural sciences. We thought that, with the breakthroughs made by Planck, Heisenberg and Einstein, the sciences were once again on their way to God. The antireligious orientation that had reached its climax with Haeckel had now been broken, and this gave us new hope. Aloys Wenzel, a philosopher from Munich who had first specialized in physics, wrote a much-read work, his *Philosophy of Freedom*, in which he tried to show that the determinist world view of classical physics, which left no room for God, had been dispelled by an open conception of the world in which there was room for something new, something unforeseen and incalculable. In the domain of theology and philosophy, the voices that moved us most directly were those of Romano Guardini, Josef Pieper, Theodore Hacker and Peter Wust [...]. I read Steinbüchel's two volumes on the philosophical foundations of moral theology which had just appeared in a new edition, and in them I found a first-rate introduction to the thought of Heidegger and Jaspers as well as to the philosophies of Nietzsche, Klages and Bergson. Almost more important for me was Steinbüchel's book *Der Umbruch des Denkens* (The Revolution of Thought): here I read how, just as now we could affirm that physics was abandoning the mechanistic worldview and turning toward a new openness to the unknown—and hence also to the known Unknown, namely, God—so, too, in philosophy we could detect a return to metaphysics, which had become inaccessible since Kant.[43]

Several things stand out from this narrative that help one better appreciate the thinking of Ratzinger: Firstly, one senses a certain philosophical curiosity regarding the new ways of thinking about the questions of metaphysics and epistemology on Ratzinger's part. In this vein, the question of being as the ultimate question of metaphysics is linked to the question of knowing, which is the ultimate question of epistemology. Given this philosophical integration, both metaphysics and epistemology are tied to anthropology, to the human subject, who as a concrete being is a seeker of knowledge, either through empiricism, rationalism or, living in a post-Kantian world, the transcendental idealism of Kant. In addition, this tying together of the different strands of philosophy, in this case metaphysics, epistemology and anthropology, are indicative of Ratzinger's instincts of overcoming compartmentalization and seeking a reconciliation of positions and specific disciplines. This sense of a synthesis of truth, as Hegelian as it appears, could very well be described as Ratzingerian.

Second, present in Ratzinger's explanation of his educational landscape is the reality of the science of theology in dialogue with the non-theological sciences. Ratzinger prefers theology to be in dialogue with what one might refer to as the other hard scientific disciplines, because the place of God in physics ought to be protected if physics is to serve its noblest and truest goals and expectations. In other words, matter was not eternal, an autonomous entity, capable of ordering itself, but a creation of the Divine Mind who orders all things into being. In this sense, the truths of physics cannot exclude God on the grounds of the very hermeneutics of the physical sciences.[44] This explains his clear excitement with what he perceives to be the opening of science to God in the works of Planck, Heisenberg, and Einstein, in that matter is not closed in itself but is in the process of bursting forth with energy; it still unfolds under a cosmic sense of transcendence.

In other words, the interplay of philosophy and theology constitutes an interpretive trajectory that provides Ratzinger with the context thanks to which he is able to nurture and sustain his Christian faith and scholarly undertakings. Faith cannot be severed from reason, as shown in the early church's decision in favor of the God of philosophy over and against the gods of pagan myths and piety. More so, faith cannot be severed from reason because the decision for the God of philosophy, as will be seen in chapter three, guarantees, for Ratzinger, that the fateful demolition of pagan religious piety that followed paganism's rejection of philosophy, does not recur with the Christian religion:

> Early Christianity boldly and resolutely made its choice and carried out its purification by deciding *for* the God of the philosophers and against the gods of the various religions. Wherever the question arose as to which god the Christian God corresponded, Zeus perhaps or Hermes or Dionysius or some other god, the answer ran: to none of them. To none of the gods to whom you pray but solely and alone to him to whom you do not pray, to that highest being of whom your philosophers speak [...]. When we say God, we do not mean or worship any of this; we mean only Being itself, what the philosophers have expounded as the ground of all being, as the God above all powers—that alone is our God.[45]

Ratzinger's interest in philosophy, therefore, naturally finds good company not in something extrinsic to theology or the life of faith, but in the very experience of the Christian faith itself, viz., the life of the early Church and its embrace of Greek philosophy. In other words, the relationship between philosophy and theology, faith and reason, appeared to Ratzinger as that which grounded Christian faith as it struggled to emerge in a world of competing religious affiliations, pieties and contradictory myths.

In effect, philosophy aided Christianity in its struggle to wrestle humans from the worship of nature, for by inserting reason into piety it introduced what Kant would later describe as critical reason into the discourse of faith helping to expose the latent irrationalities and blind anthropomorphisms of pagan piety and religion.[46] To quote Ratzinger,

> The movement of the *logos* against the myth, as it evolved in the Greek mind in the philosophical enlightenment, so that in the end it necessarily led to the fall of the gods, has an inner parallelism with the enlightenment that the prophetic and Wisdom literature cultivated in its demythologization of the divine powers in favor of the one and only God.[47]

Clearly, Ratzinger feels indebted to philosophy, and this chapter offers the opportunity to take a closer look at this in terms of Ratzinger's academic formation, not only in the Hellenistic sense of Greek philosophy of *logos*, but also in the philosophical spirit closer to Ratzinger and contemporary German Catholicism, namely, the Enlightenment. Ratzinger's particular reading of this relationship between philosophy and theology is presented in the formal structure of a dialogue between the God of philosophers and the God of theologians. This interchange between philosophy and theology was so significant to Ratzinger that he took it up in his inaugural lecture as a university professor. This will be dealt with in the next chapter.

At this point, one can pose the question: What kind of philosophical position best describes Ratzinger? The possibilities are many. In the first place, Ratzinger characterizes himself as a Platonist: "To a certain extent I am a Platonist. I think that a kind of memory, of recollection of God, is, as it were, etched in man, though it needs to be awakened. Man doesn't simply know what he is supposed to know, nor is he simply there, but is a man, a being on the way."[48] Perhaps it suffices to say here that amongst the ancient philosophers Plato comes closest to Christian theology, and hence Ratzinger's affinity could very well be because of the discernable possibilities Platonism and Neo-Platonism offer Christian theology, beginning with the Fathers. One can recall here that when narrating the incident of his conversion in Book VIII of the *Confessions*, Augustine tells us that Simplicianus congratulates him for not falling into "the writings of other philosophers which are full of vain deceits, according to the elements of this world, whereas in the Platonists God and his Word are everywhere implied."[49] Given Ratzinger's affinity for Augustine, perhaps such a ringing endorsement of Platonism from the latter might have predisposed Ratzinger toward Platonism.

A second philosophical category that one discerns in Ratzinger is that of Personalism, understood as a position of active engagement with the personhood of the other as other, as someone thanks to whose being I am able to delve into the profound depths of my own existence. The person stands in the light of truth, with all of his or her brokenness, strengths, and struggles. This explains Ratzinger's devotion to Augustine and Martin Buber. Ratzinger recounts in his memoirs:

> We then found the philosophy of personalism reiterated with renewed conviction in the great Jewish thinker Martin Buber.

> This encounter with Personalism was for me a spiritual experience that left an essential mark, especially since I spontaneously associated such personalism with the thought of Saint Augustine, who in his Confessions had struck me with the power of all his human passion and depth. By contrast, I had difficulty penetrating the thought of Thomas Aquinas, whose crystal-clear logic seemed to me to be too closed in on itself, too impersonal and ready-made.[50]

For Buber, Personalism is essentially a relationship that takes the form of an I-Thou, in such a way that the center of one's being is taken up not only in the You of God but in the You of the Other. And all these encounters are graced happenings.[51] Personalism for Buber is both theocentric and anthropocentric, engaging the neighbor, the stranger, the other person.[52] These encounters are not primarily self-orchestrated: "The You encounters me by grace—it cannot be found by seeking [...]. Thus, the relationship is election and electing, at once passive. An action of the whole being must approach passivity, for it does away with all partial actions and thus with any sense of action."[53] From this encounter with God comes the mission into the world, in which other comfortable tendencies such as the *I-I*, *I-it*, and *Us-Them* are re-centered and given new meaning by the I-Thou relationship. This Personalism of Buber caught the attention and affection of the young Ratzinger, especially as it corroborated his spontaneous instincts of the dialogical nature of Christian revelation and salvation history, as seen in his habitation thesis on Bonaventure.

Recently, Benedict reaffirmed his profound affection for Buber in his conversations with Peter Seewald:

> I revered Martin Buber very much. For one thing he was the great representative of Personalism, the I-Thou principle that permeates his entire philosophy. Of course, I have also read his complete works. He was a bit fashionable at that time. He had newly translated the Holy Scriptures together with Rosenzweig. His personalistic viewpoint and his philosophy, which was nourished by the Bible, were made fully concrete

> in his Hasidic tales. This Jewish piety, completely uninhibited in faith and simultaneously always standing in the center of the concerns of this time, his mode of having faith in today's world, his whole person—all this fascinates me.[54]

It is not difficult to see why Ratzinger has remained fascinated by Buber, for both men share that sense of *pietas*, of a profound humility before the mystery of God, not only from a philosophical perspective, but from their active life of faith and worship.

Going further to Augustinian existentialism, Ratzinger says in *Salt of the Earth: The Church at the End of the Millennium*: "From the beginning, St. Augustine interested me very much, precisely insofar as he was, so to speak, a counterweight to Thomas Aquinas."[55] But what form of Thomism was Ratzinger reacting against? Ratzinger explains that what he and his peers eschewed was the post-war "rigid, Neo-Scholastic Thomism that was simply too far afield from my own questions."[56] Perhaps the Neo-Thomism of the post-World War II Europe had become a caricature of what Thomas envisaged in the larger picture of his *Summa*—God, Man and Christ, to the extent that it had taken on the coloring of an uninspiring, dry, syllogistic system of theologizing fixed on logical coherence and precision and did not seem to encounter the flesh and blood, real spiritual choices of everyday Christians. In his *Last Testament* conversations, Benedict once more emphasizes this, although here gives a more measured demonstration of his Augustinian sensibilities over and against Thomas:

> The personal struggle which Augustine expresses really spoke to me. Thomas' writings were textbooks, by and large, and impersonal somehow. That said, there is of course a personal struggle standing behind them, which you only discover later. Augustine battles with himself, and indeed continues to do so after his conversion. And that is what makes the subject compelling and beautiful.[57]

Here, one finds in the later Ratzinger a much more generous appreciation of the scholasticism of Thomas.

Nevertheless, though finding the Neo-Thomism too abstract for his liking, Ratzinger's memories of the course on the history of philosophy is much warmer and more appreciative: "More helpful, on the other hand, was a four-semester course of lectures on the history of philosophy by a young professor, Jakob Fellermeier, who provided us with a comprehensive overview of the intellectual struggle, beginning with Socrates and the pre-Socratic up until the present. This gave me a foundation in philosophy for which I am still grateful today."[58] This testifies to a broad and perhaps comprehensive philosophical perspective for the young Ratzinger, a foundation that seemingly never left him.

Overall, one can make the claim that the early Ratzinger's interest in philosophy was due in large part to the link that he saw between history and metaphysics, for at the center of Ratzinger's thought is salvation history and the place of the Incarnation as the defining moment in salvation history. Metaphysics, dealing with the question of the reality of being as being, provided a helpful possibility of engagement of the facticity of the Incarnation as a real event, not something Gnostic, but a reality, a being, that precisely by happening in real history changed history. In effect, because metaphysics deals with being, and because for Ratzinger the question of being is essentially Christological in a historical context since it ultimately amounts to the being of Christ in salvation history, it is therefore possible to read in Ratzinger a close relationship between metaphysics and the historical sense of liberation.[59] In this sense, one can talk of a theological metaphysics in describing Ratzinger, for he opens up the question of being to the question of truth and freedom, which he ultimately ties to God. Says Ratzinger:

> When man poses the questions that are most vital to him, questions that are inescapable, i.e., about truth and freedom, he is asking ontological questions. The question of being, which is so slandered today, arose for no other reason than the desire for freedom, which cannot be divorced from man's need for truth. So, it cannot be said that the question of being belongs only to a particular phase of mankind's intellectual development, to the age of metaphysics, which A. Comte, in accordance with this three-stage law, allots to the middle

> phase, between the mythical age and the positive age. (In Comte's view, we are now in the latter stage, in which the erstwhile metaphysical question is obsolete.)[60]

One can deduce in this text the classical formulations of metaphysics regarding the so-called transcendental properties of being, in which being is identifiable with truth, goodness, beauty and oneness. If Ratzinger is restating this position here in emphasizing that the path to truth must pass through being and that by rejecting truth modern philosophy is jettisoning being, the consequence for this rejection of truth through the rejection of being comes into bolder relief. This is explainable in that once the question of being is shown the exit sign, there is no longer anything left for humans to stand on, for the ground of existence is that there is being. In effect, we become people lacking firm roots, and as Ratzinger points out in another text, humans will become "tools of self-alienation and hence of man's enslavement. The question of truth and the question of freedom are involved in the question of being and therefore also in the question of God. Indeed, they *are* the question of God."[61] Herein emerges a theological metaphysics, that is, tying the question of truth to being and tying both, truth and being, to God, seen by Ratzinger as the source of both.

Ultimately, Ratzinger believes that truth and being are too important to be left exclusively to the whims and caprices of modern subjective philosophy, for in the final analysis, if they are not tied to God, then life becomes a matter of the strongest imposing their "truth" on everyone. This is the sense in which we can understand Ratzinger's eagerness to argue for a space for God, for as we have seen in the afore-cited texts, without truth and being as its complementary component, humans face self-alienation and enslavement, for the question about being and truth is essentially the question about the dignity of the human being, in terms of origin, identity, and mission. Ratzinger attributes to socio-praxis modes of thinking the abandonment of the metaphysical considerations of life, and calls them a consequence of the excesses of the post-*Aufklärung*.[62] In summary, Ratzinger emerges from his philosophical formation as one with affinities for Platonism, Personalism, and Augustinian Existentialism, and these three philosophical trends, coincidentally, will find themselves, in one form or another, engaged and challenged by German Enlightenment philosophers. Much of this will be dealt with in the subsequent section dealing with these philosophical figures.

1.4 Ratzinger's Theological Formation

On the theological plane, Joseph Ratzinger found his bearings as a protégé of Gottlieb Söhngen, who served as the supervisor of Ratzinger's doctoral thesis as well as his habilitation.[63] Ratzinger found his seminary curriculum of theology to be profoundly open to new questions and theological possibilities, rooted in the tradition and yet not stifled by the tradition: "It was defined by the fact that it was completely biblically orientated, working from Holy Scripture, the Fathers, and the liturgy, and it was very ecumenical. The Thomistic-philosophical dimension was missing; maybe that was its real benefit."[64] There was, certainly, in Ratzinger's theological faculty in Munich, an enthusiasm for a new way of doing theology that sought to provide answers to the burning questions of post-World War II Europe, in the description of Elio Guerriero, an "existential theology." Guerriero explains:

> The traditional apologetics with its rational formulas had proved to be inadequate now. Modern man is not the only one to be shaken in his faith; the theologians, too, cannot avoid confronting the doubt that his contemporaries seek to stifle by immersing themselves in the noise of life and the anxiety of work. The theologian, in contrast, leaving neo-Scholastic thought behind because merely rational assurances are no longer enough, must look at existence, at *his* existence, because theology is not just a course of studies to complete as soon as possible, but rather an encounter, a dialogue through which he must tune in to God's wavelength. And if God is love and generosity, it is necessary to respond to him with the same attitude.[65]

Post-war Europe had therefore provided a profound challenge to not only the way of doing theology in terms of the Scholastic method, but even more, the contents that theology must concern itself with under the given circumstances, such as the question of the meaning of human existence, the struggle between good and evil, Christian responsibility for the evil of the Shoah and the fragility of peace and the temporal order, the necessity for a theology of hope and renewal, to cite a few. For Ratzinger and his fellow seminarians, returning to the seminary after the war was a declaration of their conviction of the crucial role that the Church had to play in the new Germany and the new Europe. As Guerriero points out regarding the batch of post-war seminarians, "all, however, were united by their great love of the Church, which they considered the true bulwark against Nazi barbarity, and by their desire to leave behind them the tragedy of the conflict so as to start a new life."[66] Therefore, the underlining motivation for Ratzinger and his peers was that of hopefulness and optimism, rooted in a deep Christian faith and piety.

Quite naturally, one senses in Ratzinger's appraisal of his theological studies, an earnest perception of the ecclesial character of theology, as it engages Ratzinger beginning with Scripture through the Fathers, the liturgy, and ecumenism. To Ratzinger, the contents of the science of theology precede the individual theologian, owing to the nature of the Church that is studied by the theologian under the discipline of theology. Thus, theology, like the Church that it studies, is not something devised by us, but something that precedes us. Ratzinger remarks:

> If theology wishes and should be something other than religious studies [...] then it can only be based on starting from an answer that we ourselves have not yet devised; yet in order for this to become a real answer for us, we have to try to understand it, not to resolve it. That is what is peculiar to theology, that it turns to something we ourselves have not devised and that is able to be the foundation of our life, in that it goes before us and supports us; that is to say, it is greater than our own thought. The path of theology is indicated by the saying, "*Credo ut intelligam*": I accept what is given in advance, in order to find, starting from this and in this, the path to the right way of living, to the right way of understanding myself.[67]

Similar to the divine origins of the Church, the discipline of theology, for Ratzinger, is not restricted to the subjective strengths of any given theologian. That is, there is more that explains what the theologian can do given his or her human capabilities. Therefore, "without what was given in advance, which is always greater than we can devise ourselves and never becomes part of what is just our own, there is no theology."[68] Thus, the reality of the substance of the faith that we seek to understand is not imagined and created by us, but is something that we receive from outside of us, precisely because we humans could not have created such a mystery that certainly eludes our full comprehension. It is with this sense of expectancy of the more, of that which transcends my particularity, that one should view the theology of Joseph Ratzinger in general, and his ecclesiological convictions in particular.

For Ratzinger, the starting point for theology is reason, understood as being much more than an intellectual faculty. Drawing on John's Prologue, Ratzinger maintains that "theology is based on the assumption, accepted by faith, that what is believed, that is, theology's own foundation, is reasonable, is, indeed, reason itself." [69] Further developing this rational character of theology, Ratzinger opines: "Theology necessarily follows from the blending of biblical faith and Greek rationality upon which historical Christianity is based, already in the New Testament."[70] Ratzinger sees this blending between the Gospel and Greek rationality in the Prologue of the Gospel of John, in which Jesus is described as the *Logos*: "The passage (Jn 1:1) expresses the conviction that what is reasonable, indeed, fundamental reason itself, comes to light in the Christian faith; it means to say that the very foundation of being is reason, and that reason is not a random byproduct of the ocean of irrationality from which everything actually sprang."[71] By implication, Christian faith brings reason (*logos*) to light because as faith it demands reason for its own self-understanding and self-actualization.

Precisely because faith seeks to understand itself in terms of its contents, methodology, structure and sources, reason is an essential part of this process of faith that we call theology. Ratzinger therefore draws this conclusion, "This means that theology takes up the fundamental question of Greek philosophy, with which the human mind had entered into a new stage of its history: the question about truth itself, about being itself. The

Christian theologian does not merely interpret texts but inquires about the truth itself, and he regards man as capable of apprehending the truth."[72] The primacy of reason for theology inadvertently leads to the question of truth, for what does reason search for; what is the purpose of the questions asked, if not to arrive at the truth? In other words, if theology is in its core an undertaking in faith, does it not become impossible to ground it on reason, granted that it belongs to reason to question while it belongs to faith to believe, that which has already been revealed? Is it not the case that because theology already has its answers even before it debates; if theology is offering only ready-made certainties, then theology cannot really claim the autonomy and freedom that belong to the faculty of reason?

Theology's conviction that there is truth that can be known and adhered to becomes an irrational position that does not fit into the culture of the modern university that is now guided by the creed of radical skepticism regarding both reason and truth. It suffices to recall here that not even the forebears of modern philosophical skepticism, for example, Nietzsche,[73] went as far as giving up on the possibility of truth. In this context, theology faces a serious temptation:

> Instead of searching for the truth itself in its authoritative texts, theology can explain the historical conditions in which these texts came into being, attempt to reconstruct their original meaning by historical methods, and critically compare them with the interpretations that have come to light in their history of the influence of the texts. This means that theology can retreat into a thoroughgoing professionalism and thus prove that it completely measures up to the canon of positivistic reason. In this way it attains the same rank as the other specialized disciplines of scholarship. The only problem is that the special task originally assigned to it and to philosophy now drops out: the question about the whole, transcending the separate disciplines, is no longer asked.[74]

Given the classical Western Pre-Reformation position that, following Aquinas, held that truth is convertible with being,[75] all truth is one, even if looked at from different perspectives or from the different academic disciplines. The difficulty today, however, is that metaphysics does not hold sway over contemporary thinking even in Western societies as was previously the case.

1.4.1 Ratzinger's Doctoral Thesis: The People and House of God in St. Augustine's Doctrine of the Church

Why did Ratzinger choose to write on the topic of the Church in his doctoral thesis? Aidan Nichols, O.P., suggests that it was because Ratzinger shared the conviction with Romano Guardini that, theologically speaking, the twentieth century was the "century of the Church." From this conviction, Ratzinger turned to no other than Augustine, the Father of Western theology, to see what he had to say on the nature of the Church.[76] Overall, from a theological perspective, Ratzinger is a decided Augustinian. In Augustine, Ratzinger found an existential liveliness of the faith put forth with an amazing erudition.

To Ratzinger, Augustine of Hippo (354–430) is not just one theologian amongst others, but the theologian whose life and thought shaped and defined Ratzinger's own life down to particular details, as well as shaping the life of Western Christianity. Ratzinger says: "This man of passion and faith, of the highest intelligence and tireless in his pastoral care, a great saint and Doctor of the Church, is often known, at least by hearsay, even by those who ignore Christianity or who are not familiar with it, because he left a very deep mark on the cultural life of the West and on the whole world."[77] Augustine fought and won many consequential battles, from Manichaeism to Donatism, Arianism to Paganism, and certainly Skepticism. On many counts, Augustine taught the Church what the Church believed in sacramental theology, creation, Christian anthropology, original sin, predestination, ecclesiology, eschatology, epistemology, theodicy, Trinity, and psychology.

Augustine defined Western Christianity and the Western world in an inimitable way, for after all, here was a man who through the vicissitudes of his life had presented the world of his time and future generations with an unprecedented trilogy of history. Firstly, a "history" of God (*De Trinitate*): Augustine gives a full picture of the story of God as a Trinity of Persons. The Father as Lover loves the Son, the Beloved, and the love between the Father and the Son is the Holy Spirit. Augustine produced a history of the world (*De Civitate Dei*), in which world history is presented as a battle between two loves which define life's choices and life's destiny. And finally, Augustine produced a history of the human being *(Confessiones)*, which tells the story of fallen man's quest for happiness and meaning in life. And in *De Doctrina Christiana*, Augustine left the Church with the basic principles of interpreting Scripture, which continue to be relevant today. Commenting on the timeless character of these main texts and the entire literary legacy that Augustine bequeathed to the Church and to the world in the disciplines of philosophy, theology, psychology, sociology and politics, Ratzinger writes:

> When I read Saint Augustine's writings, I do not get the impression that he is a man who died more or less 1,600 years ago; I feel he is like a man of today; a friend, a contemporary who speaks to me, who speaks to us with his fresh and timely faith. In Saint Augustine, who talks to us, talks to me in his writings, we see the everlasting timeliness of his faith; of the faith that comes from Christ, the Eternal Incarnate Word, Son of God and Son of Man. And we can see that this faith is not of the past although it was preached yesterday; it is still timely today, for Christ is true yesterday, today, and forever.[78]

Therefore, by engaging Augustine from an ecclesiological perspective in his doctoral thesis, *The People and House of God in St. Augustine's Doctrine of the Church*, Ratzinger treated issues that were significant to theology, viz. the relationship between the Old and New Testaments; how the law is related to the sacraments; and the life of Christians under pagan or secular rule. In accordance with this path of Scripture, the sacraments and Christian living, the sense of the Church that emerges from Augustine, at least in Ratzinger's reading of him, is that of a people and house of God that is intently connected to the concept of the Body of Christ, "founded on the Christological reinterpretation of the Old Testament and on the sacramental life centered on the Eucharist, in which the Lord gives us his Body and transforms us into his Body."[79] Given this realization, Ratzinger maintains, "it is, then, fundamental that the Church, the People of God in a Christological and not a sociological sense, be truly inserted into Christ."[80] Augustine exposes this Christological character of the Church as the people and house of God when, talking about Christian prayer and Christian liturgical worship, the Bishop of Hippo writes that Christ "prays for us, prays in us, and prays by us; he prays for us as our priest; he prays in us as our head, and he prays by us as our God: let us therefore recognize him as our voice and ourselves as his."[81] It is this Christic character of the Church that Ratzinger sought to study Augustine's thought in his doctoral work.

Nichols points out that Ratzinger's engagement with Augustine places the latter head-on in the trajectory of the history of religion in Augustine's age.[82] Certainly, Augustine's Neoplatonism set the framework for Augustine's theological conclusions. Added to his philosophical background was Augustine's experience of the Church in Roman Africa, with all its never-ending concomitant theological controversies. In Ratzinger's reading of the Bishop of Hippo, what was of paramount importance was not merely the philosophical or theological formative influences on Augustine's ecclesiology, but an examination of the role that Augustine's ecclesiology performed. Ratzinger explains his motives:

> I began with the theme of the Church, and it is present in everything. Only, in dealing with the Church it was important to me, and it has become increasingly important, that the Church not be an end in herself but exist so that God may be seen. In that respect I would say that I study the theme of the Church with the intention of opening a vista onto God. And in this sense, God is the real central theme of my endeavors.[83]

In this doctoral thesis, therefore, Ratzinger sought to offer what he saw as a necessary correction to the horizontalization of the Church by grounding the Church in its Christic foundation, which emerges along the two lines of faith and love.

From the brief summary presented above, Augustine's life showed an adventure with different schools of thought, in which, while consistently seeking the truth, he heavily relied on reason, that is, his own intellect, as the path to truth. His initial rejection of Christianity after reading Cicero's *Hortensius* was due in large measure to the fact that Augustine found the Old Testament to be rationally and literarily weak, especially with its numerous accounts of wars waged between Israel and the surrounding kingdoms.[84] At some point, Augustine had to let himself be taken over by the hand of the Lord. He had to believe in order that he might understand—*crede ut intelligas*.

In this context, the Church's rites and sacraments ushered in a new path for Augustine. He learned to focus not on the physicality of the rites, but on what was invisibly conveyed. The interior life of grace with God became something real for Augustine, and this for him is what defines and shapes the Church as the People of God. For in baptism we seek faith from the Church which is the invisible doorway that we enter into this new people of God with Christ as head. As Nichols points out, for Ratzinger it is not difficult to comprehend why the young Augustine, struggling to find truth and engaging intensely with issues of authority and skepticism, would have been struck by the conception of "faith" incorporated by a universal Church, capable of fulfilling a mediatory role and a uniquely magisterial function.[85] Thus, there is an idea of a necessary relationship between the Church and "faith," illustrated by Ratzinger's interpretation of Augustine's struggle to faith and the Church:

> This Church is the place where God gives us the Invisible to feed upon in visible form, thus leading us ever more toward the Invisible until we become adults in his presence. Because of man's wounding through sin, the Church now becomes a necessary stage in the ascent of the soul to Wisdom. All must pass through the triad of *credere*, *auctoritas*, *humilitas*. "have faith, accept authority, practice humility," if they are to see the divine wisdom in its beauty.[86]

Thus, faith is the doorway through which one ascends to God through the People of God, the Church, which occupies an indispensable place in this journey to God, through her sacramental life, meaningful only through the eyes of faith. In other words, membership in the Church is born from faith, nurtured and sustained in faith.

In addition to faith, love as the bond of unity shapes the Church as the house of God. For Augustine, this unity must be *catholica* in character, not sectarian, provincial or national, for a household divided within itself cannot not be sustained. This explains Augustine's fierce battle with the Donatists in North Africa. Ratzinger describes the anti-Donatists ecclesiological exegesis of Augustine in this way:

> The multitude of nations who live within the earth's girdle now stands forth as the single people of Abraham, brought together out of their mutually separating multiplicity and bound together in an inner unity through the Seed of Abraham, Jesus Christ.[87]

For Ratzinger, therefore, the unity of the Church in Augustine is not a later, accidental development, but something that is integral and constitutive of the very life and fabric of the Church. As Nichols points out, Ratzinger maintains that the greatest sin of the Donatists, at least according to Augustine, was what Ratzinger describes as the lack of "objective charity which does not betoken a subjective attitude, but rather belonging to the Church, and more specifically to that Church which itself lives in Charity,"[88] that is, in "Eucharistic love-relationship with other Christians in the whole world."[89] To belong to the Church is therefore to participate in this universal life of *caritas*, which binds the whole Church together.

In Augustine, maintains Ratzinger, even the presence of sinners in the Church—something that elicited very strong sentiments from the Donatists—was not a sufficient justification to sever the bonds of love, charity, and unity in the Church. This in no way denies the reality of the anti-witness of sinful living by those professing to be Christians. In fact, Ratzinger maintains, Augustine does not hesitate to denounce the sinful lives of Christians, as seen in Augustine's homily on the weeds and wheat, for which Ratzinger provides this interpretation in his thesis:

> Augustine can say: The Catholic Church is the true Church of the holy. Sinners are not really in her, for their membership is only a seeming reality, like that of the *mundus sensibilis*.

> But on the other hand, he can stress that it is no part of the Church's business to discharge such sinners, just as it is not her affair to cast off this body of flesh. It is the Lord's task, who will awaken her (at the End) and give her the true form of her holiness.[90]

Rather than adopting a schismatic position toward sinners as demanded by the Donatists, Augustine, as Ratzinger reads him, sees in the Church the place of encounter with God's merciful love that is patient, benign, and salvific. In his catechesis on Augustine, Benedict XVI characterizes this Augustinian realization of the presence of sin, even in the Church, as a third stage in Augustine's conversion, the other two stages being his intellectual conversion, and his conversion to humility and simplicity—in other words, his pastoral conversion. Speaking about this third stage, that is, Augustine's realization that sin does not completely cease to be even after baptism, Ratzinger declares:

> But there is a last step to Augustine's journey, a third conversion, that brought him every day of his life to ask God for pardon. Initially, he thought that once he was baptized, in the life of communion with Christ, in the sacraments, in the Eucharistic celebration, he would attain the life proposed in the Sermon on the Mount: the perfection bestowed by Baptism and reconfirmed in the Eucharist. During the last part of his life he understood that what he has concluded at the beginning about the Sermon on the Mount—that is, now that we are Christians, we live this ideal permanently—was mistaken. Only Christ himself truly and completely accomplishes the Sermon on the Mount. We always need to be washed by Christ, who washes our feet, and renewed by him. We need permanent conversion. Until the end, we need this humility that recognizes that we are sinners journeying along until the Lord gives us his hand definitively and introduces us into eternal life.[91]

This Augustinian realization of the continuous need for God's mercy, in opposition to Donatism, leads Ratzinger to draw the conclusion that the conflict between Augustine and Donatus was an "inner-dogmatic affair," because—in Ratzinger's reading of Augustine—Donatism is not a heresy because it promulgated re-baptism, which is clearly a departure from the practice of the universal Church. Rather, Donatism is a heresy because it is *schisma inveteratum*—that is, on the basis of rejecting sinners or those who refused to withstand persecution of the faith—and had separated itself from the *ecclesia catholica*, from the universal Church. It fractured love and unity. This is a grave situation because as Augustine himself often stated, "I am in the Church, whose members are all those Churches about which we know in truth from Holy Scripture that they originated and grew by the activity of the apostles. I will never give up *communio* with her, neither in Africa nor anywhere else, so help me God."[92] With this manner of professing the Catholic faith, Ratzinger maintains that Augustine became the doctor of catholicity.[93] Thus, this context of a schismatic experience for Augustine becomes a locus thanks to which the Church emerges as a People and House of God.

Patrick McGlinchey raises an important question relating to Ratzinger's handling of Augustine's conversion experience, and what that says to us about the ecclesial consequences of this experience of Augustine for Ratzinger. In other words, what can we deduce from Ratzinger's ecclesiology from the way in which he incorporated and integrated the conversion experience of Augustine into his general understanding of Augustine's thought? This question is crucial because Ratzinger is clearly aware of the puzzle regarding Augustine's 386 AD conversion. That is, was Augustine's conversion to the Gospel, specifically his garden experience, a conversion to spirituality or to the historic Christian faith?[94] Ratzinger offered a conclusive picture of where he stands in relation to this question in his catechesis on Augustine as Benedict XVI. Talking about the garden scene in which Augustine is exhorted *tolle*, *lege*, *tolle*, *lege* (the text turns out to be from Paul's Letter to the Romans, chapter 13:13–1), Ratzinger comments:

> He (Augustine) understood that those words in that moment were addressed personally to him; they came from God through the Apostle and indicated to him what he had to do at that time. Thus, he felt the darkness of doubt clearing, and

> he finally found himself free to give himself entirely to Christ: he described it as "your converting me to yourself" (*Confessions* VIII, 12, 30). This was the first and decisive conversion.[95]

For Ratzinger, this decisive experience of Augustine was possible because of Augustine's passion for the human being and for the truth. Augustine's search for God was driven by passion, and when Augustine allowed Christ to find him and placed his life in the hands of Christ in faith, Augustine suddenly discovered that his search for God, his pursuit of truth, had come to an end. For truth is Christ, God made flesh.[96] But we should note that this recent rendition or interpretation of Augustine's conversion experience by later Ratzinger is markedly different from an earlier construing of the same text by Ratzinger.

In his *Introduction to Christianity*, the young professor Ratzinger offers this reading of Augustine's conversion experience: "The program of the early Augustine—God and the soul, nothing else—" is impracticable: and it is also un-Christian. In the last analysis there is no religion along the solitary path of the mystic, but only in the community of proclaiming and hearing."[97] It is not immediately clear how the middle Ratzinger arrived at this reading of Augustine, but what stands out in his later reading cited above, is that by relating Augustine's personal conversion, not primarily to spirituality or at worst, simply to an inner development along the path of Neoplatonism, Ratzinger makes the case that the individual's search for God, for truth, in this case Augustine's, is incomplete when it bears no reference to the visible Church. Speaking on the centenary of the death of John Henry Newman, Ratzinger returns to this theme of Augustine's solitary conversion vis-à-vis the Church:

> When Augustine was converted in the garden at Cassiacum he understood conversion according to the system of the revered master Plotinus and Neo-Platonic philosophers. He thought that his past sinful life would now be definitively cast off; from now on the convert would be someone wholly new and different, and his further journey would be a steady climb to the ever-purer heights of closeness to God.[98]

As McGlinchey points out, the words employed in the preceding citation by themselves "suggest that Ratzinger saw even Augustine's Christian conversion as being heavily overlaid by philosophical presuppositions drawn not from the deposit of faith, but from a philosophical/spiritual worldview derived from the mystical experience of Plotinus."[99] In effect, Ratzinger leads the reader of his doctoral thesis into the nuances of Augustine's conversion by highlighting the two strands of conversion present in Neo-Platonism, that is, the regal path known only by the philosophers which entails a metaphysical search for the truth and undertaken by the few, and the universal way, with lesser standing, meant for the masses and undertaken via the religious *cultus*.[100] While the former is clearly esoteric and elitist, the latter was clearly commonplace and accessible to all.

For Ratzinger, therefore, the great moment in Augustine's conversion was the movement from the regal path of philosophy, limited and restricted to the few, to the universal way of salvation, opened to the masses. Ratzinger guesses that it must have been impressive and at the same time questionable to Augustine that the Christian religion lays claim to be both popular salvation (*salus populi*) and the regal path.[101] Nevertheless, grace gets the better of Augustine and he is able to realize that the Church mediates full salvation for all, for the masses, salvation that was presumed by the philosophers to be for a select few of the high and regal path. Ratzinger considers this a significant change in Augustine, for this, to Ratzinger, is when faith begins—that is, when one is no longer the architect of one's salvation, but rather one opens the self to what comes from the outside, receiving it in faith, a faith similar to the attitude that one displays, for example, toward one's parents.[102] Faith as the fundamental attitude in which one does not rely on one's strength but opens the self to the help that comes from the other, from outside, is the defining and determining attitude of being a Christian.

Augustine, therefore, cannot rely only on his own strength to sustain the mystical vision of God. He has to depend on the Church, his new mother who now plays the maternal role Monica played in his pre-conversion life. As Ratzinger points out, "in his weakness, Augustine cannot bear the divine 'food' in its pure form. Therefore, the divine Word has mingled itself with flesh so that humanity can enjoy it."[103] In other words, the possibility of the human being experiencing the life of divine bliss comes about only if God himself takes the initiative to reach out to humans, to stretch out a helping hand and lift humans up to the level of the divine. And for Ratzinger, this appears to be the role of the Church, that is, the helping hand that God stretches out to humans by means of the sacraments, thanks to which the Church is able to mediate God's saving presence for humanity. This is the context in which one should understand the Church as that People and House of God, in the midst of the world, the nations.

Ratzinger identifies three fundamental representations of this Augustinian concept of the Church as the People and House of God. In the first place, this categorization refers to Israel, the first people called by God, the people of the promises, of the patriarchs. Secondly, granted that Israel was not called to be closed in on itself but to be a sign for the nations, for the people of God for the future, the designation People and House of God refers as well to the spiritual Church of all those baptized in Christ Jesus, from all the nations of the world. Lastly, the people and house of God is the heavenly and eschatological counterpart of the spiritual Church, that is, the Church triumphant in heaven.[104] The final stage of this people of God is therefore the heavenly Church, which is the longing of all those on the way. Perhaps it is worth noting how remarkably similar this trajectory is to what one will find in the structure of the Second Vatican Council's Dogmatic Constitution on the Church, *Lumen Gentium*, especially in chapter one, "On the Mystery of the Church." Not only is the Church traceable to Israel as the *qahal YHWH*, but chapters seven and eight, on eschatology and Mary, bring the reality of the Church to its definitive fulfillment in the *communio sanctorum*, in which the earthly Church reaches its definitive realization.

Ratzinger also sees in the mosaic art of Church architecture in the North Africa of Augustine's day a representation of the ecclesiological description of the Church as the People and House of God. Ratzinger points out that one of Augustine's mosaics had the inscription *Ecclesia mater*. Seen this way, the church building is the visible form of Mother Church, whose stones and mosaics constitute an image of the living stones of God's people: *ecclesia dicitur locus, quo ecclesia congregatur*. The Spirit of God makes a dwelling in this people, as the Spirit did in the temple of Zion of old. Mutual charity is what binds the bricks of this house of God, absent which the house will not be constructed.[105] Charity or love is therefore the internal form of the People and House of God.

Another aspect that Ratzinger takes on in his doctoral work is the theme of the life of the Church in the midst of a pagan world—that is, Augustine's *De Civitate Dei*. In 410 AD, Rome fell into the hands of the Goths. The charge was then leveled against the Christians: Rome had fallen because Rome had abandoned its pagan gods for the Christian God, who clearly was unable to protect Rome. This devastation could only be remedied with a renewal of the pagan cult. Sacrifices had to be offered to the pagan gods of Rome for atonement and restoration of Rome and for the welfare of the citizens of Rome. With *De Civitate Dei*, Augustine offers a robust defense of the Christian faith that sheds a crucial light on his liturgical ecclesiology, at least from a Ratzingerian perspective. For Ratzinger, the central nexus of Augustine's argument is that sacrificial worship is the offering of a human life, that is, a life lived according to the precepts of God. In other words, sacrifice is right living. Roman sacrifices were futile because the Romans themselves were living immoral lives. Owing to sin, the human relationship with God has been severed. This calls for a mediator who will not only share mortality with us, but likewise blessedness with God. This mediator, out of mercy for humanity, will save humanity from subjection to the demonic, from the futile sacrifices made to the Roman gods.[106] This insight of the determinacy of the cult of Christ to replace not only pagan Roman cults but all cults before it, will be further developed in chapter five, which studies Ratzinger's liturgical ecclesiology of the Word and *Logos*, that is, the true sacrifice as *oratio*, prayer, the worship and sacrifice of the mind and spirit.

Accordingly, by his life, death, Resurrection, and the sending of the Holy Spirit, Jesus Christ is the sacrifice that should be offered but it could not be so because of the Roman decision for pagan cult. Nichols comments: "It is this sacrifice of the Mediator, which is to be, in the polis that no being lives outside, the true worship, the *cultus* of the City of God."[107] How does this sacrifice of Christ bring about or relate to the Church as the People and House of God? Tracing Augustine's analysis through Justin, Athanasius, and other Anti-Arian Fathers, Ratzinger gives a *pneumato-ecclesia* response, to the effect that, as Nichols summarizes it:

> We are united with Christ by faith whereby his Spirit dwells in us; yet the Spirit of Christ is no other than the grace of Christ, the *caritas* which is spread abroad in our hearts by the Holy Spirit; in referring to such caritas we overstep the boundaries of the individual to enter the realm of the community, the Church which is Christ's body. And while that *ecclesial Corpus Christi* is not directly accessible to us, it may be found in its holy sign, its sacrament, the Eucharist.[108]

This synthesis shows the essential characterization of the Eucharistic ecclesiology of Ratzinger, for in the sacrament of the Eucharist, the true sacrifice of the Church, is contained the inner *Leib-Christi-Sein* of the holy people of God in Christ Jesus, and their existence as a body of Christ. The hub of this people is *caritas*, which is the animating principle of the whole body. In this light, what is most interior is what is most exterior, in living out Christian *caritas*, as Ratzinger points out:

> Charity is the unity of the Church, and more; it is the real, sober, working love of the Christian heart. And that means that every act of genuine Christian love, every work of mercy, is in a real and authentic sense a sacrifice, a celebration of the one and only *sacrificium christianorum*.[109]

In other words, the moral life of Christians is shaped by and lived through the Eucharistic fellowship. Charity, therefore, is the link between Church and Eucharist. When Ratzinger reflects on *caritas* as the mark of the House of God for Augustine, Ratzinger understands *caritas* to mean objective charity not contingent, restricted, or defined by subjective dispositions.

Christianity sees charity as the defining principle of what it means to be a Christian. The Church is perceived as subsisting in charity, that is, "in Eucharistic love-relationship with other Christians in the whole world."[110] But this does not imply a blanket pass to all the members of the universal Church, Ratzinger notes. In fact, Ratzinger maintains that though by virtue of membership in the universal Church one shares in the outward and visible participation in charity, there abound in the universal Church those who in reality belong with the Donatist schismatics owing to their nature as "sinners,"[111] precisely because by opting out of the mother Church, they have severed the bounds of charity.

Clearly, what Ratzinger seeks to achieve with his reading of Augustine's *caritas* as defining the universal Church as the House of God, is essentially to establish a firm basis for the mediatory role of the Church. Given that the spiritual goods of the Church, that is, the sacraments, are not regional in character but universal, it can only be sensible that such a Church, in order to correspond to the universal character of her goods must of necessity be universal as well. And this universality is verifiable thanks to the concreteness and visibility of the Church. In addition, this reading of Augustine by Ratzinger offers a realistic picture of the presence of the mystery of iniquity, of sin, in the lives of believers and in those who enter the portals of the Church. In this sense, the Church emerges as that space wherein healing is offered to the wounded and the sinful, and the sacraments are therefore healing remedies offered by the Church to the sinful and the broken that enter her gates.

Going further, for Augustine *caritas* serves as a unifying force for humanity to the extent that men and women recognize God as the *summum bonum* of the entire world.[112] If love is severed from God, it becomes self-serving. This worldly love fundamentally differs from the love that animates the *civitas Dei*, for not only is the latter love oriented toward the good of the other, *agape*, but it is a love that hopes for something beyond this world. It is transcendental love. In this Augustinian reading, therefore, two loves are discernible: the *cupido* of the earthly city and the *caritas* of the heavenly city. These two cities, the earthly and the heavenly, differ in their origin, development, and ends.[113] To Ratzinger, the reality of the *earthly colony* in the objective sense and character as it stands in contra-distinction to the heavenly city has profound implications for historical theology, which was something of great interest to the *Aufklärung* thinkers, who tended to advocate for an autonomous earthly city with little, if any, reference to the heavenly city.

In all, it might be important to note that although Ratzinger adopts the position of physicality in the reading of Augustine—that is, the Church is visible and concrete and because of this visible presence we can access the life in Christ through the sacramental experience of the Church—Ratzinger is not oblivious of the fact that present in Augustine is also the sense of an interior, spiritual, invisible, and I dare say mystical Church. This appears to give support to the position that Augustine's conception of the nature of the Church is not monolithic. If anything, it appears dialectical. Ratzinger cites *De Magistro,* where the Bishop of Hippo declares that the temple of the spiritual God is the interiority of the human being.[114] This appears especially concerning for Ratzinger, for as McGlinchey points out, if one were to adopt *De Magistro* as the hermeneutical key to Augustine's doctrine on the Church, realities like Church and sacraments are noticeably absent.[115] No doubt, as Nichols observes, Ratzinger sees this as a serious shortcoming on Augustine's part in *De Magistro*, which was rectified by a more ecclesial notion of God's temple in the later Augustine, especially when Augustine confronted the regional schismatics of North Africa, the Donatists.[116] The true Church is the Church of the nations, the *ecclesia omnium gentium*, visible in all parts of the world and not just restricted to the pure of Roman Africa. From the perspective of Ratzinger's reading of Augustine, therefore, to believe with the Church is an indispensable part of the interior journey of faith.

In a word, Ratzinger's doctoral thesis portrays his conviction that the Church is visible and concrete, containing both saints and sinners, over and against the Donatist position of a more spiritual Church of the pure. Ratzinger wholly adopts the Augustinian position. We also encounter a Church in battle for the soul of the world, a battle waged by the *corpus Christi* against the *corpus Diaboli*. This Augustinian sense of battle never actually leaves Ratzinger, for as we will see later on in the thesis in Ratzinger's treatment of *logos* as unity of love in his response to the *Aufklärung's* critique of Christian love, Ratzinger emphatically argues from the perspective of a love that is torn in opposite directions, earthly and heavenly, and yet a love that can only find its fullest expression and meaning in God, in the heavenly city, whose foretaste is encountered in the *corpus Christi*. All taken together, visibility, universality and *caritas* are the defining traits that stand out in Ratzinger's study of Augustine's ecclesiology, and these will become handy in the later engagements that will emerge following the appeal to a primacy of the sense of the historical, of the expressive understanding of love, and of the particularizing ecclesiological positions that, following the spirit of the *Aufklärung*, will become dominant in the post-World War II and post conciliar Church, especially in the heartland of Europe. When the *Aufklärung* places human rationality front and center, it thereby places the human being as the center of faith, as one sees in Kant's *Religion* and Hegel's *Phenomenology*. Ratzinger warns of the dangers of a one-sided horizontal ecclesiology. In his reading of Augustine's ecclesiology, faith constitutes the People of God, while *caritas* or love constitutes the House of God.

1.4.2 Ratzinger's *Habilitation*: The Theology of History in St. Bonaventure (AD 1221–1274)

Ratzinger wrote his post-doctoral thesis or *Habilitation* on *The Theology of History in St. Bonaventure*. As earlier pointed out, metaphysics, existentialism, and personalism were Ratzinger's philosophical preferences for the simple reason that he has always been interested in the nature of salvation history, and saw in these philosophical resources the possibility of constructing a theological response to what he perceived as the discontents of contemporary civilization and world history, especially with the religious and socio-political analysis that emerged with the *Aufklärung* and subsequent modern secular thinking. In Bonaventure's theology of revelation, Ratzinger was able to arrive at the conclusion that the saving plan of God is embedded in history, for revelation is not something of the past but was an ongoing reality of the Spirit in the life of the Church.

However, and this is what landed Ratzinger in hot water, Ratzinger argued that revelation refers to the act in which God shows God's self to a creature, not to the objectified result of this act. In this sense, the receiving subject is always also a part of the concept of revelation. Therefore, concludes Ratzinger, "where there is no one to perceive 'revelation,' no re-*vel*-ation has occurred, because no veil had been removed. By definition, revelation requires a someone who apprehends it."[117] If Bonaventure is right that the receiving subject of revelation constitutes an integral part of revelation, then it follows that revelation precedes Scripture and is deposited in Scripture, while not identical with Scripture. It also implies that revelation is always more than what is written down. This further implies that *sola scriptura* is an untenable option, because an "essential element of Scripture is the Church as understanding subject, and with this the fundamental sense of tradition is already given."[118] In other words, without a recipient of revelation, there is no revelation, there is no pulling off of the veil so that the human being can clearly see the face of God. Ratzinger writes:

> In Bonaventure (as well as in theologians of the thirteenth century) there was nothing corresponding to our conception of "revelation," by which we are normally in the habit of referring to all the revealed contents of the faith: it has even become a part of linguistic usage to refer to Sacred Scripture simply as "revelation." Such an identification would have been unthinkable in the language of the High Middle Ages. Here, "revelation" is always a concept denoting an act. The word refers to the act in which God shows himself, not to the objectified results of this act. And because this is so, the receiving subject is always also a part of the concept of "revelation." [...] If Bonaventure is right, then revelation precedes Scripture and becomes deposited in Scripture but is not simply identical with it. This in turn means that revelation is always something than what is merely written down.[119]

For Michael Schmaus, Ratzinger's *Habilitation* thesis reader, this Ratzingerian reading of Bonaventure amounted to a modernist subjectification of the concept of revelation that had to be rejected outright. Schmaus, schooled in the scholastic spirit that was dominant in the Neo-Thomism of the pre-conciliar era, must have seen in Ratzinger's push for the indispensable place of the receiving subject in the process of Divine revelation a creeping anthropocentric notion of God and the whole concept of God's self-disclosure to humans, that is, divine revelation. But what was probably overlooked by Schmaus was the indispensability of the ecclesial context that Ratzinger sought to establish, vis-à-vis revelation, in that revelation is not a closed-in act. Revelation, at least in Ratzinger's interpretation of Bonaventure, is such that it *arrives* and it is *perceived* in the *Ecclesia*.[120] This implies that "the living organism of the faith of all ages is then an intrinsic part of revelation."[121] Rather than a failed grade, the compromise was for Ratzinger to rework the thesis taking into consideration these objections advanced by Schmaus.[122] Ratzinger eliminated the "controversial" section on Bonaventure and revelation, leaving Bonaventure's reading of history to stand as the corrected version of the thesis. This revision passed, and Ratzinger was awarded a professorship in dogmatic theology on February 21, 1957, after "weeks of restless waiting."[123] Following the successful end of his *Habilitation* drama, Ratzinger became a lecturer at the University of Munich and in the philosophical-theological college in Freising.

This experience of his *Habilitation* clearly left an indelible mark on Ratzinger, in that, as he himself says in *Milestones*:

> At the moment I could hardly feel any joy, so heavily did the nightmare of what had happened weigh me down. But slowly the anxiety that had taken root in me began to dissolve [...]. I made the resolve not to agree easily to the rejection of dissertation or habilitation theses but whenever possible—and respecting the integrity of the procedure—to take the side of the weaker party. This attitude will later play a role in my academic career, as we will see.[124]

With the drama of his *Habilitation* defense over, what insights can one glean from Ratzinger's study of Bonaventure that might be pertinent to Ratzinger's ecclesial engagements with the *Aufklärung*? To respond to this question, it is helpful to recall, as Ratzinger himself points out, that the context of Bonaventure's theology of revelation is very much the controversy stirred up by the interpretations of Joachim of Fiore (c. AD 1132–1202), a Cistercian abbot, mystic, and apocalyptic writer. In synthesis, Joachim put forth a Trinitarian philosophy of history in which history was seen from the perspective of three periods or ages, viz., the Age of the Father, the Age of the Son, and the Age of the Spirit.[125] This Trinitarian reading has a very scriptural imprint.

The Age of the Father (*ordo conjugatorum*) corresponded with the Old Testament and was defined by the Mosaic Law. The Age of the Son (*ordo clericorum*) spanned from the advent of Christ to circa AD 1260. This era is marked by the mediation of God's grace through the rituals and sacraments of the Church as administered by priests. Finally, the Age of the Spirit (*ordo monachorum*) began around the mid-thirteenth century, ushered in by St. Francis (c. AD 1181/1182–October 3, 1226), and his community of Friars. This Age of the Spirit will see a new outburst or flourishing of universal brotherly love that will render ecclesiastical organizations and structures superfluous.[126] To Joachim, it was only within the Age of the Spirit that the full import of God's revelation in Christ would be properly comprehended. Thereafter will come an era of peace and tranquility, with the Franciscans being instrumental in bringing about this new era of tranquility and world peace.[127] The Franciscan movement would be interpreted as the new people of God, the *ecclesia contemplativa*, a new charismatic condition heralded by Francis, of an unmediated access to grace by all, that called for the following of the poor Christ poorly.

When Bonaventure became Master General of the Franciscan Order in 1257, he replaced John of Parma who had been forced to resign, owing to the tensions that were facing the Franciscan movement in terms of those calling for a radical following of the poor Christ, the Spiritualists, on the one hand, and those preferring a more accommodating spirit with the materialistic, opulent, medieval Church, on the other hand. Ratzinger maintains that though Bonaventure never mentions the name "Joachim" in the *Hexameron*, Bonaventure "had debated Joachim's ideas extensively and, as a man of the center, had striven to keep what was useful in order to integrate it into the ecclesial order."[128] And Ratzinger was apparently sympathetic with this approach of Bonaventure, in which a conscious attempt is made to preserve the good while eschewing what is unhelpful.

In the context of this conflict-ridden reading of the prophecies of Joachim by the so-called Spiritual Franciscans, Ratzinger maintains that Bonaventure reinterpreted Joachim back into tradition against the Joachimites that were interpreting him in opposition to tradition. This helped preserve the unity of the Franciscan Order.[129] Thus, Ratzinger not only clearly admired the method of Bonaventure, of marking what was salvageable in the theology of history of Joachim, but, more profoundly, Ratzinger admired the unity and harmony Bonaventure restored to the Franciscan Order.

Ratzinger's study of Bonaventure concentrates on the *Collationes in Hexaemeron* (1273). The overriding theme of the study is ecclesiological and eschatological, in the sense that it concerns itself with the ultimate destiny of the world and the responsibility of the Church in bringing about this destiny. The point of departure is the priestly account of creation in Genesis, in which the six days of creation becomes the six periods of salvation history: Adam to Noah; then Abraham; then David; and then the Babylonian Captivity and the Return from Exile; then Christ; and finally, the *Finis Mundi*, or the end of the world. The first four periods correspond to the Old Testament, while the last two are of the New Testament.[130] By looking at history through the epochal events that marked salvation history, Bonaventure thus provides a link between history and theology, as Ratzinger points out: "In this way, Bonaventure arrives at a new theory of scriptural exegesis that emphasizes the historical character of the scriptural statements in contrast to the exegesis of the Fathers and the Scholastics that had been more clearly directed to the unchangeable and the enduring."[131] What can we deduce from this Ratzingerian study of Bonaventure?

Firstly, one gains the sense of a historical ecclesiology heading toward a fulfillment in the future. The Church for Bonaventure was not something of the past. In fact, the full meaning of the Church was such that it could only be grasped when viewed from the perspective of the consummation of the journey of the Church through history, through time and space. From Bonaventure's reinterpretation of Joachim's prophecies in which the figure of Christ is moved from the end to the center of history, the eschatological character of the Church becomes something that is not set over and against the institutional and sacramental dimension of the Church. In effect, because Christ is the center of the Church, it is the case that the Church will eventually emerge triumphant or victorious at the consummation of history. This Church, as part of human history, rises from Abel the Just, *ecclesia ab Abel*, goes through the vicissitudes of history, making men and women into a community of persons capable of living with God forever.

As Ratzinger points out, "the historical ascent of the Church from the Patriarchs at the beginning to the People of God of the final days is simultaneously a growth of the revelation of God."[132] In evidence in this text is the influence of Bonaventure on Ratzinger, in that not only does Ratzinger again assert the indispensable place of the human subject, in this case the Patriarchs and Israel, in the unfolding of God's revelation, but unlike Joachim and following Bonaventure Ratzinger harbors a broader sense of the consummation of history that clearly transcends the Joachimites. But still within the Franciscan school of history and revelation, one can assert, regarding the destiny of the Church and the world, that truth will triumph over falsehood, good over evil, in the Church of the Perfect or the Triumphant Church. But this sense of the eschaton should not be mixed up with any present political utopia aimed at bringing about such a definitive reading of the pilgrim Church in the sense of its future to the present.

Remaining within this historical perspective of the Church, Ratzinger adopts the Bonaventurian position on this historical evolution of the Church, which evolves according to the Seven Seals of the Apocalypse: The White Horse is symbolic of Christ; the Red Horse symbolizes the Age of the Martyrs; the Black Horse stands for the time of the heretics; the Pale Horse is the Age of the False Christian and concomitantly the time of the founding of the religious orders; the Earthquake is the Age of the persecution by the Anti-Christ; and the Silence is the Age of the Eternal Vision.[133] In this sense, the history of salvation is the history of the Church, with Christ marking a new and decisive beginning in this history whose climaxing point is the Church of the Perfect, beyond time, in eternity:

> With this it becomes decisively clear that the revelation of the final age will involve neither the abolition of the revelation of Christ nor a transcendence of the New Testament. Rather, it involves the entrance into that form of knowledge which the Apostles had; and thus, it will be the true fulfillment of the New Testament revelation which has been understood only imperfectly up till now. And so, the final age will be truly and in the full sense of the word, the New Testament.[134]

This conviction of Ratzinger of the decisive finitude of the New Testament might be indicative of his attitude to questions pertaining to interreligious dialogue. Ratzinger clearly believes that because of the figure of Christ whose mission is passed down in the Church, the presence of the Church in history is already a sign that awaits the final consummation of salvation history, the Sabbath rest of the Church.

Secondly, in Bonaventure Ratzinger discerns a historical reading of Scripture in which Scripture is understood not as an act, an artifact closed in on itself and impenetrable, but rather as a witness or testament to the act of revelation. In this sense, though the word of revelation as recorded in Scripture is definitive, nonetheless, because Scripture is a "book of the Church" in that the Church is the reading subject of Scripture, new depths of meaning must be uncovered in every age through the Church's reception of Scripture. As Ratzinger points out:

> At no time does Bonaventure refer to the Scriptures themselves as 'revelation.' He speaks of *revelare* and *facies revelata* primarily when a particular understanding of Scripture is involved, namely that "manifold divine wisdom" which consists in grasping the three-fold spiritual sense of Scripture—the allegorical, the anagogical and the tropological. These three are understood in analogy with the three divine virtues of faith, hope and love.[135]

In the light of this understanding, the role of the Spirit does not close with any particular age, as Joachim had maintained, but the Spirit is present in every age. The Spirit continuously opens the Church to a deeper understanding of the Scripture. While being attentive to the Spirit, the senses of Scripture enables the Church to discern her future, says Ratzinger:

> Scripture points to the future, but only the one who has understood the past can grasp the interpretation of the future because the whole history develops in one unbroken line of meaning in which that which is to come may be grasped in the present on the basis of the past [...]. In this way, the

> exegesis of Scripture becomes a theology of history, the clarification of the past leads to prophecy concerning the future.[136]

This new way of historical exegesis opens up a new interpretation of salvation history within the life of the Church. Between the fifth and the sixth ages, that is, between Jesus Christ and the *finis mundi*, there will be space for what Ratzinger calls an "inner-historical transformation of the Church."[137] The sign of this inner-historical transformation, obviously for Bonaventure, was Francis of Assisi, the Seraphic Father. Francis marked the time of peace preceding the final storm foretold in the seventh chapter of the Book of Revelations. In line with Joachim of Fiore's prophecy that the Angel of the Seal would receive the full power to renew Christianity, Francis was understood both by Joachim and Bonaventure, Ratzinger maintains, as marked with the seal of the living God, the stigmata, the very impress of the crucified Christ. Given this understanding, the final people of God, the 144,000, would be the community of contemplative men and women, for whom the form of life realized in Francis is the norm. The Franciscans will therefore enjoy the peace of the seventh day that will precede the Parousia.[138] Predictably, Ratzinger is cautious about a wholesale identification of the Franciscan Order with the final era, even if intrigued by Bonaventure's analysis:

> Though this new people of God may rightfully be called Franciscans, and though it must be said that it is only in this new people that the real intention of the *Poverello* will be realized, nonetheless, this final Order is in no way identical with the present Order of Franciscans. It may be that the present Order was originally destined to inaugurate the new people immediately. But even if this had been the case, the failure of its members has frustrated this immediate determination. For the present, the Dominican and the Franciscan Orders stand together at the inauguration of a new period for which they are preparing, but which they cannot bring to actuality by themselves. When this time arrives, it will be a time of *contemplatio*, a time of the full understanding of Scripture,

> and in this respect, a time of the Holy Spirit who leads us into the fullness of the truth of Jesus Christ.[139]

In other words, though Ratzinger clearly sees the significance of the figure of Francis in the life of the Church, and how the inner life of Francis, the contemplative life, will eventually triumph in the Church, Ratzinger is not eager to read in the person of Francis an immediate sign of the end of history or the culmination of the Church's life. Ratzinger is no doubt clearly sympathetic to the life of Francis. To Ratzinger, Francis, the *simplex*, the *idiota*, at the consummation of the Church and history, will turn out to have a more penetrating and profound view of life, because Francis loved God more.[140] This love for God remains a central leitmotif in Ratzinger's theological landscape. Even as pope, he felt his most pressing attention was to remind the Church and the world that God is love, as his first encyclical proclaims.

Thirdly, by placing Christ at the center of the Church and of history as Bonaventure does, Ratzinger reads in this centrality of Christ, the pattern for the Church in the midst of world history. The Mystical Body of Christ, that is, the Church, must tread the same path as Christ, the center and head of the Church. The rejection that Christ faces should likewise be expected of the Church. This rejection and persecution prepare the Church for the final Sabbath rest.[141] Ultimately, therefore, with the eyes of faith and focusing on Christ as the Sun that enlightens the Church, we can already see the ultimate triumph of Christ and the Church in the spirit of the poor friar of Assisi whose angelic life is a triumph over the anti-Christ forces of the world.

Fourthly, Bonaventure provides Ratzinger with a nuanced reading of the institutional dimension of the Church. We should recall, as shown above, that in the prophecies of Joachim which Bonaventure engaged, the Age of the Spirit was such that Christian life was going to be unmediated, with a direct access to grace by all the members of the evangelical community. Joachim was therefore suspicious of attempts at structuralizing the Franciscan Order, in fidelity to what he perceived to be the original intent of Francis of Assisi. But when Bonaventure took over as Superior General, he adopted a realistic vision of the necessity of some form of structure or institution if the Franciscan Order was to remain in existence. As Ratzinger points out, "without feeling any infidelity toward the holy Founder, Bonaventure could and had to create institutional structures for his Order, realizing all the while that Francis had not wanted them."[142] Pragmatically, Bonaventure saw that the eschatological form of life advocated by Francis could not literarily be adapted to the here and now. The life of Francis, that is, a life without structures and institutions that relies solely on unmediated grace, could only be realized as a break-through of God's grace in the soul of the individual, till such a time as the completion of history with the final eschaton.

This Bonaventurian reading of history has proven helpful to Ratzinger in his response to opinions that are overly critical of the structural form of ecclesial life, more precisely, the hierarchical organism of the Church. Ratzinger points out that through institutionalization, Bonaventure was able to preserve the eschatological character of what could be preserved.[143] But such a defense of the hierarchical structure of the Church by Ratzinger does not imply a blindness or deafness on his part to the excesses of institutionalism in the life of the Church. In fact, Ratzinger has been a frequent critic of the large bureaucracies that continue to expand in the post-conciliar Church, especially in his native Germany:

> Nowadays the opinion surfaces occasionally even in ecclesiastical circles that a person is more Christian the more he or she is involved in Church activities. We have a kind of ecclesiastical occupational therapy: a committee, or any rate some sort of activity in the Church, is sought for everyone. People—according to this way of thinking—must constantly be busy about the Church, they must always be talking about the Church, or doing something to or in her. But a mirror that reflects only itself is no longer a mirror; a widow that no longer lets us see the wide-open spaces outside, but gets in the way of the view, has lost its reason for being [...]. The more administrative machinery we construct, be it the most modern, the less place there is for the Spirit, the less place there is for the Lord, and the less freedom there is.[144]

Ratzinger is therefore, very much conscious of the dangers of institutionalism, that structures could easily become self-serving if not non-evangelical. For Ratzinger and in line with Bonaventure, it is critical to keep the instrumental value of ecclesial structures on the radar—that is, they are never to be ends in themselves, but rather the means that the pilgrim Church employs in the service of the mission of the Church.

Finally, it is worth noting that Ratzinger is lukewarm regarding the assertion regarding the "Church of the poor" that stands as the foundation of the Age of the Spirit, especially in the interpretation of this "poor caste" as replacing the mediatory priestly class of the Church. This objection is based on the fact that Ratzinger does not believe in separating the Church into classes of sacramental dispensers in distinction of the poor. Maximilian Heim suggests that this Ratzingerian reading of Bonaventure "had key importance for Ratzinger in the later debate about the eschatological aspects of the Constitution on the Church and about the different ways in which it was received in ecumenical circles as well as by proponents of Latin American liberation theology."[145] Following Bonaventure's re-evaluation of Joachim's Age of the Spirit which had put forth a *this-worldly* eschatological fulfillment of history, Ratzinger is suspicious of *this-worldly* claims of economic, political, or religious messianism.

To Ratzinger, this promise within history of Joachim that Bonaventure refuted, nevertheless, marked a synthesis of utopia and eschatology that set the stage for subsequent philosophical and socio-economic trends: "Joachim concretely formulated such a promise and so prepared the way for Hegel [...]. Hegel, in turn, furnished the intellectual model for Marx."[146] In a word, if Ratzinger showed hesitance toward some aspects of present-day liberation theology, it might be traced back in large measure to what he sees as a divide between Christological and sacramental Church on the one hand, and the pneumatological and prophetic Church of the poor on the other, which claims to be able to bring about a utopia through their way of life. Ratzinger has certainly shown multiple positions toward liberation theology overtime,[147] which, even if not always coming across as sympathetic, reveal two things: Firstly, Ratzinger definitely takes liberation theology seriously, especially in the promises it offers in the continent of Latin America; and secondly, Ratzinger is conscious of the socio-economic factors that necessitated liberation theology—that is, he might agree with the diagnosis, but he disagrees with the prescription.

Certainly, the question of history and faith takes on a sharper focus with the challenges brought about by the *Aufklärung*, in terms of its penchant for the historical-critical method of approaching not only Scripture but the doctrinal contents of faith as a whole. With the above insights in mind, one might say that Bonaventure and Augustine played no small roles in preparing Ratzinger for the challenges based on the nature of historically verifiable claims that were characteristic of the *Aufklärung*. As we will see in the subsequent treatment of the engagements between Ratzinger and the postulates of the *Aufklärung* on love, person, creation, and reason that Ratzinger takes up on account of the flexible character of the Greek concept of *logos*, the concern for Ratzinger will not be to deny the import of these concepts from the philosophical point of view, but to open these concepts up to the rationality of faith and love, through Augustine, and dialectical claims of history in an ongoing transcendental sense, through Bonaventure. In all, the fulfillment of all human hopes and aspirations on this side of history presents a false hope, for human hopes rightly experienced in history will find their ultimate fulfillment in a Christological completion at the end of history.

In confronting the historical claims of the *Aufklärung* on love, person, reason, word, and the rational understanding of Jesus' sonship as one finds, for example, in Hegel's *Spirit of Christianity* and the *Positivity of Religion*, Ratzinger clearly engages these positions with Augustinian insights, as will be seen later in this work. Chapter two thus sets the philosophical foundations and framework in which these Augustinian ecclesiological convictions in Ratzinger will play out in the field of the post-*Aufklärung* context.

Notes — Chapter One

1 Some biographical texts include: Stephen Mansfield, *Pope Benedict XVI His Life and Mission* (New York: Penguin Group USA Inc. 2005); Brennan Pursell, *Benedict of Bavaria An Intimate Portrait of the Pope and His Homeland* (New Haven, CT: Circle Press, 2008); Lawrence Paul Hemming, *Benedict XVI: Fellow Worker for the Truth: An Introduction to his Life and Thought* (London: Burns & Oates, 2005); Georg Ratzinger, *My*

Brother, The Pope (San Francisco: Ignatius Press, 2011); Peter Seewald, *Benedict XVI An Intimate Portrait* (San Francisco: Ignatius Press, 2008); Marco Bardazzi, *In the Vineyard of the Lord, The Life, Faith, and Teachings of Joseph Ratzinger/Benedict XVI* (New York: Rizzoli International Publications Inc. 2005).

2 Vincent Twomey, S.V.D., *Pope Benedict XVI, The Conscience of Our Age: A Theological Portrait* (San Francisco: Ignatius Press, 2007), 55–61.

3 Mary McCaughey, *The Church as Hermeneutical Community and the Place of Embodied Faith in Joseph Ratzinger and Lewis S. Mudge* (Bern: International Academic Publishers, 2015), 202.

4 Ratzinger, *Introduction*, 11.

5 Joseph Ratzinger, *Milestones: Memoirs 1972–1977* (San Francisco: Ignatius Press, 1998), 8.

6 Benedict XVI, *Last Testament in His Own Words with Peter Seewald*, trans. Philip Jacobs (New York: Bloomsbury, 2016), 43.

7 Benedict XVI, *Last Testament*, 43.

8 Benedict XVI, "Homily for the Beginning of the Petrine Ministry of the Bishop of Rome" (April 24, 2005), at www.vatican.va, accessed April 5, 2018.

9 William Congdon, *The Sabbath of History: With Meditations on Holy Week by Joseph Ratzinger* (New Haven, CT: Knights of Columbus Museum, 2012), 135–136.

10 Congdon and Ratzinger, *Sabbath of History*, 136.

11 Congdon and Ratzinger, *Sabbath of History*, 137.

12 The *Schott* was the German translation of the Missal from the Latin original, undertaken in the nineteenth century by the Benedictine monk, Anselm Schott, of Beuron Abbey.

13 Ratzinger, *Milestones*, 20.

14 Congdon and Ratzinger, *Sabbath of History*, 147.

15 Congdon and Ratzinger, *Sabbath of History*, 147.

16 Congdon and Ratzinger, *Sabbath of History*, 147–148.

17 Benedict XVI, *First Messages of His Holiness Benedict XVI* (Nairobi: Pauline Publications Africa, 2005), 16–17.

18 Benedict XVI, *The Door of Faith: Motu Proprio Porta Fidei* of the Supreme Pontiff Benedict XVI for the Induction of the Year of Faith (Nairobi: Pauline Publications Africa, 2012), 2.

19 Congdon and Ratzinger, *Sabbath of History*, 148.

20 Congdon and Ratzinger, *Sabbath of History*, 148.

21 Congdon and Ratzinger, *Sabbath of History*, 148–149.

22 Ratzinger, *Milestones*, 12.

23 Benedict XVI, *Last Testament*, 46.

24 Georg Ratzinger, *My Brother, The Pope*, trans. Michael J. Miller (San Francisco: Ignatius Press, 2011), 65.

25 Joseph Ratzinger, *Joseph Ratzinger with Vittorio Messori, The Ratzinger Report: An Exclusive Interview on the State of the Church*, trans. Salvator Attanasio and Graham Harrison (San Francisco: Ignatius Press, 1985), 45–46.
26 Ratzinger, *The Ratzinger Report*, 46.
27 Ratzinger, *Pilgrim Fellowship of Faith*, 183.
28 Joseph Ratzinger, *Behold the Pierced One: An Approach to a Spiritual Christology*, trans. Graham Harrison (San Francisco: Ignatius Press, 1986), 127.
29 Joseph Ratzinger, *Being Christian*, trans. David Walls (Chicago: Franciscan Herald Press, 1970), ix.
30 Ratzinger, *Being Christian*, 17.
31 Ratzinger, *Being Christian*, 19.
32 Ratzinger, *Being Christian*, 7–8.
33 Ratzinger, *Being Christian*, 8.
34 Ratzinger, *Being Christian*, 8.
35 Ratzinger, *Being Christian*, 10–11.
36 Ratzinger, *Being Christian*, 12.
37 Ratzinger, *Being Christian*, 15.
38 Benedict XVI, Interview by Jacques Servais, S.J., October 2015, 12, at www.catholicworldreport-text-of-benedict-xvis-recent-rare-and-lengthy-interview/, Accessed July 10, 2018.
39 Benedict XVI, Interview by Jacques Servais, S.J., 1–2.
40 Benedict XVI, *Last Testament*, 78.
41 Ratzinger, *Salt of the Earth,* 55.
42 Ratzinger, *Milestones*, 42.
43 Ratzinger, *Milestones*, 42–44.
44 Ratzinger, *Milestones*, 42–44.
45 Ratzinger, *Introduction*, 138.
46 Kant's *Critique of Pure Reason* and *Religion Within the Boundaries of Mere Reason* essentially makes the case for a rational faith that ultimately replaces revealed religion with the moral law, inherent in each person. This moral law is antecedent and superior to all works of piety or postulates of revealed religion.
47 Ratzinger, *Introduction*, 139.
48 Ratzinger, *Salt of the Earth*, 41.
49 Augustine of Hippo, *Confessions*, trans. F. J. Sheed (Cambridge: Hackett Publishing Company Inc, 2006), VIII, ii, 3, 142.
50 Ratzinger, *Milestones*, 44.
51 Martin Buber, *I and Thou*, trans. Walter Kaufmann (New York: Touchstone, 1970), 54–66.
52 Buber, *I and Thou*, 62.
53 Buber, *I and Thou*, 62.
54 Benedict XVI, *Last Testament*, 99.

55 Ratzinger, *Salt of the Earth*, 60.
56 Ratzinger, *Milestones*, 44.
57 Benedict XVI, *Last Testament*, 79.
58 Ratzinger, *Milestones*, 44–45.
59 Ratzinger, *Behold the Pierced One*, 33–35.
60 Ratzinger, *Behold the Pierced One*, 34.
61 Ratzinger, *Behold the Pierced One*, 34–35.
62 Ratzinger, *Introduction*, 58–75.
63 About his theological mentor, Gottlieb Söhngen, Ratzinger says, that he "had originally wanted to be only a philosopher and had begun his career with a dissertation on Kant. He belonged to that dynamic current in Thomism that took from Thomas the passion for truth and the habit of asking unrelenting questions about the foundation and goal of all the real: but all of this he consciously placed in relation to the questions that philosophy asks today. With his phenomenology, Husserl had opened the door for metaphysics, at least a crack, a door others were now throwing wide open, although in very different ways. Heidegger was asking questions concerning being, Scheler concerning values, and Nikolai Hartmann was attempting to develop a metaphysics in a rigorously Aristotelian spirit. External circumstances directed Söhngen toward theology. Being a child of a mixed marriage and deeply concerned with the ecumenical question on account of his origins, Söhngen took up the debate with Karl Barth and Emil Brunner [...]. Characteristic of Söhngen above all was the fact that he always developed his thought on the basis of the sources themselves, beginning with Aristotle and Plato, then on to Clement of Alexandria and Augustine, Anselm, Bonaventure and Thomas, all the way to Luther and finally the Tübingen theologians of the last century. Pascal and Newman too, were among his favorite authors. What particularly impressed me about him was that he was never satisfied in theology with the sort of positivism that could usually be detected in other subjects. Rather, he always asked the question concerning the truth of the matter and hence the question concerning the immediate reality of what is believed." Ratzinger, *Milestones*, 56.
64 Benedict XVI, *Last Testament*, 83.
65 Elio Guerriero, *Benedict XVI His Life and Thought*, trans. William J. Melcher (San Francisco: Ignatius Press, 2018), 65.
66 Guerriero, *Benedict XVI His Life and Thought*, 62.
67 Ratzinger, *Pilgrim Fellowship of Faith*, 31.
68 Ratzinger, *Pilgrim Fellowship of Faith*, 31.
69 Ratzinger, *Pilgrim Fellowship of Faith*, 150.
70 Ratzinger, *Church, Ecumenism and Politics*, 148.
71 Ratzinger, *Church, Ecumenism and Politics*, 148.
72 Ratzinger, *Church, Ecumenism and Politics*, 150.

73 Friedrich Nietzsche, *On the Genealogy of Morals*, trans. Walter Kaufmann (New York: Vintage Books, 1967), I, 1.
74 Ratzinger, *Church, Ecumenism and Politics*, 152.
75 Thomas Aquinas, *Summa Theologiae*, I, q. 16, art. 3. ad 1. trans. Laurence Shapcote, O.P. (Lander, Wyoming: The Aquinas Institute, 2012).
76 Aidan Nichols, O.P., *The Thought of Benedict XVI: An Introduction to the Theology of Joseph Ratzinger* (New York: Burns & Oates, 2005), 18.
77 Pope Benedict XVI, *Church Fathers: From Clement of Rome to Augustine* (San Francisco: Ignatius Press, 2008), 167.
78 Benedict XVI, *Church Fathers*, 178.
79 Benedict XVI, *Church Fathers*, 182.
80 Benedict XVI, *Church Fathers*, 182.
81 Augustine, *Enarrationes in Psalmos*, trans. Maria Boulding, OSB (Vienna: Austrian Academy of Sciences Press, 2004), 85, 1.
82 Nichols, *The Thought of Benedict XVI*, 30.
83 Ratzinger, *Salt of the Earth*, 65–66.
84 Augustine of Hippo, *The Confessions*, trans. F. J. Sheed (Indianapolis, IN: Hackett Publishing Company, Inc. 2006), III, v). Augustine writes: "When I first read those Scriptures, I did not feel in the least what I have just said: they seemed to me unworthy to be compared with the majesty of Cicero. My conceit was repelled by their simplicity, and I had not the mind to penetrate into their depths."
85 Nichols, *Thought of Benedict XVI*, 33.
86 Joseph Ratzinger, *Volk und Haus Gottes in Augustine Lehre von der Kirche*, (Munich: EOS-Verlag, 1954), 9–10, trans. Nichols, *Thought of Benedict XVI*, 33.
87 Ratzinger, *Volk und Haus Gottes*,133–134, trans. Nichols, *Thought of Benedict XVI*, 42.
88 Nichols, *Thought of Benedict XVI*, 42.
89 Ratzinger, *Volk und Haus Gottes*, 138, trans. Nichols, *Thought of Benedict XVI*, 43.
90 Ratzinger, *Volk und Haus Gottes*, 146, trans. Nichols, *Thought of Benedict XVI*, 43.
91 Benedict XVI, *Church Fathers*, 194–195.
92 Augustine of Hippo. *Against Cresconius the Grammarian*, trans. Allan Fitzgerald (Michigan: Eerdmans Publishing, 1999), 3, 35, 39: PL 43, 517.
93 Ratzinger, *Called to Communion*, 86.
94 Patrick McGlinchey, *Ratzinger's Augustinianism and Evangelicalism* (Bletchley, Milton Keynes: Paternoster Lightning Source, 2017), 78–79.
95 Benedict XVI, *Church Fathers*, 193.
96 Benedict XVI, *Church Fathers*, 193.
97 Ratzinger, *Introduction*, 60.
98 Joseph Ratzinger, "Presentation on the Occasion of the Centenary of the

Death of Cardinal John Henry Newman," Rome, April 28, 1990, at www.vatican.va, accessed October 2, 2018.

99 McGlinchey, *Ratzinger's Augustinianism and Evangelicalism*, 80.

100 Ratzinger, *Volk und Haus Gottes*, 7–8, trans. Nichols, *Thought of Benedict XVI*, 31.

101 Ratzinger, *Volk und Haus Gottes*, 8, trans. Nichols, *Thought of Benedict XVI*, 32.

102 Ratzinger, *Volk und Haus Gottes*, 8–9, trans. Nichols, *Thought of Benedict XVI*, 32.

103 Ratzinger, *Volk und Haus Gottes*, 82, trans. Nichols, *Thought of Benedict XVI*, 32.

104 Ratzinger, *Volk und Haus Gottes*, 167–168; 175–177, trans. Nichols, *Thought of Benedict XVI*, 45.

105 Ratzinger, *Volk und Haus Gottes*, 170, trans. Nichols, *Thought of Benedict XVI*, 45.

106 Ratzinger, *Volk und Haus Gottes*, 173, trans. Nichols, *Thought of Benedict XVI*, 47.

107 Nichols, *Thought of Benedict XVI*, 47.

108 Nichols, *Thought of Benedict XVI*, 47.

109 Ratzinger, *Volk und Haus Gottes*, 213, trans. Nichols, *Thought of Benedict XVI*, 48.

110 Ratzinger, *Volk und Haus Gottes*, 138, trans. Nichols, *Thought of Benedict XVI*, 43.

111 Ratzinger, *Volk und Haus Gottes*, 146, trans. Nichols, *Thought of Benedict XVI*, 43.

112 Augustine of Hippo, *The City of God*, trans. Gerald G. Walsh, S.J., Demetrius B. Zema, S. J., Grace Monahan, O.S.U. and Daniel J. Honan, (New York: Image Books, 1958), XI – XXII.

113 Nichols, *Thought of Benedict XVI*, 49.

114 Ratzinger, *Volk Und Haus Gottes*, 36, trans. Nichols, *Thought of Benedict XVI*, 33.

115 McGlinchey, *Ratzinger's Augustinianism and Evangelicalism*, 83.

116 Nichols, *Thought of Benedict XVI*, 36–40.

117 Ratzinger, *Milestones*, 108.

118 Ratzinger, *Milestones*, 109.

119 Ratzinger, *Milestones*, 108–109.

120 Maximilian Heim, *Joseph Ratzinger, Life in the Church and Living Theology: Fundamentals of Ecclesiology with Reference to Lumen Gentium*, trans. Michael J. Miller (San Francisco: Ignatius Press, 2005), 161.

121 Ratzinger, *Milestones*, 127.

122 Ratzinger, *Milestones*, 109–112.

123 Ratzinger, *Milestones*, 111.

124 Ratzinger, *Milestones*, 112–113.
125 Ratzinger, *Milestones*, 110. It is important to note the growth in scholarship around the question of the influence on Joachim of Fiore on the Spiritual Franciscans from the time that Ratzinger defended his habilitation in 1957. Joachim wrote three major works, namely, the *Exposition on the Apocalypse*, the *Book of Concordance*, and the *Ten-stringed Psaltery*. In these writings, Joachim shares much with the Jewish and Christian apocalyptic writers in the biblical times. *Apocalyptic Spirituality: Treatises and Letters of Lactantius, Adso of Montier-en-der, Joachim of Fiore, the Franciscan Spirituals, Savonarol*, trans. Bernard McGinn (New York: Paulist Press, 1979), 97–98.
126 Matthew Bunson, ed. *Encyclopedia of Catholic History* (Huntington, IN: Our Sunday Visitor, Inc. 1995), 458–459.
127 Bunson, *Encyclopedia of Catholic History*, 459.
128 Ratzinger, *Milestones*, 111.
129 Joseph Ratzinger, *The Theology of History in St. Bonaventure*, trans. Zachary Hayes, O.F.M. (Chicago: Franciscan Herald Press, 1971), V.
130 Ratzinger, *The Theology of History*, 17.
131 Ratzinger, *The Theology of History*, 7.
132 Ratzinger, *The Theology of History*, 92.
133 Ratzinger, *The Theology of History*, 104.
134 Ratzinger, *The Theology of History*, 93.
135 Ratzinger, *The Theology of History*, 62–63.
136 Ratzinger, *The Theology of History*, 8–9.
137 Ratzinger, *The Theology of History*, 14.
138 Ratzinger, *The Theology of History*, 54–55.
139 Ratzinger, *The Theology of History*, 55.
140 Ratzinger, *The Theology of History*, 161–162.
141 Ratzinger, *The Theology of History*, 28.
142 Ratzinger, *The Theology of History*, 50.
143 Ratzinger, *The Theology of History*, 51.
144 Joseph Ratzinger, *Called to Communion* (San Francisco: Ignatius Press, 1996), 46.
145 Heim, *Joseph Ratzinger: Life in the Church and Living Theology*, 160.
146 Ratzinger, *Salt of the Earth*, 63.
147 Some of Ratzinger's positions on liberation theology would be found in: Joseph Ratzinger, *Principle of Catholic Theology: Building Stones for a Fundamental Theology* (San Francisco: Ignatius Press, 1989), 378–393; Joseph Ratzinger, *Church, Ecumenism and Politics: New Endeavors in Ecclesiology* (San Francisco: Ignatius Press, 2008), 237–254; Joseph Ratzinger, "Eschatology and Utopia" in *The Ratzinger Report: An Exclusive Interview on the State of the Church* (San Francisco: Ignatius Press, 1986), 169–190.

Chapter Two: *Ratzinger: From Augustine and Bonaventure through the* Aufklärung *to the God of Faith and the God of the Philosophers*

Chapter one of this work delved into the biographical outline of Ratzinger's life, and how, following the reading which Ratzinger himself makes of the circumstances of his birth, there emerges a sense of openness to the provisionality of this side of human existence and likewise the sense of the sacred, even in what could appear ordinary events of life. Chapter one also considered in greater detail Ratzinger's engagements with Augustine and Bonaventure, the two figures that largely shaped and defined Ratzinger's theological outlook especially regarding the question of the Church. For Augustine, love or *caritas* is the defining characteristic of the Church, while Bonaventure's view of the Church is one of a Christo-centric character. Likewise, in chapter one, the theological contours of the Church for Ratzinger emerge thanks to the insights drawn from Augustine and Bonaventure. For the former, the Church is the People and House of God in the midst of the world. For the latter, the emphasis is on the ultimate triumph of the Church as the community of the just, brought about and sustained thanks to the historical and supernatural revelation beginning with Israel and finding its culmination in the figure of Christ, the center of the new community whose life is nourished by the gifts bestowed upon her by the Holy Spirit.

In this sense, one could say that Ratzinger's engagement with Augustine and Bonaventure was not only an intra-ecclesial experience, but also prepared him for a more robust public engagement in terms of the life of faith that is the life of the Church in the public arena. That said, it might be noteworthy to remark that just as Augustine's ecclesiological positions were shaped by historical events such as the sack of Rome by the Barbarians or the Pelagian controversy, so too with Ratzinger, only in this instance, the ecclesial context will no longer be the spirit of the Barbarians but the spirit of the *Aufklärung*. In this sense, one can talk of Ratzinger's theological formation as thereby having a contextual character.

And again, chapter one shows that while, on the one hand, Ratzinger affirms the rational spirit of the *Aufklärung*, he is not caught up in a tug of war between faith and reason, but seeks to go beyond, transcending the antithesis into a reconciliation of both. Along these introductory lines and insights, therefore, one can recall the famous question that Tertullian posed centuries ago, viz. what has Athens got to do with Jerusalem? Ratzinger's response could very well be summarized as: Everything. Such a conclusion is likely in the sense that if an academic's inaugural lecture is anything to go by, then Ratzinger already pointed to this direction of the relationship between philosophy and theology as constitutive of the hermeneutical framework of his theology.

Indeed, as seen in chapter one, this reading of theology with the help of philosophy and history is something that emerges from Ratzinger's study of Augustine and Bonaventure and his wide reading of modern philosophy. This is very much evident in Ratzinger's 1959 Inaugural Lecture at the University of Bonn, titled "The God of Faith and the God of Philosophers." In this lecture, Ratzinger sought to foster a dialogue between faith and reason, an interchange that he sees as necessary for both if faith and reason are to attain their highest aspirations in the essential roles that both are called to play in the world. This lecture offers a profound insight into Ratzinger's thinking particularly on modern philosophy as an indispensable interlocutor with theology. But before delving further into Ratzinger's ecclesial reading of the philosophical currents that came with modern thought in the *Aufklärung*, what are the defining qualities of the *Aufklärung* with which Ratzinger engages?

2.1 The Peculiarities of the *Aufklärung*

The *Aufklärung*, as the German strand of the pan-European Enlightenment movement, marked a conclusively irrevocable change in the political, religious, and social life of the old continent.[1] Europe was taken over by the ideas of liberty, fraternity, and equality, which translates into individual freedom, religious toleration, and the equality of citizens before the law. Europe witnessed the flowering of culture and polite society in the eighteenth century. As a philosophical system, the *Aufklärung* marked "the attempt to establish the authority of reason in all walks of life, whether in the state, the church, the universities, or society at large."[2] The *Aufklärung* also reflected an optimism in the belief in social progress.[3] But this optimism regarding human potential was not blind, for even in the positivism and optimism that characterized the *Aufklärung*, Europe was still conscious of the potentials of debasement rooted in the human heart. As Nicholas Till points out:

> The *philosophers* and the *Aufklärer* were certainly believers in progress; but while one eye of the Enlightenment was always focused gladly on the bright future, the other eye was trained uneasily on the recent past. For the Enlightenment had been born in the shadow of the disintegration of social order which had occurred throughout Europe in the seventeenth century, following what seemed like an almost total collapse of political and religious authority. Civil war on a scale hitherto unknown had riven nations and overthrown established political powers; religious doubt had come to assail those not possessed and consumed by the new fanaticisms; status and property no longer offered security and certainty. The unrest of the mid-seventeenth century forced a fundamental reappraisal of the principles of social order, which led people to ask whether the traditional bounds could ever again be adequate.[4]

Given this atmosphere of socio-political and economic uncertainties, the *Aufklärung* as a pan-European movement sought to offer new interpretations of human nature, of society and of the moral life, in an otherwise uncertain Europe.[5] One can therefore read two sides regarding the *Aufklärung* coin: on the one hand, the awareness that the medieval social order which saw a harmony between throne and altar was no longer sustainable became a position held by large sectors of the intelligentsia class. On the other hand, there was an eagerness or optimism to forge a new basis for the social order that had to emerge from the ruins of the collapsed medieval order.[6] Thus, both pessimism and optimism characterized the emergence of the *Aufklärung* spirit across Europe.

Added to this sense of social change as a contributory factor to the development of the *Aufklärung* was the rise of capitalism in early modern Europe. In the medieval period, Till writes:

> Most people had been born into a predetermined social position that defined them throughout their life, and placed them within a network of hierarchies and institutions understood to be part of the divine, unchanging order: a person was inseparable from his or her role in society; he or she was a peasant, an artisan, a knight, and not an individual who happened to have this or that occupation; and the medieval person's role carried with it a number of pre-ordained obligations such as those of kinship or feudal duty. Binding this multiplicity of institutions and hierarchies together was the authority and power of the Church[...]. The stability of medieval society was undermined from within by the dynamics of economic growth—the opening-up of markets, the widening circulation of commodities, the accumulation of wealth by a new class that derived its power from money rather than status. This in turn forced into being another class without status obligations, which sold its labor in exchange for a wage. Thus, the demands of economic activity gave rise to some of the basic ideals of the Enlightenment itself: individual freedom, legal equality, religious toleration.[7]

One can therefore make the case that the *Aufklärung* was a rejection of socio-economic determinism. People were eager to move upward in the social strata of society. People felt hard work had to be rewarded and the sense of a privileged economic class eschewed. And with free markets came newfound wealth for the masses, and with wealth came the desire for power, in this case, political power, which inevitably meant the discarding of monarchical and royal power, in what one might consider a clash of irreconcilable wills. The emerging socio-political order that came into being with material prosperity was articulated *via* the language of equality, and sustained by the spirit of freedom, liberty, and fraternity amongst the emerging business class.

Underlying all of Europe in terms of characterizing the *Aufklärung* was what Ernst Cassirer described as the *libido sciendi*, that is, the lust for knowledge, which, as Cassirer claims, "theological dogmatism had outlawed and branded as intellectual pride."[8] The eighteenth century saw the search for knowledge as a prerogative of the soul, and the *Aufklärer* largely felt that it was his duty to defend this right of every person to knowledge, without any censors. A proof of this was the emergence of the *Encyclopedia*, championed by the French thinker Diderot, which Diderot saw not only as a source of a body of knowledge, but more importantly as a tool meant to change the way people thought about all of reality.[9] And this is quite understandable, for it would have been meaningless to champion the usage of reason without allowing for an unbridled access to all knowledge, especially in the broad sense of reason that the concept took in the mind of the *Aufklärer*.

Notwithstanding these pan-European orientations, the *Aufklärung* had its own peculiar German character that distinguished it from its French and English counterparts, some of which we can identify to be the following.

2.1.1 The *Aufklärung*'s Alertness to Christianity as a Religious-Cultural Phenomenon

Firstly, unlike the French Enlightenment, the *Aufklärung* cannot be assessed as specifically an anti-religious or anti-Christian movement:

> The Church was much more than its institutions and doctrines, and it was impossible for reformers to conceive of their culture as divorced from its religious context. There persisted the belief in the possibility of a harmony between the civil and religious authority—the *concordia sacerdotii et imperii*—in which the sum was greater than its parts. This is

> evident, first of all, in the reformer's interest in ecclesiastical and religious history.[10]

Thus, the *Aufklärung* showed a keen interest in the religious dimension of the German society, albeit with a critical and reformist orientation.

In this sense, "the theologians of the *Aufklärung* were concerned to reformulate Christian doctrines upon the basis of premises more justifiable upon rational grounds, either by reducing them, reinterpreting them, or eliminating them."[11] In other words, the *Aufklärung*, particularly in its initial stages of the eighteenth century, was not representative of an adversarial and confrontational relationship between faith and reason, philosophy and theology, Church and State, even if it tended to subordinate faith to reason, theology to philosophy, and called for a healthy autonomy in the intertwining relationship between Church and State.[12] Alister McGrath explains that the reason for such a benevolent attitude toward faith and hence toward the Church was owed to the conviction that "God is the ontological principle or being which determines what exists, and the structure of existence."[13] *Aufklärung* thinkers therefore saw reason, faith, and the institutional Church through a harmonious lens, albeit maintaining that revelation, faith, and the practices of faith as put forth by the Church had to be judged on the basis of reason, which occupies the first place in the grand scheme of things.

The bottom line at this point, in terms of the relationship between Christianity and the *Aufklärung,* on the part of the latter is that "truth is not something which can be regarded as mediated to man from outside (for example, on the basis of a recognized authority), but something which arises within man on account of its conformity with his rationality."[14] McGrath thus concludes based on this subsequent parting of ways between faith and reason, that, even with Kant, Hegel, and perhaps Heidegger, "it will therefore be evident that there was an inherent tendency within the *Aufklärung* to regard the concept of supernatural revelation with suspicion."[15] How so? I think because of the sense of the historical vis-à-vis revelation that eventually emerges with the *Aufklärung*. And at the center of this dialectics between history and revelation stands the question of the historical verifiability of religious truth claims.

2.1.2 The *Aufklärung* and the Sense of the Historical-Religious Experience

In effect, as the spirit of the *Aufklärung* further developed the disconnecting of reason from faith it raised the question of whether the concept of divine revelation was historically defensible, especially under the claims of autonomous rationality. In this light, and as McGrath points out, Hermann Samuel Reimarus (1694–1768) applied the *Aufklärung* insights to the nature of truth and history, with very astonishing results for the claims of Christian faith.[16] In effect, the *Aufklärer* called into question the historicity and accuracy of the life of Christ as presented in the Scriptures. They argued for the insufficiency of the events recorded in Scripture, particularly the New Testament, even if they were eyewitness accounts. As McGrath points out, "The origins of the 'Quest of the Historical Jesus' may be seen in the *Aufklärung* conviction that the gospels contained material concerning Jesus which was unacceptable (because it was immoral, or supernatural) and which thus required correction in the light of modern thought."[17] The real Jesus was clearly different from the Jesus of the gospels. As McGrath maintains, the *Aufklärer* "attempted to evolve methods of internal and external criticism by which an historical re-evaluation of dogma might proceed, leading ultimately to the exclusion of doctrines which were considered to be irrational or morally indefensible."[18] An example of such a doctrine will be the divinity of Christ, which was often reinterpreted in purely moral terms. And even when other truths of revelation such as the Incarnation of *Logos* in Christ were accepted, they were represented as a recognition of the fact that spiritual truths can take palpable and historical forms.[19] Thus, one must note the distinction between the concept acceptable to the *Aufklärer*, and the content that was subjected to a radical historical criticism. A good example of this is Kant's treatment of the *Gestalt* of Jesus in *Religion Within the Boundaries of Mere Reason*, in which the supernatural claims of Christianity were rationalized and reduced to categories of rationality.

Albert Schweitzer offers a trenchant analysis of the salient points in his *The Quest of the Historical Jesus*. Given that this reading of the figure of Jesus and the Church marks the monumental shift of the assumptions and presuppositions of hitherto unquestionable orthodox Christological dogmas, and granted that these positions are largely engaged by Ratzinger albeit with the intent of rebuttals, we can state the salient points here as captured and enunciated by Reimarus. With Reimarus, we find a rational presentation of Jesus as a Jewish prophet within the Jewish messianic history of expectation of the breaking forth of the kingdom of God, in the life of Israel. From the extant fragments or writings of Reimarus, Schweitzer points out that for Reimarus' historical reading, the starting point was the content of the preaching of Jesus, which is markedly different from the teachings or preaching of the apostles. Jesus preaching might be synthesized in this proclamation: "Repent, for the kingdom of God is at hand." This "kingdom of God" must be understood in a completely Jewish sense, given that neither John nor Jesus himself bothered to explain it in their preaching. The assumption is that their audience knew what it meant. Jesus is therefore an eschatological preacher of the kingdom of God.[20] Owing to this "kingdom" character of Jesus' preaching, the assumption was that under the leadership of Jesus, the promised Messiah was about to be brought in—messianism understood here in the political sense.

Giving voice to Reimarus, Schweitzer explains that for the Jews listening to Jesus, "there was no difficulty in accepting the belief that he was the Messiah, the Son of God, for this belief had no metaphysical content. The nation was the son of God; the kings of the covenant-people were sons of God; the Messiah was in a pre-eminent sense the son of God. Thus, even in his messianic claims, Jesus remained within the limits of humanity."[21] Within this human limit of Jesus, Reimarus claims that a proper historical reading of Jesus is one in which Jesus' preaching is understood as a summons to righteousness as a prerequisite for the kingdom of God.

Put differently, Jesus did not intend to found a new religion. His was an ardent desire to bring about the eschatological reality of the kingdom of God, and this is the spectrum through which one has to read the events in Jerusalem that culminated with his death. Jesus wanted to forcefully bring about the messianic prophecy of Zechariah in Jerusalem. The cry of Jesus, "My God, my God, why have you forsaken me?" is a glaring pointer to Jesus' realization and acknowledgment that God had not aided him as he had hoped. The cry shows that Jesus had not intended to die, but to politically liberate the Jews from Roman oppression.[22] With Jesus' death, all the sensual hopes of messianism on his part and on the part of his disciples came to an unexpected end. In order to earn a living—given that they had abandoned their trades when they accepted to follow Jesus—the disciples took on the second strand of Jewish messianism in a supernatural sense. They offered a spiritual interpretation of Jesus' death, hence, the necessity of the Resurrection motif.[23] Armed with this spiritual messianism explainable thanks to the Resurrection, the Parousia became the next logical step.

In this sense, the second coming of Jesus offered the disciples the content which they could preach to a gullible first-century Palestinian audience. The Parousia was therefore a creation of the early Church to explain away the failure of Jesus to bring about the kingdom of God, a failure of Jesus the eschatological prophet. The Parousia was a product meant to sustain hope, rather than a teaching of Jesus. Owing this, Christianity is therefore built on a false premise. Christianity is a fraud because it is a creation by Jesus' disciples for the sole purpose of ensuring their usefulness, after the mistaken and failed project of their teacher, Jesus of Nazareth. To put it more precisely, "inasmuch as the non-fulfilment of its eschatology is not admitted, our Christianity rests upon a fraud."[24] In sum, Jesus is a failed prophet whose understanding of Jewish messianism landed him into a premature and unexpected death, over and against his wishes and expectations.

This is certainly not the place to evaluate these claims and positions advanced by Reimarus, as spelled out by Schweitzer. But it suffices to say that while one must certainly acknowledge, to Reimarus' credit, a strong sense for the historical and a keen attention to exegesis, it must be stated, as Schweitzer does, that overall, Reimarus saw eschatology from a wrong perspective, namely, the political. Reimarus can only read Jesus as the son of David, nothing more. And not only that, Reimarus' assumption that the eschatology was earthly and political is not only restrictive, but in pursuing this narrow reading of eschatology, Reimarus largely ignored the account of other New Testament texts such as the Gospel of John.[25] And such a reductionist reading of Jesus does injustice both to any historical reading of the figure of Jesus and the Christological confession erected on such a history.

On this basis, therefore, McGrath points out, the *Aufklärung* poses three Christological challenges: Firstly, the traditional two natures of Christ were called into question, following the naturalistic and rationalistic logic of the *Aufklärung*. Modern reason could jettison this "relic" of the early Church without much controversy.[26] Secondly, if following the logic of the *Aufklärung*, Christ's significance had to be conceived in purely naturalistic terms, how would the Church represent the unicity of Christ? The *Aufklärung* generally presented Christ as a moralist, a teacher of the good life whose superiority over other moral teachers is based upon the supremely moral character of Christ's teachings.[27] As McGrath points out, "there seemed to be no way in which his uniqueness could be established without resorting to a discredited supernaturalism."[28] Such a view during the *Aufklärung* of Christ as an ethics teacher would naturally be a concern to someone of a spiritual and intellectual temperament like Joseph Ratzinger. Thirdly, another Christological challenge of the *Aufklärung* vis-à-vis the Christian faith has to do with the certainty of our knowledge of Christ.[29] How can we be sure about the Christ of the gospels when, following the dialectics of history, one cannot ascertain with objective certainty that what we read in the Scriptures is true?

2.1.3 The *Aufklärung* and the Duel between Divine and Human Rational Supremacy

McGrath maintains that "the ultimate foundation of the theology of the *Aufklärung* may be regarded as the doctrine that the natural faculty of human reason is qualitatively similar to (although quantitatively weaker than) the divine reason."[30] The world of the *Aufklärung* is in essence a rational cosmos in which the human being works out his or her own moral perfection by conforming the self to the moral structures of the cosmos. Moral activity is therefore the highest destiny of the human being, and reason is the only practical guide to this destiny. This rationality of the *Aufklärung* is best summarized in these three propositions: firstly, all reality is rational; secondly, the human being has the necessary epistemological capabilities to unearth the rational *Ordnung* of reality; and thirdly, the human being is adept at acting upon this cognition of reality in order to achieve his or her rational destiny by acting morally.[31] In this light, the human being is capable of attaining morality without any external assistance, and revelation and the authority of God was perceived to be such an extrinsic assistance. In other words, unaided reason was capable of bringing about a just and moral society. In this worldview, religious faith as a source and sustainer of morality was no longer essential, for one could be moral or ethical without being religious.

Such a view of the *Aufklärung* naturally runs contrary to the Christian orthodoxy that, over the years of observation, reflection, and pondering the actions of the human being vis-à-vis the moral law, had come to discern in revelation the woundedness of human nature in the doctrine of original sin. While not rejecting the value of human rationality in discerning and arriving at moral truths, Christianity recognized as well the place of God's revelation in the moral landscape. The orthodox position, following Augustine, has been that on account of original sin, the human intellect is blinded and the will is weakened, so much so that the human being cannot function as an autonomous moral agent.[32] As fallen creatures, therefore, God's moral law in historical revelation purifies and strengthens reason's natural reflections and discernments. In the eyes of the *Aufklärung*, this doctrine of original sin certainly posed a conceptual obstacle to moral perfection and even smacked of Manichean dualism. The doctrine clearly had become obsolete and warranted abandonment.[33] Therefore, in order to counteract doctrines like original sin, the science of the development of dogma emerged from the *Aufklärung* movement.[34] In this sense, it was not sufficient to simply believe what the Church teaches as doctrine. A critical understanding of the formulation and historical evolution of a given doctrine was as essential as the doctrine itself.

2.1.4 The *Aufklärung*, the Nature of Reality and its Christological Implications

Another distinguishing characteristic of the *Aufklärung* was its understanding of the nature of reality. As McGrath points out, the theologians of the *Aufklärung* regarded rational truth as necessary, eternal, and universal in the sense that "it was axiomatic that such knowledge could not be had through an historical religion, in that history was not capable of conveying the necessary, unchanging, and eternal core of rational reality. Historically mediated rational truth was regarded as a contradiction in terms."[35] This was because the spirit of the *Aufklärung* read history as conditionally shaped, relative to a specific time and space.

If the truths of revelation were to be necessary, that is, unchanging and eternal, they could not be historically revealed because that would have meant they were conditioned. Spinoza captures this interpretive dynamic when he declares that knowledge of God "should be derived from general ideas, in themselves certain and known, so that the truth of an historical narrative is very far from being a necessary requisite for our attaining our highest good."[36] Or, to phrase the mindset more pointedly as Lessing does, the "accidental truths of history (*zufällige Geschichtswahrheiten*) can never become proof of necessary truths of reason (*notwendige Vernunftwahrheiten*)."[37] Underpinning this *Aufklärung*'s reading of history is a static perspective of reality, in which history is interpreted in a relative sense, with no absolutes. If all things in history and from history are relative and conditional, how must we now understand God and the truths of faith, given that God is, by nature, timeless? The likely conclusion could be that it would be impossible to derive the truths of God from history or historical events, as recorded in the gospels.

The *Aufklärung* therefore placed history and revelation in a tense dialectical relationship, for following this relativization of history, Christ is primarily understood as a moral teacher in his lifetime, a moral exemplar whose main goal was to call people to excel in the moral life. Jesus' death is a supreme example of self-giving. In addition, the *Aufklärung* interpreted Christ as embodying the potentials of every human being toward perfection.[38] Put differently, the moral perfection possessed by Christ is latent in every human being. Christ therefore inspires every human being to strive to realize this latent perfection.[39] In the final analysis, this position of Christ as moral exemplar and inspirer implies a discrepancy between the historical Jesus and the apostolic Church from whom the accounts recorded in the gospels emerged.

2.1.5 The *Aufklärung* and the Educated Classes of German Society

To Michael Printy, the *Aufklärung* "must be understood as the product of the growth of a literate, educated class of readers and writers, who more and more found themselves in the service of the state or the church."[40] The *Aufklärung* is traceable to the universities and the world of academia. Many of the main proponents of the *Aufklärung* were university professors. Already in the eighteenth century, Germany was filled with unusually large universities that filled the semi-autonomous regions due to political and religious fragmentation that saw to the establishment of courts and bureaucracies. Most of these universities were almost always economically independent, and therefore paved intellectual paths of their own.[41] German university intellectuals tended to view with suspicion certain religious devotions that had marked the faith experience of their fatherland for long periods of time. And the universities possessed a sway over the religious culture because the universities were key institutions in the intellectual life of the established churches, Protestant and Catholic alike.[42] What is more, as Printy points out, "the power struggle over educational reform lies at the core of the German Catholic Enlightenment in the eighteenth century."[43] This implies that the universities actively sought to bring about the religious changes that they felt were more in sync with the modern spirit of the *Aufklärung*. We see this trend on full display in Kant's *Vernunftglauben* with its objective moral categories, and Hegel's religious ladder, moving from consciousness through self-consciousness to reason, spirit, religion, and absolute knowing. In addition to universities, books and periodicals largely focused on philosophy, theology, and history and constituted another layer of influence on *Aufklärung* by the educated elite class.

One can see in these realities the attentiveness to the religious experience called Christianity; the active role of the educated classes of Germany; the rationalization and modernization of historical truth claims of Christianity so as to give it a more natural character; the question of the supremacy of divine versus human reason; the nature of reality in terms of its cosmic identity; and German nationalism and piety.[44] Ratzinger sought, in his theological works, to respond to these *Aufklärung* concerns through differing, agreeing, pushing, and integrating the different strands, with the overall goal of helping the spiritual and evangelical life of a modern Catholicism. It is also critical to see to what extent the issues at play were of interest to Ratzinger and how they formed and engaged him.

2.2 Ratzinger's 1959 Inaugural Lecture: God of Faith and God of the Philosophers

On June 24, 1959, in the lecture hall VIII located in the main building of Bonn University, Ratzinger delivered his inaugural lecture as a university professor titled "The God of Faith and the God of Philosophers: A Contribution to the Problem of *Theologia Naturalis*."[45] With hindsight, Benedict XVI would declare this lecture as containing the main themes of his thought—*Der Leitfaden meines Denkens*.[46] Ratzinger sought in this lecture to investigate the ways in which the God of revelation is different from the God of the philosophers, in order to ascertain the kind of rationality that might be suitable for Christian theology.[47] Clearly, the inaugural lecture can be seen as a synthetic logical development of Ratzinger's intellectual formation and development, from Augustine to Bonaventure. Armed with the ecclesiological insights taken from Augustine and the Christo-ecclesial gains from Bonaventure, Ratzinger appears comfortable placing the God of faith in an open and unfiltered dialogue with the God of the philosophers. As will be seen in the subsequent analysis, the relationship between ancient Greek philosophy and biblical faith is critical in answering this question. In other words, does Greek rationality belong to the essence of Christianity or was the alliance formed between Athens and Jerusalem an unfortunate, disastrous misunderstanding?

To highlight the two approaches to the question, Ratzinger offers as paradigmatic the positions of Thomas Aquinas, who brings the God of faith and the God of the philosophers together, on the one hand, and the Swiss Protestant dialectical theologian Emil Brunner (1889–1966), a staunch defender of the *theologia naturalis*, on the other hand.[48] For Aquinas, philosophy represents the welcoming, highest point that the unaided human mind can reach regarding the question of God. On the other hand, for Brunner, the God of the philosophers cannot arrive at what the human spirit ultimately seeks, namely, a communion with the divine. Such is the case because *physici*, the domain of the *theologia naturalis* that properly belongs to the philosophers, cannot make the leap to communion with the God of faith. As Emery de Gaál points out, for Ratzinger, "Brunner infelicitously develops an irreconcilable contradiction between the God of the philosophers and the one of faith."[49] Ratzinger therefore hopes, by his lecture, to overcome this chasm between the dialogical God of the Bible and the monological God of Greek philosophy, showing points of convergence and the eventual transformation that biblical faith brought to the God of philosophy, moving being *qua* being into being in relation with the other.

The lecture not only stresses the necessity for a dialogue between faith and reason, religion and philosophy, but likewise points out that though the relationship between faith and reason is as old as humanity, humanity would cease to exist were we to consider this question as once and for all settled. The dialogue of faith and reason therefore constitutes one of the serious issues of our times, especially given the different conceptions of God that emerge from both philosophy and theology.[50] And hence, Ratzinger hoped by this lecture to once again invite both sides of the aisle, the believer and the rational *Aufklärung* thinker, into a conversation.

In calling for such a dialogue, it is important to note from the outset that Ratzinger does not assume a simplistic identification between philosophy and theology, faith and reason, regarding the question of the nature of God. Ratzinger acknowledges the fundamental difference between the God of philosophy and the God of theology. He writes:

> In it then at the same time an important contrast to the Greek philosophical relationship with God becomes clear: In philosophy it is man who seeks God on his own initiative, in biblical faith it is God himself and God alone who in creative freedom establishes the relationship between man and God. So now the contrast between the name of God and the concept of God, the God of faith and the God of philosophers becomes clearer and more definite. The God of the philosophers "is the God to whom one does not pray, the God with whom there is unity—namely the unity which thinking itself thinks" as the deepest truth—"but no community"—community which is founded by God himself.[51]

Here, Ratzinger makes two arguments. Firstly, Greek philosophy was able to achieve the unity of God, later a cornerstone of Israel's faith, as one finds in the *Shema O Israel* proclamation. Secondly, this unity, while an achievement was also a limitation, for in the intrinsic fidelity to itself philosophy could not make space for communication with this unity, for this unity was a self-subsistent being, closed in on itself. So, while on the one hand, there is a meeting point between philosophy and theology regarding the oneness or unity of the Biblical God, on the other hand there appears an unbridgeable gap between the two. For one, that is, theology, is capable of going beyond unity into communion, into communication, while philosophy remains simply at the level of an ineffable idea. This is the framework of Ratzinger's inaugural lecture, that is, how to bring these two seemingly irreconcilable positions together in order to attain a harmony that serves the human person, since it is the human person who is simultaneously a thinker and a believer.

In a word, Ratzinger's position is essentially Thomistic. Having been critical of the neo-Thomism of his seminary days, Ratzinger still finds in Thomas the philosophical principle on which a dialogue between faith and reason, theology and philosophy, might be cultivated and should be cultivated, for the simple reason that for Thomas philosophy is the highest possibility of the human spirit:

> For Thomas, the God of religion and the God of philosophers are completely intertwined, whereas the God of faith and the God of philosophy are partially different; the God of faith exceeds the God of philosophers, adds something to it. The *religio naturalis*—and that means any religion outside Christianity—has no higher content and can have no higher content than the philosophical doctrine of God offers it. On the contrary, all it contains beyond or contrary to it is apostasy and aberrance. Outside the Christian faith, according to Thomas, philosophy is the highest possibility at all of the human spirit.[52]

So it is, for as Aquinas taught grace does not destroy but perfects nature—*gratia non tollit naturam, sed perficiat*.[53] It is therefore only with Greek philosophy that unaided human reason was capable of arriving at the notion of the oneness or unity of the divine Being, the Unmoved

Mover or First Cause, whom Thomas will call God in his demonstrations of the existence of God as Prime Mover, First Cause, Necessary Being, Absolute Being and Designer.[54] Though Thomas demonstrates the existence of God with these five ways or proofs, such demonstrations in no way imply that the finite intellect can know the essence of the infinite God, given that cognition is contingent on the mode of the knower, in this case, finitude standing before infinitude. These demonstrations simply point to Thomas' conviction that the human intellect *qua* intellect can arrive at rational grounds for the postulate for the existence of God, in other words, that reason can back the claims of faith in God. Put differently, to believe in God is not an irrational act. Modern philosophy, responding to Anselm of Canterbury, will more or less crystalize the idea of the proofs of the existence of God into three categories—the cosmological, teleological, and ontological proofs—with arguments largely aimed at dismantling the proofs, weighing their merits and demerits, strengths and limitations, as seen in the altercation between Kant and Hegel on Anselm's ontological argument for the existence of God.

However, though interrelated, the God of faith is not just identical with the God of philosophy or reason, because faith adds something to reason. Ratzinger thus introduces a new analogical mirroring of the bond between Aquinas and Aristotle:

> The Christian faith in God absorbs and perfects the philosophical idea of God. To put it bluntly, the God of Aristotle and the God of Jesus Christ are one and the same. Aristotle has recognized the true God, whom we are permitted to grasp more deeply and more purely in faith, just as we will grasp God's nature more intimately and closer in the beatific vision of God. One could perhaps say without violence to the facts: Christian faith relates to the philosophical knowledge of God in the same way as the beatific vision of God relates to faith. It concerns three stages of a single path.[55]

Three insights are evident here. Firstly, following Aquinas' reading of Aristotle, Ratzinger states that the God of philosophy, the God recognized by Aristotle as Supreme Being, Prime Mover, is the true God.

Secondly, what Aristotle was capable of discerning thanks to philosophic reason, the believer is able to grasp by faith. This Supreme Being is the One God of Christian monotheism. And thirdly—and this is where Ratzinger starts going beyond Thomas and Aristotle—Ratzinger makes the point that the relationship between the God of Aristotle and the God of faith mirrors the relationship that faith in the present has with eschatological faith. In other words, that faith which is full, supreme, and in need of no other, which we will experience in the eschaton, might be seen as what happens when philosophy turns toward faith. Such is the case because it does not lose sight of what it has already attained, but sees before it, in faith, a fuller picture of what is to come. In other words, Christian faith is related to the philosophical knowledge of God, as the eschatological vision of God is to faith.

To Ratzinger, the name revealed to Moses commonly transliterated in English as *Ehyeh asher ehyeh*—"I am who I am" (Ex 3:14)—was certainly mysterious, and he is sympathetic to a mysterious translation interpretation of the tetragrammaton. The tension is whether to interpret the tetragrammaton as pertaining to essence, that is, being in this case, the "I Am," or whether to interpret it as presence, in this case as "I will be with you in the manner in which I will be with you." As Leora Batnitzky points out regarding the issue of the translation of Exodus 3:14, Martin Buber and Franz Rosenzweig in their translation of the Bible into the German language insist that "I am that I am" misunderstands the Hebrew, which from their perspective is not about God's essence but about God's presence. Buber and Rosenzweig translate Exodus 3:14 as *Ich werde Dasein, als der ich Dasein werde* ("I will be there, howsoever I will be there"). Batnitzky comments: "God's presentation of God's self to Moses is not for the sake of clarifying philosophically what kind of being God is or is not. Instead, God presents God's self to Moses to let him know that God is literally there with him, and the children of Israel."[56] Perhaps, precisely because what is under consideration is the sacred name, one could find space enough for both essence and presence as containable therein, together, without excluding either positions. Isn't the inability to fully comprehend and translate the tetragrammaton a pointer to the *Deus absconditus*, that remoteness of God, who, though present, continues to elude the full comprehension and grasp of finite intellect? Yet the sense of the mysterious and the transcendent should not lead to a theological agnosticism before the tetragrammaton. On the contrary, God is mysterious because God is also being, the One who is, the I Am. There is a surprising agreement between biblical faith and Greek philosophy, between divine existence and essence, in the sense that what human metaphysical reflection sought to achieve and what Scripture (the LXX translation) reveals about God coincides. As Ratzinger points out, if there is no positive connection between monological philosophy and dialogical revelation, then the *analogia entis* ought to be considered illegitimate and incomprehensible.[57] The ontological and the pragmatic-existential, therefore, coincide in the religious experience and manifestation of the tetragrammaton.

Ratzinger thus safeguards both positions, that is, the Greek Fathers' sense of mystery and transcendence, on the one hand, and the philosophical sense of being, of ontology, on the other:

> On the one side there is the God, who grants himself to be known as You in the naming of his name and opens himself to man, presents himself to him, to the community. On the other side, there is philosophical thinking, which sees an anthropomorphism in the revelation of the name, but with which, however, the revelation itself rejects sufficient reason-thinking itself does not want to recognize anything that comes from beyond its own possibility.[58]

Therefore, the possibility of mystery and concreteness, of transcendence and immanence is not simply a matter of the highlighting or preferring one over the other, but is essentially a realization that comes from revelation. In other words, God is both mystery and being because God has revealed himself to us that way. Without revelation, Moses would not have had the experience of not only being capable of knowing God's name, but likewise of knowing that the name is not non-being, not nothing, but signifies the ground of all being, is being *par excellence*. But more importantly, because God is also being and not just an ineffable name, it is possible to enter into communion with God. This marks a major distinction between the God of faith and the God of the philosophers, for whom the self-subsistent being, though one, a unity, cannot enter into a relationship with creatures.

With this distinction in mind, Ratzinger then poses the question as to whether the suspicion of some of the Greek Fathers had any value or was warranted in any form. He offers a nuanced response:

> In view of such serious and far-reaching consequences, the question must be asked once again and anew whether and to what extent the dash drawn by the Fathers of the Church between the God of Faith and the God of Philosophy, whose justification and necessity had hitherto been demonstrated by the general problem of monotheism, was justified especially with regard to the biblical concept of God. This can first be answered: It was justified if and insofar as the biblical faith in God wanted and ought to be monotheism.[59]

In effect, the Fathers were able in their theology to communicate Christian biblical monotheism, a monotheism that resonated with the philosophical monotheism of Greek philosophy. The Fathers were aided in this process thanks to their embrace of Greek philosophy, thereby establishing a rapport between the God of philosophy and the God of faith. But this rapport does not imply a complete identification, for biblical faith's monotheism conveys a personal God, while the God of philosophy is an impersonal God. With the tetragrammaton, Israel had to come to the realization that God was not a God of a given location but was going to accompany them as a personal God. Such an existential realization could only be possible thanks to the notion of this God who will be with Israel in the manner in which he will be with them. This God was, primarily, a God who is, a God who, precisely because he is being, is able to accompany them beyond the geographical limits of Egypt, the land of slavery, and into Canaan, the promised land.

Besides the question of a personal God who is such because he is in the first place being and hence is able to accompany Israel, Ratzinger likewise points out that the suspicion toward philosophy likewise contributed in large measure to severing the relationship between nature and grace, a severing which finds its crescendo in Luther's battle cry of *sola scriptura*. Herein lies a fundamental difference between Catholicism and Protestantism, in which the latter, by following Luther, tended to relegate philosophy and consequently reason. What solution does Ratzinger offer to this impasse posed, on the one hand, by Luther against the God of Philosophy, and, on the other hand, by *Aufklärung* scholars against the God of Faith? Ratzinger goes beyond the mere concept of faith and reason as standing independently, each as an autonomous self-subsistent being, into a relationality between the God of philosophy and the personal life of the believer:

> Let us start from the philosophical concept of God, which now, in contrast to the God of faith, presents itself to us in a sharpened way as the concept of God in Greek philosophy. It is not sufficient to know and adopt a certain form of definition in order to understand it. Rather the relationship must be seen in which this concept of God stands to the spiritual and religious world in which it was found and in which it was classified in this way or in another way. For the pre-Christian philosophical concept of God undoubtedly also stood in some relation to religion, which there too was something different from philosophy, and only when this relationship is seen, is the philosophical concept of God seen by the Greeks as such and as a whole correctly; in principle the same applies to any philosophical concept of God.[60]

Ratzinger makes the case for the difference between the pre-Christian God of philosophy and philosophy itself in the sense that the concept of this pre-Christian God is a religious concept, utterly different from a non-confessional sense of philosophizing. In effect, it is not simply a question of intellectual cognition or rational clarity, but one of a person-centered relationship that effects and shapes our conception of God.

For Ratzinger, it is only when this pre-Christian philosophical concept of God of the Greeks is seen through the religious lens that a sensible relationship between the God of philosophy and the God of religion can thus be perceived, apprehended, and appreciated. Ratzinger probably had before him the argument of Paul in his Letter to the Romans: "For what can be known about God is perfectly plain to them since God himself has made it plain. Ever since God created the world his everlasting power and deity—however invisible—have been there for the mind to see in the things he has made. That is why such people are without excuse" (Rm 1:20). Along this line of thinking, not only is it possible that pre-Christian philosophy such as that of the Greeks was capable of rightly accessing the truth of God as the Supreme Being or the One Beyond Being, but, following Ratzinger, it was incumbent on unaided reason to necessarily arrive at the truth of God because the grammar of God is written in the human intellect and in creation.

Quite certainly, Ratzinger would have seen the 1998 encyclical *Fides et Ratio* by John Paul II, in which the pope sought a rapprochement between the God of philosophy and the God of religious faith, as a magisterial stamp on the essential insights of his inaugural lecture. In this light, therefore, the relationship between the God of philosophy and the God of faith is further buttressed by the primacy of truth that is not only antecedent to both material subjects, but does not separate reason and faith. Ratzinger therefore concurs with John Paul II when the latter writes that "faith and reason are like two wings on which the human spirit rises to the contemplation of truth; and God who has placed in the human heart a desire to know the truth—in a word, to know himself—so that, by knowing and loving God, men and women may also come to the truth about themselves."[61] To Ratzinger, this relationship of two wings is connatural. It comes to him almost effortlessly, like a self-evident proposition, given Ratzinger's penchant for overcoming any dichotomy between faith and reason, as demonstrated in his push for the reconciliation between the God of faith and the God of philosophers.

An example of such a rapprochement would be how philosophy and theology perceived the being of God, as the ultimate foundation of all proof on which every thought rests. Such a foundation is never measured but only perceived. That both philosophy and reason hold the unverifiable nature of God is significant for Ratzinger: "We cannot verify God as we would verify some measurable object. There is question here also of an act of humility: the acceptance of the fact that one's own intellect has been called by the eternal intellect."[62] Common areas between faith and reason therefore caution against an excessive distinction between the two, which, to Ratzinger, will deprive faith of its objectivity and again split object and subject, that is, the individual person with his human rationality who is also a believer, into two different worlds.

Along the lines of Ratzinger's propensity to argue for a rapprochement between faith and reason, the *spirit* of Ratzinger's Regensburg Lecture provides an opportunity of accessing how he views and expects faith and reason to be interwoven:

> The university was also very proud of its two theological faculties. It was clear that, by inquiring about the reasonableness of faith, they too carried out a work which is necessarily part of the "whole" of the *universitas scientiarum*, even if not everyone could share the faith which theologians seek to correlate with reason as whole. This profound sense of coherence within the universe of reason was not troubled, even when it was reported that a colleague had said there was something odd about our university: it had two faculties devoted to something that did not exist: God. That even in the face of such radical skepticism it is still necessary and reasonable to raise the question of God through the use of reason, and to do so in the context of the tradition of the Christian faith: this, within the university as a whole, was accepted without question [...]. Not to act in accordance with reason is contrary to God's nature.[63]

Clearly subscribing to this synthesis of faith and reason, Ratzinger traces the lamentable process severing this synthesis to the sixteenth-century reformation movement, in what he called the dehellenization of the Christian faith. *Sola scriptura* was clearly a rejection of the framework of philosophy that had hitherto nurtured the nascent faith right up to the scholastic era. Ratzinger writes that "when Kant states that he needed to set thinking aside in order to make room for faith, he carried this program (of dehellenization and severing of the synthesis of faith and reason) forward with a radicalism that the Reformers could never have foreseen. He thus anchored faith exclusively in practical reason, denying it access to reality as a whole."[64] And opposing faith and reason is not exclusive to Kant. Such opposition is also noticeable in Heidegger, who states what he considers to be the classical position regarding faith and knowledge, revelation and reason, thus:

> Philosophy is that interpretation of the world and of life that is removed from revelation and free from faith. Theology, on the other hand, is the expression of the creedal understanding of the world and of life—in our case a Christian understanding. Taken as such, philosophy and theology give expression to a tension and a struggle between two worldviews. This relationship is decided not by scientific argument but by the manner, the extent, and the strength of the conviction and the proclamation of the worldview.[65]

Though clearly acknowledging these divergent worldviews regarding philosophy and theology or faith and reason, Heidegger offers a puzzling resolution, in that he appears not to see the possibility of an intrinsic connection between the two, but rather draws the conclusion that theology as a positive science is radically different from philosophy.[66] And to buttress the incompatibility of the two, Heidegger goes on to declare that there is no such a thing as Christian philosophy, which to him, amounts to an attempt to square a circle.[67] To Heidegger, therefore, the God of theology does not feature in philosophy. In other words, the *Logos* of St. John has no relationship with the *logos* of Greek metaphysics.

According to Ratzinger, positions of incompatibility between faith and reason such as that expounded by Heidegger do a disservice to both faith and reason. While not oblivious to the proper sphere of competence of philosophy and theology, he argues that the distinction between the two need not have such accents of differentiation, because the net result would be a psycho-social schizophrenia in which the individual person is torn between the energies of faith and reason that, otherwise, could have afforded an inspiring life synthesis. Even reason detached from faith cannot account for the ethical foundations of society and could end up being very destructive, Ratzinger argues:

> If we have noted the urgent question of whether religion is truly a positive force, so we must now doubt the reliability of reason. For in the last analysis, even the atomic bomb is a product of reason; in the last analysis, the breeding and selection of human beings is something thought up by reason. Does this then mean that it is reason that ought to be placed under guardianship? But by whom or by what? Or should perhaps religion and reason restrict each other and remind each other where their limits are, thereby encouraging a positive path?[68]

This text reflects a clear call for a mutual relationship of correction and support between faith and reason. It seems to be in the nature of the human being to seek unity, to understand the whole picture, to seek commonality, for as Thomas Aquinas observes in the *Summa Theologica* all persons have the same last end.[69] This appears to be the case, so much so that even for a philosopher like Heidegger inclined to drawing a strict line between philosophy and theology, faith and reason, one still finds expressions that reflect a desire for a rapprochement between faith and reason. This is the context from which one can understand Heidegger's famous claim, "*Nur ein Gott kann uns noch retten*"—"only a god can save us now"—a confession he made in his *Der Spiegel* interview shortly before his death in 1976:

> Philosophy cannot produce an immediate effect which would change the present state of the world. This is not only true for philosophy but for all specifically human endeavors. Only a God can save us now. The only possibility remaining to us in thought and in poetry is to remain available for the manifestation of this God or for the absence of this God in our decline.[70]

Speaking from a post-Nazi and post-war Germany, clearly evident here is Heidegger's restlessness, almost sense of despair, in the face of the inability of reason alone to provide a solution to Germany's woes, to resolve the tribulations plaguing the modern world. But it need not be the case, if one were to recognize the limits of reason, while acknowledging its strengths. Whether Heidegger meant by his "only a God can save us now" the Judeo-Christian God is debatable, for Heidegger discerns three gods: God as Creator who is the God of Revelation; God as the First Cause who is the God of Metaphysics; and God as Sacred who is the God of poetry. His preference for the poetic God is noticeable, granted that firstly, one cannot burn incense or dance before the *causa sui* God of metaphysics, and secondly, the God of Revelation has no business with philosophy.[71] Nevertheless, that Heidegger turns to the God of poetry for salvation is indicative of the insufficiency of philosophy, of sequestered rationality. And it is this dialogue, this interaction between faith and reason, that Ratzinger has sought to establish in his vocation as a theologian on the many fronts that he has engaged.

2.3 The Reconciliation of the God of Faith and the God of Philosophers

How does Ratzinger reconcile the divergent positions regarding God by philosophy and theology in his lecture? Ratzinger becomes heavily Pascalian, for in the experience of Pascal the mathematician and scientist, reason is not rejected per se, but reaches its limits and has to make room for something, or more precisely for someone, that one can existentially relate to, and in a personalistic and pragmatic sense. Ratzinger explains the experience of Pascal:

> It begins after a very careful indication of day and hour with the words: "Fire. God of Abraham, God of Isaac, God of Jacob, not of philosophers and scholars." The mathematician and philosopher Pascal asked the living God, the God of faith, to awake and, in such living encounters with the You of God, to grasp in dismay and joyful astonishment how different the epiphany of the reality of God is compared to what the mathematical philosophy of a Descartes, for instance, knew to say about God.[72]

Thus, Pascal's cry to God is an epiphany, to the extent that it shows that the God of mathematics, of mere rationality as one finds in Descartes and later on in Kant, is incapable of meeting the highest aspirations of the human heart, the greatest longings of the human heart, namely, the ability to love and be loved, the ability to enter into communion, of communication between the "I" and the "You." Two things, therefore, stand out in this text: Firstly, Ratzinger's ringing admiration for the experiential nature of Pascal's faith, in which Ratzinger discerns the experiential model of religious faith, of Christianity that engages the whole person and not just the rational faculty, a Christianity that struggles through the vicissitudes of being human in a complex and unpredictable world; And secondly, the contrast between Pascal's faith and the rationalism of Descartes, for whom the experience of God came about thanks to a process of rational deductions from clear and distinct ideas,[73] as put forth in Descartes' *Meditations on First Philosophy*.

In the first and second mediations, Descartes makes a distinction between three sets of ideas. Firstly, there are what he calls *adventitious ideas*, which are the ideas that come and go in an overpowering manner in the human mind. The second set of ideas, what Descartes calls *fabrications*, are ideas that are produced by him. The third kind, *innate*, are ideas merely of thought, such as the idea of the self and the idea of infinity.[74] Descartes' underlining methodology is to cast each and every idea, be it adventitious, fabricated, or innate, into doubt, for the simple reason that he could be mistaken by either imagining the idea himself, or by a miscalculation. By so doing, as Peter Markie points out, Descartes rejects both the Deceptive God Hypothesis and the Dream Hypothesis: "The Deceptive God Hypothesis does not give him a reason to doubt his beliefs that he thinks and exists; for it entails them and so fails to indicate how they might be false despite his clear and distinct perception. The same is true of the Dream Hypothesis."[75] What is the next step for Descartes?

Descartes therefore discards all other ideas, as they all could have originated from him, except the idea of God. But how is the idea of God different from the other ideas? In terms of objective reality, the idea of God has more reality than him. God is: "A certain substance that is infinite, independent, supremely intelligent and supremely powerful, and that created me along with everything else that exists—if anything else exists."[76] Based on this definition, the idea of God could not have originated from Descartes alone, because the idea is of an infinite substance, while he is of finite substance. The idea of God must necessarily proceed only from an infinite substance. As Jean-Marie Beyssade points out, "the idea of God precedes, at any rate, in terms of its status in the argument, the aspiration of the human mind to perfection. It is not human aspiration which defines the idea of the infinite; rather, the idea of the infinite is what arouses that aspiration."[77] In this sense, the idea of an infinite substance must have come from an infinite substance himself. And this idea would not have been present in Descartes from God, unless God exists—that is the conclusion that Descartes draws. Descartes thus concludes that the idea of an infinite substance does not originate from Descartes himself, because finitude cannot give birth to infinitude. This idea does not convey nothingness, but fullness of being. The Cartesian system, at least from Descartes' point of view, succeeds in establishing three existential claims: "I am, I exist (the Cogito); God exists (divine veracity); corporeal things exist (the foundations of physics)."[78] These existential claims constitute the central nexus of the Cartesian architectonic system.

However, while this Cartesian ontological, rational proof of God's existence was a commendable achievement,[79] the eighteenth century *Aufklärung* movement moved beyond this proclivity for an *a priori* system of thought, to a more experiential mode of thinking, based much more on the phenomena in terms of a rational reading of the phenomena. In other words, despite its merits, eighteenth century German philosophers, the Pietists in particular, tended to eschew the methodology of mathematics that characterized the Cartesian system as a way of philosophizing. As Frederick C. Beiser points out, "according to the Pietists, the method of philosophy should be empirical and inductive rather than mathematical and deductive; the philosopher cannot construct concepts according to definitions, like the mathematician, but must analyze concepts given to him in experience."[80] Hence, in terms of its reception, German metaphysicians of the eighteenth century were already moving beyond Cartesianism's mathematical outlook on philosophy. In all, Cartesianism was not without its critics, notwithstanding its influence.[81] And as Cassirer points out, "this new methodological order characterizes all eighteenth century thought. The value of system, the '*esprit systematique*' is neither underestimated nor neglected; but it is sharply distinguished from the love of system for its own sake, the *esprit de système*."[82] In other words, the problem with seventeenth century rational idealism was not that it made use of reason and the cognitive faculties. The issue that was confronted and largely rejected with the scientific experiential rational methodology of Newton and the spirit of the *Aufklärung* was that the former tended to raise individual concepts such as the concept of the clear and distinct idea of Descartes, to the status of a dogma, so much so that such a concept became a determining hermeneutical principle in explaining reality, such as the reality of God's existence.

And such an understanding by the *Aufklärer* is understandable, for reason to them, as we saw in the introduction, is not simply one faculty but everything, that which connotes all of reality, the ground thanks to which we can access all of reality. In this sense, because reason possesses such a broad connotation, it cannot be limited or restricted to a closed system. Cassirer offers a trenchant explanation worth citing at length, for this marks the dichotomy between the seventeenth and eighteenth centuries, between the rational idealism of Descartes, which Ratzinger rejects, and the rationalism of faith, of the experiential, as seen in Pascal, which Ratzinger embraces:

> One should not seek order, law, and "reason" as a rule that may be grasped and expressed prior to the phenomena, as their *a priori*; one should rather discover such regularity in the phenomena themselves, as the form of their immanent connection. Nor should one attempt to anticipate from the outset such "reason" in the form of closed system; one should rather permit this reason to unfold gradually, with ever increasing clarity and perfection, as knowledge of the facts progresses. The new logic that is now sought in the conviction that it is everywhere present on the path of knowledge is neither the logic of the scholastic nor of the purely mathematical concept; it is rather the "logic of facts." The mind must abandon itself to the abundance of phenomena and gauge itself constantly by them. For it may be sure that it will not get lost,

> but instead it will find here its own real truth and standard. Only in this way can the genuine correlation of subject and object, of truth and reality, be achieved; only so can the correspondence between these concepts, which is the condition of all scientific knowledge, be brought about.[83]

Thus, whereas Descartes took mathematics as the governing principle of reason, the eighteenth century took contemporary natural science, as particularly espoused by Newton, as the starting point of reasoning. Reason could not be understood from the point of view of a system, but as the mind's critical reflection on all of reality. This is the sense by which reason thus becomes capable of capturing whatever is in existence. To dare to use reason therefore is to dare to be engaged with all of reality, with reality in terms of its causes, processes, evolutions, and *telos*.

Seen from this perspective, reason is no longer the sum total of "innate ideas" that are given prior to all human experiences, which reveal the absolute essence of all things. Reason is now very much seen as an acquisition rather than as a heritage. As Cassirer points out, reason is not the treasury of the mind in which the truth, like a minted coin, is stored. On the contrary, reason is the original intellectual force which guides the discovery and determination of truth. As Cassirer concludes, "the whole eighteenth century understands reason in this sense; not as a sound body of knowledge, principles, and truths, but as a kind of energy, a force which is fully comprehensible only in its agency and effects."[84] Given this perspective, what reason is and what reason can do can only be known by its function, that is, by what reason does.

In this light, the *Aufklärung* moved reason from a purely speculative to a practical realm, in which conclusions are drawn thanks to what emerges from the reality of experience, even if this must be processed by the rational mind. And as Cassirer points out, nothing is excluded from this function of reason as it analyzes all—revelation, tradition, and authority—which must all face the scrutiny of reason.[85] In this sense, the *Aufklärung*, even if respectful to Cartesianism, moved beyond it with the embrace of Newtonian principles of physics and rational thinking. As Cassirer points out:

> The Enlightenment does not take the ideal of this mode of thinking from the philosophical doctrines of the past; on the contrary, it constructs its ideal according to the model and pattern of contemporary natural science. The attempt to solve the central problem of philosophic method involves recourse to Newton's "Rule of Philosophizing" rather than to Descartes' Discourse on Method, with the result that philosophy presently takes an entirely new direction. For Newton's method is not that of pure deduction, but that of analysis. He does not begin by setting up certain principles, certain general concepts and axioms, in order, by virtue of abstract inferences, to pave the way to the knowledge of the particular, the "factual." Newton's approach moves in just the opposite direction. His phenomena are the data of experience; his principles are the goal of his investigation.[86]

Hence, with Newton, philosophy moved away from an arbitrary starting point, from a hypothesis to logical conclusions emanating from it, for the simple reason that a hypothesis can be invented or modified as desired by the subjective thinker. A hypothesis can become a tool opened up indefinitely, to be manipulated at will. As Cassirer points out, "a scientific abstraction or 'definition' cannot serve as a really unambiguous starting point, for such a starting-point can only be obtained from experience and observation."[87] In other words, Cartesianism as a rational system could not sustain the greatness and profundity of all that is encompassed in the historical revelation of God in the *Gestalt* of Jesus of Nazareth, in terms of all that is accessible thanks to faith.

Clearly, for Ratzinger, the God of Jesus Christ is such that rational processes of deductions, as commendable as they might be, cannot lead the individual into a life-changing and life-orienting engagement. In other words, the Cartesian mathematical God that Pascal knowingly moves beyond is a God that cannot know me as an individual. A God that cannot know my name, that cannot enter into a relationship with me, that cannot comprehend my struggles, challenges, joys, and sorrows, cannot save me. Such a God is irrelevant. He might be useful in terms of mental clarity and apologetic reasoning, but when the chips are down I cannot count on such a God for help.

Therefore, while Ratzinger appreciates this Cartesian demonstration that faith is not irrational, he does not see the warmth, enthusiasm, and personalism in the "mathematical philosophy" of Descartes that he so much appreciates and relishes in Pascal. Ratzinger does not reject Kant's rational faith, for as he argues below, a faith that cannot be rationalized cannot be dogmatic, for dogma is a rational presentation of the faith, but he strives to go beyond Kant, beyond reason as well, moving from Descartes *via* Pascal to Kant, and back to Pascal:

> Only the disintegration of speculative metaphysics by Kant and the shift of the religious into the extra-rational and thus also extra-metaphysical space of feeling by Schleiermacher finally brought Pascal's thoughts to a breakthrough and only now led to the radical aggravation of the problem: Only now is the gap between metaphysics and religion unbridgeable; metaphysics, i.e. theoretical reason, has no access to God; religion has no seat in the room of *ratio*: it is experience which eludes scientific measurability; it nevertheless attempts to subtract from it an unreal scheme, the God of philosophers. This has another consequence: religion that cannot be rationalized, cannot basically be dogmatic either, if indeed dogma is to be a rational statement about religious contents.[88]

Faith, therefore, must of necessity emerge from the experience of the individual and not from a preconceived thought-project, such as one finds in Cartesianism. In this sense, Cartesianism, in spite of its best intentions, is inadequate to capture the full compass of faith, its challenges, promises and expectations. When Ratzinger argues as he does above, that religion "has no seat in the room of *ratio*," it does not imply a rejection of the rational, the cognitive, for that would create the false narrative that to be a believer is to be anti-rational, anti-reason. Rather, Ratzinger is inviting reason to go beyond reason, to allow the mind to go beyond the postulates that mere rationality has imposed on it, owing to Ratzinger's conviction that reason alone cannot account both for the grandeur of faith and for the expanse of all of what one might called the reality of life, of the world.

Therefore, going further, one can assert that reason *qua* reason is insufficient to provide the firm ground on which religious faith can flourish, if such a faith never lives itself out in concrete religious experiences. In other words, it is in the nature of faith to be existential and pragmatic. Faith engages the concrete life choices of the believer. Faith is a primordial disposition that shapes all subsequent life choices and actions of the one who opens the self to the gift of faith. Secondly, such a religious faith cannot be reduced to the rules of scientific measurability, cannot be gauged according to the mathematical, for the obvious reason that it is in the nature of faith to transcend the temporal, the here and now, and to open up the temporal to the infinite, time to eternity, and by so doing, transcend the limits of science and the mathematical.

In fact, faith is such that it must necessarily transcend the temporal and live in the simultaneity of the present and the not yet. It is in the nature of faith to abide in uncertain physical grounds, so much so that, as the Letter to the Hebrews defines it, "the assurance of things hoped for, the conviction of things not seen" (Heb 11:1). This transcendental nature of faith frees the believer from the anxieties of a self-sufficiency in the vicissitudes of life. The believer is able to allow the self to be touched by the support that comes from the outside, from the wholly Other. Due to the transcendent nature of faith, therefore, the insufficiency of reason, of the God of philosophy to account for and sustain religious faith, invites for a rapprochement between reason and faith, between the God of the philosophers and the God of faith, which the inaugural lecture offers.

From the preceding sections, there are three key insights that stand out in the lecture. Firstly, one notes the autonomy of the God of faith and the God of the philosophers. While the former is dialogical, the latter is monological, for the God of philosophy is essentially a self-enclosing One or Unity, while the God of faith is fundamentally a communion of Persons—Father, Son and Spirit—who enters into communion with human beings. Secondly, Ratzinger sees a convergence of biblical faith with Greek philosophy in the LXX translation of the tetragrammaton, in which, according to the divine name, *Being*, an otherwise ontological concept, takes on relationality. Israel's God will be with Israel in the manner in which this God will be. The God of revelation is therefore not a local deity, but a God of the entire universe, accompanying Israel and the new Israel across space and time. Thirdly, to Ratzinger, there is a conversion of this God of the philosophers into the personal God of Abraham, Isaac, Jacob, and Jesus Christ, modeled in the personalist experience of Pascal and other believers. God is not just the God of place, but is also a personal God.

This particularization has a universal significance, for Israel as a people was called for the sake of the nations, beginning with the encounter with the Hellenistic world. The fact that Biblical faith took form in Greek philosophical thought before spreading to the Gentile world was not accidental. On the contrary, it was a providential act that reason and faith were to find a synthesis such that what is common to all the nations, namely, the faculty of rationality, will not be something extrinsic to faith but will find itself in congenial rapprochement with Biblical faith. These insights from the inaugural lecture therefore lay the groundwork for the synthesis of faith and reason as mutually enriching dialogical partners.

This dialogue between faith and reason is seen in the post-*Aufklärung* era in the admixture of secular atheism and religious beliefs, in a sense a concrete mixture of the God of faith and the God of philosophers. One of the manifestations of secularism, as Charles Taylor points out, "consists in the falling off of religious belief and practice, in people turning away from God, and no longer going to Church. In this sense, the countries of western Europe have mainly become secular—even those who retain the vestigial public reference to God in public space."[89] On the other hand, given this falling away from religious practice, we find in contemporary advanced societies "a move from a society where belief in God is unchallenged and indeed, unproblematic, to one in which it is understood to be one option among others, and frequently not the easiest to embrace."[90] In this sense, materially developed societies have moved from a culture in which it was virtually out of place not to believe in God, to a culture in which faith, even for the fervent and devout believer, is simply one possibility among many. It is no longer axiomatic to believe in God, given the presence of other alternatives and possibilities.[91] These signs of a world without God, for Ratzinger, are crucial indications that, rather than resigning to a godless, secular, *fait accompli*, the question now is not only to understand the historical precedents that led to such a proclivity for unbelief, but more importantly to once again engage the post-*Aufklärung* culture of the experiential rational with the gospel message, as Ratzinger sought to do in his inaugural lecture.

2.4 Building on the Inaugural Lecture: The God of Faith and God of the Philosophers in the *Introduction to Christianity*

Ten years after the inaugural lecture of 1968, Ratzinger again takes up the question of the relationship between faith and reason, between the God of philosophy and the God of faith—in terms of the overlapping relationship between the two—in his *Introduction to Christianity*. To Ratzinger, the God of faith, that is, the God of revelation, is not in opposition to the God of philosophy in terms of oneness of the divine essence. However, the understanding of God in philosophy is not simply convertible with how religious faith understands God, for the God of faith is able to enter into communion with the believer, a relationship that cannot exist in the context of the Unmoved Mover and Greek philosophers. Such is the case because though on target as a unity, thus an equivalence of biblical monotheism, the One of philosophy is a self-enclosed thought thinking thought. Building upon his inaugural lecture, therefore, Ratzinger sought in his *Introduction* to further develop this distinction, and simultaneously the unity between the God of faith and the God of philosophers:

> On the other side, it must be noted that the ancient world itself knew the dilemma between the God of faith and the God of the philosophers in a very pronounced form. Between the mythical gods of the religions and the philosophical knowledge of God there had developed in the course of history a stronger and stronger tension, which is apparent in the criticism of the myths by the philosophers from Xenophanes to Plato, who even thought of trying to replace the classical Homeric mythology with a new mythology appropriate to the *Logos*.[92]

To Ratzinger, then, pointing out of the inner contradictions of Greek mythology was a sizeable achievement of the philosophers, akin, one might say, to the criticism of Israel by the prophets. In other words, philosophy saved Greek piety from a blind faith thanks to the introduction of reason, of *logos*, into the religious imagination of the Greeks, as seen in Heraclitus, Socrates, Plato, Aristotle, the Stoics and Plotinus. And Ratzinger finds an inner parallel here between Greek philosophy and the Enlightenment philosophy, in that "for all the differences between them, both movements coincide in their striving toward the *Logos*."[93] The *logos* as reason, therefore, was what could have saved Greek religion from its irrational and illusory myths, Ratzinger maintains, for it would have introduced the concept of truth into religious piety.

This absence of *logos* as reason and the consequent and fatal absence of truth, to Ratzinger, accounted for the demise of Greek religion and piety, for instead of treating religion as a question of truth, it treated it as a question of the regulation of life according to the whims and caprices of the gods.[94] To buttress his argument, Ratzinger cites the text in Paul's Letter to the Romans: "For what can be known about God is plain to them, because God has shown it to them [...]. But although they knew God, they did not honor him as God or give thanks to him [...]. They exchanged the glory of the immortal God for images resembling mortal man or bids or animals or reptiles" (Rom 1:19–23). Based on this Pauline text, Ratzinger concludes:

> Religion did not go the way of the *logos* but lingered in myths already seen to be devoid of reality. Consequently, its decline was inevitable; this followed from its divorce from the truth, a state of affairs that led to its being regarded as a mere *institutio vitae*, that is, a mere contrivance and an outward form of life. The Christian position, as opposed to this situation, is put emphatically by Tertullian when he says with splendid boldness: "Christ called himself truth, not custom"—*Dominus noster Christus veritatem se, non consuetudinem cognominavit* [...]. In my view, this is one of the really great assertions of patristic theology [...]. Christianity thus put itself resolutely on the side of truth and turned its back on a

> conception of religion satisfied to be mere outward ceremonial that in the end can be interpreted to mean anything one fancies.[95]

To justify this outwardly ceremonious religion of convenience, maintains Ratzinger, Greek polytheism was able to put forth three theologies—namely, physical, political, and mythical. With the aid of this trio, Greek religion was able to justify the separation of myth from the *logos* by ceding first place to the feelings of the people and the good of the political State. Mythical theology was therefore employed as a tool for political theology, weighing truth against custom and usefulness against truth. "But what can go on existing only through interpretation has in reality ceased to exist," maintains Ratzinger, for "the human mind rightly turns to the truth itself, not to what by means of devious interpretation can be shown to be reconcilable with the truth, though no longer containing any truth itself."[96] And this demise of Greek polytheism has significant lessons for today's Church.

In the first place, maintains Ratzinger, Christianity must reject the two methods Greek polytheism employed and lost the battle for its survival—namely, eschewing the inner necessity of reason in the life of faith; and secondly, cultural Christianity, or a Christianity of convenience, of the political, that works for the State. With contemporary Christianity in mind, Ratzinger warns against the temptation of repeating the errors of Greek polytheism, which he sees in the current Church in these forms:

> On one side, we have the retreat from the truth of reason into a realm of mere piety, mere faith, mere revelation; a retreat that in reality bears a fatal resemblance, whether by design or accident and whether the fact is admitted or not, to the ancient religion's retreat before the *logos*, to the flight from truth to beautiful custom, from nature to politics. On the other side, we have an approach I will call for short "Interpreted Christianity": the stumbling blocks in Christianity are removed by the interpretative method, and, as part of the process of thus rendering it unobjectionable, its actual content

> is written off as dispensable phraseology, as a periphrasis not required to say the simple things now alleged, by complicated modes of exposition, to constitute its real meaning.[97]

In effect, Christianity cannot afford to abandon reason, theology cannot abandon philosophy, for, to cite Hegel, "the task of philosophy is to show forth the rational content of religion [...], to reconcile reason with religion in its manifold forms, and to recognize them as at least necessary."[98] In other words, the pursuit for truth makes it incumbent that there continue to be a rapprochement between philosophy and theology, and the vehicle for such a pursuit of truth is the recognition of *logos*, rationality, as central to the Christian imagination. In his first lecture on the *Proofs of the Existence of God*, Hegel articulates a very positive view regarding this relationship between faith and thought, philosophy and theology. Hegel writes:

> This relationship presents itself in a peaceful form in the conviction that revelation, faith, positive religion, and on the other side reason and thought as such, must not be in contradiction. Indeed, not only can they exist in harmony, but also God in God's works does not contradict godself, cannot so contradict godself that the human spirit in its essential nature as thinking reason—in that which it must have come to regard as divine in itself from the very beginning—could come into conflict with what has come to it through greater enlightenment about the nature of God and the relationship of humanity to the divine nature.[99]

Is Hegel here making the case that the oneness of truth necessitates a harmony between faith and reason? Likely, but on a much more pragmatic note, the level of the argument might be viewed from the perspective of the futility that an antagonistic perspective of the relationship between faith and reason serves. Such is the case, for on the part of the believer faith necessitates knowledge of God and the contents of revelation, and to know that God, as Hegel points out, belongs to the domain of the philosophy of religion, to philosophy, and to reason.[100] From the

Ratzingerian perspective and closely allied to the Hegelian reading of the question of faith and reason, the pragmatic utility of the necessity of this rapprochement between faith and reason boils down to the need for theology to stick with reason, truth, logic, and language—that is, with the God of philosophy, as did the early Christians.

2.5 The Transformation of the God of Philosophers by Faith in Ratzinger's *Introduction to Christianity*

Summing up the organic development from Ratzinger's inaugural lecture to the *Introduction to Christianity*, De Gaál writes that for Ratzinger, "both faith and reason stand to gain from relating to one another time and again. Were faith to retreat from rationality into the realm of 'mere piety,' it would betray the Incarnation of the eternal *Logos*, Jesus Christ, as Ratzinger later demonstrates in his classic *Introduction to Christianity*."[101] As with his inaugural lecture, Ratzinger in his *Introduction* does not simply embrace the God of philosophy as philosophy, that is, in accordance with the material and object senses of philosophy. In other words, when the Christian faith adopts the God of philosophy over and against the myths of pagan religions, something happens to the God of philosophy. Something changes. There is a transformation that occurs with the Prime Mover, Pure Being, of the God of philosophy:

> The God who had previously existed as something neutral, as the highest, culminating concept; this God who had been understood as pure Being or pure Thought, circling around forever closed in upon itself without reaching over to man and his little world: this God of the philosophers, whose pure eternity and unchangeability had excluded any relation with the changeable and transitory, now appeared to the eye of faith as the God of men, who is not only thought of all thoughts, the eternal mathematics of the universe, but also *agape*, the power of creative love.[102]

Effectively, therefore, Christianity did not only appropriate the God of philosophy, but it radically transformed the whole notion of the God of philosophy, removing this God from the mere intellectual or academic realm to the realm of the living experiences of believers. This movement does not imply that natural reason *qua* natural reason could not lead to a worship of God, for as Aquinas points out: "It belongs to the dictate of natural reason that man should do something through reverence for God. But that he should do this or that determinate thing does not belong to the dictate of natural reason, but is established by Divine or human law."[103] However, the encounter between the God of natural reason and the God of revelation introduces a living and dynamic accessibility and relationality that was hitherto absent in the realm of natural reason alone. The God of philosophy, the God of natural reason, through the encounter with Christianity has become a living, accessible, and approachable Being. Ratzinger writes:

> So, in this sense there is the experience that the God of the philosophers is quite different from what the philosophers had thought him to be, though he does not thereby cease to be what they had discovered; that one only comes to know him properly when one realizes that he, the real truth and ground of all Being, is at one and the same time the God of faith, the God of men and women.[104]

Given this transformation, the God of philosophy, like the God of faith, becomes capable of emotions, can rejoice, and seeks to enter into human relations. Ratzinger maintains that the God of philosophy is no longer the "unfeeling geometry of the universe, neutral justice standing above things undisturbed by a heart and its emotions; he has a heart; he stands there like a person who loves, with all the capriciousness of someone who loves."[105] It is therefore, not naïve anthropomorphism to believe that the Supreme Being of philosophy cares about the human person and really wants to cultivate a relationship with the humans. To Ratzinger, it is precisely in the fact that the Supreme Being of philosophy, the greatest, takes interest in what is small, in the human being, that the true divinity of the Supreme Being stands out:

> Precisely this overstepping of the greatest and reaching down into the smallest is the true nature of absolute spirit. At the

> same time, we see here a reversal in value of maximum and minimum, greatest and smallest, that is typical of the Christian understanding of reality. To him who as Spirit upholds and encompasses the universe, a spirit, a man's heart with its ability to love, is greater than all the milky ways in the universe. Quantitative criteria become irrelevant; other orders of magnitude become visible, according to which the infinitely small is the truly embracing and truly great.[106]

This process of the great taking interest in the small, of the supreme becoming little, constitutes the germ of the transformation of the God of philosophy when this philosophical apprehension encounters faith. While faith accepts the intuitions of reason in its postulation of the Supreme Being as utterly different and the highest form of existence, faith liberates the God of philosophy from its unbridgeable distance, and in the process, "corrects philosophy and lets us know that love is higher than mere thought."[107] Not only does faith move philosophy's God from the point of a self-contemplative thought, a thought thinking itself, to a position of relationship, but thanks to this movement faith is able to present the God of philosophy as a God of love. In the final analysis, therefore, the absolute Being of philosophy is creative love, based on the conviction that to love is divine, a position Ratzinger analyzes as the Creative *Logos*: "The *logos* of the whole world, the creative original thought, is at the same time love; in fact, this thought is creative because as thought, it is love, and, as love, it is thought."[108] This bonding of the truth of philosophy's intuition of the Supreme Being with love, therefore, ensures the identification of truth with love.

With the new way of thinking that comes with the new sciences and the prominent philosophers that emerged from the spirit of the *Aufklärung*—either employing reason to make the case for reason, or reason to make the case for what they saw was the irrationality of the *Aufklärung*, such as one finds with Nietzsche—reason, *logos*, becomes the possible concept through which Ratzinger is able to bring his Augustinian, personalist, and existentialist philosophical background to bear on the questions of Christology and Ecclesiology, as promoted by the *Aufklärer* and their successors. That the *Aufklärer* adopted reason to connote a broad spectrum—that is, nature, science, consciousness, social, and political life—the metaphysical domain, the moral order, and finally the supernatural order of revelation open the way for a concomitant appropriation of reason or *logos* by Ratzinger from a theological perspective.

As will be seen in chapter three, underlining these Ratzingerian appropriations of *Aufklärung* reason or *Logos* as creative Reason, Person, unity of love, Word, and Son, is the conviction, as de Gaál points out, that for Ratzinger, "philosophical truth becomes personal, divine-human truth in Jesus Christ as the *Logos*. Truth and charity become synonymous in Christ."[109] With this Christological outcome comes the realization of human insufficiency without the God of Jesus Christ who is continuously mediated by an imperfect Church. Christology and ecclesiology are therefore the overriding hermeneutical framework. Ratzinger therefore opens up the *Aufklärung* concept of reason to the horizons of the highest human aspirations regarding such sublime concerns regarding the source of all things, that is, creation by creative Reason; secondly, who the human being is as a person, that is, *logos* and Personhood; the human vocation of love, that is, *Logos* as unity of Love; what does it mean to speak, that is, *Logos* as Word; and finally, the definitive opening of the finite to the infinite, or more precisely, the breaking forth of the infinite into the realm of finite existence, with the *Logos* becoming Son, at the fullness of time (Gal 4:4). These theological appropriations eschew the attraction of a superstitious human self sufficiency motivated by an unwarranted amplification of the concept of reason.

However, it is important to note that Ratzinger would not have been able to make these appropriations if he had not first demonstrated, as he did in both his inaugural lecture and in the *Introduction*, the possibility of faith actively engaging reason and shaping it from within, and vice versa. Hence, de Gaál asserts that Ratzinger's inaugural lecture is the best demonstration of the remarkable theological consistency of Joseph Ratzinger regarding the positions, insights and lines of argumentation of the theologian Ratzinger over the decades.[110] Not only does the inaugural lecture build on the personalist conception of the God of revelation and Christian faith that is largely Augustinian in texture—a debt to Ratzinger's doctoral studies as seen in chapter one—but more so, it opens up this personal God of faith to the gains of the secular *Aufklärung* by acknowledging the achievements of what Kant will call *mere reason*, especially the achievement of the monological God of Greek philosophy attained through unaided reason. And Ratzinger carries these insights from his doctoral work through his inaugural lecture and into his *Introduction to Christianity*, as seen in the first two chapters of this work. Under this ambiance of the dialogue between faith and reason, Ratzinger can thus make the five-fold theological appropriations of *Logos*, of reason, which is constitutive of chapter three. This is done bearing in mind that reason is not understood as a mere rational faculty, but the ground for all being, that which encompasses all and holds all in being.

Notes — Chapter Two

1 Alister E. McGrath, *The Making of Modern German Christology: From the Enlightenment to Pannenberg* (Oxford: Basil Blackwell, 1986), 9.

2 Frederick C. Beiser, "Kant's intellectual development: 1746–1781," in Paul Guyer (ed). The Cambridge Companion to Kant (New York: Cambridge University Press, 2008), 29. Beiser points out that we can explain Kant's initial devotion to metaphysics from Kant's desire to escape the dilemma posed by the Pietists to the Wolffians, that is, either a rational skepticism or an irrational fideism, based on the argument that reason cannot demonstrate the basic principles of our thought because reason cannot provide us with any knowledge beyond sense experience. As Beiser maintains, "only metaphysics, the young Kant believed, could rescue the *Aufklärung's* faith in reason from the attacks of the Pietists. Only it could provide a rational justification for our moral and religious beliefs, and thus a middle path between skepticism and fideism" (p. 30).

3 Ian R. Boyd, *Dogmatics Among the Ruins: German Expressionism and the Enlightenment as Contexts for Karl Barth's Theological Development* (Bern: Peter Lang, 2004), 205.

4 Nicholas Till, *Mozart and the Enlightenment* (London: Faber and Faber, 1992), 1.

5 Boyd, *Dogmatics Among the Ruins*, 205.

6 Boyd, *Dogmatics Among the Ruins*, 205–206.

7 Till, *Mozart and the Enlightenment*, 207.

8 Ernst Cassirer, *The Philosophy of the Enlightenment*, trans. Fritz C. A. Koelln and James P. Pettegrove (Princeton, NJ: Princeton University Press, 2009), 14.

9 Cassirer, *Enlightenment*, 14.
10 Michael Printy, *Enlightenment and the Creation of German Catholicism* (Cambridge: Cambridge University Press, 2009), 156.
11 McGrath, *The Making of Modern German Christology*, 10.
12 McGrath, *The Making of Modern German Christology*, 10.
13 McGrath, *The Making of Modern German Christology*, 10.
14 McGrath, *The Making of Modern German Christology*, 11.
15 McGrath, *The Making of Modern German Christology*, 11.
16 McGrath, *The Making of Modern German Christology*, 14.
17 McGrath, *The Making of Modern German Christology*, 17.
18 McGrath, *The Making of Modern German Christology*, 13.
19 McGrath, *The Making of Modern German Christology*, 13.
20 Albert Schweitzer, *The Quest of the Historical Jesus* (Minneapolis: Fortress Press, 2001), 17.
21 Schweitzer, *The Quest*, 17–18.
22 Schweitzer, *The Quest*, 20.
23 Schweitzer, *The Quest*, 21.
24 Schweitzer, *The Quest*, 22.
25 Schweitzer, *The Quest*, 22–24.
26 McGrath, *The Making of Modern German Christology*, 17.
27 McGrath, *The Making of Modern German Christology*, 17.
28 McGrath, *The Making of Modern German Christology*, 17–18.
29 McGrath, *The Making of Modern German Christology*, 18.
30 McGrath, *The Making of Modern German Christology*, 11.
31 McGrath, *The Making of Modern German Christology*, 11.
32 McGrath, *The Making of Modern German Christology*, 11.
33 McGrath, *The Making of Modern German Christology*, 12.
34 McGrath, *The Making of Modern German Christology*, 11.
35 McGrath, *The Making of Modern German Christology*, 11.
36 Baruch Spinoza, *Tractatus theologico-politicus* 4, in *Works*, Vol. 1, trans. R. H. M. Elwes (New York: Rowman & Littlefield Publishers Inc., 1951), 61.
37 Henry Chadwick, ed., *Lessing's Theological Writings* (Redwood City, CA: Stanford University Press, 1956), 53.
38 McGrath, *The Making of Modern German Christology*, 13.
39 McGrath, *The Making of Modern German Christology*, 14.
40 Printy, *Enlightenment*, 127.
41 Printy, *Enlightenment*, 127.
42 Printy, *Enlightenment*, 141.
43 Printy, *Enlightenment*, 142.
44 Printy, *Enlightenment*, 125. It should be noted that the list is clearly not exhaustive, for there are other factors such as the anti-Jesuit character that

largely defined this movement; however, engaging the anti-Jesuit question takes us too far afield from the subject matter under consideration.

45 Emery de Gaál, *O Lord, I Seek Your Countenance: Explorations and Discoveries in Pope Benedict XVI's Theology* (Steubenville, OH: Emmaus Academic, 2018), 71.

46 De Gaál, *Explorations*, 71.

47 De Gaál, *Explorations*, 71.

48 De Gaál, *Explorations*, 73.

49 De Gaál, *Explorations*, 73–74.

50 Joseph Ratzinger, *Der Gott des Glaubens und der Gott der Philosophen* (Bonn: Johannes-Verlag Leutesdorf, 2005), 23: "Das Problem ist schwer und ernst. Man kann ihm nur näherkommen, wenn man beide Gottesbegriffe genau und gründlich ins Auge faßt, um ihr Wesentliches zu erkennen."

51 Ratzinger, *Der Gott des Glaubens*, 18: "Darin wird dann zugleich ein wichtiger Gegensatz zum griechisch-philosophischen Gottesverhältnis deutlich: In der Philosophie ist es der Mensch, der von sich aus nach Gott sucht, im biblischen Glauben ist es Gott selbst und Gott allein, der in schöpferischer Freiheit das Mensch-Gott-Verhältnis herstellt. So wird nun der Gegensatz zwischen Gottesname und Gottesbegriff, Gott des Glaubens und Gott der Philosophen schon deutlicher und bestimmter. Der, Gott der Philosophen 'ist der Gott, zu dem man nicht betet, der Gott, mit dem es wohl Einheit gibt – namlich die Einheit, die das Denken als –' tiefste Wahrheit 'selbst denkt—aber keine Gemeinschaft—Gemeinschaft, die von Gott selbst gestiftet wird."

52 Ratzinger, *Der Gott des Glaubens*, 15: "Fur Thomas fallen Gott der Religion und Gott der Philosophen vollig ineinander, dagegen sind Gott des Glaubens und der Gott der Philosophie teilweise unterschieden; der Gott des Glaubens übersteigt den Gott der Philosophen, fügt ihm etwas hinzu. Die religio naturalis - und das heißt: jede Religion außerhalb des Christentums - hat keinen höheren Inhalt und kann keinen hoheren Inhalt haben als die philosophische Gotteslehre ihn bietet. Im Gegenteil, alles was sie daruber hinaus oder im Widerspruch zu ihr beinhaltet, ist Abfall und Verirrung. Außerhalb des christlichen Glaubens ist nach Thomas die Philosophie die höchste Moglichkeit des menschlichen Geistes uberhaupt."

53 Thomas Aquinas, *Summa Theologiae*, Ia, q.1 art. 8, ad 2. trans. Laurence Shapcote, O.P. (Lander, Wyoming: The Aquinas Institute, 2012).

54 Thomas Aquinas, *Summa Theologiae*, Ia, q. 2 art. 3, trans. Laurence Shapcote, O.P. (Lander, Wyoming: The Aquinas Institute, 2012).

55 Ratzinger, *Der Gott des Glaubens*, 16: "Der christliche Gottesglaube nimmt die philosophische Gotteslehre in sich auf und vollendet sie. Scharf gesagt: Der Gott des Aristoteles und der Gott Jesus Christi ist ein und derselbe, Aristoteles hat den wahren Gott erkannt, den wir im Glauben

tiefer und reiner erfassen dürfen, so wie wir in der jenseitigen Gottesschau abermals inniger und näher Gottes Wesen erfassen werden. Man könnte vielleicht ohne Vergewaltigung des Tatbestandes sagen: Der christliche Glaube verhält sich zur philosophischen Gotteserkenntnis etwa so wie sich die endzeitliche Gottesschau zum Glauben verhält. Es handelt sich um drei Stufen eines einheitlichen Gesamtweges."

56 Martin Buber, *Eclipse of God*, trans. Leora Batnitzky (Princeton, NJ: Princeton University Press, 2016), xii.

57 Ratzinger, *Der Gott des Glaubens*, 22.

58 Ratzinger, *Der Gott des Glaubens*, 21–22: "Da steht auf der einen Seite der Gott, der sich in der Nennung seines Namens als Du zu erkennen gibt und sich öffnet auf den Menschen hin, sich ihm zur Gemeinschaft darbietet. Da steht auf der anderen Seite das philosophische Denken, das in der Namensoffenbarung einen Anthropomorphismus sieht, damit aber letzterdings die Offenbarung selbst ablehnt. "– Das sich selbst genügende Vernunftdenken will nichts anerkennen, was von jenseits seiner eigenen Möglichkeit kommt. – "

59 Ratzinger, *Der Gott des Glaubens*, 29: "Angesichts so ernster und weittragender Konsequenzen ist die Frage noch einmal und neu zu stellen, ob und inwieweit der von den Kirchenvätern gezogene Bindestrich zwischen Glaubensgott und Philosophengott, dessen Berechtigung und Notwendigkeit bisher vom allgemeinen Problem des Monotheismus her aufgewiesen wurde, speziell im Hinblick auf den biblischen Gottesbegriff berechtigt war. Darauf kann zunächst geantwortet werden: Er war berechtigt, sofern und soweit der biblische Gottesglaube Monotheismus sein wollte und sollte."

60 Ratzinger, *Der Gott des Glaubens*, 23–24: "Gehen wir aus vom philosophischen Gottesbegriff, der sich uns nun, im Gegenüber zum Gott des Glaubens, in zugespitzter Weise als der Gottesbegriff der griechischen Philosophie darstellt. Es genügt zu seinem Verständnis nicht, eine bestimmte Definitionsformel; zu kennen und zu übernehmen. Es muß vielmehr die Beziehung gesehen werden, in der dieser Gottesbegriff zu der geistigen und religiösen Welt steht, in der er gefunden und in die er so oder anders eingeordnet wurde. Denn in irgendeiner Beziehung hat ja zweifellos auch der vorchristliche philosophische Gottesbegriff zur Religion gestanden, die auch dort etwas anderes war als Philosophie und erst wenn diese Beziehung gesehen ist, ist der philosophische Gottesbegriff der Griechen als solcher und ganzer richtig gesehen; im Prinzip gilt Gleiches für jedweden philosophischen Gottesbegriff."

61 John Paul II, *Encyclical Letter on the Relationship between Faith and Reason Fides et Ratio* (Vatican City: Libreria Editrice Vaticana: 1998), 3.

62 Joseph Ratzinger, *Principles of Catholic Theology: Building Stones for a*

Fundamental Theology, trans. Mary Frances McCarthy, S.N.D. (San Francisco: Ignatius Press, 1987), 73.

63 Joseph Ratzinger, *The Regensburg Lecture* (South Bend, IN: St. Augustine's Press, 2007), 5–7, 14.

64 Ratzinger, *The Regensburg Lecture*, 35.

65 Martin Heidegger, *Phenomenology and Theology*, John C. Caputo (ed.) *The Religious* Blackwell Readings in Continental Philosophy (Malden: Blackwell Publishers, 2002), 50.

66 Heidegger, *Phenomenology and Theology*, 51.

67 Heidegger, *Phenomenology and Theology*, 60.

68 Habermas & Ratzinger, *The Dialectic of Secularization*, 65–66.

69 Aquinas, *Summa Theologica*, I-II, i, 7.

70 Martin Heidegger, "Only a God," D*er Spiegel*, 31 May 1976, in Richard Kearney, *Strangers, Gods and Monsters, Interpreting Otherness* (London: Routledge Taylor & Francis Group, 2002)215.

71 Richard Kearney, *Poetics of Modernity Toward a Hermeneutic Imagination* (*Philosophy and Literary Theory*) (New York: Humanity Books, 1995), 58.

72 Ratzinger, *Der Gott des Glaubens*, 11–12: "Es beginnt nach einer sehr sorgfältigen Angabe von Tag und Stunde mit den Worten: " – Feuer. '– Gott Abrahams, Gott Isaaks, Gott Jakobs –' nicht der Philosophen und Gelehrten." Der Mathematiker und Philosoph Pascal hatte den lebendigen Gott, den Gott des Glaubens erfahren und in solch lebendigem Begegnen mit dem Du Gottes offenbar in bestürztem und freudigem Erstaunen erfaßt, wie anders der Einbruch der Wirklichkeit Gottes ist im Vergleich zu dem, was die mathematische Philosophie etwa eines Descartes über Gott zu sagen wußte."

73 René Descartes, *Meditations on First Philosophy*, trans. Donald A. Cress (Indianapolis, IN: Hackett Publishing Company, Inc., 1993), III, 38, 26.

74 Descartes, *Meditations*, III, 38, 26.

75 Peter Markie, "The Cogito and its importance," in John Cottingham (ed.), *The Cambridge Companion to Descartes* (New York: Cambridge University Press, 2005), 156. In this article, Markie points out that

Descartes dismisses the evidence of the senses, arriving in his famous *cogito ergo sum* maxim, derived thanks to the process of intuition and deduction, in which the *cogito* in the primary sense is self-evident, not derived from a syllogism and, in the final analysis, the first principle of philosophy (Markie, *The Cogito*, 140). Descartes has absolute certainty that he thinks and therefore he exists, because Descartes clearly and distinctively perceives the fact of his thinking. Though a phenomenal epistemological achievement which places us in Descartes debt, it is important to note with Markie, that not all clear and distinct perceptions produce certainty (Markie, *The Cogito*, 152). For example, an atheist who has a clear and distinct idea of the non-existence of God does not make God's non-existence a self-evident proposition or idea.

76 Descartes, *Meditations*, III, 45, 30.

77 Jean-Marie Beyssade, "The idea of God and the proofs of his existence" in John Cottingham (ed.), *The Cambridge Companion to Descartes* (New York: Cambridge University Press, 2005), 181.

78 Beyssade, "The idea of God and the proofs of his existence," 183.

79 It is worth noting that critiques of the Cartesian system have described it not only as a metaphysical castle in the air, but, in terms of the immediate worldview of seventeenth-century France and Holland, as dangerous for the Christian faith. The charge of a philosophical foe to Christianity was largely attributed to Descartes' anti-scholasticism. In 1663 Descartes works were placed on the *Index Librorum Prohibitorum* with the provision *donec corrigantur—until they are corrected*. In addition, Descartes has also been charged for lack of originality in his thought, in that his doubt as perceived to have been drawn from the Greek skeptics, his Cogito from Augustine, and the ontological argument from Anselm. For the insights in this footnote, see Nicholas Jolley's "The reception of Descartes' philosophy" in John Cottingham (ed.), *The Cambridge Companion to Descartes* (New York: Cambridge University Press, 2005), 393–394, 398 and 410.

80 Beiser, "Kant's intellectual development," 28.

81 In Paul Guyer, "Introduction: The starry heavens and the moral law," in Paul Guyer (ed.) *The Cambridge Companion to Kant*," (New York: Cambridge University Press, 2008), 8, Guyer remarks about the movement beyond Cartesian mathematical conception of God as follows: "[...] Contrary to the dream of all rationalist philosophers since Descartes, philosophy could not use the same method as mathematics. Mathematics could begin with definitions and then prove indubitable results by constructing objects in accordance with those definitions and performing various operations upon them; philosophy, however, could never begin with definitions but only with 'certain primary fundamental judgments' the analysis of which could lead to definitions as its conclusion, not its commencement." In other words, the question of method is germen to the difference between mathematics and philosophy, and hence, to the possibilities that come with a mathematical perception of the question of God vis-à-vis a philosophical conception of the God-question.

82 Cassirer, *Enlightenment*, 8.

83 Cassirer, *Enlightenment*, 9.

84 Cassirer, *Enlightenment*, 13.

85 Cassirer, *Enlightenment*, 13.

86 Cassirer, *Enlightenment*, 7.

87 Cassirer, *Enlightenment*, 8.

88 Ratzinger, *Der Gott des Glaubens*, 12–13: "Erst die Zertrümmerung der spekulativen Metaphysik durch Kant und die Verlagerung des Religiösen in den außerrationalen und so auch außermetaphysischen Raum des Gefühls durch Schleiermacher brachte den pascalschen Gedanken endgültig zum Durchbruch und führte nun erst zur radikalen Zuspitzung des Problems: Jetzt erst ist der Graben zwischen Metaphysik und Religion unüberbrückbar, Metaphysik, d.h. theoretische Vernunft hat keinen Zugang zu Gott; Religion hat keinen Sitz im Raum der ratio: Sie ist Erleben, das sich der wissenschaftlichen Meßbarkeit entzieht; diese dennoch versuchen, bedeutet aus ihr ein unwirkliches Schema abziehen, den, 'Gott der Philosophen.' Das hat eine weitere Folge: Religion, die nicht rationalisierbar ist, kann im Grunde auch nicht dogmatisch sein, wenn anders Dogma eine rationale Aussage über religiöse Gehalte sein soll."

89 Charles Taylor, *A Secular Age* (Cambridge, MA: Harvard University Press, 2007), 2.

90 Taylor, *A Secular Age*, 3.

91 Taylor, *A Secular Age*, 12.

92 Joseph Ratzinger, *Introduction to Christianity*, trans. Michael J. Miller (San Francisco: Ignatius Press, 2004), 138–139.

93 Ratzinger, *Introduction*, 139.

94 Ratzinger, *Introduction*, 140.

95 Ratzinger, *Introduction*, 140–141.

96 Ratzinger, *Introduction*, 141–142.

97 Ratzinger, *Introduction*, 142.

98 G. W. F. Hegel, *Lectures on the Philosophy of Religion, Vol. III: The Consummate Religion*, ed. by Peter C. Hodgson and trans. by R. F. Brown, P. C. Hodgson and J. M. Stewart with the assistance of H. S. Harris (Oxford: Clarendon Press, 2007), 175.

99 G. W. F. Hegel, *Lectures on the Proofs of the Existence of God*, ed. and trans. Peter C. Hodgson (New York: Oxford University Press, 2011), 230.

100 Hegel, *Lectures on the Proofs of the Existence of God*, 228.

101 De Gaál, *Explorations*, 80.

102 Ratzinger, *Introduction*, 143.

103 Thomas Aquinas, *Summa Theologiae*, IIa-IIae q. 81, art. 2, ad 3. trans. Laurence Shapcote, O.P. (Lander, Wyoming: The Aquinas Institute, 2012).

104 Ratzinger, *Introduction*, 144.

105 Ratzinger, *Introduction*, 145.

106 Ratzinger, *Introduction*, 146–147.

107 Ratzinger, *Introduction*, 147.

108 Ratzinger, *Introduction*, 148.

109 De Gaál, *Explorations*, 80.

110 De Gaál, *Explorations*, 81.

Chapter Three: *A Ratzingerian Reading of the Historico-Philosophical Trajectory of the Concept of* Logos *as the Bridge to the* Aufklärung

Thus far, we have seen how Ratzinger has sought to maintain a rapprochement between faith and reason, between the God of philosophy and the God of theology. Chapter two also exposes the broad understanding of the concept of reason that came with the *Aufklärung*. Reason is not *mere rationality*, but a concept designating all of reality. Nothing was excluded from the gaze of reason, not even revelation. As seen from Ratzinger's treatment of the synthesis between the God of faith and the God of philosophers, Ratzinger is not opposed to reason. However, to Ratzinger, the light of reason alone is insufficient in terms of enlightening human concerns. Reason has its limits, and the depths of reason are all the more discovered under the stimulus of revelation, irrespective of the legitimacy of human reflection, philosophy and the sciences. On cru cial life questions, one quickly comes to terms with the limits of the mere rational, for example: Why do I exist? What is my destiny? Why is there suffering in the world? Why do bad things happen to good people? What is there when this earthly life is over? These questions and more cause us to come to terms with the insufficiency of reason in terms of explaining all phenomena.

That is not to say that proponents of mere reason do not raise these sorts of questions and seek to answer them. The bone of contention is that their answers, if they are to remain *within the boundaries of mere reason,* to use Kantian terminology, still leave many questions unresolved. In other words, because mere reason must limit itself to pure reason, it must be satisfied with the empirically accessible only. But the human mind remains curious of possibilities beyond reason, which could be available to us, as Maurice Blondel demonstrates in *L'Action (1893)*. Blondel seeks to establish the supernatural or transcendental as a hypothetical necessity to resolve the dialectic opened up by Blondel's synthetic analysis of the phenomenon of willed human action as it opens up in human subjectivity, that is, what Blondel refers to as the *one thing necessary*.[1] To Blondel, this *one thing necessary* is the inevitable transcendence of human action. This is the consciousness of reason that transcends all particular motives and, to Blondel, pushes toward the infinite.[2] This orientation of the natural order towards the supernatural is grounded in the inability of the natural order to be self-sustaining, hence, the inevitability for the need for the supernatural in human life. Faith therefore extends to where reason cannot reach. This is the sense in which one can assert that without the light of Christ, the light of reason is insufficient in the face of the most penetrating questions of human life. Blondel characterizes the tendency of excluding the horizon of faith as the human display of a superstitious self-sufficiency, which, to Blondel, is not sustainable, for it forces an infinite desire into the cloak of finitude – a futile attempt at turning a blind eye to a mystery that outlasts the apparently full use of all of human powers. We are therefore faced with a dilemma, Blondel writes: "Man aspires to be a god: to be god without God and against God, to be god through God and with God, that is the dilemma."[3] This impasse, from the Blondellian reading of things, constitutes the trial of the modern period – to view God and religion in a manner that, while not always explicitly rejecting God and religion, effectively transforms humans into the supernatural through absolute claims of the finite and the temporal.

Having established a broad reading of reason, this third chapter gets to the crux of the matter; it studies Ratzinger's employment of the Greek philosophical concept of *logos* in the theological categories that serve the purpose of taking his reconciliatory movement of what one could describe as the counter-*Aufklärung* to a level in which the Greek philosophical heritage is opened up to the gains of the *Aufklärung*, with both brought into the theological service of Ratzinger's ecclesiological and Christological conclusions, of creative Reason, Person, Son, Word, and unity of love. These areas are not meant to be exhaustive or comprehensive, that is, there is no intention of stating that these five areas cover all of Ratzinger's engagements with the positions that are representative of the *Aufklärung* movement. On the contrary, creative Reason, Person, Son, Word, and unity of love are meant to be representative of the central concerns of modern theology. And to the extent that Ratzinger engages them, one can find, as will be seen, many points of convergence and divergence with the central concerns, arguments, and presuppositions of the *Aufklärung*.

The concept of *logos* is therefore the consistent thread underpinning and undergirding Western philosophical reasoning, a concept that, as we will see shortly, was already taken up into the language of theological reflection and Christian apologetics, as early as Justin Martyr. From the root λεγ, the word *logos* designates a plurality of meanings, such as, to speak, to report, to select, to collect,[4] across the biblical, philosophical, and theological spectrum, as this chapter will demonstrate. As Heraclitus pointed out in antiquity, everything happened in accordance with the *logos*,[5] thereby giving *logos* a universal import and application. Following this Heraclitan reading, it is on target to conclude that the "failure to understand the *logos* results in an epistemic state that is both child-like and apparently not significantly different from sleep."[6] If ignorance of the *logos* is likened to being asleep, then knowledge of the *logos* is awakening. It means *logos* provides a sense of epistemic cognition of things, of the truth of things.

In line with Heraclitus, the Stoics will see in *logos* the divine reason that was inherent and which permeated the entire cosmos.[7] With the Stoics, therefore, accentuation was given to the cosmological dimension of *logos* from the perspective of rationality, especially as pertains to wisdom and virtue. The Stoic good and wise man, the sage, was the one who had arrived at the consciousness of *logos* within him, and hence lived according to *logos*, that is, according to virtue. The Stoics made a distinction between things that were within human control, such as anger, jealousy, lust—in a word, vices and passions, things demanding the application of the human intellect and will, on the one hand, and, on the other hand, things that were beyond human control, such as money, health, and reputation, toward which the sage was called to cultivate an attitude of radical indifference, as seen in the *Meditations* of the Roman Emperor Marcus Aurelius.[8] When, for instance, a person wishes to acquire wealth that is not accorded to that person by the divine will, that person becomes unhappy and will always lament. For the Stoics, therefore, the human being is likened to a dog tied to a moving cart that can either trot along carefully or be dragged along uncomfortably but must go along with the cart in any case.[9] The Stoics held that the internal world of rationality, the mind, was within human control. A proper attitude in life is reflected in self-control, not letting oneself be dependent on the ever-changing external world. This meant a life of rationality, the good life, which was perceived as the philosophical life, the life of *logos*. *Logos*, reason, is therefore the highest function of the human being, and a life directed by reason is the highest good for the human being. A harmonious life, lived according to virtue, is a life lived according to *logos*. Thus, reason, *logos*, is the tool that the gods have placed under human control, which ought to help the virtuous person or sage to make right judgment about the appearance of things, to distinguish between things that are within and those that are beyond the sage's power. Morality is thus contingent on the rightful application of *logos*.[10] The Stoic stage must therefore always live in accordance with *logos*.

In the light of these assertions regarding *logos* in Greek philosophy, such as its commonality, universality, and foundations for cognition and hence for the possibility of truth, one can see why such a concept, preeminent as well in the Western mode of thinking, must have been readily attractive to Ratzinger. The Ratzingerian body of texts is therefore replete with examples of his appropriation of the Greek concept of *logos*. For example, in Ratzinger's trilogy on Jesus and the post-synodal apostolic exhortation *Verbum Domini*, Ratzinger makes a case for the primacy of the Prologue of John's Gospel, which clearly stands out for him as his favorite hermeneutical key because of the concept of *logos* contained therein. In *Verbum Domini*, Benedict XVI ties together the different layers of meaning of *Logos* in a harmonious, interrelated symmetry:

> As the Prologue of John clearly shows us, the *Logos* refers in the first place to the eternal Word, the only Son, begotten of the Father before all ages and consubstantial with him: *the Word was with God, and the Word was God*. But this same

> Word, Saint John tells us, "became flesh" (Jn 1:14); hence Jesus Christ, born of the Virgin Mary, is truly the Word of God who has become consubstantial with us. Thus, the expression "Word of God" here refers to the person of Jesus Christ, the eternal Son of the Father, made man. While the Christ event is at the heart of divine revelation, we also need to realize that creation itself, the *liber naturae*, is an essential part of this symphony of many voices in which the one Word is spoken. We also profess our faith that God has spoken his Word in salvation history; he has made his voice heard; by the power of his Spirit, "he has spoken through the prophets." Finally, the Word of God, attested and divinely inspired, is sacred Scripture, the Old and New Testaments.[11]

In all, at the center of Ratzinger's *logos* theology stands the figure of Christ, the one who gives the multiple theological appropriations of *logos* their ultimate bearing. This is crucial in understanding Ratzinger's theological appropriation of the philosophical concept of the rational *logos* because, as Christopher Collins, S. J., points out in *The Word Made Love*:

> If Jesus is not the Eternal Word who has descended from above and is really made known in the flesh, in history, there is, for Ratzinger, ultimately no spiritual meaning and efficacy in him. It is precisely the fact that the Eternal *Logos* is expressed in history as *sarx* in Jesus Christ, that makes the hope of salvation within history real. In Christ, the *Logos* that had been understood as the principle of coherence for all of creation is now seen as a person: The *Logos* made flesh, manifested in love.[12]

In other words, Ratzinger's appropriation of *logos* is not just a pragmatic, this-worldly sense of utilitarianism, but is because the same *Logos* now present in history is simultaneously the source or originator of history. The event of the Incarnation is therefore not something extrinsic to the inner contours of history. It is *Logos*, creative Reason, that is behind the start of history, entering history to bring history unto a new level of being, shaped by the humanizing and concomitant divinizing of history, thanks to the *Gestalt* of the Eternal *Logos*, Jesus Christ. Collins is therefore right in emphasizing the interrelationship between faith and historical consciousness in Ratzinger's thought.

As Benedict XVI himself emphasizes in *Verbum Domini* when talking about *Logos* and historical consciousness, the *Logos* has been "abbreviated," that is, it has become "shorter" in that it has become historical in order to be apprehended and understood by human beings.[13] And as Benedict puts it again in his Christmas homily of 2006, "the eternal word became small—small enough to fit into a manger. He became a child, so that the Word could be grasped by us."[14] Collins comments: "This is the classic kind of Benedict-ine formulation that is startling in its tenderness and pastoral sensitivity, drawing the suspicious contemporary audience into a highly intimate encounter—the kind of encounter for which the contemporary person longs."[15] Therefore, one notices a strong sense of the eternal in Ratzinger's appropriation of the philosophical concept of *logos*. And this vantage point of eternity is what makes the entry into history comprehensible and possible, for the Incarnation of the *Logos* is the meeting point between eternity and time, between the pre-historical and the historical.

Given this sense of eternity and history, therefore, one can make an interpretive reading of the historical evolution of the philosophical concept of *logos* through a Ratzingerian lens. This is possible because Ratzinger's theological usage of the *logos* concept, as indicated above, is profoundly historical, even if pre-historical and simultaneously trans-historical, since, in the final analysis, what one is dealing with here is the *Gestalt* of Christ, the Eternal Son who is the new present Adam who opens the way to the future. It is thanks to this line of thinking that we can bring Ratzinger into contact with Greek philosophers that had a great influence in the development of the concept of *logos*, such as Heraclitus. The aim is not to make the case that Ratzinger explicitly cites Heraclitus, for example, but to show that the Ratzingerian sense of the eternity of the *Logos* who as *Logos* in eternity is likewise present in history and has been guiding history as its originator, was much present in the history of thought, even before the event of the Incarnation.

In other words, it is not out of place to study Heraclitus as a prelude to getting to the gist of Ratzinger's theological appropriation and actual usage of the concept of the *logos*. If anything, by placing the Ratzingerian reading of the concept of the *logos* in its twin dimensions of eternity and history in the middle of Greek philosophy, a new possibility might open up for theological and philosophical dialogue and rapprochement, which, as seen in chapter two, remains an underlining concern for Ratzinger. Consequently, the historical-philosophical trajectory of the concept of *logos* that puts Ratzinger and the Greek philosophical heritage of *logos* together is another concrete example of the possible dialogue between the God of faith and the God of philosophers, between faith and reason, always paying attention to the Ratzingerian principle of faith as providing a wider framework and not obstructing or impeding the dictates of reason *qua* reason.

3.1 Heraclitus of Ephesus (circa 500 BC) and *logos*

The Greek philosophical tradition of *logos* is traceable to Heraclitus, otherwise known as the philosopher of *logos*.[16] As Edward Hussey points out, ancient perceptions about Heraclitus are mixed. For some like Aristotle and Theophrastus, Heraclitus is a kind of eccentric figure, "a deranged denier of the law of non-contradiction, who in more lucid moments sketched an incomplete cosmology in Milesian style. On the other hand, the Stoics, followed by some early Christian writers, saw Heraclitus as a sage and a precursor."[17] As Hussey remarks, neither position regarding the figure of Heraclitus should be discarded, but what should ultimately determine the position one assumes regarding the legacy of Heraclitus, whether seen as a sage or not, should depend on one's encounter and interpretation of the surviving fragments of his writings.[18] That said, though Heraclitus is considered the philosopher of *logos* owing to the prominence that *logos* finds in his fragments, it is helpful to note, as pointed out above in the introductory paragraphs preceding this section, that *logos* was a commonly used Greek word, with varied meanings—for example, "word," "story," "measure," "calculation," "right reckoning," "reasonable proportion."[19] From these multiple usages, the term *logos* in its Greek context found a home not only in social settings, but in historical, mathematical, and scientific thinking as well. As Hussey observes, for Heraclitus,

> [...] *logos* has a special significance, in which each of its ordinary uses is allowed some resonance and is exploited as occasion serves. At the most basic level, Heraclitus' *logos* coincides with what Heraclitus is saying: it is his story about the way things are. Yes, as in the remark just cited (that is, Fragment B50: "*When one listens not to me but to the logos, it is wise to agree (homologein) that all things are one*"), it (that is, *logos*), must also be distinguished from Heraclitus' words: it is not *as* Heraclitus' "story" that it commands assent, but because it shows what is *wise* to think. (It is, though, still something that speaks, and that can be listened to; it still is the story of somebody or something, with language as its vehicle). Heraclitus is not laying claim to any merely private revelation or purely personal authority.[20]

Logos, from the perspective of Heraclitus, was not a principle that could be personalized and privatized. It belongs to the nature of *logos* to be shared by all, to be present in all and to be for all. It is in the nature of *logos* to be universal. This is a sense in which listening to Heraclitus is not listening to Heraclitus, for the story is not Heraclitus', but of a common reasonableness that is universally deducible. And this universality of *logos* sets out the foundation upon which there could and should emerge a common interaction and dialogue of ideas in the marketplace of public discourse. Heraclitus clearly underscores this point in Fragment B2: "Though the *logos* is shared, the many live as though they had a private source of understanding."[21] Hence, this universality of *logos* eschews all pretensions to any sense of privileged privacy or occultist revelation. To Heraclitus, not to be conscious of *logos*, as we read in Fragment B1 and as remarked above, is to live a life that is in a state of sleep-walking:

> Of this *logos* [...] people prove to have no understanding, both before they hear it and when once they have heard it.

> For though all things come about according to logos, (people) are as though they had no experience, though they experience such words and deeds as I set forth, marking off each thing according to its nature and pointing out how it is. But other people do not notice what they do when awake—just as they do not notice all the things they forget about when asleep.[22]

And what is lamentable, from the perspective of Heraclitus of Ephesus, is that many people live through life sleeping, since many are unconscious of the experience and workings of *logos*. David Wiggins makes an insightful comment regarding the Heraclitan metaphor of sleep-walking and *logos*: "Regarding Heraclitus' several fragments about sleeping and waking and grasping how things are, one is struck by the similarity between the state of ordinary men as Heraclitus conceives them and men sleep-walking. If one sleep-walks, one finds one's way without knowing what one is doing."[23] If Wiggins is right, then the implication could be that underlying the consciousness of *logos* is an intrinsic epistemological character, in the sense of what would be the capacity to interpret one's experiences, especially when one bears in mind Hussey's interpretation of Heraclitus' "listening to the logos" as grounded on the certainty that *logos* is what accounts and explains the nature of things.[24] In this light, the inability to be interpretive and analytic, to participate in the breadth of reasoning that comes with a life lived according to *logos*, amounts to sleepy existence, a dogmatic slumber, a state of mental inertia, while being fully awake and physically conscious.

In this sense, one could read Heraclitus to be implying that logos offers a system of rationality, as Hussey attests and explains:

> Heraclitus, then, is claiming that his way of seeing things is the only *rational* way [...]. He (Heraclitus) is committed to the recognition that there is a system, though a concealed one, in things, and a systematic way of thinking about them, once the clue, the "latent structure," has been found. For Heraclitus, the clue consisted in the structural pattern that may conveniently be called "unity-in-opposites." This is what gives substance to his claim that "all things are one."[25]

But what is the content of this unity-in-opposites of Heraclitus? Hussey points out three features. Firstly, that unity is more fundamental than the opposites, which is suggestive of the fact that Heraclitus might have nurtured monistic ambitions with focus on an underlying unity that, as Hussey puts it, "incorporates and manifests the opposites."[26] Secondly, unity-in-opposites reveals itself in that opposites are essential features of the unity, for, "in whatever way the opposites are present in the unity, what matters is that their presence is of the essence of the unity. The unity could not be what it is without them."[27] There is therefore a functional sense in which unity harmonizes opposites, for they are opposites because they stand in unity to one another. Finally, Hussey writes that "the manifestation of the opposites involves a process, in which the unity performs its essential function."[28] In other words, what appears opposite now could simply be a step toward unity, opposites in potency of unity. Be as it may, I do not think it necessary to go into the intricacies in terms of the reception of this Heraclitan principle of unity-in-opposites by later philosophers, who have judged Heraclitus to be indeterminate in his language and having inevitably fallen victim to the principle of non-contradiction.[29] But what could be interesting to a Ratzingerian reader of Heraclitus' unity-in-opposites is the thought process behind the principle, that is, *how all, in their diversity and difference, eventually fit together*. In other words, it would not be too much of a stretch of the imagination to see a certain similarity of thinking between unity-in-opposites undergirded by the logic of how everything fits together, though different, on the part of Heraclitus, and Ratzinger's Christological reading of the human history, with all its differences, uncertainties, and aspirations, all fitting together around the center of Christ, the omega point of history.

In the one-hundred-and-thirty-one surviving fragments from Heraclitus, the concept of *logos* takes on multiple roles of meaning that very well serves a Ratzingerian appropriation and reading, at least from a theological point of view. An analysis of the multiple senses of Heraclitan *logos* and the theological roles that these usages can play in the Ratzingerian Christological and ecclesiological structure would include the following: Firstly, we have the sense of *logos* as the verb *legein* on which the noun *logos* is built. In this context, *logos* connotes the sense of picking up, laying down, lay by, to collect, to count up, to tell as in a tale, and hence, to give account.[30] These largely are related to speech, which, from a philosophical perspective, is the vehicle for human rationality, in that thanks to speech, we can get to know what the mind was thinking in and by itself. The word that says it, the saying that expresses it, the sentence that states it, and the sense of meaning conveyed by it, as well as the explanations expanded and the arguments enforced, are further expatiations of the activity of the mind.[31] Given this rational character, *logos* moves from being simply speech that is uttered to reason as rationality.

From a theological point of view, this sense of *logos* as speech that becomes creative reason *in the beginning* is readily useful in John's Prologue, which Ratzinger appeals to both in his *Introduction to Christianity* and in *Jesus of Nazareth*, particularly volumes I and III, in putting forth the figure of Christ as the culminative omega point of the aspirations of Greek philosophy and pagan cosmology. As the *Logos* of God, declares Ratzinger, "the man Jesus is the dwelling-place of the Word, the eternal divine Word in this world [...]. Jesus' origin, his provenance, is the true 'beginning'—the primordial source from which all things come, the light that makes the world into the cosmos. He comes from God. He is God."[32] Because he is from God, Jesus is able to communicate God to the world:

> The God who revealed his face only in Israel, even though he was also honored among the pagans in various shadowy guises. It is this God, the God of Abraham, Isaac, and Jacob, the true God, whom he has brought to the nations of the earth. He has brought God, and now we know his face, now we can call upon him. Now we know the path that we human beings have to take in this world. Jesus has brought God and, with God, the truth about our origin and destiny: faith, hope, and love. It is only because of our hardness of heart that we think this is too little.[33]

Thanks to this presence of *Logos* as Jesus of Nazareth in history, we can now see the face of God and call upon God. God is no longer so distant and remote from us, but has become one of us, Immanuel, establishing an anthropological relationship of communicability and mutuality with human beings: "For to all who received him, who believed in his name, he gave power to become children of God; who were born not of blood nor of the will of the flesh nor of the will of man, but of God" (Jn 1:12).

A second philosophical component of *logos* has to do with relationality, for as Brann points out, telling is relating: "The *logos* brings terms into relations to each other, particularly the ratio-relation that connects two terms in mutually determining juxtaposition, especially in respect to their common measurability."[34] *Logos* is therefore a relation in the sense that brings together two terms without merging them. It puts together a thinking and speaking capacity, so much so that they can "say the same," *homo-logein*, all the while remaining different.[35] One does not cease to be because of the other. The sameness of love between the Father, Son and Spirit speak one word, love, but their individual persons do not cease to be owing to this sameness. On the contrary, the sameness of love connects them in a relationship of mutual love and self-giftedness, as amplified by Augustine of Hippo.

In addition to *logos* as speech-reason and *logos* as relation, the third facet of *logos* that emerges from Greek philosophy is *logos* as unity, oneness. In the fiftieth fragment of Heraclitus cited above in the introduction to this section, we read: "*ouk emou, alla tou logou akousantas homologein sophon estin hen panta einai* (Listening not to me but to the *logos*, it is wise to acknowledge that all things are one)."[36] Everything is one—*hen, panta*. In the Greek philosophical concept of *logos*, therefore, there are present the roots from which biblical faith could relate its belief in a monotheistic God. Ratzinger attests as much:

> However, there remains the fact that monotheism consists in nothing else than this hyphen, which connects the Absolute—the "God of the Philosophers"—and the God of man—the God of Abraham, Isaac, and Jacob. The hyphen, which St. Augustine put "between neo-Platonic ontology and the biblical Knowledge of God," is legitimate in the case of Monotheism; it is the tangible way in which the hyphen between the God of the Philosophers and the God of Faith and mankind had to manifest itself.[37]

In this text, Ratzinger draws a link between the unity of Greek philosophical principle and biblical monotheism. It is helpful to bear in mind that at the height of Greek philosophy stands the principle of unity or singularity, articulated in varied ways, namely, the unity of the Good, for Plato, the unity or singularity of the Prime Mover or Unmoved Mover, for Aristotle, or the ecstatic ascent toward the unity or singularity of the immateriality of the Plotinian One who is beyond all being, as enunciated in the *Enneads*.[38] As Christian Mofor attests, "in Greek classical thought [...], the One beyond being in Plotinus' philosophy is identified with the ultimate Good in Plato's noetic world in the *Republic*."[39] And again, with reference to the principle of derivation and aspiration, that is, all as coming from Plotinus' One and returning to the One, Mofor again testifies that "in this particular respect the One beyond being in the *Enneads* is comparable to Aristotle's Unmoved Mover. The latter, in its primary position in Aristotle's *Metaphysics*, is also conceived as the object of desire and of thought."[40] Certainly, there is a sense in which one can see an intrinsic parallel between *Logos*, the Good, the Unmoved Mover, and the One, that is, between Heraclitus, Plato, Aristotle, and Plotinus.

However, for the sake of philosophical precision, it is significant to underscore the fact that while in the *logos* of Heraclitus there is a sense in which the *logos* as the creative principle pervades all things and is in all things, such omnipresence cannot be said of the Plotinian One in particular. For in the Plotinian framework, the One, far removed from all being and the source of all being in those who owe their existence and subsistence through contemplation of the One, is far removed from Matter, which is the principle of plurality and evil, unlike the unity and pure good of the One. There is no immediate or direct connection between the One beyond all being and Matter, for as "the region of unlikeness," there is a "sheer negativeness of matter, as opposed to the principle from which it derives."[41] In this grand scheme of things, therefore, there is a twofold movement of descent, from the One beyond being through the Intellect-Intelligible through the Soul-of-the-All to Matter, and the movement of ascent from Matter through the Soul-of-the-All to the Intellect-Intelligible and finally to the One beyond being. The movement of descent is the process of generation, while the movement of ascent is the process of contemplative return.[42] But besides these, what could be characterized as katabatic and anabatic movements, it is important to note as well regarding particular souls, which abide in the Soul-of-the-All, that Plotinus attributes a triple movement: a "going down," a "going about," and a "going up."[43] These triple movements of particular souls underscore the difference between the particular souls and the Soul-of-the-All in the *Enneads*, which is always transcendent,

Therefore, though the One beyond all being is "the first principle of causal dependence and the source of derivation and aspiration of being,"[44] Mofor rightly observes that "the One beyond being is neither "this" nor "that" particular reality in the world which it generates. In other words, the One beyond being transcends the activity which is generated from the perfection in it."[45] The One surpasses all attributes that could be made of the One. The One is Indeterminateness. The One is nameless because we can say nothing of the One. As John Bussanich remarks, the One is "everything and nothing, everywhere and nowhere [...], the indemonstrable first principle of everything [...]. Efforts to understand or to define the nature of the One, Plotinus believes, are doomed to be inadequate."[46] Hence, given this sense of this ineffability of the first principle, the One, it can be spoken about only in terms of what it is not, rather than in terms of what it is. In this sense, this absolute transcendence of the One is quite strikingly similar to the Judeo-Christian understanding of God as an absolute transcendent being, whose essence cannot be captured by the finite intellect of creatures. This explains why in talking about God in relation to creatures, one must employ the principle of analogy of being. Given this Plotinian insight, it is certainly remarkable that philosophy was able to attain this perceptiveness of the unity and uniqueness of the One or God. This philosophical achievement, in a sense, laid the groundwork for the monotheism of biblical faith, from the Supreme Being or the One Beyond All Being of Greek Philosophy, to the One God of Abraham, Isaac and Jacob. In a word, there is a correlation between biblical monotheism and philosophical monotheism.

The fourth aspect of *logos* deducible from the philosophical fragments of Heraclitus is that of the *logos* as a speaker. Heraclitus declares: "Listening not to me but to The Speaker, there is a Wise Thing to agree with—One: Everything."[47] Expressed in this text is the subordination of the human being to the *logos*, in which the human being is the faithful listener to a chosen speaker. Given this context, the listener becomes capable of uttering what he or she has heard from the *logos*-speaker, after the experience of profound listening. It will not be stretching the imagination too much to see in this understanding of *logos* as Speaker and the human being as the recipient of the speech of *logos*, the inner dynamics of Ratzinger's understanding of the process of revelation in his habilitation thesis on Bonaventure, as seen in chapter one. Just like the speech of the Greek *logos*, Ratzinger, in his habilitation work, makes the case that revelation is not the Bible itself, but that the Bible is the medium or channel of revelation who is God. Revelation is God revealing God's self through the speech of the Bible. Ratzinger found in Bonaventure that revelation transcends the written text:

> If Bonaventure is right, then revelation precedes Scripture and becomes deposited in Scripture, but it is not simply identical with it. This in turn means that revelation is always something greater than what is merely written down. And this again means that there can be no such thing as pure *sola scriptura* (by Scripture alone), because an essential element of Scripture is the Church as understanding subject, and with this the fundamental sense of tradition is already given.[48]

There is, therefore, a clear dynamic between subject-object, between revelation and the recipient of revelation, speaker and the listener, between speech uttered and the recipient of the uttered word, that, all the while describing Ratzinger's reading of Bonaventure's theology of revelation, largely resonates with similar dynamics in the treatment of *logos* as speech uttered by Heraclitus and the Greek philosophical tradition. Ratzinger can thus conclude:

> By its application to Jesus of Nazareth, the concept of *logos* acquires a new dimension. It no longer denotes simply the permeation of all being by meaning; it characterizes this man: he who is here is "Word." The concept of *logos*, which to the

> Greeks meant "meaning" (*ratio*), changes here really into "word" (*verbum*). He who is here is Word; he is consequently "spoken" and, hence, the pure relation between the speaker and the spoken to.[49]

In this sense, *logos* as speaker constitutes the basis for relationality in the Christian economy, for the art of speaking presupposes a recipient or audience vis-à-vis the one who speaks or what is spoken.

The fifth quality of *logos* that one finds in the fragments of Heraclitus denotes *logos* as wisdom: "Of all whose *logoi* I have heard, not one has come this far—to know that 'Wise' is separated (*kechorismenon*) from everything." And in another fragment: "The Wise Thing, one and only, wants and does not want to be called by the name of Zeus."[50] These senses of *logos* as wisdom indicate that as wisdom, as the wise thing, *logos* is not only separated from all things, but is likewise at work within everything. Brann ties the aspect of *logos* as wisdom with *logos* as speech that is uttered and listened to by an active recipient thus:

> Our *logos* and our *logoi*, the sense we receive and the words we in turn say, should be informed by our having heard *the Logos*. This great *Logos* has a wisdom, or rather it *is* the Wise Thing, and this Wise Thing has a maxim, or rather it *is* that practical principle which guides everything through everything, relates all things to all things, which says One: Everything.[51]

Following classical tradition and continuing with a Christic reading of *logos*-wisdom, Ratzinger reads *logos* as wisdom personified in the Son of God who, assuming flesh, entered the world as Jesus of Nazareth, whose heart is the heart of God. Jesus is the *Logos* who, as wisdom, enables us to be logical, and this wisdom, maintains Ratzinger, is a sharing in God's way of perceiving reality which only comes about thanks to our unity with God in the person of Christ Jesus.[52] Certainly, this goes beyond the Greek conception of *logos*, but it is not completely foreign to the concept of personhood being introduced into the concept of *logos*, for as we saw when we highlighted the fourth aspect of the Heraclitan *logos*, the consciousness of *logos* as speaker is likewise present in Greek philosophy.

The sixth characteristic of *logos* in Heraclitus that resonates with Ratzinger is that of *logos* as common to all creatures. Heraclitus declares: "Therefore one must follow what is common (*toi xynoi*). But although *logos* is common (*xynou*) the many live as if they had a private mind (*phronesin*), in the sense of mindful insight."[53] The charge made here by Heraclitus is that though *logos* is common to all creatures in that all are naturally endowed with understanding that presupposes the gift of reasoning, many are inattentive to the presence of *logos* in their lives. This understanding of *logos* from the perspective of rationality opens up the window through which one can read the human soul as the locus of *logos*, as Heraclitus writes: "The bounds of soul you would not find by going about, though you traveled over every road; so deep a *logos* does it have" (Fragment B45); and again, "To the soul belongs a *logos* that increases itself" (Fragment B115)."[54] As Hussey points out, the "*logos* of the soul is the true, rational account of the soul, but it can also be understood as the account given *by* the soul."[55] The *logos* of the soul endows the soul with the potential of reflectivity and self-introspection. It makes it possible to speak rationally, to be able to discern and articulate an orderly grammar in the unfolding of human experience. Given this insight of the universality of *logos* that is found in every human soul, hence anthropological in character as well, one can find a precedent of the argument that Ratzinger made in Regensburg, when he argued against the dehellenization of the Christian faith. It is my reading that Ratzinger was in no way rejecting the genuine novelties and significant contributions of other cultures vis-à-vis the Christian faith. Rather, Ratzinger, looking at the picture of the whole of human history in its complex diversities and particularities, was pointing to *logos* as a common ground that could serve as the foundation for the dialogue between cultures and religions.[56] And such a pointer to the common ground of *logos*, understood as reason, is the possibility of any speech aimed at bringing the other to the experience of faith, without resorting to violence. Ratzinger cites the erudite Byzantine emperor Manuel II Paleologus to underscore his point:

> Violence is incompatible with the nature of God and the nature of the soul. "God," he says, "is not pleased by blood—and not acting reasonably (σὺν λόγω) is contrary to God's nature. Faith is born of the soul, not of the body. Whoever would lead someone to faith needs the ability to speak well and to reason properly, without violence and threats [...]. To convince a reasonable soul, one does not need a strong arm, or weapons of any kind, or any other means of threatening a person with death.[57]

Thus, a reasonable soul can understand a reasonable God, and this is a component of what it means to be human, that makes the propositions of faith rationally accessible as well. As Ratzinger observes regarding the relationship between *logos* and biblical faith in terms of its synthetic commonality, "A profound encounter of faith and reason is taking place here, an encounter between genuine enlightenment and religion. From the very heart of Christian faith and, at the same time, the heart of Greek thought now joined to faith, Manuel II was able to say: Not to act 'with *logos*' is contrary to God's nature."[58] In this light, Ratzinger appears to make the argument that this commonality of *logos* has an inherent potential, if considered by the various religions, to foster religious tolerance and overcome religious extremism in which violence is perpetuated in the name of God. Why Ratzinger displays such a trust in reason and reason's ability to bring about a peaceful engagement between different religious adherents in a manner that eschews selfish fundamentalism could very be an open question subjected to different interpretations. However, that Ratzinger has such faith in reason, in the rational, is clearly not in doubt. In precis, these six insights provide a platform from Greek philosophy that clearly resonate with theological appropriations by Ratzinger, as put forth above. Let us now turn to Philo of Alexandria for a further development of the philosophical principle of *logos*, after which we will consider the Fathers, and how the Church Fathers were able to make the transition from *logos* as a principle, a philosophical principle found in Greek philosophy, to *Logos* as a Person, Jesus of Nazareth.

3.2 Philo of Alexandria (circa BC 20 – AD 50) and *logos*

The Jewish-Hellenist philosopher, Philo of Alexandria, offers us an interpretation of *logos* that fits into his wider scheme of interpreting the Old Testament in the light of Greek philosophy, in order to provide an allegorical reading of the history of the human soul and its relation to God. This philosophical methodology enabled Philo to establish a link between Judaism and Hellenism, forging spiritual and mystical bonds between the former and the latter. Being the eclectic philosopher that he was, Philo saw God as both transcendent and immanent, and the bridge between God's transcendence and immanence, between the uncreated and the created, is the *Logos* or Divine Reason.[59] Notwithstanding the similarity and dissimilarity between Philo's *Logos* and the *Logos* of the Prologue of John's Gospel, Philo's treatment of *Logos* explains why Philo would be perceived as an ally by later Christian thinkers such as Justin the Martyr, Clement, Origen, and Ambrose.[60] The affinity with Christian thought certainly helped in popularizing Philo's writings.

It is important to note that the hermeneutical framework of Philo's treatment of *logos* is both Stoicism and Platonism, in that, while Philo relies on the Stoic idea of *logos* as the principle of rationality, his interpretation of *logos* and creation in his commentary on the book of Genesis is largely based on Plato's theory of ideas. Just as Plato gives priority of place to the reality of pre-existing ideas, so does Philo, who sees God as a great architect who, before setting out to build a city, first conceives the detailed plan of the city in his mind. As Philo explains, before creation, "The incorporeal world, then, was now finished and firmly settled in the Divine Reason, and the world patent to sense was ripe for the birth after the pattern of the incorporeal."[61] The world, like the city, pre-exists in the mind of the architect, and only later is the idea of the world or the city that is in the mind of the architect brought to realization in the concrete act of the city being built, or the world being created.[62] Given this analogy, God is the Architect with the world in the Divine Mind of God, - Θεία Λόγος. To Philo, therefore, the invisible has come into being as an image of the Divine Word in the creation of the world.[63] This coming into the world of the Divine Idea in the act of creation that brings the world into being, this appearing of the invisible in visibility, clearly echoes the Christian theology of the Incarnation.

For Philo, the human being stands out in this process of the appearing of *logos* in visibility, a process called creation. Though conscious of the Stoic idea of the presence of *logos* in all of nature, hence, the Stoic maxim to live according to nature, the fact that the human being is created in the image and likeness of God brings with it a different level of particularity and intentionality regarding the presence and operation of *logos* in humans. What precisely is this kinship between humans and *logos*, the divine Reason? Philo explains:

> Every man, in respect of his mind, is allied to the divine Reason, having come into being as a copy or fragment or ray of that blessed nature, but in the structure of his body he is allied to all the world, for he is compounded of the same things, earth, water, air, and fire, each of the elements having contributed the share that falls to each, to complete a material absolutely sufficient in itself for the Creator to take in order to fashion this visible image.[64]

In this text, Philo makes an interesting distinction between the corporeality of the human flesh, the human body (the component that he grounds, following pre-Socratic cosmology, on the elements of earth, water, air, and fire) and the immateriality of the human intellect (reason, which, to Philo, is the locus or ground of *Divine Logos*). In this sense, the human intellect reflects the divine Intellect or *Logos*, and the divine *Logos* is the source of the intelligibility of both the universe and the human being.

An intriguing aspect of the *logos* cosmology of Philo has to do with the distinction that he makes between the *heavenly man*, pertaining to the creation of man in the priestly account of creation, by the *speech* or Word of God, and the earthly man, taken or created from dust, pertaining to the Yahwist account of creation, that is, Genesis 1:26–27 and Genesis 2:7, respectively. This text is very significant for it demonstrates the limits Philo could not transgress, in fidelity to his heart as a pious, believing Jew. And Philo's interpretation, fascinating as it is, leaves him, in the final analysis, not as a Christian philosopher, but, if appropriation of

Philo is permissible, a Jewish philosopher with a Christian soul—*anima naturaliter Christiana*. Philo writes:

> The heavenly man, being made after the image of God, is altogether without part or lot in corruptible and terrestrial substance; but the earthly one was compacted out of the matter scattered here and there, which Moses calls "clay." For this reason, he says that the heavenly man was not molded but was stamped with the image of God; while the earthly is a molded work of the Artificer, but not His offspring.[65]

For Philo, this heavenly man, created by God's Word, *Logos*, is the model for the creation of the earthly man in chapter two of the book of Genesis. Is Philo applying here the same reasoning of an archetypal idea in the divine Mind from which and in accordance to which the world was created, so much so that the heavenly man is to the earthly man what the divine idea of the world in the divine Mind is to the created cosmos? It seems likely, given the Platonic character of this aspect of Philo's thought. However, what is enthralling for the Christian reader is why Philo refuses to name or identify any historical figure with the heavenly man? That will be left for Christian theology to do, and that is what the author of the Fourth Gospel does with the Prologue to the Gospel: the heavenly man, entirely different from the earthly man, the man of the speech or Word, *Logos*, becomes incarnate in Jesus of Nazareth. This task was left for the New Testament to accomplish, and if Philo had crossed this threshold, he would have gone beyond the limits of Judaism, and that, whether he was ever conscious or not of Jesus and the teachings of Jesus, that, Philo did not do. But his reasoning laid the groundwork and set the pace for the Fathers like Justin, Irenaeus, and Ambrose, to make just that transition of identifying the *Logos* heavenly man with Jesus of Nazareth, certainly oriented as well by the Prologue of John's Gospel.

3.3 Justin Martyr (AD 100 – 165) and the *Logos*

With Justin, the treatment of *logos* takes on a sense of historical fulfillment. Justin sought to expose the similarities between Christian thought and Greek philosophy, with the ultimate goal of showing Christianity as the true and safe philosophy worth adhering to. In terms of the *Logos*, Justin's point of departure is first of all the transcendence of God, who as God, is an ineffable Father who is without origin or beginning. There is therefore an insurmountable gap between God and creatures. Only the *Logos* is capable of bridging this abyss between finite creatures and an infinite and transcendent God. The *Logos* is therefore the guide to God and the instructor for man and woman. Justin sought to illustrate that creation and salvation were fulfilled in Jesus Christ, the *Logos*, that is, the eternal Word and creative Reason:

> For whatever either lawgivers or philosophers uttered well, they elaborated by finding and contemplating some part of the *Logos*. But since they did not know the whole of the Word, which is Christ, they often contradicted themselves. And those who by human birth were more ancient than Christ, when they attempted to consider and prove things by reason, were brought before the tribunals as impious persons and busybodies. And Socrates, who was more zealous in this direction than all of them, was accused of the very same crimes as ourselves [...]. For no one trusted in Socrates so as to die for this doctrine, but in Christ, who was partially known even by Socrates (for He was and is the *Logos*) who is in everyman, and who foretold the things that were to come to pass both through the prophets and in His own person when He was made of like passions, and taught these things, not only philosophers and scholars believed, but also artisans and people entirely uneducated, despising both glory, and fear, and death, since He is a power of the ineffable Father, and not the mere instrument of human reason.[66]

In this sense, the same *Logos* who revealed himself to the Hebrew prophets, as we find in the *First Apology*, likewise manifested himself in seeds of truth in Greek philosophy, especially in Socrates. Hence, "the doctrine of the *Logos* is the most important doctrine of Justin because it forms a bridge between pagan philosophy and Christianity."[67] Justin writes:

> I confess that I both boast and with all my strength strive to be found a Christian, not because the teachings of Plato are different from those of Christ, but because they are not in all respects similar, as neither are those of the others, Stoics, and poets and historians. For each man spoke well in proportion to the share he had of the spermatic word, seeing what was related to it. But they who contradict themselves on the more important points appear not to have possessed the heavenly wisdom, and the knowledge which cannot be spoken against. Whatever things were rightly said among all men, are the property of Christians.[68]

Therefore, though Justin disputed Greek philosophy and its contradictions, and although Justin affirms that the fullness of the *Logos* only took form in Christ, Justin maintains that the seed of the *Logos* was already very much present in much of humankind, long before the arrival of Christ on the historical scene, for all humans possess a seed of the *Logos* in their rational faculty. Justin is therefore decisive in orienting all philosophical truths to the *Logos*, thereby making a claim regarding the universality and veracity of the Christian religion. The Old Testament and Greek philosophy are therefore two paths pointing to Christ, and this happens thanks to the presence of seeds of the *Logos* in these historical antecedents to the Christian era. Commenting about this approach of Justin to philosophical fulfillment in Christ, Benedict XVI declares:

> Overall, the figure and work of Justin mark the ancient Church's forceful option for philosophy, for reason, rather than for the religion of the pagans. With the pagan religion, in fact, the early Christians strenuously rejected every compromise. They held it to be idolatry, at the cost of being accused for this reason of "impiety" and "atheism" [...]. Philosophy, on the other hand, represented the privileged area of the encounter between paganism, Judaism and Christianity, precisely at the level of the criticism of pagan religion and its false myths [...]. In fact, the pagan religion did not follow the ways of the *Logos* but clung to myth, even if Greek

> philosophy recognized that mythology was devoid of consistency with the truth. Therefore, the decline of the pagan religion was inevitable: it was a logical consequence of the detachment of religion—reduced to an artificial collection of ceremonies, conventions and customs—from the truth of being. Justin, and with him other apologists, adopted the clear stance taken by the Christian faith for the God of the philosophers against the false gods of the pagan religion.[69]

With this line of interpretation of Justin by Benedict, it follows that the choice of philosophy in opposition and even in contrast to pagan mythology by the early Church as embodied in Justin, was a choice in favor of truth as opposed to contradictory myths of the pagan religions. In other words, Justin's choice for the *logos*, for reason, was a choice for the object of the intellect, which is truth.

Another aspect of Justin's theology of the *Logos* that anticipates Ratzinger's is understanding of *logos* in terms of a theology of worship. In the *First Apology*, Justin writes: "The only honor that is worthy of him is not to consume by fire what he has brought into being for our sustenance, but to use it for ourselves and those who need, and with gratitude to him to offer thanks by praises and hymns for our creation."[70] As Johannes Quasten points out, one cannot understand Justin's concept of sacrifice except one takes into consideration Justin's doctrine of the *Logos*. To Quasten, what Justin rejects is the material sacrifice of the Jews and pagans. By means of the concept of sacrifice, Justin intends to bridge the gap between pagan philosophy and Christianity. To quote Quasten:

> [Justin's] ideal is the *logikē thusia*, the *oblatio rationabilis*, the spiritual sacrifice which the Greek philosophers declared to be the only veneration worthy of God. Here, as in the case of the *Logos*, Christianity represents the fulfilment of a philosophical ideal because it possess such a spiritual sacrifice.[71]

For Justin, therefore, there is no longer any need for bloody material sacrifices, for the Eucharist is the long-desired spiritual sacrifice. In the

Eucharist, the *logikē thusia*, the *Logos* himself, Jesus Christ, is the victim. To Quasten, this insight of the *logikē thusia* by Justin was a tremendous achievement with profound implications, for thanks to it, Justin was able to appropriate the highest achievements of Greek philosophy for Christianity, while simultaneously stressing the newness and uniqueness of Christian worship. Justin "retained an objective sacrifice while, on the other hand, he emphasized the spiritual character of Christian worship. Thus, the term *oblatio rationabilis*, in the canon of the Roman Mass expresses better than any other word Justin's concept of sacrifice."[72] The Eucharist, as the *logikē thusia*, the *oratio rationabilis*, is the true sacrifice that has brought all material, animal sacrifices to their completion. As will be seen in chapter five, Ratzinger builds on this insight of Justin in his treatment of *logos* as Word, which essentially captures the core content of Ratzinger's theology of worship.

3.4 Irenaeus of Lyons (AD 130–202) and the *Logos*

With Irenaeus, one finds the appropriation of the *Logos* as a *Recapitulation*, in which the *Logos* is identical with the Son of God, with the God-man Jesus, with our Saviour and Our Lord. The heart of Irenaeus' claim is that since by the fall of Adam the whole human race was lost, the *Logos* had to become man in order to effect a recreation of humankind: "When he became incarnate and was made man, he recapitulated in himself the long history of man, summing up and giving us salvation in order that we might receive again in Christ Jesus what we had lost in Adam, that is, the image and likeness of God."[73] Christ is thus the true prototype of the human person, for it is in Christ that humanity becomes liberated from the condition of sin and oriented toward becoming more and more like God.

This reality of the person of Christ has a cosmic dimension, involving both creation and redemption. Therefore, in Christ, the New Adam, creation is not only remade, but endowed with the ultimate potential for divinization. In other words, as Irenaeus explains, the Incarnation of the *Logos* is the singular event that brought about not only the divinization of the human being, but likewise, the entry into divinity of human nature. Irenaeus writes:

> And for this reason did the Word become the dispenser of the paternal grace for the benefit of men, for whom He made such great dispensations, revealing God indeed to men, but presenting man to God, and preserving at the same time the invisibility of the Father, lest man should at any time become a despiser of god, and that he should always possess something toward which he might advance; but, on the other hand, revealing God to men through many dispensations, lest man, falling away from God altogether, should cease to exist. For the glory of God is a living man; and the life of man consists in beholding God.[74]

This is the perspective, that is, of the divine-human meeting in Christ, that one can understand Irenaeus' doctrine of recapitulation (*anakephalaiosis*), in which the whole of reality is gathered into Jesus Christ. In this light, Jesus is an embodiment of human history. Jesus shares and sums up all of human reality except sin. By his humanity in which he passes through all stages of human development from childhood to full adulthood, Jesus redeems humanity in all its stages of growth and development.

What then, did the *Logos* now incarnated as Christ Jesus bring? And more importantly, what did the Christ leave behind to continue to bring about this work of recapitulation? This is the meeting point between Christology and ecclesiology, for God sums up in Christ (recapitulation) not only the past but the future as well, and therefore has made the incarnated *Logos* the head of the Church in order to perpetuate through the Church God's work of reimaging the world, until the consummation of the ages. As Irenaeus writes, "The invisible is become visible, the incomprehensible is become comprehensible, and the impassible passible; and the *Logos* is become man, recapitulating all things in himself [...]. He takes the primacy to himself and by making himself the head of the Church, he will draw all things to himself at the appointed time."[75] Here, one notices not only that Irenaeus is emphasizing the entrance of the *Logos* into history, but likewise that the *Logos* comes forth in the Church. In this wise, the Church becomes the locus of encounter with the *Logos*, especially in the sacramental life of faith of the Church.

Two central aspects, therefore, stand out, in Irenaeus' theology of the *Logos*. Firstly, there is the refutation of Gnosticism and the insistence of the true bodily nature of the man Jesus. As Ratzinger comments, "firmly rooted in the biblical doctrine of creation, Irenaeus refuted the Gnostic dualism and pessimism which debased corporeal realities. He decisively claimed the original holiness of matter, of the body, of the flesh no less than of the spirit."[76] It is truly as man that Christ saves us. The earthly life of Jesus of Nazareth was not simply a mirage, an appearance. Jesus truly took on flesh in the Incarnation. Jesus truly experienced the human conditions of biological existence. And Jesus truly suffered, died, and rose from the dead. In a word, in the Incarnation of the *Logos*, Jesus experiences and sums up all of human reality in his person.

The second aspect, as indicated above, has to do with the Church, which, for Irenaeus, finds its authenticity in the apostolic tradition that is public, one and pneumatic. There is no secret doctrine of Christianity that is meant for the intellectuals. The only doctrine that the Church has is her simple faith, meant for all. And this faith is the preaching of the apostles, guaranteed in an unbroken line of apostolic succession thanks to the presence of the Spirit in the Church.[77] Benedict's admiration for Irenaeus is clear, as he even describes Irenaeus as the first systematic theologian of the Church, the one who created systematic theology.[78] From his theology of the *Logos*, therefore, Irenaeus bequeathed to the Church a Christology that is anthropological and an anthropology that is likewise Christological. And these two realities, a Christological anthropology and an anthropological Christology flourish in the locus of the community of the Church, hence making room for a Christological ecclesiology.

3.5 Origen of Alexandria (AD 184–253) and the *Logos*

Still within this historical trajectory of the concept of *logos*, one finds very early on Origen, an outstanding teacher and intellectual of the early Church who served as head of the Catechetical School of Alexandria. Origen was the successor to Clement of Alexandria. Benedict says about Origen: "He was a true 'maestro,' and so it was that his pupils remembered him with nostalgia and emotion: he was not only a brilliant theologian but also an exemplary witness of the doctrine he passed on."[79] For Origen, the foundations of theology lay in the interpretations of the Scriptures. Origen's magisterial work, *De Principiis*, testifies to the primacy of the Scriptures in his soul. In Origen, one finds what Benedict calls a "perfect symbiosis between theology and exegesis."[80] Owing to his extant writings that extended from exegesis to dogma, to philosophy, apologetics, ascetical theology and mystical theology, Benedict characterizes Origen as the "most prolific author of Christianity's first three centuries."[81] Personally, it can come across as symbolic that during his apostolic visit to Cameroon and Angola in March 2009, Benedict, in his address to the Bishops of Africa, called for the reopening of Origen's Catechetical School of Alexandria, albeit in a different form today.[82] Perhaps this is a dream for the African Church awaiting fulfillment.

In terms of Origen's theology, one could point out that with language reminiscent of Platonism, Origen maintains that just as the soul dwells in the body and gives life to the body, so does the *Logos* dwell in the Church, the mystical Body of Christ. In other words, the *Logos* is the life-giving principle that not only brings about the Church, but animates and sustains the Church in being:

> We say that the Holy Scriptures declare the body of Christ, animated by the Son of God, to be the whole Church of God, and the members of this body—considered as a whole—to consist of those who are believers; since, as a soul vivifies and moves the body, which of itself has not the natural power of motion like a living being, so the Logos, the Word, arousing and moving the whole body, the Church, to befitting action, awakens, moreover, each individual member belonging to the Church, so that they do nothing apart from the Word.[83]

To Origen, this intrinsic relationship between *Logos* and Church finds its ultimate point of convergence in the Cross of Christ, which Origen sees as the narrow way of salvation that is diametrically opposed to the wide and easy way of worldly philosophy. In this sense, maintains Origen, the vision of the *Logos* is attainable only at the point at which we as members of the Church die to the world. The cross is therefore the fullest expression of the *Logos*, the crucified Jesus, at once priest and victim.[84] One can thus describe the *Logos* theology of Origen as a *Logos-Cruxis*, in which what is most central is the ultimate self-gift of the *Logos* on the wood of the Cross.

In synopsis, while one might certainly allude to other patristic figures that provide historical evidence of the appropriation of the Greek concept of the *logos*, what emerges from the above analysis of Justin, Irenaeus, and Origen is clearly the Christological and ecclesiological bridges that the concept of *logos* served in their theologies. In the first place, it is about the person of Christ, who as the eternal Son of the Father, predates creation and yet enters creation as Jesus of Nazareth. In a sense, the Christologies of these Fathers prepared the Church for the eventual formulations of Nicaea (325), Ephesus (431), and Chalcedon (451).

In addition, this Christological reading of *Logos*, of reason, Incarnate, finds in the community of the Church, the place wherein the believer can enter into the mystical body of Christ, as explained by Origen above. This implies that for the Fathers, there is always an ecclesiological dimension to their Christology. In other words, one cannot have Christ, encounter Christ, the *Logos* of God, while excluding the Church. Irenaeus stressed the pneumatological character of the Church, to the extent that the degree of the presence of the Spirit in the life of the believer is made visible in the love for the Church that emanates from the believer's life.

In commenting on Ratzinger's appropriation of *logos*, Roland Millare points out that "the key to understanding Ratzinger's use of the word *Logos* throughout his works is to underscore that *logos* is to be understood as truth and love."[85] These two aspects of truth and love coincide in the person of Jesus of Nazareth, and this, as Millare points out in his reading of Ratzinger, partly explains the limitations of rationality, of reason in the face of revelation, owing to the fact that "truth is a person and not simply an abstract idea."[86] Given this personalistic reading of truth, more has to be demanded of reason if reason is to fully grasp the profundity of truth. And it is at this point that love comes in, for love opens reason beyond reason by establishing a personalist relationship with truth embodied, that is, with Jesus, who promises to reveal himself to those who love (Jn 14:21).

One notes that this view of a personalistic perspective of love is clearly a fruit of Benedict's engagement with Bonaventure as seen in chapter one, and as Benedict pointed out in his General Audience of March 3, 2010, "for St. Bonaventure the ultimate destiny of the human being is to love God, to encounter him, and to be united in his and our love."[87] Love does not erase reason, but propels reason to embrace truths that go beyond the mere rational. In this same General Audience, Benedict XVI points out the influence of Pseudo-Dionysius on Bonaventure regarding the realization of love as exceeding the capacity for reason. Benedict writes:

> Whereas for St. Augustine the *intellectus*, the seeing with reason and the heart, is the ultimate category of knowledge, Pseudo-Dionysius takes a further step: in the ascent toward God one can reach a point in which reason no longer sees. But in the night of the intellect love still sees; it sees what is in accessible to reason. Love goes beyond reason, it sees further, it enters more profoundly into God's mystery.[88]

This is the framework by which one ought to read the various appropriations of *logos* by Ratzinger, namely, that notwithstanding the merits of reason, left to itself reason cannot grasp the full picture of revelation. This therefore calls for a metamorphosis of reason, of *logos*, into other theological consciousnesses, such as creative Reason, Son, Person, unity of love, and Word as one finds in Ratzinger. Ratzinger explains this theological appropriation and transformation thus:

> God is *Logos*. But there is a second characteristic. The Christian faith in God tells us also that God—eternal Reason—is Love. It tells us that he is not a being turned in on himself, without relation to others. Precisely because he is sovereign, because he is Creator, because he embraces everything, he is Relation and he is Love. Faith in the Incarnation of God in Jesus Christ, and in his suffering and death for mankind, is the

> supreme expression of a conviction that the heart of all morality, the heart of being itself and its deepest principle, is love.[89]

Once again, in this text, one finds Ratzinger interpreting *logos* at its most profound level to be an experience of the creative love of God, which finds its fullest expression in the sacrificial life of Jesus of Nazareth. In Christ, *logos* is not only love, but likewise relation, for love invites into relationship, love brings about communion, companionship. Thus, wherein the eighteenth-century *Aufklärung* saw reason, rationality, as the ground of all reality as seen in chapter two, Ratzinger, thanks to a retrieval of the classical multifaceted concept of the *logos* that he gives a Christological reading as love, sacrifice and relationship, puts forth this Christological reading of *logos* as the steady ground of all reality. Ratzinger explains:

> Two features characterize this concept of God. God himself is *Logos*, the rational primal ground of all that is real, the creative reason that gave birth to the world and that is reflected in the world. God is *Logos*—meaning, reason, and word, and that is why man corresponds to God when his reason is open and he pleads the cause of a reason that is not allowed to be blind to the moral dimensions of existence.[90]

In this sense, God is *Logos* as evident in the rational framework of natural reality such as in creation. Chapter four of this text will engage this in more detail. In addition, God is *Logos* as evident in the ability of humans to enter into a relationship with God, thanks to word, to speech that is spoken. Chapter five will offer a fuller treatment of this theological concept of *Logos* as love, in its varied forms pertaining to the individual and communal dimensions of love.

3.6 *Logos* in the Gospel of John: An Epochal Theological Inculturation

Given all that has been said above regarding *logos* in Greek philosophy and a sampling of the Fathers, it is very significant to underscore that the overarching difference between *logos* from a philosophical perspective as opposed to *logos* from a theological perspective found its most explicit amplification and presentation in the Prologue to the Gospel of John in which the appearing of the person of Jesus is presented in *logos*-language, when the author of the Gospel of John writes ὁ λόγος σὰρξ ἐγένετο καὶ ἐσκήνωσεν ἐν ἡμῖν—"The Word became flesh and made his dwelling among us" (Jn 1:14). With this declaration of *logos* becoming flesh, the author of the Gospel of John introduces a new relationship between rationality, reason, and human existence, a principle that has metamorphosed into personhood. Ratzinger explains:

> John takes up again here a paradigm of theological thought that is extremely widespread in both the Greek and the Jewish intellectual world and naturally adopts a series of connotations that are already developed within it, so as to apply them to Christ. Perhaps one could maintain, however, that the new element that he imparted to the *Logos* concept lies significantly in the fact that what was decisive to him was not the idea of an eternal rationality—as the Greeks supposed—or whatever other speculations there might have been previously, but rather the relativity of the existence that is inherent in the concept of the *Logos*.[91]

For Ratzinger, therefore, it was this transformation, this inculturation of the Greek concept of *logos*, of reason, by the author of John's Gospel that gives reason a realistic foundation, making it an accompaniment of faith, to the extent that faith does not become a rejection or defeat of the rational, an escape from reason, but rather, "the courage to exist and an awakening to the greatness and breadth of what is real."[92] Along this line of seeing the reality of the rational from the existential being of the Incarnation and hence, as a living reality, Elio Guerriero offers a helpful commentary that sheds light on significance of this enfleshment of *logos* for Ratzinger. Guerriero writes:

> For Ratzinger, this is one of the key components of Christian thought, to which he had called attention since the time of his

> first university lecture in Bonn. The Christian faith implies no renunciation of reason but, rather, is the acceptance of the extreme depth of divine reason. In short, to believe is to take seriously the initial statement of the Gospel of John to the effect that at the origin is the *Logos,* the Divine Word, creative reason. The consequence is that not matter, but rather spirit, is at the origin of all things. By acknowledging the primacy of the spirit, man is capable of perceiving and following the traces of the reasonableness of nature, which is not subject to his absolute dominion or manipulation.[93]

No doubt, this certainly sounds very much Hegelian, and I am sure Hegel will be intrigued to read that a Bishop of Rome thinks spirit is primary to matter, even if Hegel and Ratzinger might not always agree on the precise content of the word "spirit." Nonetheless, I am inclined into thinking that both can agree on the immateriality or abstractive character of reason, even though Ratzinger will go further, with the author of the Gospel of John, to acknowledge the new dimension of reason, or to use Hegel's preferred terminology, "spirit," in the Incarnational particularity of what Hegel characterizes in his 1827 lecture on the Christianity as the Consummate Religion as the *Kingdom of the Son*,[94] albeit perceived differently from Hegel, as will subsequently be seen in this work. Owing to the inculturation of *logos* by the author of the Gospel of John, therefore, "the real essence of faith [...]," Ratzinger writes, "saves reason precisely because it grasps reason in its whole breadth and depth and protects it from the restrictions of a merely experiential verification."[95] Certainly, this assessment of reason flows from a hermeneutic of faith, and one could even say, prejudices reason, at least from the perspective of the nonbeliever. But for Ratzinger, it is a position that is positive and affirmative of reason, stretching reason beyond the limits of reason.

Summarily, therefore, even though *logos* provided a common ground for both philosophy and theology, faith and reason, for philosophy or unaided reason, *logos* remains a principle, a philosophical principle largely understood and characterized as reasonableness. In other words, the natural, human capacity to think things through, even questions of religion and of faith, thinking within the boundaries of mere reason, *à la manière de* Kant. On the other hand, *Logos*, from a theological perspective, as seen in the Gospel of John and the Fathers referenced above—the direction that Ratzinger certainly follows—is understood as a person, Jesus of Nazareth. There is, therefore, what one would characterize as a theological translation of a philosophical principle, clearly evident as well in the Preface which Ratzinger writes for the year 2000 edition of *Introduction to Christianity*:

> Ever since the Prologue to the Gospel of John, the concept of *logos* has been at the very center of our Christian faith in God. *Logos* signifies reason, meaning, or even "word'—a meaning, therefore, that is Word, that is relationship, that is creative. The God who is *logos* guarantees the intelligibility of the world, the intelligibility of our existence, the aptitude of reason to know God [*die Gottgemässheit Gottes*], and the reasonableness of God [*die Vernunftgemässheit Gottes*], even though his understanding infinitely surpasses ours and to us may so often appears to be darkness. The world comes from reason, and this reason is a Person, is Love—this is what our biblical faith tells us about God.[96]

This text displays Ratzinger's movement from *logos-principle* to *logos-person*, all the while maintaining the underlining current of rationality or reasonableness, both from the point of reflective reasoning, that is, philosophy, and from the point of creative reason, that is, theology, in reference to the Person of the Incarnate Word. While the philosophical *logos* is impersonal, non-animate rational principle, the theological *logos* is an incarnate, animate person, who as the Eternal Son of God recapitulates history within himself, as we find in the thought of Irenaeus, and ultimately brings history to its climax and fullest expression, as Ratzinger points out in his exegesis of the Apostles' Creed in his *Introduction to Christianity*.

In synopsis, therefore, the concept of *logos* that originated in Greek philosophy as seen in Heraclitus' treatment of it above, finds a home in the thought of the Fathers as sampled above, and they cannot simply be interchanged, one for the other. There is certainly a point of convergence in which one can theologically employ the multiple senses of philosophical *logos* as seen in what one could labeled a speculative interactive engagement between Heraclitus and Ratzinger, seen above. But there is a limit to how far one can go with such a philosophical-theological engagement, a limit which, while remaining an open question, leaves things open for discussion and further engagement. Thus, this treatment of the concept of Greek *logos* and the Fathers as seen in this third chapter, exemplifies the coming together of what one might characterize as the autonomous regions of faith and reason, of the God of philosophers and the God of faith. Chapters four and five will therefore proceed to examine how Ratzinger, building on these philosophical blocks, constructs a Christological and ecclesiological edifice that, while taking the reinterpretation of traditional Christian claims from the perspective of *logos* understood as 'mere reason' by the *Aufklärung*, will seek to engage these positions as well. He does so with the aid of a reason widened by faith, in its scientific sense, a reason that flows from an experiential model of a Christianity that is active in the here and now, a Christian faith that is not something of the past or something privatized by noeticism.

Notes — Chapter Three

1 Maurice Blondel, *L'Action (1893)*, trans. Oliva Blanchette (South Bend, IN: Notre Dame Press, 2007), 339–341.

2 Blondel, *L'Action (1893)*, 117.

3 Blondel, *L'Action (1893)*, 356.

4 Hubert Ritt "λόγος," in *Exegetical Dictionary of the New Testament*, ed. Horst Robert Balz and Gerhard Schneider (Grand Rapids, Michigan: William B. Eerdmans, 1990) 2: 356–359.

5 Joel Wilcox, *The Origins of Epistemology in Early Greek Philosophy: A Study of Psyche and Logos in Heraclitus* (New York: Edwin Mellen Press, 1994), 50.

6 Wilcox, *The Origins of Epistemology*, 53.

7 Anthony J. Kelly, "Logos," in *The New Dictionary of Theology*, ed. Joseph Komonchak, Mary Collins and Dermot A. Lane (Collegeville, Minnesota: The Liturgical Press, 2000), 601–602.

8 Marcus Aurelius, *The Meditations*, trans. Haines, M. A. (Cambridge: Harvard University Press, 1987), II, 7; II, 10.

9 Armstrong, Arthur Hilary, *An Introduction to Ancient Philosophy*, (London: Methuen & Co Limited, 1968), 125.

10 Aurelius, *Meditations*, V, 14.
11 Benedict XVI, *Verbum Domini*, 7.
12 Christopher Collins, S. J., *The Word Made Love: The Dialogical Theology of Joseph Ratzinger/Benedict XVI* (Collegeville, MN: Liturgical Press, 2013), 70.
13 Benedict XVI, *Verbum Domini*, 12.
14 Benedict XVI, "Solemnity of the Nativity of the Lord: Homily of His Holiness Benedict XVI," St. Peter's Basilica, December 24, 2006, at www.vatican.va, accessed January 10, 2019.
15 Collins, *The Word Made Love*, 71.
16 Heraclitus of Ephesus was around by 500 B.C. His thoughts, contained in fragments of aphorisms that survived, do not have any formal linkage. They are like aphorisms. Grouped with the Ionian natural philosophers, Heraclitus was concerned with cosmic processes, that is, with the nature of things: Cf. Edward Hussey, "Heraclitus" in A. A. Long, *The Cambridge Companion to Early Greek Philosophy* (New York: Cambridge University Press, 2011), 88–89.
17 Edward Hussey, "Epistemology and Meaning in Heraclitus" in Malcolm Schofield & Martha Nussbaum, (eds.) *Language & Logos: Studies in Ancient Greek Philosophy* (New York: Cambridge University Press, 2006), 35.
18 Hussey, "Epistemology and Meaning in Heraclitus," 35.
19 Hussey, "Heraclitus," 91.
20 Hussey, "Heraclitus," 92.
21 Hussey, "Heraclitus," 92.
22 Hussey, "Heraclitus," 92.
23 David Wiggins, "Flus, Fire and Material Persistence," in Malcolm Schofield & Martha Nussbaum, (eds.) *Language & Logos: Studies in Ancient Greek Philosophy* (New York: Cambridge University Press, 2006), 30.
24 Hussey, "Epistemology and Meaning in Heraclitus," 57.
25 Hussey, "Heraclitus," 93.
26 Hussey, "Heraclitus," 96.
27 Hussey, "Heraclitus," 96.
28 Hussey, "Heraclitus," 96.
29 Hussey, "Heraclitus," 97.
30 Brann, *The Logos of Heraclitus*, 10.
31 Brann, *The Logos of Heraclitus*, 10.
32 Joseph Ratzinger/Benedict XVI, *Jesus of Nazareth, The Infancy Narratives*, trans. Philip J. Whitmore (New York: Image Books, 2012), 11.
33 Ratzinger/Benedict XVI, *Jesus of Nazareth, From the Baptism in the Jordan to the Transfiguration*, trans. Adrian J. Walker (New York: Doubleday, 2007), 44.
34 Brann, *The Logos of Heraclitus*, 10.
35 Brann, *The Logos of Heraclitus*, 38–39.
36 Brann, *The Logos of Heraclitus*, 15.

37 Joseph Ratzinger, *Der Gott des Glaubens und der Gott der Philosophen* (Bonn: Johannes-Verlag Leutesdorf, 2005), 28: "Aber es bleibt dabei, daß den Monotheismus nichts anderes ausmacht als gerade der Bindestrich, der das Absolute – den "– Gott der Philosophen – " – und den Menschgott den Gott Abrahams, Isaaks und Jakobs – miteinander verbindet. Der Bindestrich, den Augustin " – zwischen neuplatonischer Ontologie und biblischer Gotteserkenntnis – " gesetzt hat, ist also von der Sache des Monotheismus her legitim, er ist die konkrete Weise, wie sich für ihn der Bindestrich zwischen Gott der Philosophen und Gott des Glaubens, Gott der Menschen darstellen mußte."

38 Plotinus, *Enneads*, I, trans. A. H. Armstrong (Cambridge, MA: Harvard University Press, 1989), I, 6, [7] 10–20: "So we must ascend again to the good, which every soul desires. Anyone who has seen it knows what I mean when I say that it is beautiful. It is desired as good, and the desire for it is directed to good, and the attainment of it is for those who go up to the higher world and are converted and strip off what we put on in our descent [...] passing in the ascent all that is alien to God, one sees with one's self alone That alone, simple, single and pure, from which all depends and to which all look and are alive and think: for it is cause of life and mind and being. If anyone sees it, what passion will he feel, what longing in his desire to be united with it, what a shock of delight! The man who has not seen it may desire it as good, but he who has seen it glories in its beauty and is full of wonder and delight, enduring a shock which causes no hurt, loving with true passion and piercing longing; he laughs at all other loves and despises what he thought beautiful before [...]." For Plotinus, the ascent to the One beyond being, that is, beyond the intellect, is a movement that is purgatorial, freeing the soul from all worldly trappings. In addition, the language employed by Plotinus in this treatise on beauty bears a striking resemblance to the language encountered in Christian mystical writings in which discursive reasoning falls short of the visionary or mystical experiences.

39 Christian Mofor, *Plotinus and African Concepts of Evil: Perspectives in Multi-Cultural Philosophy* (Bern: Peter Lang, 2008), 24.

40 Mofor, *Plotinus and African Concepts of Evil*, 24.

41 Mofor, *Plotinus and African Concepts of Evil*, 49.

42 Maria Luisa Gatti, "Plotinus: The Platonic Tradition and the Foundation of Neoplatonism" in Lloyd P. Gerson (ed.) *The Cambridge Companion to Plotinus* (New York: Cambridge University Press, 1999), 30–34. In these pages, Gatti offers us what I find to be a comprehensive account of the creative contemplationist metaphysics of Plotinus.

43 Plotinus, *Enneads*, III, trans. A. H. Armstrong (Cambridge, MA: Harvard University Press, 1993) III 9 [13] 3, 6.

44 Mofor, *Plotinus and African Concepts of Evil*, 19.

45 Mofor, *Plotinus and African Concepts of Evil*, 20.
46 John Bussanich, "Plotinus' Metaphysics of the One" in Lloyd P. Gerson (ed.). *The Cambridge Companion to Plotinus* (New York: Cambridge University Press, 1999), 38.
47 Brann, *The Logos of Heraclitus*, 17.
48 Joseph Ratzinger, *Milestones*: Memoirs 1927–1977, trans. Erasmo Leiva-Merikakis (San Francisco: Ignatius Press, 1998), 109.
49 Joseph Ratzinger, *Introduction to Christianity*, trans. J. R. Foster (San Francisco: Ignatius Press, 2004), 189.
50 Brann, *The Logos of Heraclitus*, 20.
51 Brann, *The Logos of Heraclitus*, 21.
52 Peter John Cameron, *Benedictus: Day by Day with Pope Benedict XVI* (New York: Magnificat, 2006), 204–205.
53 Brann, *The Logos of Heraclitus*, 22.
54 Hussey, "Heraclitus," 104.
55 Hussey, "Heraclitus," 105.
56 Benedict XVI, *The Regensburg Lecture* (South Bend, IN: St. Augustine's Press, 2007), 139.
57 Benedict XVI, *The Regensburg Lecture*, 133–134.
58 Benedict XVI, *The Regensburg Lecture*, 137.
59 Philo, Volume I: *On the Creation and on the Allegorical Interpretation of Genesis*, trans. F. H. Colson and G. H. Whitaker (Cambridge MA: Harvard University Press, 1929), Introduction, xix.
60 Philo, Volume I, Introduction, xxi.
61 Philo, Volume I, *On the Creation*, 36, X.
62 Philo, Volume I, *On the Creation*, 20 V.
63 Philo, Volume I, *On the Creation*, 31 VIII.
64 Philo, Volume I, *On the Creation*, 146 LI.
65 Philo, Volume I, *On the Allegorical Interpretation of Genesis*, 31 XII.
66 Justin the Martyr, *Second Apology*, 2, 10, in Johannes Quasten, *Patrology* Vol. I (Westminster, MD: Christian Classics Inc. 1993), 210.
67 Quasten, *Patrology*, 209.
68 Justin, *Second Apology*, 2, 13 in *Patrology*, 210.
69 Pope Benedict XVI, *Church Fathers: From Clement of Rome to Augustine* (San Francisco: Ignatius Press, 2008), 19–20.
70 Justin Martyr, *First Apology*, 13, in Johannes Quasten, *Patrology* Vol. I (Westminster, MD: Christian Classics Inc. 1993), 218.
71 Quasten, *Patrology* Vol. I, 218.
72 Quasten, *Patrology* Vol. I, 218.
73 Irenaeus of Lyons, *Against Heresies*, (Washington, DC: Ex Fontibus Co., 2016), III: XVIII, I.
74 Irenaeus, *Against Heresies*, IV: XX, VII.

75 Irenaeus, *Against Heresies*, III: XVI, VI.
76 Benedict XVI, *Church Fathers*, 22–23.
77 Benedict XVI, *Church Fathers*, 24–26.
78 Benedict XVI, *Church Fathers*, 23.
79 Benedict XVI, *Church Fathers*, 32.
80 Benedict XVI, *Church Fathers*, 33–34.
81 Benedict XVI, *Church Fathers*, 34.
82 Benedict XVI, "Address to Members of the Special Council for Africa of the Synod of Bishops (Yaoundé, 19 March 2009), in Benedict XVI, "Post-Synodal Apostolic Exhortation On the Church in Africa in Service to Reconciliation, Justice and Peace *Africae Munus*" (Vatican City: Libreria Editrice Vaticana, 2011), 137.
83 Origen of Alexandria, *Against Celsius*, 6, 48 ANF, in *Patrology* Vol. II, by Johannes Quasten (Westminster, MD: Christian Classics Inc. 1993), 82.
84 Origen of Alexandria, *On First Principles*, trans. G.W. Butterworth (South Bend, IN: Ave Maria Press, 2013), xxx.
85 Roland Millare, "The Wedding Feast of the Lamb Has Begun: The Relationship Between Eschatology and the Liturgy in the Logoscentric Theology of Joseph Ratzinger" (STD Dissertation, University of St. Mary of the Lake, Mundelein, IL, 2018), 59.
86 Millare, "The Wedding Feast of the Lamb Has Begun," 59.
87 Benedict XVI, *Doctors of the Church: Wednesday General Audiences from June 20, 2007 – April 6, 2011* (Huntington, IN: Our Sunday Visitor, 2001), 190.
88 Benedict XVI, *Doctors of the Church*, 192.
89 Joseph Ratzinger, *Europe: Today and Tomorrow*, trans. Michael J. Miller (San Francisco: Ignatius Press, 2007), 97.
90 Joseph Ratzinger, *Values in a Time of Upheaval*, trans. Brian McNeil (San Francisco: Ignatius Press, 2006), 112.
91 Joseph Ratzinger, *Dogma and Preaching: Applying Christian Doctrine for Daily Life*, ed. Michael J. Miller; trans. Michael J. Miller and Matthew O'-Connell (San Francisco: Ignatius Press, 2005), 188.
92 Joseph Ratzinger, *A Turning Point for Europe? The Church in the Modern World: Assessment and Forecast*, trans. Brian McNeil, C.R.V (San Francisco: Ignatius Press, 1994), 142.
93 Elio Guerriero, *Benedict XVI His Life and Thought*, trans. William J. Melcher (San Francisco: Ignatius Press, 2018), 367–368.
94 G. W. F. Hegel, *Lectures on the Philosophy of Religion, Vol. III: The Consummate Religion*, ed. by Peter C. Hodgson and trans. by R. F. Brown, P. C. Hodgson and J. M. Stewart with the assistance of H. S. Harris (Oxford: Clarendon Press, 2007), 234–251.
95 Ratzinger, *A Turning Point for Europe?* 106.
96 Ratzinger, *Introduction*, 26.

Chapter Four: *A Christological Reading of Ratzinger's Theological Appropriation of* Logos *as Creative Reason, Son, and Person, vis-à-vis the* Aufklärung

Thus far, it has been ascertained, as seen in chapter three, that the Greek concept of *logos* is very versatile. With Heraclitus it became evident that *logos*, for Greek philosophy, meant the ground of everything, the field on which all can stand. Chapter three also demonstrates that the Church Fathers did not hesitate to embrace this metaphor, following the clear lead in the Prologue of the Gospel of John, in which the Eternal Word becomes the Incarnate *Logos*. Owing to the all-encompassing character of the concept of *logos*, it is not surprising that it serves as the bridge Ratzinger uses to ground his own Christological positions when confronting the *Aufklärung* reinterpretations of the classical declarations of orthodoxy. This chapter therefore studies *logos* from a Christological perspective, in the light of creative Reason, Sonship, and Personhood. The goal is not only to arrive at a deeper Christological picture of the Ratzingerian positions, but even more so to see what Ratzinger makes of these positions beyond the theological formulas in which they are contained.

4.1 *Logos* as Creative Reason: Ratzinger's Engagement with the *Aufklärung*'s Necessary Causality of Nature and Dialectical Materialism

This section will study Ratzinger's theological appropriation of *logos* in the light of the *Aufklärung*'s understanding of nature as an autonomous principle in need of no divine help, in the sense that nature itself is eventually a divine principle, a spirit, a process, unfolding in history. In other words, as will be seen, the theological metaphor of *logos* as Creative Reason captures Ratzinger's theology of creation as a response to the *Aufklärung*'s understanding of nature as autonomous and self-driving.

Regarding nature in terms of cosmology, the *Aufklärung* sought for a rapport between the sensible world and the intelligible world because the natural world had to be read from the perspective of the physical laws of the sciences, especially after Newton. Given this reading of nature by the *Aufklärung*, one notices two things. Firstly, there is a certain continuity in terms of understanding with the preceding scholasticism of the middle ages, an age that saw reality as constitutive of God, the human soul, and he world. All of knowledge, in the scholastic point of view, had to be oriented toward these three realities.[1] When the *Aufklärung* talked of nature or creation, therefore, it was not a new concept out of the blues. Rather, they were taking on a concept that was central to medieval scholasticism.

Going further, it is worth noting that the *Aufklärung* radically transformed the scholastic understanding of nature, in that it sought to give nature an independent grammar that had to be profoundly severed from a religious undercurrent. In other words, there had to be no other foundations of certainty about the world. In the worldview of the *Aufklärung*, there had to be an inner affinity between nature and the intellect that was freed from any religious constraints. In other words, the natural world was not simply an ontological phenomenon. Nature was likewise an epistemological phenomenon. It was not just a way of being, but it was a way of seeing life. Nature defined and imposed its own perspective of life. Nature had its own eyes that it wanted used in the seeing of reality. As Cassirer points out:

> Nature, therefore, does not so much signify a given group of objects as a certain 'horizon' of knowledge, of the comprehension of reality. To nature belongs everything in the sphere of 'natural light' (*lumen naturale*), everything whose understanding and confirmation require no other aid than the natural forces of knowledge.[2]

This insistence, as it were, on the autonomy of nature by the *Aufklärung* ushered in a new dichotomy between the realm of nature and the realm of grace. While the former is communicated to us through sense perception through processes of logical judgments and inferences as seen in Kant, for example, the realm of grace, on the other hand, is accessible through divine revelation.

Such a sharp distinction between nature and grace certainly marked a remarkable rupture of human thinking about reality or nature, which preceded the *Aufklärung*. If anything, it was a given to the Scholastic mode of thinking to see nature and grace in terms of the latter being completing the former. Though grace overshadows nature, it does not impinge on the existence of nature. Grace rather completes nature.[3] To the scholastics, this perfection of nature had to be sought not in nature itself but in the supernatural sphere. To perfect nature, one had to go beyond nature. Supernatural assistance is a *conditio sine qua non* to bring nature to nature's perfection. Medieval scholasticism consequently articulated this understanding of nature from the perspective of natural law (*lex naturalis*) and divine law (*lex divina*). Natural law is accessible to and dominated by human reason. By itself, however, *lex naturalis* is unable to restore the original knowledge of reality that was lost thanks to the fall of man and woman, at the dawn of creation. Thus, while reason is critical in the understanding of nature and nature's laws, reason essentially plays an auxiliary role to revelation, to the *lex divina*.[4] Thus, it was in the nature of philosophy not to be an autonomous science, but one that had to be in lure of another, namely, theology. And even in this intrinsic relationship between the two, it had to be that one constantly had correct the other and bring the other to its fullest potentials, that is, faith leading reason to fullness.

Looking at this scheme of things, therefore, when the *Aufklärung* assumed the battle cry to dare to use one's reason, it was an implicit and explicit rejection of the subordination of nature to grace, of philosophy to theology, of reason to faith, and in the words of Ratzinger's inaugural lecture, of the God of the philosophers to the God of faith. As Cassirer comments, the basic tendency of the *Aufklärung* was that "the true essence of nature is not to be sought in the realm of the created (*natura naturata*), but in that of the creative process (*natura naturans*)."[5] In other words, nature is much more than just creation in terms of an objective, substantial matter. Rather, nature was a process, an ever-unfolding process in which the divine was an intrinsic part of nature. The divine was in the essence of nature as a principle inherent in nature. The dualism between creator and creation as seen in Scholasticism and all of Judeo-Christian religious experience is now abolished in the *Aufklärung* mode of thinking. Nature is now an original divine power, a formative principle moving from within. As Cassirer states:

> Through its capacity to unfold and take on form from within itself, nature bears the stamp of the divine. For God is not to be conceived as a force intervening from without and exerting its influence as a moving cause on matter foreign to itself; God Himself enters directly into the processes of nature.[6]

In this process, God is an internal principle of motion within nature, with this nature being God's own nature. Creation is thus elevated into the sphere of the divine. Creation enters into the infinity of the divine nature. And this includes the individuality, particularity and independence of all of creation. This is the understanding which Kant brings into the conversation, when he asserts that the categorical imperative be such that it is not only universal and human, but above all, that it be autonomous.[7] In other words, the universal moral maxim should be such that everyone can endorse it. It makes room for autonomy as opposed to heteronomy. No distinction ought to be between the lawgiver and the law, for the law must be such that it is of the same nature with the lawgiver. The *Aufklärung* therefore took a step toward essentially reducing the independent being of God to the level of nature or creation as a whole, so much so that nature or creation becomes divinized. As Cassirer explains, "the law which governs individual entities is not prescribed by a foreign lawgiver, nor thrust upon them by force; it is founded in, and completely knowable through, their own nature."[8] This self-legislation avoids constraint on the subject, affirming the primacy of the individual over any external principles or persons, which was very much an expression of the spirit of the *Aufklärung*. Also, nature becomes a first principle with an inherent causality. Nature or creation causes itself to be, given that there is no God outside nature or creation to cause it to be. Where Scholasticism following Aristotle had explained nature in terms of causality with God as the Uncaused Cause, the *Aufklärung* pivoted to the position of creation as an eternal process unfolding in, and generating history, with and in self-motion.

The challenge of this new mode of thinking about nature for Christian orthodoxy that catches Ratzinger's attention resides in the fact that not only is nature or creation now accorded an eternal, divine status, but more importantly, nature or creation becomes a new source of truth, independent of God and of revelation, since God at this point is understood to be the natural processes of history. As Cassirer explains:

> This truth is revealed not in God's word but in his work; it is not based on the testimony of Scripture or tradition but is visible to us at all times. But it is understandable only to those who know nature's handwriting and can decipher her text. The truth of nature cannot be expressed in mere words; the only suitable expression lies in mathematical constructions, figures and numbers. And in these symbols' nature presents itself in perfect form and clarity. Revelation by means of the sacred word can never achieve such brightness and transparency, such precision, for words as such are always varicolored and ambiguous admitting a variety of interpretations. Their meaning must always be given them by man and must therefore be fragmentary. In nature, on the other hand, the whole plan of the universe lies before us in its undivided and inviolable unity, evidently waiting for the human mind to recognize and express it.[9]

This *Weltanschauung* reflects not only the triumph of the scientific mindset over the religious, but likewise the substance of science, namely, the order of matter, over the voice of revelation in the apprehension of the truths of creation. Mathematics and physics are seen as paramount in explaining the deeper processes of creation, more so than any theology of creation in biblical physics. Human knowledge therefore emerges as victorious over divine knowledge or divine science. Consequently, "the correlation between nature and human knowledge has now been established once and for all and the bond between them is henceforth inseverable."[10]

Put differently, nature in the human being meets nature in the cosmos half way and discovers its own essence there. The human being is therefore called not to impose the person's subjective ideas on creation, but to follow creation's own course and determine it by observation and experimentation, by measurement and calculation. There is therefore a self-sufficiency of nature and the human intellect, given that "the autonomy of the intellect corresponds to the pure autonomy of nature."[11] If such is the state of things, any mediation based on a transcendental power or a transcendental being between nature as cosmos and nature as human becomes superfluous, for it does not add anything to the bond already in existent between the former and the latter.

Quite the contrary, the intervention of the transcendent being or God loosens the bond between nature and the subjective mind and must therefore be absolutely precluded. As Cassirer renders it, "against this relapse into transcendence the philosophy of the Enlightenment proclaims the pure principle of immanence both for nature and for knowledge."[12] To the *Aufklärung*, therefore, the eighteenth century was the time that had come to force nature to give up its secrets, for creation was no longer a mystery to be left in the dark, to be marveled at as an unfathomable mystery. Creation had to be brought under the bright light of reason in order for it to be analyzed in all its essential potencies. And to attain such a critical apprehension of creation by reason, the bond between theology and physics had to be severed, once and for all. Biblical physics and theological physics had to be completely eschewed.[13] This was certainly a remarkable new point for the *Aufklärung*, as Cassirer notes:

> This was the first important victory of the philosophy of the Enlightenment. It finished in this respect what the Renaissance had begun; it marked off a definite field for rational knowledge within which there was to be no more restraint and authoritative coercion but free movement in all directions. By virtue of this freedom philosophy could attain to full self-knowledge and to knowledge of its inherent forces.[14]

This newfound philosophical project of unmasking creation according to nature's laws in terms of stylometry employed as tools, experimentation, deduction and analysis, for the mind had to critically observe creation, test out these observations and then draw conclusions from these observatory tests. Sense perception therefore played a crucial role in this process, as empirical phenomena held sway on many counts. Finally, the question of God has been settled as a question of nature—*deus sive natura*—Spinoza provided the formula that captured the sentiments of this *Aufklärung* achievement.[15] The laws of creation that govern and determine all phenomena are nothing but the eternal decrees of God.

In this sense, materialism understood in terms of the absolute primacy of matter is justified and defended, not just as a scientific dogma, but more so, as an imperative that seeks to establish a thesis concerning the nature of things. It also sought to command and to forbid the inclusion of any reference to the transcendent being as different from nature and as the interpreter of nature. Theology thus appears as a superstitious manifestation: "Man must free himself from all idols, from all illusions concerning the original cause of things, for only by do doing can he succeed in ordering and establishing the world according to his own ideas."[16] Theology is thus construed as an inhibiting force against the sciences, who must shed the shackles of theology if they are to make any real progress: "The notions of God, freedom, and immortality are to be uprooted once and for all, so that the rational order of nature shall not be threatened and overthrown by constant intervention from the supernatural world which these notions seem to construct."[17] In the final analysis, reason, or *logos*, has turned nature into a necessary cause unto itself, and in the process excludes God and divinizes nature or the material universe.

In engaging this position of the *Aufklärung* vis-à-vis the natural order, Ratzinger displays a profound appreciation of the employment of reason or the rational mind in presenting the natural order, which Ratzinger sees as a product of the *logos*. Ratzinger writes:

> For *Logos* designates a reason that is not merely mathematical: it is the basis of the good and guarantees the dignity of the good. Faith in the God who is *Logos* is at the same time faith in the creative power of reason. It is faith in the Creator God and faith that man is created in the likeness of God and therefore shares in the inviolable dignity of God himself.[18]

This text reveals the framework by which one begins to understand the theological contours of Ratzinger's appropriation of the concept of *logos* as creative Reason, namely, that creation is not an arbitrary, accidental, or evolutionary product, but a reality that is thought-through and willed by God. In this sense, while appreciating the *Aufklärung*'s scientific presentation of nature from a rational perspective, Ratzinger still makes the case that Scripture's account of God's creative act at the start of history is the true Enlightenment because it is a work of Reason:

> Hence, this creation account may be seen as the decisive "Enlightenment" of history and as a breakthrough out of the fears that had oppressed humankind. It placed the world in the context of reason and recognized the world's reasonableness and freedom. But it may also be seen as the *true* Enlightenment from the fact that it put human reason firmly on the primordial basis of God's creating Reason, in order to establish it in truth and in love, without which an "Enlightenment" would be exorbitant and ultimately foolish.[19]

To its credit, therefore, the *Aufklärung*, by seeking to interpret the phenomenon of the natural world through the prism of reason, of *logos*, liberated nature from the perception of an arbitrary and capricious entity. But employing reason or *logos* in the manner in which it does, that is, to the exclusion of creative reason or reason as an act of God over matter, swings the pendulum to another extreme that distorts the harmony which ought to exist between faith and reason vis-à-vis the subject matter of nature or material creation. What emerges in place of this excessive amplification of *logos* by the *Aufklärung* is what Ratzinger describes as human beings as creators, replacing God the Creator: "God's creation and 'nature' are having to defend themselves against the limitless pretensions of human beings as creator. Human beings want to understand the discovered world only as material for their own creativity."[20] In this new scenario, the doctrine of creation appears as the cause of the pillage of the world.

And what drives this sense of humans as creators via mere rationality—at least in the Ratzingerian reading of things—is that the question of what humans can do has replaced the question of who humans being are. To Ratzinger, these two questions are inseparable, that is, the question of who we are and the question of what we can do.[21] And the two questions bear a striking semblance to the question of being and time that so much concerned the Eleatics. To Ratzinger, Plato and Aristotle will later on resolve this question in favor of being, that is, given primacy to who we are before what we do or can do, which shows itself in time.[22] Ratzinger argues that it is with Hegel that the decisive turning point against being happens, for with Hegel's phenomenology of the human spirit as spirit returning to itself in history, being itself is now regarded as time. The *logos* becomes itself in history. The *logos* "cannot be assigned, therefore, to any particular point in history or be viewed as something existing in itself outside of history. All its historical objectifications are but movements in the whole of which they are parts."[23] All of history is therefore a self-evolution of the *logos* as it seeks to bring about a universal reconciliation, from consciousness to self-consciousness through to reason to spirit, to religion and finally to absolute knowing. Through these stages, faith emerges as knowledge, in which one shares God's knowledge of himself and his world, or when our knowledge becomes constitutive of what God is. God is appearing as pure Spirit, not extrinsic to the self, but within the self.

Unfortunately, Ratzinger maintains, whereas the *Aufklärung* clearly focused on what we can do, on humans as actors as is evident in the Hegelian dialectic that Ratzinger invokes as highlighted above, the *Aufklärung* largely neglected the question of being in favor of the question of doing, of activity. As seen in Hegel, for example, spirit is an active process of consciousness in a circle of unfolding unto itself, bringing action to the level of absolute knowing. However, even when the human being in this process of nature becomes the absolute self to the extent that human beings eschew God the Creator for human creators, the effect, as Ratzinger sees it, is that humans end up sawing off the branch on which they sit, for who we are as humans is rooted in the unique and transcendental origins in God the Creator of heaven and earth. It is as a consequence of our dignity in God that we can live a life of hope, for hope is a theological virtue in which the believer places his present and his future into the hands of a good and loving God.

Ratzinger sees the development of the rejection of the doctrine of creation by the mode of thinking of the *Aufklärung* as having emerged in three stages, in what he describes as culminating in the crisis of modern consciousness or modernity. Firstly, the starting point for Ratzinger is with the philosophy of Giordano Bruno in the sixteenth and seventeenth centuries. Bruno was responsible for the emphatic rediscovery of the cosmos in its divinity. To Ratzinger, it is precisely this reversion to a divine cosmos that brings about the recession of faith in creation. Here, "re-naissance" means "relinquishing the Christian so that the Greek can be restored in all its pagan purity."[24] The world thus appears as a divine fullness at peace within itself. By contrast, creation makes the world to depend on something other than itself, so much so that for Bruno, as per Ratzinger's reading of him, the Christian idea of the world's dependence on this something else seems to deprive the world of its power. The world must therefore be protected against this divine threat, for the world in fact is self-grounding. The world itself is divine. While one can acknowledge the contingency of individual things, any talk of contingency of the world as a whole cannot be accepted. Ratzinger maintains that in the final analysis, this perspective of seeing the world as a whole as self-sufficient and contingent on no other is an aesthetic prelude to an increasingly dominant idea in the modern mind which increasingly views religious faith with suspicion, seeing it "as the real barrier to human freedom, that basis of all other restrictions, the first thing needed to be eliminated if humankind is [to be] effectively liberated."[25] Hence, the rejection of the doctrine of creation is an expression of the *Aufklärung*'s quest for liberty, understood as the absence of any reliance on an external God.

The second phase of this journey away from faith in creation by the modern mind coincides with the figure of Galileo. Ratzinger maintains that with Galileo, one encounters the return to Greece, not in its aesthetic and emancipatory form, but in a reversion to the mathematical side of platonic thought: "God does geometry is the way he expresses his concepts of God and nature as well as his scientific ideal. God wrote the book of nature with arithmetic letters. Studying geometry enables us to touch the traces of God."[26] To Ratzinger, Galileo's position implies that the knowledge of God is turned into the knowledge of the mathematical structures of nature. The concept of nature as science therefore takes the place of the concept of creation. Given this state of affairs, the whole of knowledge is hereby fitted into the schema of subject and object, so much so that what is not objective is subjective. The challenge this position poses is that only the object is defined by natural science as objective, that is, only the things that can be concretely exhibited and examined are defined as objective. As Ratzinger comments:

> The subjective is everything arbitrary and private, everything outside of science; as arbitrary, it is unworthy of knowledge. "God does geometry." Determined by this axiom, God has to become platonic. He dwindles away to be little more than the formal mathematical structures perceived by science in nature.[27]

Thus, even if Galileo does not explicitly reject God as First Cause of nature, the fact that God as First Cause reveals itself only in nature, in the mathematics of nature and not to humans in revelation, is clearly a God that has abandoned humans to a realm of beyond the sphere of influence of this God. In the final analysis, such a First Cause is no longer God but a scientific hypothesis. On the other hand, maintains Ratzinger, a God who is likewise restricted to the inner world of piety with nothing to do with the rationality of creation is also no longer God, for he is devoid of reality and ultimately meaningless. As Ratzinger argues:

> Only when creation and covenant come together can either creation or covenant be realistically discussed—the one presupposes the other. A mere first cause does not express the idea of creation because it thinks of *causa* in terms of the scientific idea of causality. Such a cause is not God, but just a cause—a hypothetically postulated active member of a series of things that can be postulated in science.[28]

Once again, Ratzinger's penchant for the synthesis of faith and reason comes into play here. While the mathematical God of Galileo is insufficient in terms of explaining nature, a pietistic God that has nothing to do with mathematics is likewise inadequate, for such a God will have nothing to say about matter, and a God that has nothing to say about matter is irrelevant and useless, for the materiality is essential to what it means to be. One must therefore find a common ground between the geometrical God of Galileo, the God of reason, and the pietistic God of the believer who is open to the voice of revelation, the God of faith. Only with such a rapprochement are we able to find the full breadth of meaning in creation as nature and the covenant as God's invitation to humans to participate in the act of co-creating the world. Thus, it is by acknowledging the limitation of the subject/object schema of Galileo and the limitation of pietistic irrational sentimentalism that we can arrive at a fuller picture of reality as created and yet in need of human rationality to bring nature to its full potentials.

To Ratzinger, the third phase of the movement away from creation that we have seen in Bruno and Galileo finds its locus in Martin Luther. With Bruno and Galileo, one finds a passionate desire to return to a pre-Christian Greek and pagan world, as it were, beyond the synthesis of Jerusalem and Athens that had been formed over time. They thus laid the foundation of the post-Christian world of reason. For Luther, the Greek element symbolizes the alienation of Christianity which must be gotten rid of, in order to establish a pure Christianity: "The Greek element that he tries to eliminate from Christianity he finds above all in the concept of the cosmos, in the question of being, and therefore in the area of the doctrine of creation."[29] Being for Luther is an expression of the burden of the past, of the shackles and chains of one's damnation.

Redemption happens when one is liberated from the chains of the past, from the shackles of being. Redemption is the rejection of nature and the embrace of the nothingness of God, for the human being cannot help the self, for there is nothing good in nature. Only faith and hope in God's saving goodness, that is, grace, can save one. As Ratzinger sees things, "grace is seen here in radical opposition to creation, which is marked through and through by sin; it implies an attempt to get behind creation."[30] Luther must hold on to grace in opposition to creation because the world for him is one of intrinsic corruption. Without the mystery of redemptive love, therefore, the world inevitably becomes dualistic, for by nature, the world is geometry; but as history, the world is the drama of evil, from which Luther cries out for a merciful God that can save his soul.

To Ratzinger, only with Hegel do we arrive at a crescendo of the currents building up from Bruno, Galileo, and Luther. "It was Hegel," Ratzinger writes, "who made the systematic attempt to resolve this antimony and thereby to achieve the supreme philosophy. Hegel's system is ultimately a gigantic theodicy."[31] Hegel's *Phenomenology of Spirit* reveals a God who must not be seen as the eternal self-existent almighty Being, different from the reality of the world. Rather, God for Hegel exists in the process of reasoning. This God comes into being only in the other and in exchange with the other. In other words, God is the spirit of the community, as Hegel himself explains in his understanding of the meaning of religion. All cultural and intellectual activities, Hegel points out, "find their ultimate center in the *one* thought of *God*, God is the beginning of all things and the end of all things."[32]

For Hegel, therefore, the whole universe, the whole of history, is in this process of reason, and the individual moments in this process from consciousness to absolute knowing find their meaning as parts of the whole, as spirit unfolding in various processes and coming home to itself. As Peter C. Hodgson points out, "spirit" or "mind" (*Geist*) is in fact the ultimate Hegelian category, descriptive of that process of embodied consciousness that encompasses finitude and yet is itself intrinsically infinite, universal, and absolute.[33] In this Hegelian sense of spirit, God is spirit, but so is the human being, though in the modality of finitude and differentiation, for ultimately, the very meaning of God lies in the unfolding process of consciousness that goes on in the human being, in an awakening in which spirit comes evermore to itself and for itself, in the communion of the whole. Hegel therefore writes that,

> Religion is defined generally as the consciousness of God, of God the absolute object; but God's consciousness and subjectivity—the genuine object—is the whole. That God whom we designated as a mere object *over against* consciousness is an abstraction. God is this whole; hence he is the universal, the absolutely universal power, the substance of all existence, the truth—but as consciousness, as infinite form, infinite

> subjectivity, that is, as *spirit*. God's infinite form is (a) an object, content, or spirit; and (b) one, God *is* as a process, he is self-consciousness, he is as an object, as truth.[34]

Spirit, therefore, first appears in the form of finite consciousness, and the *telos* of both logical idea and finite spirit is the actuality of God as absolute spirit. Hegel makes a distinction between God as the absolute idea in and for itself—God in eternity, that is, the immanent or pre-worldly trinity, which is differentiated from the economic or worldly trinity, which makes its appearance in creation, Incarnation, reconciliation, reaching its apex in the spiritual community.[35] To Hegel, the absolute idea of God makes its appearance in three forms. The first form is what Hegel calls universality, that is, God as pure thought as God is in and for God's self, God in God's eternal essence. This is the divine history that outside the world, outside finitude, Hegel describes as "God as he is in and for himself."[36] This element of God as universality, God in and for himself, God as pure thought, is God outside of time, God as pure thought of eternity as set against time. The second form of the appearance of the idea of God is what Hegel refers to as particularity, in which "consciousness is entrapped in its relation to the other."[37] This is divine history as revealed in the world, God being in a determinate form in the world, that is, the appearing of the Christ of God in the world, Jesus of Nazareth. Hegel maintains that this appearance is a *past time*, "for appearance means something that is, that has being, but it has a mode of being that has been reduced to a mere show,"[38] for the fact that it is a mode of being of history, of the past. The third appearance of the absolute idea is what Hegel calls singularity, the thinking of the free spirit, that is, "the *inner place*, the community, first of all in the world, but also the community insofar as it simultaneously raises itself to heaven, or already has heaven within itself on earth—the community which, as the church, is full of grace, and in which God is active and present."[39]

To Hegel, this community of the church is the present that differentiates past and future from itself, a present that is distinctive from the eternity of universality and the past of particularity, a present that brings about a reconciling consummation that must necessarily open this present to the future. In this sense, we have the idea of God unfolding as universality, that is, the Father, appearing in the particular; that is, the Son, reconciling and consummating in the singular present-future; and the Spirit, though Hegel considers the appellation of "Father," "Son," and "Spirit" to be childlike.[40] Therefore God, as an absolute idea, is the beginning of all things. God, as absolute spirit, is the end of all things. Finitude is the appearance of God in finite spirit, which embodies the history of redemption and reconciliation. Hegel explains:

> The definition of God is that he is the absolute idea—i.e., that he is Spirit, However, three things may be said about Spirit as the absolute idea: (a) It *is* only as the *unity of concept and reality*, so that the concept in itself is the totality, and likewise the reality. (b) But this reality, as was previously shown, is *revelation*—the manifestation that has being on its own. Finite self-consciousness, or what is called human nature, (stands) over against this concept. Since we call the absolute concept the divine nature, the idea of spirit is to be the unity of divine and human nature. Humanity has arrived at this intuition. But the divine nature is itself only this, to be absolute spirit; hence precisely the unity of divine and human nature is itself absolute spirit.[41]

For Hegel, therefore, the manifestation of the reality of God, that is, divine nature, happens in revelation, in which the totality of the divine nature makes itself known, a reality that is antithetical to finite consciousness, that is, human nature. What is intriguing is how Hegel brings finite consciousness or human nature together with divine nature, that is, through spirit, or more precisely, the idea of spirit, of the absolute spirit. Hodgson points out that, "at each stage of consciousness, spirit remains unfulfilled and is constantly drawn beyond itself in the quest for a more adequate and encompassing reconciliation of estranged antithesis."[42] Looking at Hegel's ladder, therefore, one sees consciousness as being in constant motion, with each stage following the next. There is no possibility of being static. As Paul Ricoeur points out, each form of consciousness in Hegel's ladder finds its meaning in what follows. What is before us, therefore, is a teleology of consciousness in which spirit is constituted as spirit in the very dialectic of transition from one figure to the next.[43] And this quest for spirit is essentially a religious quest.

Given this Hegelian religious dialectic, Ratzinger writes that the historical religious data, such as Good Friday as the day of Christ's crucifixion, becomes, in the Hegelian scheme of things, an expression of the speculative Good Friday, that is, of the necessity of rising up to oneself after the experience of defeat.[44] This is the sense in which the Hegelian system appears as a gigantic theodicy, in which the problem of theodicy is resolved. Insight replaces sin, and evil is bound up with finitude and therefore is unreal vis-à-vis infinitude. Suffering is the pain of limitation and when taken up into the whole of reality, suffering is abolished.[45] The Hegelian system is therefore largely idealistic, though not devoid of political motivation,[46] as seen in the Marxist call to action.

To Ratzinger, this Hegelian theoretical dialectic finds concreteness with Marx, in whose thought it becomes a call to action. Redemption is now construed as the "praxis" of the human being, a denial of creation or indeed, as per Ratzinger's reading, as an antithesis to faith in creation.[47] Ratzinger makes his case of the Marxist fulfillment of the Hegelian dialectic with two arguments:[48] Firstly, "the individual is taken up and abolished in the whole."[49] The individual as individual "is robbed of reality."[50] The instrument of operation within history is the party, "the organized form of class."[51] The "I" of the individual ceases to be of any significance, as the individual consciousness is taken up into class consciousness, in which individual suffering no longer counts.[52] What matters is the logic of the system and sustaining that system through human work understood as human creation.

Secondly, creation is defined as dependence, origin *ab alio*.[53] Creation is taken over by the category of self-creation, accomplished through work. Ratzinger concludes: "Since creation equals dependence, and dependence is the antithesis of freedom, the doctrine of creation is opposed to the fundamental direction of Marxist thought."[54] To Ratzinger, therefore, creation is the total antithesis to Marxism.[55] This rejection of dependence and life as encountered is the strongest fuel for the Marxist movement. These points aside, it must be noted that Ratzinger's reading of Marxism places accent on its perceived weaknesses, perhaps to the point of overlooking the issues in need of redress that might have motivated Marx, such as the socio-economic imbalances in the world.

Overall, however, it is clear that to Ratzinger, the historical trajectory of Bruno, Galileo, Luther, Hegel, and Marx is indicative of the fact that the concept of creation constitutes a crossroads in the intellectual development that marked the *Aufklärung*. Ratzinger identifies three strands or modes of concealment of creation exhibited by the intellectual character of the *Aufklärung*. Firstly, the concept of creation is concealed by the scientific concept of nature, understood exclusively in the sense of the object of science, admitting of no other meaning. Given this positivistic view of "science," Ratzinger points out that "theological arguments about the 'nature of humans' or 'natural rights,' resting as they do on the concept of creation, meet a look of blank incomprehension; in fact, they seem nonsensical, the relic of an archaic 'natural philosophy.'"[56] But this naturalness of science does not correspond to reality, for life is about daily choices, and this implies that decision-making must find a criterion beyond mere naturalness. Without a criterion for decision-making, humans would appear "condemned" to a formless freedom.[57] Life could easily degenerate into a meaningless cycle.

Ratzinger thus concludes antithetically to the *Aufklärung*'s self-sufficiency of nature, that "if creation cannot be recognized as the metaphysical middle term between nature and artificiality, then the plunge into nothingness is unavoidable."[58] Secondly, the concept of creation is further concealed in modern enlightenment mode of thinking in the form of a resentment against humans, seen as a disease of nature. Humans are perceived as disturbing the beautiful balance of nature, diseased by their mind and its consequence, that is, freedom. As Ratzinger claims, mind and freedom are the sickness of nature, and humans and the world must be delivered from these if there is to be a redemption. To restore the balance, humans must be healed of being human. This is seen, Ratzinger contends, in various forms of nihilism becoming an ever-greater temptation for the youth of the West.[59] A third and final form of concealment against the concept of creation by the *Aufklärung* mode of thinking takes place on the theological level. Ratzinger asserts that here, "nature is undermined for the sake of grace; it is robbed of its belongings and gives way, so to speak, before grace. Here we should recall the crucial text of 1 Corinthians 15:46: 'It is not the spiritual which is first but the physical, and *then* the spiritual.'"[60] To Ratzinger, therefore, and in line with St. Paul, the logic does not flow such that the spiritual precedes the physical. It always has to be the other way around if we are not to be absorbed into a monism of grace. Once we skip over the physical, creation is denied and grace is deprived of its foundation:

> A selflessness that tries to abolish one's own "I" degenerates into "I-lessness," and then "Thou-lessness" follows directly. This undermining of creation can never become a vehicle of grace, but only of an *odium generis humani*, a Gnostic disenchantment with creation, which ultimately does not and cannot desire grace any longer.[61]

In other words, the valuable contribution of Thomas Aquinas that grace builds and does not destroy nature, continues to be irrevocable for Ratzinger, for as he asserts above, creation in this case, or embodiment, constitutes a unique source of grace in its own right.

In defending the human body and in arguing against what could be characterized as Christian spiritualism, Ratzinger invokes the foundational quality of love in the Christian religious experience. In other words, Christian love presupposes faith in the Creator, for it implies an acceptance of the self as God's creature and a love of the Creator's creation in me. This love for the Creator must lead one to the freedom of accepting oneself and any other person as equal members of the Body of Christ.[62] In a word, one might say that love for the Creator implies not only a total rejection of ancient Gnosticism, but likewise a conscious appreciation of the beauty of human embodiment.

Following Ratzinger's thinking, therefore, it would not be wrong to draw the conclusion that the *Aufklärung*'s rejection of creation as a conscious act by a benevolent God, opting rather for a self-sufficiency of nature as ordered by an inherent necessary causality, is a return of the ancient heresy of Gnosticism that the early Church had to deal with, albeit this time under the guise of mere rationality of nature. With this rebirth of Gnosticism comes a rejection of "the mystery of suffering, of love, of substitutionary redemption, in favor of a control of the world and of life through knowledge."[63] Isn't this what one encounters in Kant, Hegel and Nietzsche, for example, that is, this rejection of redemptive substitutionary suffering, and love? This rejection of the whole Christian experience of a personal God who, though utterly different from one, knows one because this God is both Creator and Redeemer.

Because faith in God as Creator implies dependence on God and given that such a dependence is an antithesis to the *Aufklärung*'s objective of knowledge and power through knowledge, nature as necessary causality not needing a Creator is the only logical exit. Consistency demands that the *Aufklärung* not entrust the self to a world already created. It could only entrust one to a world still to be created, so that skill, and not trust or religious faith, constitutes the only requirement or precondition for participation in such a world.

For the believer, the option is the exact opposite of this Gnostic model of the *Aufklärung*, for all of nature is a fruit of God's creative love. In biblical revelation the very first line introduces the theme of creation. Holy Writ begins with the words: "In the beginning, God created the heavens and the earth. The earth was without form and void, and darkness was upon the face of the deep; and the Spirit of God was moving over the face of the waters. And God said, 'Let there be light'; and there was light" (Gen 1:1–2). The priestly account continues with the beautiful refrain that accompanies the narrative, "and God saw that it was good." For much of orthodox Christianity, particularly Roman Catholicism, these words constitute the first reading of the series of readings that constitute the Solemnity of the Easter Vigil. This biblical text is "translated" into the first article of the Nicene Creed, as revelation continued to unfold as the tradition of the church developed. These first lines of the Creed constitute at once a prayer of praise and a confession of one of the core beliefs of the church: that God is the "maker of heaven and earth, of all that is seen and unseen." The creation theme recurs again and again in the prophetic and wisdom literature, in the Pauline writings, and in the Gospels. Finally, in the Apocalypse we find a hymn in praise to the Creator: "You are worthy, our Lord and God, to receive glory and honor and power, for you created all things, and by your will they existed and were created" (Rev 4:11).

On the other hand, because the words of Genesis belong to Israel's faith—though its contents are shared with all the great civilizations of the world—it is worth noting that a proper theological understanding of Israel's faith in creation ought to be located during the Babylonian Exile of Israel's geo-political and religious history.[64] Israel had lost its land and temple, and according to the mentality of the time this was something incomprehensible, for it meant that the God of Israel was vanquished—a God whose people, whose land, and whose worshipers could be snatched away from him.[65] A God who could not defend his worshipers was seen as a weak God. Indeed, he was no God at all; he had abandoned his divinity. Thus, being driven out of their land and being erased from the map of the earth was for Israel a terrible trial: "Has our God been vanquished, and is our faith void?" Israel wondered![66] One could say that Israel's exile posed a fundamental threat to Israel's conviction about her understanding of God.

Something unique happens at this stage of Israel's faith: "The prophets opened a new page and taught Israel that it was only then [in exile that] the true face of God appeared and that he was not restricted to that particular piece of land. He had never been."[67] Though God had promised this piece of land to Abraham before Abraham settled there, he had been able to bring his people out of Egypt. God could do both things because "he was not the God of one place but had power over heaven and earth."[68] He could, therefore, drive his faithless and disobedient people into another land in order to make himself known there. In her seeming defeat, Israel entered a new understanding of her God.

In the context of real physical suffering, Israel came to understand that her God was unlike the other gods, that he was the God who held sway over every land and people. He could do this, however, because he himself had created everything in heaven and on earth. It was in exile and in the seeming defeat of Israel that there occurred an opening to the awareness of the God who holds every people and all of history in his hands, who holds everything because he is the creator of everything and the source of all power. This faith now had to find its own contours, and it had to do so precisely in opposition to the seemingly victorious religion of Babylon, vis-à-vis the great Babylonian creation accounts of Enuma Elish, marked by splendid displays in liturgies like that of the

New Year, in which the re-creation of the world was celebrated and brought to its fulfillment.[69] The world was said to be produced out of a struggle between opposing powers.

The world assumed its form when Marduk, the god of light, appeared and split into two the body of the primordial dragon. Heaven and earth came to be from that sundered body, the firmament and the earth from the sundered body of the dread dragon, and the human beings from the blood of the Marduk.[70] In other words, the world is a dragon's body, and human beings have dragon's blood in them. As Ratzinger points out, "at the very origin of the world lurks something sinister, and in the deepest part of humankind there is something rebellious, demonic, and evil."[71] Given this milieu, only a dictator, the king of Babylon and Marduk's representative, can repress the demonic and restore order to the world. Ratzinger makes a nuanced synthesis of this state of things of the ancient Near East religions:

> Such views were not simply fairy tales. They expressed the discomfiting realities that human beings experienced in the world and among themselves. For often enough it looks as if the world is a dragon's lair and human blood is dragon's blood. But despite all oppressive experiences the scriptural account says that it was not so. The whole tale of these sinister powers melts away in a few words: "The earth was without form and void." Behind these Hebrew words lie the dragon and the demonic powers that are spoken of elsewhere.[72]

It is only with the context of the confusing myths of Babylon that one can see in bolder relief, the dramatic confrontation implicit in the biblical text. The world emerges as a creation of God's Reason and God's Word. The sun and the moon are no longer gods, but lamps placed by God in the sky for the measurement of time—a sacrilegious statement to make, to near Easterners. The world was not a product of a demonic confrontation but of God's *Logos*. Creation therefore places the world in reason and freedom. This is the context in which Ratzinger sees the theology of creation as the true *Aufklärung* dispelling the darkness of fear, violence, darkness, and the demonic.[73] Reason, love and freedom are the enlightened fruits that characterize faith in Creation as opposed to the violence of the Babylonian and pagan myths of the near-Eastern religions. Creation as an act of the *Logos* of God, God's Word, as one finds in Genesis, finds its fulfillment as testified in the New Testament, in which the Creator becomes the Redeemer, at the fullness of time (Gal 4:4). Creation and Redemption are therefore not extrinsic to each other, but mutually enrich and complement each other. One can make the argument that creation itself is God's redemption of the material from the non-God of violence, chaos, and contradictory and irrational mythologies.

Summarily, Ratzinger's argument is that by understanding nature as an object, the *Aufklärung* sought to explain the self-sufficiency of nature in order to dispense of the necessity of God, of creatural dependence on God, which is a precondition for faith in the Creator God. But nature on its own cannot explain the being of creation, for nature as objectified by the *Aufklärung* denies the indispensable place of the subjective which gives meaning and interprets the objectified. By rejecting faith in creation in reference to the necessary causality of nature, it rejected love, the only reason for God to create the world. By rejecting faith in creation, it likewise rejected the transcendental dignity of the human being created in the image and likeness of God, leaving the human being at the mercy of the dragon's blood, a product of the carcass of creation. And finally, by rejecting creation for the concept of causality as natural and necessary, which takes the determination of things in themselves to be the determination of things in time, this conception of necessary natural causality of the *Aufklärung* cannot explain how character is built and how one can hold someone responsible outside the framework of free action that characterizes the theology of creation, as expressed in the Genesis accounts of creation. Given these, it is difficult not to see why faith in God, Creator of heaven and earth, offers a more compelling alternative or proposition to the necessary causality or self-sufficiency of matter as propounded by the *Aufklärung*, as specifically illustrated by Hegel, as demonstrated in this section.

From a Christological perspective, what emerges from the above considerations, in the first place, is the realization that for Ratzinger, the figure of Christ who as creative Reason is at the source of creation, reflects what one might call a Christological rationality of love and freedom. Because Christ is at the origin and center of creation, there is no room to view creation from the perspective of fear and irrationality, from the view of Marduk. Who is Christ? Christ is the Eternal *Logos*, Reason, and by his Word, the heavens were made (Ps 33:6). This implies that faith in the person of Christ is not antithetical to reason, does not diminish the value of matter, of nature and of creation. On the other hand, rather than asserting that creation emanated from a chaotic, evil, irrational principle, the Christological orientation of the creation theology of Ratzinger asserts that creation is not only reasonable, a conscious act of God, but is likewise good. Creation is a fruit of the benevolence and rationality of the *Logos* who is Creative Reason.

This implies that even from an evolutionary perspective, God is not absent from creation as an ongoing process. In Christ, God is intrinsic to creation. Deism is not the Christian option. God remains Immanuel, with us. This points to the fact that Christ is not distant from the world, but, in recreating the world in the act of redemption, Christ is forever a part of creation. In other words, the fact of the Incarnation has opened up a new dimension in the creation. The entrance of the figure of Christ into creation marks an evolutionary leap. In Christ, creative Reason, creation has transcended the boundaries imposed by time and space, the *a priori*-ness of time and space, to reference Kant, and has entered into a new phase of infinity, of boundlessness, precisely because the Incarnation and the Resurrection have forever opened the limits of creation to the limitlessness of divine power.

Christologically speaking therefore, the new creation in Christ is the opening of the present of creation into the infinity and freedom of the Spirit that comes with the fact of the Resurrection. It means that in the Resurrection of Christ, creation has been liberated, as Paul says, from bondage, from slavery (Rom 8:21), into freedom. Only in this sense does creation not only return to its pristine form of goodness, beauty, and innocence, but even more, enters into the definitive form of divinization that comes with the Incarnation, the Resurrection, and the sending of the Spirit who breathes life into the new creation in Christ, into all of creation.

At this point, Christology opens to pneumatology, for creation becomes remade and taken over by the Spirit of Christ, sent forth to renew the face of the earth and all creation (Ps 104:30). The Christology of Ratzinger's theology of the *Logos* as creative Reason can therefore be characterized as a Christological pneumatology, to the extent that creation is freed from fear, is liberated from the darkness of the pagan myths, and enters into the free spirit of Christ who imparts his Spirit unto creation. The person of Christ and the historical entrance of that person into history, into creation, forever change the dynamics of creation. One might say that the Christology of creation, built on the person of Christ, makes creation a miracle, in the sense that God's power, unleashed in its fullness in God's Incarnate Son, is capable of suspending the laws of nature, of bringing nature to a new height of boundlessness, opening all of creation into the infinite possibilities of the new Adam, so much so that creation is prepared for that consummation which no eye has seen, nor ear heard, nor the human mind conceived (1 Cor 2:9). In other words, owing to the centrality of the figure of Christ in Ratzinger's theology of creation, it is the case that creation will only reach its fullest potentials when creation enters the new heavens and the new earth (Rev 21:1-2). In this sense, Ratzinger's Christological theology of creation spans from Christology to pneumatology, while opening up to eschatology, wherein Christ as the new Adam offers up all of creation back to the Father, so that the Father will become all in all (1 Cor 15:28).

4.2 *Logos* as Son: Ratzinger's Engagement with the *Aufklärung*'s Reinterpretation of the New Testament *Gestalt* of Jesus Christ

To the extent that the *Aufklärung* sought to demystify Christianity, it is axiomatic that the figure of Christ could not be left untouched by the *Aufklärer*, especially given that Christology, as we saw in chapter two, section one, largely legitimized priesthood and mediatory religion—a bone of contention for many of the *Aufklärer*. In other words, Christology—the life, death, and Resurrection of Christ—as propagated by institutional Christianity, perpetuated an infantile religious spirit by continuously making the people dependent on the priestly class that was now acting, as classical orthodoxy understood it, *in persona Christi capitis*. The figure of Christ and his central place in Christianity therefore made revelation as understood and interpreted by the religious hierarchy and as transmitted in the living tradition of the Church, the final arbiter of truth. This is untenable to the *Aufklärung*, that saw reason, and not revelation and priesthood that propagated the tenets of revelation based on the figure of Christ, the final arbiter of truth.

To Kant, for example, this process of reason as the determinant of the existence of God and all else regarding religion constitutes the central nexus of the *Aufklärung*:

> *Enlightenment is the human being's emergence from his self-incurred minority*. Minority is inability to make use of one's own understanding without direction from another. This minority is self-incurred when its cause lies not in lack of understanding, but in lack of resolution and courage to use it without direction from another. *Sapere aude*! Have courage to make use of your *own* understanding is thus the motto of enlightenment.[74]

In other words, enlightenment for Kant is the capacity of the human being to release the self from a self-incurred tutelage, that is, to free the self from the lack of courage to think for oneself. Enlightenment is to be freed from one's thought being guided and directed by others, in the manner that parents guide and direct their children. The vocation of every human being is to get to the point in which one can think for the self. This independence in thinking is identifiable with human autonomy, which Kant understands to be "the principle of not submitting to groundless authorities."[75] Hence, that is the point of adulthood, or maturity as opposed to immaturity, which is to depend on others or to allow others to micromanage one's thinking.

But autonomy, as Kant understands it, is much more than moral independence and self-determinism. As Onora O'Neill points out, autonomy for Kant is "thinking or acting on principles that defer to no ungrounded 'authority,' hence on principles all can follow. For Kant, autonomy is living by the principles of reason; and reason is nothing but the principle that informs practices of autonomy in thinking and doing."[76] To act according to reason is to think and act according to principles that all humans can freely apprehend and adopt. And the basis for this primacy of reason in Kant's ethical-religious system is the Kantian presupposition that "normal adults are capable of being fully self-governing in moral matters."[77] Given that only autonomy in thinking can have a universal clout, autonomy is therefore not only all there is to reason, but is what gives reason is overall authority. However, and perhaps puzzlingly, Kant does not equate enlightenment with reason, but "with an oddly characterized practice of reasoning publicly."[78] The high stage accorded reason is not just for the sake of reason, but for the public and universal character and commonality that reason is called to shape in the commonwealth of peoples, ideas, and practices.

To Kant, therefore, the process of reason's ultimate autonomy is geared toward establishing a sense of equality among humans who, as humans, are called to live and work together. If Kant had such a disdain for priesthood as reflected in *Religion*, among other reasons, it is precisely because he saw the priests as depriving people from thinking for themselves, since they established themselves as mediators between God and people. Kant outright rejects this priesthood dominion of the clergy "over minds by pretending to have exclusive possession of the means of grace."[79] Priesthood represents an unacceptable infantilizing of people that must be eschewed once the religion of reason becomes commonplace in the world. As Allen W. Wood remarks regarding Kant's treatment of priesthood in the system of revealed religion, obviously with Catholicism in mind, "the plain intent (that is, in Kant's treatment of institutional religion) is that people should eventually abolish the hierarchical constitution of churches, which puts humanity in spiritual tutelage to a class of priests who usurp the authority of individuals over their own belief and conscience."[80] In the Kantian sense, therefore, *Aufklärung* means the liberation of people from religious tutelage by progressive forces, which would come about thanks to the safeguard of freedom of thought and expression by secular authorities who refuse to "support the spiritual despotism of a few tyrants within his state against the rest of his subjects."[81]

What will eventually result from this progressive current is an egalitarian ethical church with no clergy-laity distinction, in which all submit to the non-statutory autonomous law which is the will of the world ruler revealed through reason.[82] Kant is hopeful that there would come a day when "the very form of a church is dissolved; the vicar on earth enters the same class as the human beings who are now elevated to him as citizens of Heaven, and so God is all in all."[83] To set the ball rolling toward the project of such a rational, ethical, and egalitarian church under the headship of reason, Kant has to reinterpret not only the figure of Christ and the God of biblical revelation, but the entire Christological assertions built on Christ.

Specifically, for Kant the concept of the Divine Sonship of Christ is essentially humanity's desire for moral perfection. To say that Jesus Christ is the Son of God says nothing about the ontological constitution of Jesus, neither does it entail any unique sense of purpose regarding the man Christ vis-à-vis a wholly different God. For Kant, Christ is the appearance of "a person whose wisdom, even purer than that of the previous philosophers, was as though descended from heaven."[84] The virgin birth of Christ is an "idea of reason."[85] It has nothing to do with a unique revelatory phase of God's dealings with Israel, in the form of a messianic fulfillment of Old Testament prophecies. Talking about the suffering of Christ, Kant notes that it represents the contrast between the freedom of the children of heaven and a mere son of the earth, the central leitmotif being that it is profitable to die rather than compromise on virtue.[86] To Kant, therefore, the suffering of Christ for the sake of the moral duty is clear enough for every human being to recognize as his or her duty. The rational meaning of the scriptural story, therefore, is that there is absolutely no salvation for human beings except by the innermost adoption of the genuine moral principles in their disposition.[87] In effect, salvation is not about accepting God's offer of the new life in Christ Jesus, but the opening of the self to the moral law that lies within the self.

The idea of the vicarious expiation of sin by Christ is therefore superstitious, even if testified to by Scripture. In fact, it is in the nature of things for Scripture to find an inner rapport with reason, for only then can the true meaning of Scripture emerge:

> Finally, any attempt like the present to find a meaning in Scripture in harmony with the *most holy* teachings of reason must be held not only as permissible but as duty, and we may be reminded at this point of what the *wise teacher* said to his

> disciples regarding someone who went his own way, by which he would have had eventually to come to the same goal: "Forbid him not; for he who is not against us is for us."[88]

Strange as it might sound to believing ears, it is the teachings of reason, not of Scripture, that are most holy for Kant, as he points out in this passage. It is the obedience to reason that brings about the proper moral disposition necessary to live as persons. Scripture is therefore not an independent voice that gives guidance to reason, but rather is such that it can only come to its true self when it passes through the purifying route of the pure moral disposition of reason.

The *Gestalt* of the Jesus that emerges from Kant is essentially that of a moral teacher, a wise teacher, whose path is prepared not by the Hebrew prophets or by John the Baptist, but by the Greek sages. Synthetically, the Jesus of the Gospels is four things for Kant. Firstly, Jesus is the one that announces himself as sent from heaven. Secondly, Jesus is the one who declares that service faith is inherently null and void and of no consequence. Thirdly, Jesus is the preacher of the moral faith of good life and conduct. And finally, Jesus provides an example of a humanity that is well-pleasing to God.[89] The Kantian Jesus is therefore a natural, good, and wise moralist, with the sole task of teaching humans how to live a moral life that is pleasing to God.

Given this *Weltanschauung*, the Resurrection of Jesus, the central event in defining the *Gestalt* of Jesus for orthodox Christianity seemingly has no place in the Kantian scheme of things. Kant himself writes:

> The more esoteric story of his *Resurrection* and *ascension* (which, simply as ideas of reason, would signify the beginning of another life and the entrance into the seat of salvation, i.e., into the society of all the good), added as sequel and witnessed only by his intimates, cannot be used in the interest of religion within the boundaries of mere reason, whatever its historical standing.[90]

Thus, even if orthodox Christianity considers the Resurrection as the defining event of what shapes Christianity, such a position clearly does not fit in with the Kantian system of rational faith, of moral religion, which essentially invites the adherent to will one's duties as divine commands, for the sole purpose of attaining a pure moral disposition. In the Kantian scheme of things, therefore, happiness is equivalent to living the moral law as a self-willed duty, not a subservience of the self to some religious practices or cult. The rational Jesus of Kant therefore fits in with the Kantian moral religion, for to Kant, "the concept of God is valid [...] only insofar as it is based upon moral laws. We cannot prove this concept *a priori*, but are allowed to infer it only insofar as it is a precondition of the highest good."[91] To Kant, therefore, God is a principle of morality. As Wood points out,

> In many matters, Kant's religious beliefs and practices were far from orthodox. Kant was personally opposed in principle to religious ceremonies. He regarded creeds as unconscionable impositions on our inner freedom of thought, almost inevitably productive of a hypocritical frame of mind. Ceremonial praise of the Deity (the "religion of ingratiation") was for him a despicable act of self-degradation. And he saw no possible good in activities whose superstitious aim is to conjure up divine aid for our prayers, regarding petitionary prayer (the "wheedling of God') as especially objectionable in this respect.[92]

I am inclined to agree with this assessment of Wood regarding Kant, for, as will be seen in Ratzinger's treatment of the same religious postulates that Kant takes up, even if one is impressed by the Kantian position that the concept of God is natural to human reason, for example, the details of what that concept of God will constitute for Kant, when eventually dissected, will be so distant from anything close to orthodox theology about the same concept. As Wood again summarizes regarding Kant and the concept of God, the Kantian theistic framework amounts to three postulates: firstly, "I have duties"; secondly, "I have a concept of God"; and finally, "I am capable of regarding my duties as something God wills me to do."[93] Is Kant able to conceive of a religious faith that is not subsumed to ethics? And can Kant fathom a God that is outside the human being, a different being who will act as judge to human actions and choices, whose being is different from the human conscience? Assuming that Kant died and found himself before a judgment seat of a God, who will sit on the seat, Kant or God? In precis, it is very difficult to reconcile the ethical God of Kant with the God of Christian orthodoxy, hard as one might try.

Turning to Hegel as another example of the reinterpretation of the *Gestalt* of Jesus Christ, one finds again—in the spirit of the *Aufklärung's* maxim of *sapere aude*—an enterprise that seeks, according to Hegel's thinking, to make Christianity accessible to modern minds. As Laurence Dickey points out, Hegel saw his role as that of a *via media* between Protestant dogmatism that maintained a suspicious attitude toward philosophy, on the one hand, and the pretensions of liberal theology that was impatient toward the claims of dogmatic evangelicals, on the other hand.[94] Hegel saw his role as that of going beyond dogmatism and liberalism. To achieve this, Hegel puts forth the medium of speculative philosophy, clearly distinguishable from what Hegel characterizes as reflective philosophy, which is "philosophy that has not come to the true conception of philosophy, philosophy that is not really philosophy—inauthentic philosophy over against authentic philosophy which is, and cannot but be speculative."[95] Reflective philosophy gets ossified in arguments and counter arguments, unable to move to the level of freedom of consciousness that is characteristic of speculative philosophy, which transmits philosophy to the level of science, thereby making philosophy teachable. As a science, philosophy is able to give humans the dignity of a philosophical consciousness that allows humans to be reminded of the religious dimension of human nature.[96] Given the vital role that philosophy is called to play in making Christianity accessible to modern minds, in the spirit of speculative philosophy, religion, for Hegel, is construed as "a mode of consciousness that seeks to establish the truth of the relationship between man and God. That truth, Hegel implied, had expressed itself differently at different moments in human history."[97] To Hegel, therefore, given the advanced form of modern consciousness as seen in the place of prominence accorded reason, the time had come for speculative philosophy to usher in a new articulation of the same traditional religious truths of Christianity in nontraditional philosophical language.

Language thus becomes a key issue that drives the Hegelian speculative philosophy project. In this light, while the language of "feeling" and "piety" is perceived by Hegel to characterize a reflective presentation of orthodox dogmatism, on the one hand, the language of cognition is the communicative mode of speculative philosophy in its expression of religious truths, on the other hand. In other words, the *language of faith* spoke to the ordinary consciousness of peoples of all times, while the *language of knowledge or of knowing* is fitting for the consciousness of Hegel's modern age.[98] Hegel perceives the language of faith to be restrictive and narrow in its explication of religious truths, bringing about an unfortunate consequence of humans' self-perception of themselves as natural rather than spiritual beings. The only remedy for such naturalizing of humans is speculative philosophy.

It is interesting that Hegel displays a very positive attitude toward what might be characterized as a dialogical relationship, as seen in his letters, of which Laurence Dickey provides an enlightening synthesis.[99] The relationship between philosophy (in Hegel's case, speculative philosophy in particular, that is, knowing) and faith (or believing, as Hegel would prefer to call it), is nothing new to historians of Christianity. Hegel himself acknowledges this in the *Reflective Philosophy of Subjectivity*, highlighting the inner tension between faith and reason and the hitherto medieval presumption of reason as the handmaid of theology. Hegel writes:

> Civilization has raised this latest era so far above the ancient antithesis of Reason and faith, of philosophy and positive religion, that this opposition of faith and knowledge has acquired quite a different sense and has now been transferred into the field of philosophy itself. In earlier times philosophy was said to be the handmaid of faith. Ideas and expressions of this sort have vanished and philosophy has irresistibly affirmed its autonomy.[100]

Hegel, therefore, inserts himself into a debate that has been lively, from the Fathers such as Justin, Origen, and medievals like Aquinas. In fact, Ratzinger's inaugural lecture, treated earlier in this book, testifies to the perennial nature of this question.

Regarding the specific context of Hegel, the distinction and openness he advocated between knowing and believing elicited the charge, in terms of the reception of Hegel, of panlogism. Characterizing Hegel as a panlogist implied Hegel's critics read him as advocating for a supremacy of knowledge over and above faith and the human heart: "This (that is, the supremacy of knowledge over faith), Hegel's critics charged, meant that he had forsaken the real world of Christian feeling for an abstract world of concepts that had been shaped in his own, rather than God's, image and likeness."[101] From a Hegelian standpoint, however, the hermeneutical tool of speculative philosophy that brings about the language of knowledge provides the unique opportunity of modern accessibility to Christianity. Such is the case because, with speculative philosophy, God is conceptualized, such that in the language of modern science God is conceived as an abstract truth, the highest idea, a logical concept that people are now free to discuss and engage, rather than a reflection by peoples of certain times and places on their conception of God.[102] To Hegel, therefore, believing, that is, faith, had to be translated into reason, that is, knowing, into abstraction, and only after this translation has taken place, can we enter into the final stage of doing, hence, a trilogy of believing, knowing, and doing. As Hegel argues in *The Philosophy of Religion*, believing, knowing, and doing not only constitute the central nexus of Christianity, but are likewise the yardsticks of the movement of speculative philosophy.[103] And it is in the light of this perspective of speculative philosophy, of abstraction, of God as the highest of ideas, that we must understand Hegel's interpretive Christological claims regarding the New Testament data of the figure of Jesus Christ.

To Hegel, theological concepts such as the divinity of Christ, take on an inelastic and an all-inclusive character that empties any sense of uniqueness vis-à-vis the person of the historical Jesus of Nazareth. The presupposition underpinning Hegel's philosophical theology is that God is not some extrinsic being, separate from humans and making demands on humans. God is the moral law latent within every human being, and the historical Jesus of Nazareth is essentially a figure that comes along to awaken the ethical consciousness within each human being. The only way Christianity had to hold itself from degenerating into folklore will be if Christianity becomes a religion of reason and virtue.[104] Given this understanding, the Jesus of Hegel is an apostle of virtue and reason. The picture that emerges is one of a Christ the moralist, whose mission appears exclusively as that of a teacher of virtue.

For Hegel, therefore, biblical theophanies like the voice from heaven that confirmed the divine sonship of Jesus were all invitations and confirmations of the foundational quality and indispensability of the moral law: "Only this voice from heaven can instruct you concerning the higher demands of reason; and only by believing in it and heeding it does one find peace of mind and true greatness and thus discover the dignity of which mankind is capable."[105] And in tandem with the general spirit of the *Aufklärung*, Hegel situates this moral law in the human being in the rational faculty:

> Indeed, by endowing man with reason the Deity so distinguished humankind from the rest of nature that man came alive with the reflected splendor of the divine essence; and only through his faith in reason does man fulfill his high destiny. Reason does not condemn the natural impulses, but governs and refines them; and whoever does not listen to it—by not duly appreciating its light, by failing to nourish it in himself—passes judgment on himself, having thus shown by his actions what sort of a fellow he is.[106]

One notices here a tension in the Hegelian dialectic regarding nature. On the one hand, Hegel, the Tübingen theologian, appears to subscribe to the notion of an *a priori* Deity or God who is the First Cause of the cosmos in general, and of man in particular. There is an action on the part of God, in that God is the source of reason in humans, a faculty that Hegel considers to be of the divine essence. On the other hand, Hegel, the Tübingen *Aufklärung* post-Cartesian and post-Kantian thinker, is eager to argue for the autonomy of reason in a manner that is independent of any religious Deity or confessional creeds and the restrictions that come with such cultic professions. It appears to be the case that, while Hegel does not want to subscribe to a God who is extrinsic to nature and hence directs nature with the resultant effect of religious absolutism and the offshoot of political despotism that accompanies it, Hegel is likewise unable to completely do away with the notion of God or of the religious. In the final analysis, a reconciliation of some sort is achieved when God becomes the spirit of the people in an all-inclusive sense.

Given this Hegelian worldview, therefore, the point of departure from which Hegel looks both at the *Gestalt* of Jesus and the New Testament presentation of Jesus, is essentially that of a moralist, an ethicist on a mission of reawakening the human race from an ethical slumber that is lethal. Clearly, even if Hegel sought to distance himself from Kant's categorical imperatives, on the question of religion, specifically the Christian religion and the figure of Jesus of Nazareth, Hegel, like the rest of much of the *Aufklärer*, is heavily Kantian in his reinterpretation of Christianity. Notwithstanding, Hegel clearly displays a much more nationalistic bent in his divinization of what he considers to be the spirit of socio-political and cultural order, so much so that Hegel can be considered as the philosopher of the Prussian state.[107] God becomes the spirit of the people, as resolved in the *Phenomenology*.

Discussing Christ's divinity in his *The Life of Jesus*, for example, Hegel writes:

> When you regard your ecclesiastical statutes and positive precepts as the highest law given to mankind, you fail to recognize man's dignity and his capacity to derive from his own self the concept of divinity and the comprehension of the divine will. Whoever does not honor this capacity within himself does not revere the Deity.[108]

Divinity is therefore not a unique prerogative of Jesus Christ that he makes available to us. On the contrary, divinity is already in each and every one of us. What Jesus does is to awaken us to that consciousness. Jesus brings this about by pointing to the moral law, by calling us to a prioritization of ethics and the moral life through the aid of reason, for "pure reason, transcending all limits, is divinity itself—whereby and in accordance with which the very plan of the world is ordered (in John 1). Through reason man learns of his destiny, the unconditional purpose of his life."[109] This purpose of human life is to discover the moral law within and to live a life of virtue based on this moral law. For example, in his reinterpretation of the confrontation between Jesus and the Pharisees when the latter asked the former about his authority to teach publicly in the temple, Hegel has Jesus say to the Pharisees: "Do you really believe that the Deity threw the human species into the world and left it at the mercy of nature without a law, without awareness of the purpose of its existence, and without the possibility of discovering within itself how it might become pleasing to him?"[110] Here again, the tension in the Hegelian dialectic regarding the being of God as a creative Deity emerges: On the one hand, Hegel acknowledges God's existence, but what precisely does Hegel mean by the Deity? It seems that even if such a Deity existed as creator, the most the Deity can be is a watch maker who allows the watch, or in this context creation or nature, to unfold based on an inner, unaided causality.

To turn to the central event of Jesus' passion and crucifixion, Hegel has Jesus explain his passion in exclusively moral terms, that is, Jesus gives his life to awaken humans to the moral law. Hegel's Jesus says:

> This inner law is a law of freedom to which a person submits voluntarily, as though he had imposed it on himself. It is eternal, and in it lies the intimation of immortality. Obliged as I am to awaken men to this law, I, like any responsible shepherd, am prepared to give up my life for my flock. Perhaps you will take my life; but if you do, you will not be robbing me of it, because I offer it freely. You, however, are slaves. You stand yoked by a law imposed on you from without; and this is why you are powerless to wrest yourself free of bondage to your inclinations through self-respect.[111]

Jesus' passion is therefore a consequence of Jesus' dedication to virtue, to his efforts to summon his confreres to the path of virtue that is inbuilt in them, but which, over time, had become clouded owing to Jewish national prejudices and cultic adulterations and ruinations. And the crux of Jesus' eschatological discourse consists in this:

> But now that I depart from you, I am not leaving you behind as though you were orphans; I leave you with a guide within

> yourselves. The seed of goodness that reason has sown inside you I have awakened in each of you, and the memory of my teaching and love for you will sustain in you this spirit of truth and virtue—a spirit which people do not embrace only because they are ignorant of it and do not search for it within their souls. You have become men, able at last to trust in yourselves without having need of external restraints. Once I am no longer with you, your developed moral sense shall be your guide [...]. The Holy Spirit of virtue will keep you from stumbling.[112]

For Hegel, therefore, Jesus, the moralist and virtue ethician has by his historical life awakened in his disciples the consciousness of the moral law, which constituted the sole mission of his coming into the world. Hegel is not concerned that his *Life of Jesus* finds no historical anticipations in the Old Testament, nor any equivalence in the thoughts of the Fathers or early Christian writers. And reducing Christianity to morality leaves Hegel with no qualms. If anything—and very much like Kant—such is the ultimate destiny of Christianity, that is, a moral reawakening of a people lost in religious absolutism.

It is perhaps striking that, like Kant, Hegel has no space for the Resurrection of Jesus as a particular trans-historical event in the subjective person of Jesus of Nazareth, with repercussions for world history, at least for the believing Christian. If the Resurrection is the Father's vindication of the mission of the Son ("You are my Son, today have I begotten you," Heb 5:5), then its existential absence in the Kantian and Hegelian systems is a further indication of the erosion of the unique sense of sonship that Christian orthodoxy understands Jesus as the *Logos* of God to be. The *Aufklärung* paradigm that emerges from both Kant and Hegel, in the final analysis, is one that empties sonship from any exclusive meaning in terms of relationship between the Father and Jesus of Nazareth. Sonship is replaced with the category of a moralist or an ethicist. It will not be completely out of place to conclude that the Hegelian system is a further development of the *Aufklärung's* anthropological rendition of religion, in which the human being not only replaces God, but "God" as Feuerbach logically concludes from the development of Kant to Hegel, essentially becomes a projection of the human mind.[113] Christianity is essentially an endless striving for religious perfectionism that is centered on the self, and in this sense, egocentric. One can make a distinction between, on the one hand, the theocentric faith of orthodox Christianity, and, on the other hand, the anthropocentric faith of the *Aufklärung*, as seen in the preceding paragraphs, embodied in Kant and Hegel. But what precisely emerges when the figure of Christ is reinterpreted as one finds in the *Aufklärung*? Essentially, it amounts to a rejection of the historical uniqueness of the man Jesus of Nazareth, with the ultimate goal of denying Jesus' divinity. This is the challenge to which these philosophical theological reconstructions of Jesus eventually lead, and this is for Ratzinger what constitutes a profound challenge in need of an engaging response.

To Ratzinger, the challenge of these reinterpretations of the figure of Christ lies not so much in apprehension and engagement by these philosophical constructs or reconstructions, critical as such a task might be if theology is to remain in dialogue with theology. The issue, as Ratzinger sees it, resides in the insurmountable gulf that such philosophical theological attempts bring about between the historical Jesus and the Christ of faith, first, in Protestant liberal theology, and later on, in Roman Catholicism. Ratzinger wonders: "But what can faith in Jesus as the Christ possibly mean, in Jesus as the Son of the living God, if the *man* Jesus was so completely different from the picture that the Evangelists painted of him and that the Church, on the evidence of the Gospels, takes as the basis of her preaching?"[114] In effect, reinterpretations of Jesus such as Hegel's *The Life of Jesus* and Kant's *Mere Religion* as shown above, while certainly constituting a remarkable rational achievement in terms of reason's self-understanding of Jesus of Nazareth, fail to explain why the believer must now trust Hegel's reading of the *Gestalt* of Jesus rather than the portraits of the gospel writers.

Such a questioning is necessary for any meaningful evaluation for the added reason that the portraits of Jesus that one finds in the gospels constitutes an integral part of the living faith experience, from the early Christians to the post-modern world. Following the *Aufklärung* and the spirit of modernity that came with it and the subsequent reconstructions of the life of Jesus that followed, Ratzinger points out, "if you read a number of these reconstructions one after the other, you see at once that far from uncovering an icon that has become obscured over time, they are much more like photographs of their authors and the ideals they hold."[115] Thus, the Jesus of Kant is a moralist exclusively bent on calling us toward the fulfillment of the moral law. The Jesus of Hegel is likewise an ethicist, a moral exemplar meant to point to the moral law within, thanks to which the community spirit is the divine spirit. Clearly, what is set aside regarding the person of Jesus is his divine sonship in the sense of a reflection of Jesus' intimate and exclusive relationship and communion with the Father, and secondly, in the sense of Jesus' self-description of himself in a way that marks both Jesus' origin and the destiny of his mission.

But what does Ratzinger make of all these, and how does he feel about these historical reconstructions of the life of Jesus, seen not only in Reimarus but even with others of a later date like Kant, Hegel, and Nietzsche? Ratzinger acknowledges that all these attempts have helped us gain a better insight into the reading of Scripture, as we are able to see the different layers of tradition that helped form and shape the texts. However, Ratzinger maintains that not only has the *Gestalt* of Jesus become progressively obfuscated with every innovative historical reconstruction, but, and most importantly:

> The reconstructions of this Jesus (who could only be discovered by going behind the traditions and sources used by the Evangelists) became more and more incompatible with one another: at one of the spectrum, Jesus was the anti-Roman revolutionary working—though finally failing—to overthrow the ruling powers; at the other end, he was the meek moral teacher who approves everything and unaccountably comes to grief.[116]

To Ratzinger, most of these reconstructions, rather than uncovering Jesus, ended up obscuring him.[117] In other words—and this is perhaps debatable—many of the reconstructions that followed the sense of the historical that came with the *Aufklärung* were much more subjective, and in some cases, psychologizing of Jesus, more "like photographs of their authors and the ideals they hold,"[118] rather than historical accounts, if by history we mean a disengaged reporting of events past. To summarize Ratzinger:

> All these attempts have produced a common result: the impression that we have very little certain knowledge of Jesus and that only at a later stage did faith in his divinity shape the image we have of him. This impression has by now penetrated deeply into the minds of the Christian people at large. This is a dramatic situation for faith, because its point of reference is being placed in doubt: Intimate friendship with Jesus, on which everything depends, is in danger of clutching at thin air.[119]

Thus, Ratzinger is keen on the fact that the historical reading of the figure of Jesus, when driven to extremes in the sense of the mere historical, ends up leaving us only with the personal opinions of the authors. It would seem that even with the best of intentions of Reimarus, Kant, Hegel and other *Aufklärung* figures, the Jesus of Nazareth, the Jesus who walked the dusty roads of first century Palestine refuses to become an object in the historical laboratory of writers who will subject him to the principles of mere reason. Responding to these historical reconstructions of the life of Jesus in the spirit of historical rationality rooted in the *Aufklärung*, Schweitzer incisively writes:

> Jesus of Nazareth will not suffer himself to be modernized as an historical figure. He refuses to be detached from his own time [...]. He will no longer be a Jesus Christ to whom the religion of the present can ascribe its own thought and ideas [...]. Nor will he be a figure which can be made by a popular historical treatment as sympathetic and universally intelligible to the multitude [...]. With the specific characteristics of his notions and his actions, the historical Jesus will be to our time a stranger and an enigma [...]. The mistake was to suppose that Jesus could come to mean more to our time by entering into it as a man like ourselves. But that is

> not possible. First because such a Jesus never existed. Secondly because, although historical knowledge can no doubt introduce greater clarity into an existing spiritual life, it can never call life into existence [...].[120]

And Schweitzer devoutly concludes:

> He (Jesus) comes to us as one unknown, without a name, as of old, by the lakeside, he came to those men who did not know who he was. He says the same words, "Follow me," and sets us to those tasks which he must fulfill in our time. He commands. And to those who hearken to him, whether wise or unwise, he will reveal himself in the peace, the labors, the conflicts and the suffering that they may experience in his fellowship, and as an ineffable mystery they will learn who he is.[121]

I think Ratzinger is very much in the same line of thought with Schweitzer, regarding questions not only surrounding the historical verification of the figure and deeds of Jesus of Nazareth, but even so, the value of such historical reconstructions for the overriding goal of enhancement of faith. Like Schweitzer, Ratzinger does not deny the absolute necessity of this process of historicization of the origins of the Christian faith. Ratzinger acknowledges that the *factum historicum* is not an interchangeable symbolic cipher for biblical faith, but the foundation upon which Christian faith is constructed, for when we proclaim in the Creed, *et incarnatus est*, we implicitly and explicitly acknowledge the entrance of God into history. Thus, Ratzinger maintains, "if we push this history aside, Christian faith as such disappears and is recast as some other religion. So, if history, if facticity in this sense, is an essential dimension of Christian faith, then faith must expose itself to the historical method—indeed, faith itself demands this."[122] This text is reflective of the overriding approach or spirit of Ratzinger toward the *Aufklärung*, which is one in which, while not rejecting the points that the *Aufklärung* seeks to emphasize, in this case, the historical acuteness of the religious claims regarding Jesus of Nazareth as professed by the Church,

Ratzinger, at the same time, does not allow himself to be boxed in by the claims or hypotheses of the *Aufklärer*. Ratzinger is willing to go beyond, and in the process, widens, challenges, and even offers a course correction of some sort. One finds a clear example of this Ratzingerian approach here:

> The historical-critical method—let me repeat—is an indispensable tool, given the structure of the Christian faith. But we need to add two points. This method is a fundamental dimension of exegesis, but it does not exhaust the interpretive task for someone who sees the biblical writings as a single corpus of Holy Scripture inspired by God [...]. For someone who considers himself directly addressed by the Bible today, the method's first limit is that by its very nature it has to leave the biblical word in the past. It is a *historical* method, and that means that it investigates the then-current context of events in which the texts originated[...]. To the extent that it remains true to itself, the historical method not only has to investigate the biblical word as a thing of the past, but also has to let it remain in the past. It can glimpse points of contact with the present and it can try to apply the biblical word to the present; the only thing it cannot do is make it into something present *today*—that would be overstepping its bounds. Its very precision in interpreting the reality of the past is both its strength and its limit.[123]

Certainly, such a recognition of the limits of the principle of history will definitely not sit well with some of the devotees to the *Aufklärung* who read human rationality as the final arbiter in the establishment of truth claims. Whatever position one adopts, it is difficult not to see the point that Ratzinger is driving home here, which is that history alone is insufficient to get to the deeper meaning and value of biblical texts. This is all the more because even though history studies the words of Scripture as human words, at the bottom of it, there is something to these human words that prevent them from becoming *merely human*. That something is the voice of God that human words serve as a channel or medium of expression. In fact, *Dei Verbum* renders a succinct description of this interplay between Divine and human words in the drama of revelation, to which Scripture attests to: "In the process of composition of the sacred books God chose and employed human agents, using their own powers and faculties, in such a way that they wrote as authors in the true sense, and yet God acted in and through them, directing the content entirely and solely as he willed."[124] In this light, the question of God, of faith, cannot be excluded or set aside for the purposes of historical reading of the text. In other words, faith is an integral part of the historical process.

According to Ratzinger, therefore, these enlightened reconstructions of Jesus that set aside his divine Sonship together with the New Testament witness to the divinity of Christ, leave one with the impression that one can have little certain knowledge about the historical Jesus of Nazareth who is simultaneously the Christ of faith: "This impression," Ratzinger opines, "has by now penetrated deeply into the minds of the Christian people at large. This is a dramatic situation for faith, because its point of reference is being placed in doubt."[125] Thus, the scientific research into the *Gestalt* of Jesus as Son of God made man has had the effect of obscuring the portrait of the real Jesus understood by orthodox Christianity as the Jesus of the Gospels, whose center of gravity is his communion with the Father. Without Jesus' Sonship, which can only be in relation to the Father and hence guarantee Jesus' divinity, one cannot understand Jesus at all, Ratzinger maintains. And it is only from this communion with the Father, this reality of Jesus being Son, that Jesus makes himself present even to us today.[126] Sonship is therefore the unique and defining understanding of the historical Jesus of Nazareth, for this holds both Jesus' divinity and the fact of his Incarnation at the fullness of time (Gal 4:4), in a stable, mutually correlative relationship.

Along these lines of the uniqueness of Jesus' Sonship with the Father, Benedict XVI writes in relation to the teaching ministry of Jesus: "Jesus' teaching is not the product of human learning, of whatever kind. It originates from immediate contact with the Father, from 'face-to-face' dialogue—from the vision of the one who rests close to the Father's heart. It is the Son's word. Without this inner grounding, his teaching would be pure presumption."[127] In other words, for Benedict XVI, the *Gestalt* of Jesus of Nazareth can only be understood through the lenses of Jesus' unique Sonship with the Father. Jesus' bond with the Father is the defining hermeneutical framework that alone does justice to who Jesus is. Benedict XVI writes:

> This is the context in which we need to read the conclusion of the prologue to John's Gospel: "No one has ever seen God; it is the only Son, who is nearest to the Father's heart, who has made him known" (Jn 1:18) [...]. He lives before the face of God, not just as a friend, but as a Son; he lives in the most intimate unity with the Father.[128]

To Benedict XVI, therefore, not only is sonship the defining starting point in understanding the divine origins of Jesus, but, in addition, Jesus' sonship is indispensable if one must understand the testimony of the New Testament regarding the words, deeds, sufferings, and glory of Jesus: "This is the central point, and if we leave it out of account, we fail to grasp what the figure of Jesus is really all about, so that it becomes self-contradictory and, in the end, unintelligible."[129] The challenge that the New Testament witness poses to the reader is whether one is prepared to accept the reality that this Jesus of Nazareth is different, that his being is grounded in something entirely different—namely, that of seeing and knowing face-to-face the Father, in an intimate and exclusive manner.

Benedict XVI further argues that the prayer moments of Jesus are a testimony to Jesus' unique sonship. Jesus' nights spent in prayer alone with the Father, Benedict maintains, give us a glimpse into Jesus' filial existence. Jesus' prayer moments show the Son in conversation with the Father, so much so that "his human consciousness and will, his human soul, is taken up into that exchange, and in this way human 'praying' is able to become a participation in this filial communion with the Father."[130] Thus, Jesus' words in the Gospels regarding the Father owe to the fact of his Sonship. Jesus is able to speak the way he does—*Abba, Papa*—which was seemingly impossible in the Old Testament, only because of the new form of intimacy that Jesus was expressing about his communion with the Father that he alone possesses as the Son of the Father.[131] To Ratzinger, it is the realization of Jesus' unique Sonship with the Father that made the early Christians preserve Jesus' more intimate usage of the Aramaic, *Abba*, *Papa*, in its original tongue.[132] In this sense of divine Sonship and intimacy, the Christological dimension, that is, the mystery of the Son as revealer of the Father, is therefore present in all that Jesus does and says.[133] In other words, not only is the Sonship of Jesus a mirror into Jesus' intimacy with the Father, but it is likewise indicative of Jesus' self-description.

Sonship therefore asserts Jesus' divinity and his unicity. Jesus is the eternal Son of the eternal Father, and only within this hermeneutical framework can we arrive at the right understanding of the *Gestalt* of Jesus. Only within this framework of Sonship do we discern the truth claims of the New Testament in their historical and theological significance. And while this intimacy of *Abba* distinguishes Jesus' relationship with the Father from those of all other humans, it is not meant to be so in an exclusive sense. On the contrary, Jesus' intimacy, as Ratzinger maintains, is designed to include all others in Jesus' relationship with the Father: "It wishes to incorporate them, as it were, in its own kind of attitude to God, so that with Jesus and in him they can say '*Abba*' to God just as he does; no set distance shall separate them any longer."[134] Thus, to become a disciple of Jesus is to enter with Jesus into the intimacy of the Father.

To Ratzinger, the intimacy that Jesus enjoys as Son of the Father is a pointer to the total relationality of Jesus' existence. Jesus is a man whose essence is to be from and to be for, in total relativity with the absolute.[135] This Son-Christology, therefore, highlights the identity of work and being, of deed and person, in Jesus of Nazareth. Jesus as Son keeps back nothing from himself, but gives himself completely in his work.[136] There is no wedge between person and work, for Son means precisely that—namely, one who flows from the Father, one begotten by the Father, and the Father's gift to the world who completely offers himself to the Father in his work of redeeming the world. Ratzinger writes that, to this extent, "there is an 'ontologization,' a reaching back to the being behind the 'phenomenal' character of the mere happening."[137] What this implies is that at bottom, Jesus' teaching is himself, and as Ratzinger points out, "he as a totality is Son, Word, and mission. His activity reaches right down to the ground of being and is one with it. And it is precisely in this unity of being and doing that his special character lies."[138] In other words, the whole experience of Jesus is such that Jesus' being itself is service, a service for the world, a service of reconciling the world to God and to one another in a new radicalized and universalized understanding of mutual, inclusive love. Along these lines, Ratzinger concludes:

> And precisely because this being, as a totality, is nothing but service, it is sonship. To that extent it is not until this point that the Christian revaluation of values reaches its final goal; only here does it become fully clear that he who surrenders himself completely to service for others, to complete selflessness and self-emptying, literally becomes these things—that this very person is the true man, the man of the future, the coinciding of man and God.[139]

To speak of Jesus as Son not only brings to the fore a Sonship Christology, but likewise a service-ship Christology, for that, to Ratzinger, is what constitutes the central nexus of the person of Jesus, as a man whose intrinsic being is to be for others. Son therefore means an identity of service and being. In this Ratzingerian sense, the being of Jesus does not remain static, a mythical ontology, but is profound actuality in the concreteness of the service of love in which Jesus offers himself on the cross for the salvation of the world. "Jesus is his work,"[140] Ratzinger tersely declares, thereby capturing the core of the whole concept of the intertwining of Son and Service Christologies.

Granted this reading of the *Gestalt* of Christ and the New Testament witness to it, one can hereby draw the conclusion that the de-divinization of the *Gestalt* of Christ that emerged with the *Aufklärung*, as seen above in Kant and Hegel, and the subsequent reconstructions of the figure of Jesus and the New Testament in the nineteenth and twentieth centuries, in a sense marked a rejection of the existential implications of the Christologies of Sonship and Service-ship that is captured in the formula "Son," as detailed above. In other words, for the New Testament and the Christ portrayed in it to become essentially moral tools wanting in the religious dimension as a necessary hermeneutical framework for its interpretation to hold sway, the ontological Christology of Sonship had to be set aside by the *Aufklärung*. To Ratzinger, therefore, in spite of its best of intentions, these existential, pragmatic and phenomenological readings of Christ cannot suffice for Christology: "They do not reach deep enough, because they leave the realm of real 'being' untouched."[141] In other words, they miss the essential aspect of the person of Christ around which the whole New Testament is built, which is this man, Jesus of Nazareth, the unique Son of God whose mission in the world is his very being—that is, who Jesus is, is what Jesus is.

In this light, one clearly sees that an essential missing link in the *Aufklärung's* presentation of the *Gestalt* of Christ, while not overlooking the defects of ethical reductionism of the man Jesus of Nazareth, resides heavily in the *Aufklärung's* rejection of classical metaphysical epistemology. And as McGrath likewise attests, with the *Aufklärung*, the traditional Christian understanding of Christ that largely took on a formal shape with the orthodox Christological councils based on a language of ontology was called into question, with the aid of critical presuppositions and methods.[142] Classical orthodoxy as expressed in Nicaea, Constantinople, Ephesus, and Chalcedon had built the Christological dogmas on metaphysical language. The *Aufklärung* contested these metaphysical Christologies of orthodoxy, tilting the scale to the question of the relationship between history and revelation.[143] It is plausible that his rejection of Greek ontology as a philosophical framework helps explain in large measure Ratzinger's biting critique in his Regensburg lecture for what he calls the attempts at dehellenization of the Christian faith. Speaking of these dehellenization attempts, Ratzinger says:

> This inner rapprochement between Biblical faith and Greek philosophical inquiry was an event of decisive importance not only from the standpoint of the history of religions, but also from that of world history—it is an event which concerns us even today. Given this convergence, it is not surprising that Christianity, despite its origins and some significant developments in the East, finally took on its historically decisive character in Europe.[144]

In other words, Ratzinger reads in the synthesis between biblical faith and Greek philosophy, a providential meeting point that not only shaped and provided Christian orthodoxy with a solid framework, but likewise, with a decisive implication for Europe, the ancient heartland of Christianity. In this reading of things, Greek metaphysics was therefore essential in communicating the orthodox positions of biblical faith, placing biblical faith in its debt. But as Ratzinger sees it, the process of dehellenization not only seeks to sever this bond between philosophy and theology, but is likewise active in its aggression to exclude metaphysics as a vehicle for the communication of dogmatic truths.

Ratzinger identifies three movements or stages that exemplify this rejection of Greek philosophy and the metaphysical help that it provided to Christianity: Firstly, the sixteenth century Reformation, in which, to Ratzinger's reading, the reformers saw the rapport between philosophy and theology as basing the faith on an alien system of thought. *Sola scriptura* was precisely set against this.[145] Luther's *sola scriptura,* which became the position of the Reformation as a religious movement, bore the markings of an outright rejection of the place of philosophy in understanding and talking about the Christian faith. *Sola scriptura* was clearly a rejection of the framework of philosophy that had hitherto nurtured the nascent faith right up to the scholastic era.

The second stage of dehellenization was with Kant: "When Kant states that he needed to set thinking aside in order to make room for faith, he carried this program forward with a radicalism that the Reformers could never have foreseen."[146] Kant's *Critique of Practical Reason* essentially made faith a postulate of practical reason with no access to the entirety of reality. The consequence of this Kantian decision to sever the link between the God of faith and the God of the philosophers is seen in the liberal theologies of the nineteenth and twentieth centuries, that essentially sought to rewrite both the life of Christ and the traditional interpretations of the New Testament, more or less after the pattern of Kant and Hegel as shown above. At Regensburg, Ratzinger returned to his 1959 Inaugural Lecture, as his significant response to this process of the modern, *Aufklärung* reading of Christ, that essentially sought to create an insurmountable wedge within the distinction that Pascal had made between the God of philosophers and the God of Abraham, Isaac, and Jacob. Synthesizing this *Aufklärung* reading of the *Gestalt* of Christ, Ratzinger writes that "Jesus was said to have put an end to worship in favor of morality. In the end he was presented as the father of humanitarian moral message."[147] Ratzinger sees these reconstructions as attempts "to bring Christianity back into harmony with modern reason, liberating it, that is to say, from seemingly philosophical and theological elements, such as faith in Christ's divinity and the triune God."[148] And this is clearly evident, as seen above, in Kant's *Religion* and Hegel's *Jesus*. Ratzinger goes on to say:

> Behind this thinking lies the modern self-limitation of reason, classically expressed in Kant's "Critiques," but in the meantime further radicalized by the impact of the natural sciences. This modern concept of reason is based, to put it briefly, on a synthesis between Platonism (Cartesianism) and empiricism, a synthesis confirmed by the success of technology.[149]

In this sense, Ratzinger sees a correlation between the *Aufklärung's* position of the mathematical, intrinsic rationality of matter in terms of necessary causality, as shown in the section on *Logos* and creative Reason above, and the newfound necessity of presenting the *Gestalt* of Christ from anything other than from concepts such as sonship, that maintain Christ's divinity. The only truths that must be considered as scientifically true are those within the limits of *mere* matter, and nature therefore had to be exploited to prove this self-sufficiency and rationality through the process of human experimentation. Given this worldview, theology, philosophy, and other arts are forced to conform themselves to this enlightenment canon of scientificity. Nonetheless, Ratzinger argues, such a "scientific" mindset naturally excludes God, or at least the God of historical revelation, for since God cannot fit into a chemical reaction or test tube, God appears unscientific or pre-scientific. Consequently, says Ratzinger, "we are faced with a reduction of the radius of science and reason, one which needs to be questioned."[150] And to Ratzinger—and one sees this clearly in the works on Jesus that emerged from the spirit of the *Aufklärung*—these attempts at rendering theology "scientific" end up reducing Christianity to a meager shell of its earlier self.

The third and final stage that Ratzinger identifies in this process of wedging reason from faith is what he refers to as cultural pluralism.

This position holds that the synthesis arrived at by the early Church between Greek philosophy and biblical faith was simply an initial process of inculturation that ought not to have any lasting and binding effect. Other non-Western cultures, as they come into contact with Christianity, have to return to the simple message of the New Testament and enculturate it anew.[151] Ratzinger sees this position as not only false but also coarse and imprecise. He argues that the New Testament was written in Greek and will forever bear the Greek spirit, a spirit that had already come to maturity even in the development of the Old Testament. While Ratzinger recognizes the fact that there are elements in the early Church that need not be integrated into all cultures, he is of the opinion that "nonetheless, the fundamental decisions made about the relationship between faith and use of human reason are part of the faith itself; they are developments consonant with the nature of faith itself."[152] In other words, reason is not an added coloring to the nature of faith, but belongs to the inner dynamics of faith. To believe, therefore, is not antithetical to rationality. Kant did not have to shut the door on reason in order to make room for faith. On the contrary, Kant would have seen that faith widens the potentials latent in reason; it opens the breadth of reason beyond the limits of the scientific that Ratzinger decries in his Regensburg lecture. And given that the religious phenomenon is always with us, a view of rationality that blankets out religious faith could very well bring about an existential schizophrenia in which the human person is torn in two essential directions of faith and reason that now appear—at least in the *Aufklärung* reading of things—to be irreconcilable.

Ratzinger realizes that not all will agree to this proposition of the intrinsic nature of reason to faith, especially given that the *Aufklärung* battle cry of *sapere aude* certainly included even if not limited to, a rejection or rebellion against dogmatic religious faith. Ratzinger therefore, points out that his argument that Luther,[153] Kant and the broader spirit of the *Aufklärung* did not have to shut the door on reason or on the God of philosophy in order to make room for the God of faith, does not constitute a turning back of the clock to a pre-*Aufklärung* era. Ratzinger insists that he has no such intentions of rewinding the clock to a pre-*Aufklärung* era. If anything, as Ratzinger explains:

> This attempt [that is, Ratzinger's explanation of the dehellenization trend], painted with broad strokes, at a critique of modern reason from within has nothing to do with putting the clock back to the time before the Enlightenment and rejecting the insights of the modern age. The positive aspects of modernity are to be acknowledged unreservedly: we are all grateful for the marvelous possibilities that it has opened up for mankind and for the progress in humanity that has been granted us [...]. The intention here is not one of retrenchment or negative criticism, but of broadening our concept of reason and its application.[154]

In this light, *logos* is therefore broader and deeper than mere positivistic rationality. And this is the sense in which Ratzinger's theological metaphor of the *Logos* as Son enters into the fray of the *Aufklärung* reconstructions of the *Gestalt* of Jesus, pushing them and urging them to open themselves to the broader applications and implications of reason. To all the attempts at moralizing the figure of Christ and hence the central core of the New Testament—a moralizing that ends up rejecting the rational character of the dogmas of religious faith that is not reduced to ethics—Ratzinger insists, in clear rebuttal of the ethical reductionism of the *Aufklärung*'s *Gestalt* of Jesus, the New Testament, and the Christian faith, that:

> Being Christian is not the result of an ethical choice or a lofty idea, but the encounter with an event, a person, which gives life a new horizon and a decisive direction. Saint John's Gospel describes that event in these words: "God so loved the world that he gave his only Son, that whoever believes in him should [...] have eternal life" (Jn 3:16).[155]

This realization of Christianity as an encounter with a person certainly goes against the grain of Christianity as a moral religion, as espoused by the *Aufklärung*. And while Ratzinger does not refute the ethical demands of being a Christian in terms of a conversion to the new life in Christ, he certainly does not believe that the central nexus of Christianity lies in the ethical postulates that must be put forth as Christian narratives and dogmas are reinterpreted in the spirit of the *Aufklärung*. In this light, Ratzinger believes that the metaphor of *Logos* as Son offers the moral reductionism of the *Gestalt* of Jesus and the Christian faith—with the resultant consequence of the eschewing of reason in order to make room for faith—a possibility of entry into a more dynamic communion of love and knowledge. To Ratzinger, these two aspects capture the essential dynamics of the uniqueness that entered history with the Son of the Father.

Ratzinger points out, when commenting on the messianic *Jubelruf* of Mt 11:25–27, that knowing always involves some sort of equality, for "every process of coming to know something includes in one form or another a process of assimilation, a sort of inner unification of the knower and the known."[156] For the Son to say he knows the Father therefore, presupposes some communion with the Father, some oneness of being with the Father. Thus, the perfect communion of knowledge between the Son and the Father is likewise a perfect communion in being between the Son and the Father. As Ratzinger writes, "unity in knowing is possible only because it is unity in being."[157] In this sense of the dual unity of knowledge and being, the will of Jesus becomes the will of the Father. And the will of Jesus is that his followers unite their wills with the Father's will as well, thus becoming sons and daughters of the Father.[158] Thus knowledge, being, and will are the three defining aspects that explain the Sonship of Jesus of Nazareth.

Given the understanding that the will of the Son is to draw his followers into the filial knowledge of the Father, there is an opening here that clearly brings to the fore the limits of the *Aufklärung* readings of the *Gestalt* of Christ. Such is the case because the moral intellectualism of Kant or Hegel, for example, restrict the phenomenon of Jesus to knowledge only, leaving out being and will. In other words, the *Aufklärung* reading of the *Gestalt* of Christ makes Christ an exclusive prerogative of the intellectual experts, inaccessible to simple souls who allow their wills to be taken up by Christ into the will of the Father. For while the object of the intellect is truth, the object of the will is the good, and that is the locus of concrete action and activity. In other words, the *Aufklärung* versions of the life of Jesus and the biblical reconstructions of the quest for the historical Jesus that modeled itself on the spirit of the *Aufklärung* end up with a Jesus that is suitable only for the academicians who must, through employing their reason, arrive at self-sufficient moral truths latent within them, that render the whole experience of the being, knowledge, and will of the man Jesus of Nazareth if not irrelevant at least superfluous. Ratzinger decries these exotic interpretations of Christ, with somewhat provocative texts from the First Letter of St. Paul to the Corinthians:

> Their great learning distracts them from simply gazing upon the whole, upon the reality of God as he reveals himself—for people who know so much about the complexity of the issues, it seems, just cannot be so simple. Paul describes this same experience and then goes on to reflect upon it: "For the word of the cross is folly to those who are perishing, but to us who are being saved it is the power of God." For it is written, "I will destroy the wisdom of the wise, and the cleverness of the clever I will thwart" (Is 29:14). [...] For God chose what is foolish in the world to shame the wise [...].[159]

It might be that the gauntlet thrown by Ratzinger is the daring to embrace not just the aspect of rational knowledge regarding Christ, but more importantly the aspects of Christ's being as Son which entail an opening of a hitherto unknown experience of the being of the Father, and especially the communion of wills that follows such a unity. In precis, therefore, one could say that the issue with the *Aufklärung*'s reading of the figure of Christ is not so much its emphasis or more precisely, its moral reductionism, but that in pushing for an absolute moral or ethical reading of the historical revelation of God in Christ Jesus, it excluded other aspects. That is, the *Aufklärung*, in its quest for a moral Christ, narrowed the picture and hence, diminished the capacity of reason's greatness to go beyond in comprehending and apprehending the mere rational. In effect, the *Aufklärung*'s exclusive painting of a moral Christ, based on a rational faith, ended up closing in on itself. The *Aufklärung* became an autonomous system that severed itself from all other aspects of the reality of the life of Christ. It is in this sense that the theological metaphor of *Logos* as Son becomes handy, for Sonship, as Ratzinger repeatedly points out, involves relationality.[160] And such a relationship can only come about in a mutuality of openness of wills. To sum up in the light of the dialogical spirit between the God of philosophy and the God of theology that Ratzinger advocates, the challenge of the Ratzingerian metaphor of the *Logos* as Son, as the proper hermeneutical key to understanding both Christ and the New Testament, would be to move beyond ethical formulas into the reality of a Jesus who is flesh and blood. And the first invitation given by this Jesus is not for us to consider where we stand in a moral report card, but primarily to enter into an I-Thou intimate friendship. Only from this friendship, this communion of wills, can one properly understand the grandeur of the new moral life that the *Aufklärer* somewhat rightly emphasize.

Summarily, there emerges from Ratzinger's treatment of the *Logos* as Son the sense of uniqueness that characterizes the relationship between the Son and the Father. In other words, Jesus Christ, as unique Son of the Father, is the only One who fully knows the Father. Jesus is the One who has seen the Father face to face. And only Jesus can fully reveal the Father. Sonship is therefore not a fluid metaphor, as is wont to be perceived or characterized by some of the *Aufklärung*, as shown above. In the final analysis, the quest for humanity to "see" God which largely inspired the making of graven images, a quest given voice to by Philip, has now been met in the Sonship of Jesus, for to have seen Jesus is to have seen the Father, given that Jesus and the Father are one (Jn 14:9). In this sense, Jesus' Sonship brings about a Christological hermeneutic of Father-Son, in other words, a Christology of relationship, to the extent that the Father is Father only because of the Son, and the Son is Son only because of the Father. At the heart of the Christology of the Son, of the nature of Jesus as Son, lies relationality. And as shown above, to Ratzinger, the overriding goal of this Christology of Sonship is to invite all into the same union between the Father and the Son, to be sons and daughters in the Son, through whose being all can enter into a relationship with the Father.

Given this unicity of this Father-Son relationship, one can understand why for Ratzinger, Jesus of Nazareth is not only the unique, but the definitive, savior of the world. In Jesus, the "surplus" of God's love for humanity reaches its apogee in the sense that to be Son is intrinsically tied to God's "surplus" mission of love (Jn 3:16). To be Son is to be sent by the Father (Jn 7:16), out of love for the world. This leaves one with a sense of a mission-Christology, in which the person of Jesus is viewed primarily through the lenses of his mission in the world. In other words, mission defines person and person defines mission. One could therefore describe the person of Jesus with the language of a Christology of 'missioning,' for only in the "work" of Jesus do we finally get to the crux of his being, of who Jesus is, that is, the Savior of the world. To encounter Jesus is to encounter, concretely, not just the being of the Son of God, but salvation in the flesh. The whole nature of Jesus is salvific. When Peter says in Acts 10:38 that Jesus went about doing good, this description by Peter captures not only the function of Jesus, but the being of Jesus, for his very being brought with it goodness, healing, and salvation. In the final analysis, the Christology of the Son is a Christology of divinization of human beings. Humanity is able to call God "Father" because Jesus has opened his unique relationship with the Father to all of humanity.

4.3 *Logos* as Person: Ratzinger's Engagement with the *Aufklärung*'s Pragmatic Personalism

While the question of the *Logos* as creative Reason points to Ratzinger's theology of creation, and the question of the *Logos* as Son pertains to Ratzinger's philosophical Christology, the question concerning the *Logos* as Person considered in this chapter centers on Ratzinger's theological anthropology. Given these multiple Ratzingerian representations, in writing about Ratzinger's Christology of the *Logos* as person, Christopher Collins, S.J., points out that the pivotal moment when the metaphor of the *logos* takes on the characterization of person begins with the prologue of the Gospel of John the Evangelist. Collins writes:

> In this one pivotal moment, then, as salvation history and philosophy meet on a scriptural field, a new reality emerges. By the church's reception of the figure of Christ as the *Logos* itself in the flesh, all of creation and human history begin to be reinterpreted in light of this "*verbum*" who is actually communicated as a person.[161]

Logos is therefore not only creative Reason, but a word that is spoken, and in the process of this speech becomes a person. In the *Logos* of Christ, the Person, personhood thereby, becomes the center of humanity, as Benedict XVI writes in *Spe Salvi*:

> At the very moment when the Magi, guided by the star, adored Christ the new King, astrology came to an end because the stars were now moving in the orbit determined by Christ [...]. It is not the elemental spirits of the universe, the laws of matter, which ultimately govern the world and mankind, but a personal God governs the stars, that is, the universe; it is not the laws of matter and of evolution that have the final say, but reason, will, love—a Person. And if we know this Person and he knows us, then truly the inexorable power of material elements no longer has the last word; we are not slaves of the universe and of its laws, we are free.[162]

And because *Logos* is person, one can enter into communication with the *Logos*. One can enter into friendship with the *Logos*, into intimacy, an intimacy that gives meaning to one's life and shapes one's life in a more humane direction. And it is the *Logos*, the *prosōpon*, the Person of Christ, who calls humans into this intimacy of a dialogical encounter, by universalizing and renewing the faith of Israel to include all the nations and peoples of the world.[163] To meet the Person of Christ, therefore, is to meet the concrete reality of what personhood entails, to allow the self to be caught up into an understanding wherein all persons share a common bond of mutual love, mission, and destiny to the Father's house.

Turning to the context of the *Aufklärung*, it should be noted that for Ratzinger, the *Aufklärung's* understanding of the person, that is, its philosophical and theological anthropology, is a logical offshoot of its understanding of the autonomy of nature and matter, based on what might be described as its reductionistic view of science as that which is mathematically provable. Ratzinger declares in the Regensburg lecture:

> If science as a whole is this and this alone, then it is man himself who ends up being reduced, for the specifically human

> questions about our origin and destiny, the questions raised by religion and ethics, then have no place within the purview of collective reason as defined by "science" so understood, and must thus be relegated to the realm of the subjective. The subjective then decides, on the basis of his experiences, what he considers tenable in matters of religion, and the subjective "conscience" becomes the sole arbiter of what is ethical.[164]

It appears that Ratzinger is making the argument that to follow the logic of the autonomy of nature, of matter and of causality, eventually produces a relativistic kind of person. Such is the case because one cannot affirm the autonomy of the cosmos as an inner necessity admitting of no extrinsic causality, while simultaneously claiming some form of heteronomous guiding principle when it concerns the human person. In other words, when creation is not the work of creative Reason, of the *Logos*, as seen in the first theological usage of *logos* above, then what remains of the human being is essentially an ideologically conditioned and relativistic person.

In other words, to arrive at a proper understanding of the person from the point of view of the *Aufklärung*, any talk of creative Reason and *Logos* must be set aside. Granted the autonomy of nature and the newfound scientism of science, as Ratzinger describes it, as seen in the treatment of *Logos* as Son, the reality that now stands before the enlightened man and woman is that which Nietzsche describes as a mechanistic world based on the will to power in nature, a world in which causality is merely a psychological necessity because one finds it impossible to conceive of an event divorced from intent. Creation appears as "selection and finishing of the thing selected. This is the essential thing in every act of the will."[165] The idea of creation is an idea that came from the human being because humans could not bring themselves to understand the inner necessity of nature: "It was my hand that threw the dice,"[166] Nietzsche writes. To Nietzsche, this mechanistic world in which nature and science are absolutes, is certainly a triumph over a world of creative Reason, of *Logos*, and of the human being made in the image and likeness of creative Reason:

> It [mechanistic world] evidently has a good conscience on its side; and no science believes it can achieve progress and success except with the aid of mechanistic procedures. Everyone knows these procedures: one leaves "reason" and "purpose" out of account as far as possible, one shows that, given sufficient time, anything can evolve out of anything else, and one does not conceal a malicious chuckle when "apparent intention" in the fate of a plant or an egg yolk is once again traced back to pressure and stress.[167]

In effect, the scientific and mechanistic mindset of the cosmos or of nature produces a scientific and mechanistic human being, to the extent that the human being in the grand scheme of things simply becomes, to use Nietzschean terminology, an "analogy" to the great event of the physicists.[168] The human being is essentially submitted to the same principles of atomism which expresses "the calculability of the world, the expressibility of all events in formulas."[169] The human being is hereby reduced to norms of a logical-psychical world, especially as the idea of the transcendental dimension of the person made in the image and likeness of God with an eternal soul is jettisoned:

> Granted that the "soul" is an attractive and mysterious idea which philosophers have rightly abandoned only with reluctance—perhaps that which they have since learned to put in its place is even more attractive, even more mysterious. The human body, in which the most distant and most recent past of all organic development again becomes living and corporeal, through which and over and beyond which a tremendous inaudible stream seems to flow: the body is a more astonishing idea than the old "soul."[170]

Apparently, an "enlightened" world-view does not have room for the human soul. And once the reality of soul is done away with, the spiritual dimension that defines humans as images of God must be set aside. All that is left now is biological bodylines, and even this is not spared by the mechanistic and scientific process of the absolute atomism of all reality:

> Conversely, even those philosophers and religious teachers who had the most compelling ground in their logic and piety to consider their bodies a deception (and, indeed, as a deception, overcome and done away with) could not help acknowledge the foolish fact that the body has not gone away; of which the strangest witnesses are to be found partly in Paul, partly in the Vedanta philosophy. But what, after all, does strength of belief mean? It could still be a very foolish belief! This should be reflected on.[171]

And as Nietzsche shows, once the soul and the body are rejected, the next step is the rejection of God who is believed to have been the creator of the human being endowed with bodily and spiritual principles.

However, without the creative *Logos* in the picture, self-serving ideologies govern the human being. And very early in his papacy, Benedict XVI called attention to this: "We are not some casual and meaningless product of evolution. Each of us is the result of a thought of God. Each of us is willed, each of us is loved, each of us is necessary."[172] Humans are not the products of haphazard mistakes or forces, but a divine project from a creating Intelligence. Humans are willed. Humans are a fruit of divine love. And later on, in his Message for the World Day of Peace, January 1, 2007, Ratzinger further analyzes the current crisis of human ecology:

> Many of our contemporaries actually deny the existence of a specific human nature and thus open the door to the most extravagant interpretations of what essentially constitutes a human being. Here too clarity is necessary: a "weak" vision of the person, which would leave room for every conception, even the most bizarre, only apparently favors peace. In reality, it hinders authentic dialogue and opens the way to authoritarian impositions, ultimately leaving the person defenseless and, as a result, easy prey to oppression and violence.[173]

With the technological mindset of the scientific everything becomes possible, to the extent that the human mind can think it up and science can bring it about. The autonomy of reason has therefore moved beyond the mere ethical realm into the anthropological, so much so that what it means to be human in terms of our nature and the form which such a nature takes can no longer be spoken of objectively. Ratzinger sees a link between what he characterizes as a crisis of personhood with the ecological crisis that has gathered so much attention today. Benedict XVI writes in his World Day of Peace message for 2010: "It should be evident that the ecological crisis cannot be viewed in isolation from other related questions, since it is closely linked to the notion of development itself and our understanding of man in his relationship to others and to the rest of creation."[174] Thus, while rightfully paying attention to the crisis of environmental ecology, it is necessary to pay attention as well to the crisis of human ecology that renders uncertain not only the nature of the human being in the spiritual and bodily forms, but even more importantly the challenges that such questions raise regarding the theology of creation, the theology of the purpose of the human being in the cosmos, and eschatology, the destiny of the human being. These might constitute some of the related questions, one would imagine, that Ratzinger has in mind, in the text just cited.

To Ratzinger, every generation is called to respond to the question posed by philosophical anthropology: What is the human being? What does it mean for us to be human? The question of what a human being is, Ratzinger points out, is a task for each and every one, a task that appeals to our freedom: "We must each search into our human-beingness afresh and decide who or what we want to be as humans. In our own lives each of us must answer, whether he or she wants to or not, the question about being human."[175] In this sense, the rightful place to begin any meaningful engagement with the philosophical anthropology of the scientific, mechanistic and autonomous person that emerges from Nietzsche is the book of Genesis 2:4–9. There, one finds the essential characteristics of who the human being is and hence can arrive at an anthropological theology that finds its apogee in Christology.

To begin with, Genesis says that the human being is from the earth, from dust (Gen 2:7). This is both consoling and humbling, Ratzinger maintains, for it tells us that the human being is not God, the human being did not make the self, and the human being did not make the universe. In other words, Genesis refutes the thought of natural necessity and its radical evolutionism that often accompanies it. Genesis tells us that the human being, like all things living, is destined for death. But Genesis also tells us another truth, which Ratzinger describes as "consoling," which is, the human being is not a demon or an evil spirit, even though that might occasionally appear to be the case. One can readily think of the two world wars of the twentieth century, the Holocaust, the Rwandan genocide, Mao's communist revolution, the killing occurring in the Democratic Republic of Congo, or more recently, in the English-speaking region of Cameroon, the reality of the Latin adage, *homo homini lupus*. But as Ratzinger points out, "the human being has not been formed from negative forces, but has been fashioned from God's good earth."[176] This is the sense in which we can assert and understand the ontological goodness of the human being and the assertion that evil in all its forms is a deprivation, an absence of that creative goodness that ought to be there.

Going further, in a world still fractured by racism and ethnocentrism in all its moods and tenses, Ratzinger asserts that the Genesis declaration that all humans are from the earth points to a sameness and an equality that transcends all racial pathologies: "Despite every distinction that culture and history have brought about, it is still true that we are, in the last resort, the same [...]. Emperor and beggar, master and slave, are all ultimately one and the same person, taken from the earth and destined to return to the same earth."[177] Irrespective of all the lows and highs of history, the human being stays the same—that is, earth. The human being is formed from the earth and destined to return to earth. In this light, says Ratzinger, "the unity of the whole human race becomes immediately apparent: We are all from only *one* earth."[178] In the final analysis, humans are not fundamentally different. There certainly exists accidental differences of color, space, class, status, and more, but the basic humanness in all human beings is the same, taken from the earth and destined to return to it, as the antiphon for the imposition of ashes in the Ash Wednesday liturgy reminds all. And to cite Ratzinger again, "there is only *one* humanity in the many human beings. The Bible says a decisive "no" to all racism and to every human division."[179] In the face of so many racially-charged and ethnic divisions today, this anthropological theology of Genesis takes on a greater urgency.

But in addition to the three aspects already highlighted—that humans are creatures and not gods; that human beings are not from evil spirits or demons; and that human beings share an equality of nature in their common origin as beings taken from God's one earth—Ratzinger highlights a fourth aspect that is crucial in completing the mosaic of the theological anthropology of Genesis: Human beings are made in the image and likeness of God (Gen 1:26–27). While taken from the earth, God has breathed his breath into the nostrils of the body that was formed from the earth. Ratzinger writes: "In the human being heaven and earth touch one another. In the human being God enters into his creation; the human being is directly related to God. The human being is called by him."[180] The human being is therefore the being called, known, and loved by God. This aspect of the relationship with God provides a deeper foundation of the unity of the human race, in that God calls all human beings into a relationship with God, irrespective of their class, color, or status. Thus:

> Human life stands under God's special protection, because each human being, however wretched or exalted he or she may be, however sick or suffering, however good-for-nothing or important, whether born or unborn, whether incurably ill or radiant with health—each one bears God's breath in himself or herself, each one is God's image. This is the deepest reason for the inviolability of human dignity, and upon it is founded ultimately every civilization.[181]

In this sense, the intrinsic dignity of every human being is based exclusively on the fact that every human being is a thoughtful creation of God. Absent this, the human being risks being perceived from a utilitarian perspective. And this is the context in which the survival of the fittest mentality can set in, in which the strong trample on the weak, asserting themselves and clearing whatever happens to stand in their way. Is this not in reality the kind of person that emerges from Nietzsche's *Übermensch* in which the will to power is never satisfied, never met, but only results in an endless willing for more power? Nietzsche's preference for Dionysius, the pre-Homeric god of life, in his *On the Genealogy of Morals*, attests to his conception that the true greatness of the human being lies in a life freed of inhibitions, a life for which happiness is found in the assertion of power and the absence of *Schuld*. To the degree that human beings are less inhibited, they will be happy and healthy. For the sake of happiness, then, humans must do away with religion and its inhibitions. Christian morality, with its ascetical ideals, is a self-distraction of who humans truly are.[182] The core of human identity therefore, lies in the pursuit of the vision of *Übermensch*, of absolute power, which Nietzsche sees as the final victory over God.

It is very telling that in the process of the coming to be of the *Übermensch*, it is part of the deal that the less privileged, the less endowed, those whom one would consider to be at the margins of society, the less healthy, those unable to stand up for themselves, ought to be readily and easily set aside. Nothing could be more radically different from the Ratzingerian interpretation of the *imago Dei* as the baseline of human equality as highlighted above. In fact, Nietzsche has no scruples pointing this out:

> The sick are man's greatest danger; not the evil, not the "beasts of prey." Those who are failures from the start, downtrodden, crushed—it is they, the weakest, who must undermine life among men, who call into question and poison most dangerously our trust in life, in man, and in ourselves.[183]

Given this perception of life, the best in humans emerges to the degree that only the strongest are kept alive. And given that the weak, the poor, the infirm and those at the "bottom" of the social ladder nurse a profound resentment toward the strong, the powerful, the rich and the healthy, it is in the safety interest of the latter to crush and exclude the former, whom, if they have their way, will eliminate the latter.[184] Talk about toleration, humility, and sanctity of life are merely expressions of vanity, for Nietzsche. In this sense, therefore, "the whole morality of the Sermon on the Mount belongs here: man experiences a veritable voluptuousness in violating himself by means of exaggerated demands and in then deifying this tyrannically demanding force in his soul."[185] While one can set aside the vitriol that is characteristic of Nietzschean expressions, it is difficult not to see the effects of this line of thinking even when viewed from a "moderate" perspective, namely, the picture of an autonomous human being for whom to be human means to be absolute; and secondly, the picture of a human being who, having set the self as the measure of all things, now decide the boundaries of right and wrong.

Without going into the specifics, are the consequences of these twin realities not very much present in the experiences and happenings that marked the twentieth century and are marking the twenty-first today? Is the logic underlining this Nietzschean anthropology substantially different from the logic that marked the ideologies of Nazism, Fascism, Communism and Racism in much of the twentieth century, and more prevalent today, the throwaway ideology of abortion and euthanasia, and the indoctrination on the question of gender forcefully being pushed today? If science can do it, then it must be done, appears the acceptable norm on some of these bioethical issues. And what is startling is that the logic or reasoning being the person that must emerge from the godless Nietzschean ideology and the logic governing much of these short-listed here, are strikingly very similar. Speaking to this new technological being for whom science is bequeathing unlimited possibilities, Ratzinger says:

> The fate of all of us depends on whether this moral dignity of the human person can be defended in the world of technology, with all its possibilities. For here a particular temptation exists for our technical scientific age. The technical and scientific attitude has produced a particular kind of certitude—namely, that which can be corroborated by way of experiment and mathematical formula. This has given humankind a certain freedom from anxiety and superstition, a certain power over the world. But now there is a temptation to view as reasonable and therefore as serious only what can be corroborated through experiment and computation. This means that the moral and the holy no longer count for anything. They are considered to belong to the domain of what must be transcended, of the irrational.[186]

Consequently, while technology has opened up unlimited possibilities for humans, it is helpful to note that what is possible need not necessarily translate into what should be done. In other words, ethics must not be based exclusively on physics. Such a view, Ratzinger maintains, extinguishes what is genuinely human in humans. It crushes rather than liberates humans. Ratzinger writes:

> We must ourselves recognize what Kant recognized and knew perfectly well—that there are two kinds of reason, as he says: a theoretical and a practical reason. We may call them the physical-natural scientific and the moral-religious reason. It is improper to refer to the moral reason as gross unreason and superstition simply because its contours and the scope of its knowledge are not mathematical. It is in fact the more fundamental of the two reasons, and it alone can preserve the human dimensions of both the natural sciences and technology and also prevent them from destroying humankind.[187]

Clearly, Ratzinger is seeking room for the moral-religious reasoning in a fast-paced world that easily leaves moral and religious postulates behind. While it is possible to read Ratzinger's line of argument as containing the possibilities that could hinder the development of science and so reignite the perennial tension between science and religion, what should be noted, irrespective of where one decides to stand on, is that for Ratzinger, the central concern is not religion for religion's sake, nor science for science's sake, but the human being, made in the image and likeness of God, whose inherent dignity must always be preserved. It is therefore, not a question of being either pro-science or anti-religion and vice versa. It is a question of being pro-human-being, pro-person. This is all the more so because of the fragility of the order that has to preserve the dignity of the person, made in the image and likeness of God.

Ratzinger identifies three theological postulates from this theological assertion that human beings are made in the image and likeness of God and hence, have a dignity that must be preserved, irrespective of the scientific and religious circumstances: Firstly, the essence of an image consists in the fact that it points to something else, that it represents something else. It is in the nature of an image to go beyond itself and to manifest something other than itself. Therefore, the human being as image of God implies that humans can never be closed in on themselves, for the image of God in humans implies relationality. It points the person beyond the self. The image of God is therefore the capacity for relation.[188] Hence, humans are most profoundly themselves when they enter into familial terms with God and are capable of addressing God their Creator.

Secondly, the image of God in humans implies that humans are beings of word and of love, beings capable of thinking and praying, for without these, humans cannot enter into a relationship with God which eventually points them back to one another.[189] In effect, relationality is interwoven with communication and vice versa, and such is the case that when humans give of themselves to God and to one another in love, then and only then do they receive of themselves back. The consciousness of the *imago Dei* pushes humans away from selfishness to the discovery of the profundity of the self in the "thou" of the other. One's life is not richer when one shuts the self in. A life that is only self-referential misses out on the joy of relationality. It restricts the horizon and imprisons self in the self. Joy does not flow exclusively from self-assertion but also from relationality, from the capacity of sharing, of the giving of the self through which one discovers why one is complemented. *Imago Dei* is about self-communication and self-transcendence; the former regards other persons, the latter, the opening up to a God that is discovered to be love.

The third and final postulate of the *imago Dei* that sheds light on the theological anthropology of Ratzinger is the Christological dialectic, which encapsulates the metaphor of *logos* as person. Ratzinger proceeds by noting the exegetical principle common to the Fathers of both East and West, that is, that we must read the Old and New Testaments together, and only in the New is the full meaning of the Old revealed.[190] To Ratzinger, the fact that Christ is referred to as the Second Adam, the definitive Adam, as the image of God (cf. 1 Cor 15:44–48; Col 1:15) is very significant. Ratzinger writes:

> It implies that in Christ alone appears the complete answer to the question about what the human being is. In him alone

> appears the deepest meaning of what is for the present a rough draft. He is the definitive human being, and creation is, as it were, a preliminary sketch that points to him. Thus, we can say that human persons are the beings who can be Jesus Christ's brothers and sisters. Human beings are creatures that can be one with Christ and thereby be one with God himself.[191]

In this sense, the human being is one whose essence is to be in transition, transitioning to Christ. The mystery of Easter therefore, enters the metaphor of *logos* as person: "Human beings must die with Christ like a grain of wheat in order truly to rise, to stand erect, to be themselves (cf. Jn 12:24)."[192] The mystery of Easter is therefore the defining event in the theological anthropology that seeks to explain who and what a human being is, for not only does it say that the present and the past have a meaning, but it points to the future, a future with God forever, gathered into the body of the risen Christ. In this sense, anthropology is essentially Christology, for Christ, the new man, is the hermeneutical framework that sheds light on the grandeur of who humans are, and their ultimate destiny to live with God forever.

For Ratzinger, at the height of this Christological reading of the metaphor of *logos* as person stands the image of Christ on the cross—*Ecce homo*, "Behold the man!" Beyond the cynicism of Pilate, St. John recognizes something prophetic in these words and passed them on as part of the Christian message:

> Yes, Pilate is correct when he says: "Behold the man." In him, in Jesus Christ, we can discern what the human being, God's project, is, and thereby also our own status. In the humiliated Jesus we can see how tragic, how little, how abased the human being can be. In him we can discern the whole history of human hate and sin. But in him and in his suffering love for us we can still more clearly discern God's response: Yes, that is the man who is loved by God to the very dust, who is so loved by God that he pursues him to the uttermost toils of death.[193]

Ecce homo! In the humiliations that humans suffer, therefore, they enter into the family of God as brothers and sisters of Jesus. The question about who humans are, therefore, finds response in the following of Jesus. A patient following of Jesus, in his love and suffering, teaches humans what it means to be a human being and how to become a human being. Chalcedon (451) was therefore right in its formula of Christ as true God and true man, for not only is Jesus God's way of being human, but Jesus is God's way of teaching humans what true humanity essentially consists of, which is, self-giving love, and not the self-assertion of Nietzsche's *Übermensch*.

Summarily, therefore, the metaphor of *logos* as person provides the window thanks to which one can more profoundly appreciate the philosophical theology of Ratzinger as principally personalistic. Asked by Peter Seewald whether he considers himself a critical, modern man, in the sense and spirit of the German *critique* which is the defining quality of the *Aufklärung*, Ratzinger responds: "Well, I didn't want to operate only in a stagnant and closed philosophy, but in a philosophy understood as a question—what is man, really?—and particularly to enter into the new, contemporary philosophy. In this sense I was modern and critical."[194] This text gives us in a descriptive form the philosophical hermeneutic of Ratzinger. Firstly, it is anthropological. The starting point is about the human person, what the person is, in all humanness. Ratzinger certainly seeks to seriously engage the claims regarding personhood advanced by secular rational dialectics, and when placed side by side with Nietzsche as shown above, it is clear that his theological anthropology is an implicit refutation of certain *Aufklärung* lines of thought regarding the question of who and what is the human being. Therefore, for Ratzinger, the question about the human being, who the human being is in terms of being, life, and action, is read beyond the compartmentalizing of philosophical disciplines and branches, to what he sees as the full measure of humanity in both its anthropological, existential, and eschatological bearings.

Thus, Ratzinger's philosophical theological metaphor of *logos* as person is definitely not a dry, detached inquiry, but one that takes serious consideration of the human situation, one that is attentive to the human being in the concrete circumstances of life and not just in the mere abstract. This explains Ratzinger's affinity for personalism of Martin Buber as a philosophical interpretive key, for in it he is able to feel the sense of engagement with the practical concerns of the here and now: What is the human being? What constitutes his or her noblest goals and aspirations? How must humans live today? What happens after this earthly life is over? These are questions that concretely shape the perception that humans have of themselves as persons, and how they see others as well. And for Ratzinger, Christ is the answer to the bundle of questions that is every human being, every person.

From the point of relevance, Ratzinger's Christology of *Logos* as Person, that is, the Person of Christ with two natures, divine and human, is certainly timely today, for it establishes the intrinsic dignity of personhood, based on the divine personhood. Over and against the tendency to characterize the person in terms of utilitarian productivity, one can assert that the greatness of personhood resides in the fact that God is in fact treated as a communion of persons. And in Christ, human nature has been introduced into this community of divine persons, hence safeguarding its intrinsic dignity.

In recapitulation, these three theological metaphors—that is, *Logos* as Creative Reason, *Logos* as Son, and *Logos* as Person—provide one with what amounts to a Ratzingerian Christological portrait of the *Gestalt* of Christ, to the extent that they help one to understand what Ratzinger thinks about the nature and person of Jesus of Nazareth. In effect, they declare that this Jesus is the *Logos* at the source of all of creation. It is the merit of this eternal creative *Logos* that all of creation came to be. And this *Logos*, at the fullness of time (Gal 4:4), enters history to recreate the world. The presence of the eternal *Logos* in history brings about the consciousness that God is Father, Son and Spirit, for, as seen above, in the unique *Abba* experience of the Son, one gets to see a hitherto unknown intimacy that reveals Fatherhood and Sonship in their most profound levels in the divine Godhead.

However, though Ratzinger clearly is unwilling to push the boundaries of classical Christology regarding the person of Christ as defined by Nicaea, Ephesus, and Chalcedon, it must be noted that Ratzinger is not simply restating or reasserting classical Christology. As Ratzinger himself demonstrates in the forewords he wrote introducing the first two volumes of his trilogy on Jesus, his goal is not to reassert classical Christology, but to help post-*Aufklärung* men and women to find and enter into friendship with Jesus of Nazareth. In other words, Christology for Ratzinger is not simply a systematic science, but a path to discipleship. While one can state and repeat the formulas of Creative Reason, Sonship and Person, these formulas, if not followed by an opening of the heart, or a "yes" of one's will to the will of Jesus, remain dry, abstract, and lifeless. Christology for Ratzinger is therefore at its most intimate core spirituality. Christology attains its goal if the one who learns about the person of Christ can finally become a disciple, a friend of the Lord—*vos autem dixi amicos-* (Jn 15:15). Christology for Ratzinger is a personal search for the face of the Lord.[195] Christology is the theologian's effort to foster a living relationship with Christ, the creative Reason, Son, and Person.

And this marks the fundamental difference between the Christologies of the *Aufklärung,* be they by Kant, Hegel, or the Christology of Ratzinger. To the former, the person of Christ is largely seen, as shown above, from the perspective of a moral exemplar. There is no sense of relationality, of personal intimacy, and even less of discipleship. Christ essentially emerges as a good man who shows the example of what it means to live a moral life in a spirit of absolute heroism and fidelity. This Christ is what the *Aufklärer* wants him to be. This Christ is completely emptied of the divine nature, of the supernatural element of his being. This Christ cannot offer any help to anyone, besides pointing all to the moral law within every human being. And even when Christ's divinity is acknowledged, such as with Hegel, it is interpreted in such a way that all humans have the same divinity, and there is nothing unique about the divinity of Christ. Over and above all, this Christ cannot die for humanity. And if he cannot die for humanity, then he is likewise not raised from the dead. The Resurrection is essentially, as seen with Kant and Hegel, humanity coming to life, returning to itself, restoring itself. It has nothing to do with the Father's power raising the Son.

But with Ratzinger, one finds a completely different hermeneutic, even if he appreciates the rational interests of the *Aufklärung* in the question of the person of Jesus. As De Gaál testifies, Ratzinger's position has been that "[…] the self-communication of the absolute and sovereign God cannot be reduced or shackled to the immanent categories of the

German idealist philosopher Immanuel Kant (1724–1804)."[196] If for Kant theoretical reason could not lead to a personal relationship with God, then the Kantian Christology misses out on the most essential aspect of Christology, for in reducing the Christ to a moral exemplar, it not only reduces Christianity to ethics, but above all, it empties Christianity of its flesh and blood, concrete, life, dynamism. In precis, Ratzinger's Christology is wider and more challenging because it calls for a movement from self-centeredness to other-centeredness. One finds the self, one discovers the gravitas of one's being in meeting and entering into a relationship with Jesus of Nazareth, true God and true man, as Chalcedon rightly stated.

Notes — Chapter Four

1 Ernst Cassirer, *The Philosophy of the Enlightenment* (Princeton, NJ: Princeton University Press, 2009), 39.
2 Cassirer, *Enlightenment*, 39.
3 Cassirer, *Enlightenment*, 40.
4 Cassirer, *Enlightenment*, 40.
5 Cassirer, *Enlightenment*, 40.
6 Cassirer, *Enlightenment*, 41.
7 Immanuel Kant, *Groundwork of the Metaphysics of Moral*, trans. and ed. Mary Gregor (New York: Cambridge University Press, 2012), 4:421; 4:429; 4:431.
8 Cassirer, *Enlightenment*, 41.
9 Cassirer, *Enlightenment*, 43.
10 Cassirer, *Enlightenment*, 44.
11 Cassirer, *Enlightenment*, 45.
12 Cassirer, *Enlightenment*, 45.
13 Cassirer, *Enlightenment*, 48.
14 Cassirer, *Enlightenment*, 49.
15 Baruch Spinoza, *Tractatus Theologico-Politicus* (New York: Hebrew Union College Press, 2001), cap. Iii, sect. 7
16 Cassirer, *Enlightenment*, 70.
17 Cassirer, *Enlightenment*, 70.
18 Joseph Ratzinger, *Values in a Time of Upheaval*, trans. Brian McNeil (San Francisco: Ignatius Press, 2006), 112.
19 Joseph Ratzinger, *"In the Beginning...": A Catholic Understanding of the Story of Creation and the Fall*, trans. Boniface Ramsey, O.P. (Grand Rapids, MI: William B. Eerdmans Publishing Company, 1995), 14.

20 Ratzinger, *"In the Beginning…,"* 81.
21 Ratzinger, *"In the Beginning…,"* 82.
22 Joseph Ratzinger, *Principles of Catholic Theology: Building Stones for a Fundamental Theology*, trans. Mary Frances McCarthy, S.N.D. (San Francisco: Ignatius Press, 1987), 16.
23 Ratzinger, *Principles*, 16.
24 Ratzinger, *"In the Beginning…,"* 83.
25 Ratzinger, *"In the Beginning…,"* 84.
26 Ratzinger, *"In the Beginning…,"* 84.
27 Ratzinger, *"In the Beginning…,"* 84.
28 Ratzinger, *"In the Beginning…,"* 85–86.
29 Ratzinger, *"In the Beginning…,"* 87.
30 Ratzinger, *"In the Beginning…,"* 88. Ratzinger maintains that this rendition of Luther here certainly does not give a complete description of Luther's doctrine of creation, but only a spiritual aspect, which results from the drama of Luther's experience of grace.
31 Ratzinger, *"In the Beginning…,"* 89.
32 G.W.F. Hegel, *Lectures on the Philosophy of Religion, Vol. 1: Introduction and the Concept of Religion*, ed. P.C. Hodgson et al. (Berkeley, CA: University of California Press, 1984), 84.
33 Peter C. Hodgson, "Hegel's Approach to Religion: The Dialectic of Speculation and Phenomenology," *The Journal of Religion*, Vol. 64, No. 2. (Oxford: Oxford University Press, April 1984), 159.
34 G. W. F. Hegel, *Lectures on the Philosophy of Religion, Vol. III: The Consummate Religion*, ed. by Peter C. Hodgson and trans. by R. F. Brown, P. C. Hodgson and J. M. Stewart with the assistance of H. S. Harris (Oxford: Clarendon Press, 2007), *Ms.* 2.
35 Hegel, *Lectures on the Philosophy of Religion, Vol. III The Consummate Religion*, 15–29.
36 Hegel, *Lectures on the Philosophy of Religion, Vol. III The Consummate Religion*, 121.
37 Hegel, *Lectures on the Philosophy of Religion, Vol. III The Consummate Religion*, 121.
38 Hegel, *Lectures on the Philosophy of Religion, Vol. III The Consummate Religion*, 121.
39 Hegel, *Lectures on the Philosophy of Religion, Vol. III The Consummate Religion*, 121.
40 Hegel, *Lectures on the Philosophy of Religion, Vol. III The Consummate Religion*, 128.
41 Hegel, *Lectures on the Philosophy of Religion, Vol. III The Consummate Religion*, 6.
42 Hodgson, "Hegel's Approach to Religion," 163.

43 Paul Ricoeur, *Freud and Philosophy: An Essay on Interpretation*, trans. Denis Savage (New Haven, CT: Yale University Press, 1970), 472.
44 Ratzinger, *"In the Beginning…,"* 89.
45 Ratzinger, *"In the Beginning…,"* 89–90.
46 Ratzinger, *"In the Beginning…,"* 90.
47 Ratzinger, *"In the Beginning…,"* 90.
48 Ratzinger, *"In the Beginning…,"* 90–91.
49 Ratzinger, *"In the Beginning…,"* 90.
50 Ratzinger, *"In the Beginning…,"* 90.
51 Ratzinger, *"In the Beginning…,"* 90.
52 Ratzinger, *"In the Beginning…,"* 90.
53 Ratzinger, *"In the Beginning…,"* 91.
54 Ratzinger, *"In the Beginning…,"* 91.
55 Ratzinger, *"In the Beginning…,"* 91.
56 Ratzinger, *"In the Beginning…,"* 92.
57 Ratzinger, *"In the Beginning…,"* 93.
58 Ratzinger, *"In the Beginning…,"* 93.
59 Ratzinger, *"In the Beginning…,"* 94.
60 Ratzinger, *"In the Beginning…,"* 94.
61 Ratzinger, *"In the Beginning…,"* 95.
62 Ratzinger, *"In the Beginning…,"* 95.
63 Ratzinger, *"In the Beginning…,"* 96.
64 Ratzinger, *"In the Beginning…,"* 10.
65 Ratzinger, *"In the Beginning…,"* 11.
66 Ratzinger, *"In the Beginning…,"* 11.
67 Ratzinger, *"In the Beginning…,"* 11.
68 Ratzinger, *"In the Beginning…,"* 11.
69 Ratzinger, *"In the Beginning…,"* 12.
70 Ratzinger, *"In the Beginning…,"* 12.
71 Ratzinger, *"In the Beginning…,"* 12.
72 Ratzinger, *"In the Beginning…,"* 13.
73 Ratzinger, *"In the Beginning…,"* 14.
74 Immanuel Kant, *Practical Philosophy:* "An Answer to the Question: What is the Enlightenment? (1784)" trans. Mary J. Gregor (New York: Cambridge University Press, 2016), 8:35. Allen W. Wood points out that by the middle of the seventeenth century, the ossified form of Lutheran theology that was commonplace was challenged by two currents of thought that brought about the eighteenth-century *Aufklärung*, namely, Pietism (founded by Philipp Jakob Spener, 1635–1705) and Rationalism (derived from the philosophy of Christian Wolff (1679–1754). Pietism privileged the relational and existential character of the Christian faith, over and perhaps even against the doctrinal and propositional model. Pietism was hostile to the

intellectualization of the Christian faith. It focused on winning the heart and not the intellect. On the other hand, the Rationalism of Wolff argued for the position of the consistency, though distinct, between scriptural revelation and rational theology. Rationalism grounded its thesis on the cosmological argument, that the contingent world depended on a necessary and supremely perfect being for its existence. As Wood points out, "Wolff's philosophy was the medium in which the German Enlightenment grew." – Allen W. Wood, "Rational Theology, Moral Faith, and Religion" in Paul Guyer (ed.) *The Cambridge Companion to Kant* (New York: Cambridge University Press, 2008), 394–395.

75 Onora O'Neill, "Vindicating Reason" in Paul Guyer (ed.) *The Cambridge Companion to Kant* (New York: Cambridge University Press, 2008), 299.

76 O'Neill, "Vindicating Reason," 299.

77 J. B. Schneewind, "Autonomy, Obligation and Virtue: An Overview of Kant's Moral Philosophy," in Paul Guyer (ed.) *The Cambridge Companion to Kant* (New York: Cambridge University Press, 2008), 309. As Schneewind points out, "Autonomy involves two components. The first is that no authority external to ourselves is needed to constitute or inform us of the demands or morality. We can each know without being told what we ought to do because moral requirements are requirements we impose on ourselves. The second is that in self-government we can effectively control ourselves. The obligations we impose upon ourselves override all other calls for action, and frequently run counter to our desires. We nonetheless always have a sufficient motive to act as we ought. Hence no external source of motivation is needed for our self-legislation to be effective in controlling our behavior" (309–310). The Kantian formulation of the categorical imperative as autonomous is therefore intrinsically related to the formulation of the same as a universal maxim.

78 O'Neill, "Vindicating Reason," 298.

79 Immanuel Kant, *Religion within the Boundaries of Mere Reason*, trans. Allen Wood and George di Giovanni (Chelsea MI: Sheridan Books, 2016), 6:200.

80 Wood, "Rational Theology, Moral Faith, and Religion," 410. I find this analysis of the persona of Kant as a figure of the enlightenment very much perceptive: "[…] As a man of the German Enlightenment, Kant regarded the concerns of science and morality as *of course* also religious concerns. In Kant's milieu, there was no warfare between science and religion, only a conflict between two kinds of religious sensibility: the enlightened religious sensibility, which seeks to reconcile religion with scientific reason, and various forms of contrary sensibility, which mistrust reason, and set religion against it because they prefer either revealed tradition, or mystical experience, or enthusiastic emotionalism (414). Wood clearly accords the

respect rightly earned by the Königsberg philosopher. That said, and as shown in Ratzinger's engagement with the Kantian postulates in the specifics of this chapter, there is no denying that the rational religion of Kant, in as much as it espouses rightful ethical postulates, cannot capture the experiential mode and character of orthodox Christianity, which remains the hub of Christianity as a religious expression.

81 Kant, *Enlightenment*, 8:40.

82 Kant, *Religion*, 6:122.

83 Kant, *Religion*, 6:135.

84 Kant, *Religion*, 6:80.

85 Kant, *Religion*, 6:80.

86 Kant, *Religion*, 6:82.

87 Kant, *Religion*, 6:83.

88 Kant, *Religion*, 6:84.

89 Kant, *Religion*, 6:128.

90 Kant, *Religion*, 6:129.

91 Frederick C. Beiser, "Kant's Intellectual Development: 1746–1781," in Paul Guyer (ed.) *The Cambridge Companion to Kant* (New York: Cambridge University Press, 2008), 50.

92 Allen W. Wood, "Rational Theology, Moral Faith, and Religion" in Paul Guyer (ed.) *The Cambridge Companion to Kant* (New York: Cambridge University Press, 2008), 396.

93 Wood, "Rational Theology, Moral Faith, and Religion," 406.

94 Laurence Dickey, "Hegel on Religion and Philosophy" in Frederick C. Beiser (ed.) *The Cambridge Companion to Hegel* (New York: Cambridge University Press, 1999), 310–311.

95 G. W. F. Hegel, *Faith & Knowledge, or the Reflective Philosophy of Subjectivity in the complete range of its forms as Kantian, Jacobian, and Fichtean Philosophy*, Walter Cerf & H.S. Harris, (eds.) (New York: State University of New York Press, 1977), xvii. Cerf further points out that "in terms of the Kantian faculties, reflective philosophy is philosophy of the intellect (*der Verstand*), speculative philosophy is philosophy of Reason (*die Vernunft*), but of a Reason which has been allowed to trespass on territory Kant believed to be inaccessible to finite man. It is typical of reflective philosophy, though it does not exhaust its nature, that it relies on arguments, proofs, and the whole apparatus of logic, that it insists on clear-cut dichotomies in terms of abstract universals, dichotomies such as those of the infinite and the finite, subject and object, universal and particular, freedom and necessity, causality and teleology, etc., etc.; that it tries to solve intellectual puzzles rather than give the true conceptual vision of the whole" (xvii). Hegel definitely believed that speculative philosophy was the needed channel that could scratch the itches of modern minds left

unsatisfied by the substantial postulates articulated by the pious Lutheranism of the 1820s in Berlin. It is also worth pointing out that though being a man of reason, of spirit, Hegel shows a very critical attitude toward the *Aufklärung*, because of what he saw as its inability to rise above nature to the level of spirit. For Hegel, the *Aufklärung* as exhibited by Kant, Fichte, Jacobi and others, constituted a clear example of a failed project of rationality, of the futility of reflective philosophy or thinking, a manner of thinking that has contributed to the disintegration of thought and the human being, due to its inability to reconcile the human spirit in absolute knowing. Hegel, therefore, saw the strand of the *Aufklärung* of Kant et. al, as the formidable foe of both religion and philosophy, when the latter demonstrates the reasonableness of the contents of the Christian faith, that is, the rationality of the former. See Quentin Lauer, S.J., *Hegel's Concept of God* (Albany: State University of New York Press, 1982), 12–17. Nonetheless, this in no way dissuades from the fact that Hegel himself is through and through, a *Mann der Vernunft*, or more precisely, a *Mann der Vorstellung*, albeit different from the Kantian strand or stock, perhaps even radically so.

96 Dickey, "Hegel on Religion and Philosophy," 307.

97 Dickey, "Hegel on Religion and Philosophy," 309.

98 Dickey, "Hegel on Religion and Philosophy," 310.

99 Dickey, "Hegel on Religion and Philosophy," 310–313.

100 Hegel, *Faith & Knowledge*, 55.

101 Dickey, "Hegel on Religion and Philosophy," 315. As Dickey further points out regarding the charge of Hegel as a panlogist, quite the contrary, from a Hegelian stand point, by elevating the truth of Christianity to the sublime height of philosophical consciousness thereby putting Christian truths in teachable forms, Christian truths and values, rather than being downgraded, were made more accessible to modern critical minds (315–316).

102 Dickey, "Hegel on Religion and Philosophy," 316.

103 Hegel, *The Philosophy of Religion*, V. I, p. 456.

104 G.W.F. Hegel, ed. and trans. Peter Fuss and John Dobbins, *Three Essays, 1793–1795: The Tübingen Essay, Berne Fragments and The Life of Jesus* (South Bend, IN: University of Notre Dame Press, 2004), 13.

105 Hegel, *The Life of Jesus*, 80.

106 Hegel, *The Life of Jesus*, 80.

107 Frederick C. Beiser, ed. *The Cambridge Companion to Hegel* (New York: Cambridge University Press, 1993), 331–334.

108 Hegel, *The Life of Jesus*, 89.

109 Hegel, *The Life of Jesus*, 75.

110 Hegel, *The Life of Jesus*, 98.

111 Hegel, *The Life of Jesus*, 98.

112 Hegel, *The Life of Jesus*, 125.
113 Beiser, ed. *Cambridge Companion to Hegel*, 321–328.
114 Joseph Ratzinger/Benedict XVI, *Jesus of Nazareth, From the Baptism in the Jordan to the Transfiguration*, trans. Adrian Walker (New York: The Doubleday Broadway Publishing Group, 2007), xi.
115 Ratzinger/Benedict XVI, *Jesus of Nazareth*, xii.
116 Ratzinger/Benedict XVI, *Jesus of Nazareth*, xii.
117 Ratzinger/Benedict XVI, *Jesus of Nazareth*, xii.
118 Ratzinger/Benedict XVI, Jesus of Nazareth, xii.
119 Ratzinger/Benedict XVI, *Jesus of Nazareth*, xii.
120 Albert Schweitzer, *The Quest of the Historical Jesus* (Minneapolis, MN: Fortress Press, 2001), 478–479.
121 Schweitzer, *The Quest*, 487.
122 Ratzinger/Benedict XVI, *Jesus of Nazareth*, xv.
123 Ratzinger/Benedict XVI, *Jesus of Nazareth*, xvi.
124 Norman Tanner, S.J., ed. *Vatican Council II: The Essential Texts* Dogmatic Constitution on Divine Revelation, *Dei Verbum* (New York: Image Books, 2012), 11.
125 Joseph Ratzinger/Benedict XVI, *Jesus of Nazareth*, xii.
126 Joseph Ratzinger/Benedict XVI, *Jesus of Nazareth*, xiv.
127 Joseph Ratzinger/Benedict XVI, *Jesus of Nazareth*, 7.
128 Joseph Ratzinger/Benedict XVI, *Jesus of Nazareth*, 6.
129 Joseph Ratzinger/Benedict XVI, *Jesus of Nazareth*, 6.
130 Joseph Ratzinger/Benedict XVI, *Jesus of Nazareth*, 7.
131 Joseph Ratzinger, *Introduction to Christianity*, trans. J. R. Foster (San Francisco: Ignatius Press, 2004), 224.
132 Ratzinger, *Introduction*, 224.
133 Ratzinger/Benedict XVI, *Jesus of Nazareth*, 7.
134 Ratzinger, *Introduction*, 224–225.
135 Ratzinger, *Introduction*, 225.
136 Ratzinger, *Introduction*, 226.
137 Ratzinger, *Introduction*, 226.
138 Ratzinger, *Introduction*, 226.
139 Ratzinger, *Introduction*, 226.
140 Ratzinger, *Introduction*, 228.
141 Ratzinger, *Introduction*, 228.
142 Alister E. McGrath, *The Making of Modern German Christology: From the Enlightenment to Pannenberg* (New York: Basil Blackwell Inc. 1953), 1.
143 McGrath, *The Making of Modern German Christology*, 2
144 Joseph Ratzinger, *The Regensburg Lecture* (South Bend, IN: St. Augustine's Press, 2007), 138, 29.
145 Ratzinger, *The Regensburg Lecture*, 139, 33–34.

146 Ratzinger, *The Regensburg Lecture*, 139–140, 35.
147 Ratzinger, *The Regensburg Lecture*, 140, 38.
148 Ratzinger, *The Regensburg Lecture*, 140–141.
149 Ratzinger, *The Regensburg Lecture*, 141, 40.
150 Ratzinger, *The Regensburg Lecture*, 142, 46.
151 Ratzinger, *The Regensburg Lecture*, 143.
152 Ratzinger, *The Regensburg Lecture*, 144, 53.
153 To reference Luther here does not imply that Luther should be considered a figure of the *Aufklärung*. It simply implies that his rejection of philosophy with his principle of *sola scriptura*, laid the foundations, as Ratzinger points in his Regensburg Lecture, for a push by Kant to ultimately sever the bond between faith and reason.
154 Ratzinger, *The Regensburg Lecture*, 144, 54, and 56.
155 Benedict XVI, "Encyclical Letter *Deus Caritas Est*, On Christian Love," December 25, 2005, accessed August 8, 2018, at www.vatican.va.
156 Ratzinger/Benedict XVI, *Jesus of Nazareth,* 340.
157 Ratzinger/Benedict XVI, *Jesus of Nazareth,* 340.
158 Ratzinger/Benedict XVI, *Jesus of Nazareth,* 341.
159 Ratzinger/Benedict XVI, *Jesus of Nazareth,* 342.
160 Ratzinger/Benedict XVI, *Jesus of Nazareth*, 343.
161 Collins, *The Word Made Love*, 74.
162 Benedict XVI, "Encyclical Letter on Christian Hope *Spe Salvi*," November 30, 2007, 5, accessed January 25 2019 at www.vatican.va.
163 Joseph Ratzinger, *Behold the Pierced One: An Approach to a Spiritual Christology*, trans. Graham Harrison (San Francisco, Ignatius Press, 1986), 29–30.
164 Ratzinger, *Regensburg Lecture*, 142, 48.
165 Friedrich Nietzsche, *The Will to Power*, trans. Walter Kaufmann and R. J. Hollingdale (New York: Vintage Books, 1968), 662. In the article, "*Aufklärung und kein Ende*: The Place of Enlightenment in Friedrich Nietzsche's Thought," *German Life and Letters* 61:1 January 2008 (Malden, MA: Blackwell Publishing Ltd, 2008), 1. Nicholas Martin points out that while some have dismissed Nietzsche as an anti-Enlightenment irrationalist, Nietzsche's philosophical diagnoses are heavily informed by the critical principles of the *Aufklärung*. Martin argues that Nietzsche admires the critical spirit associated with eighteenth-century Enlightenment, notably Voltaire and Lessing, as well as representatives of earlier "Enlightenment," such as Epicurus, Petrarch and Erasmus. Nietzsche is also impressed by the audacity of the Enlightenment project and its philosophical legacy, irrespective of how flawed some parts of it might be, which somewhat explains the presence of ambivalence in the Nietzschean approach to the *Aufklärung*.
166 Nietzsche, *The Will to Power*, 659 (1885).

167 Nietzsche, *The Will to Power*, 618 (1885).
168 Nietzsche, *The Will to Power*, 619 (1885).
169 Nietzsche, *The Will to Power*, 624 (1883–1888).
170 Nietzsche, *The Will to Power*, 659 (1885).
171 Nietzsche, *The Will to Power*, 659 (1885).
172 Benedict XVI, *First Messages of His Holiness Benedict XVI*, "Homily: Mass for the Inauguration of the Pontificate of Pope Benedict XVI" (Makuyu, Kenya: Pauline Publications Africa, 2005), 18.
173 Benedict XVI, *The Human Person, The Heart of Peace*, accessed (September 20, 2018), 11, at www.vatican.va.
174 Benedict XVI, *If You Want Peace, Protect Creation*, accessed (September 20, 2018), 5, at www.vatican.va.
175 Ratzinger, "*In the Beginning …*," 42.
176 Ratzinger, "*In the Beginning …*," 43.
177 Ratzinger, "*In the Beginning …*," 43.
178 Ratzinger, "*In the Beginning …*," 43.
179 Ratzinger, "*In the Beginning …*," 44.
180 Ratzinger, "*In the Beginning …*," 44–45.
181 Ratzinger, "*In the Beginning …*," 45.
182 Friedrich Nietzsche, *On the Genealogy of Morals*, trans. Walter Kaufmann and R. J. Hollingdale (New York: Vintage Books, 1989), 65–67; 90–95.
183 Nietzsche, *Genealogy*, 122.
184 Nietzsche, *Genealogy*, 123.
185 Nietzsche, *Genealogy*, 171–172.
186 Ratzinger, "*In the Beginning …*," 46.
187 Ratzinger, "*In the Beginning …*," 46–47.
188 Ratzinger, "*In the Beginning …*," 47–48.
189 Ratzinger, "*In the Beginning …*," 48.
190 Ratzinger, "*In the Beginning …*," 48.
191 Ratzinger, "*In the Beginning …*," 48–49.
192 Ratzinger, "*In the Beginning …*," 49.
193 Ratzinger, "*In the Beginning …*," 57–58.
194 Benedict XVI, *Last Testament*, 76.
195 Ratzinger/Benedict XVI, *Jesus of Nazareth*, xxiii.
196 Emery de Gaál, *O Lord, I Seek Your Countenance: Explorations and Discoveries in Pope Benedict XVI's Theology* (Steubenville, OH: Emmaus Academic, 2018), 4.

Chapter Five: *An Ecclesiological Reading of Ratzinger's Theological Appropriation of* Logos *as Unity of Love and* Logos *as Word vis-à-vis the* Aufklärung

The preceding chapter reflected on Ratzinger's theological appropriations of *Logos* as creative Reason and as Son. These three usages, that is, creative Reason, Son, and Person, present a Christological reading of Christ, to the extent that approaching Christ as Incarnate creative Reason, as Son, and as Person, one gains a deeper insight into the nature of Christ. It emerges that this Jesus is the *Logos* of creation; the Son of the Father thanks to whom all who believe become sons and daughters of the Father; and finally, that in Jesus of Nazareth personhood has taken a dignity that transcends all human limitations, for in Jesus human nature has not only been assumed by the Second Person of the Trinity, but in the ascended Lord is forever a part of the Trinity.

This chapter therefore continues Ratzinger's further adoption of the *Logos*, only this time as unity of love and as Word. The emphasis here is ecclesiological in that not only is love the defining principle of the Church as Benedict demonstrated in the choice of his first encyclical, *Deus Caritas Est*, but likewise *Logos* as Word is central to ecclesiological thinking because, as will be seen in this chapter, not only is the Church called together in response to the Word proclaimed, but at the very center of the Church's life is the worship of God, the liturgy (whose fulcrum is the Eucharistic prayer, the *oratio*, the word). Hence, through these two usages of *Logos* as unity of love and *Logos* as Word, a deeper picture of Ratzinger's doctrine of the Church emerges, a Church defined by love, called together by listening to the Word, and she offers herself to the Father in the name of the Son and by the power of the Spirit in the *oratio rationabilis*.

It is important to note that the treatment of ecclesiology in this chapter is not exhaustive of the ecclesiological positions of Ratzinger, which might be characterized under various headings, such as: Ratzinger's *Communio* ecclesiology; Ratzinger's Eucharistic ecclesiology; Ratzinger's ecclesiology of the Second Vatican Council, that is, Ratzinger's interpretation of *Lumen Gentium* and *Gaudium et Spes*; Ratzinger's Mariological ecclesiology; and Ratzinger's pneumatological ecclesiology, to cite a few. The focus of this chapter, therefore, or what this chapter seeks to achieve, is a study of the ecclesiological question in the specific light of the *Logos* usage vis-à-vis the *Aufklärung*, particularly as it concerns what can be characterized as the ecclesiology of Love from Ratzinger's usage of *Logos* as unity of love, and the ecclesiology of the Word, from Ratzinger's usage of *Logos* as Word, which calls forth the community called the Church, and brings about the new sacrifice of praise in the Word as the *oratio rationabilis*. In sum, this chapter is in no way intended to be a conclusive treatment of Ratzinger's ecclesiology, but a setting of the stage for a further exploration of the ecclesiological dimensions and consequences of Ratzinger's Christology on his ecclesiology. This, in part, is why this study is *introductory*. But first, a word about Ratzinger's essential perception of the Church will be helpful in situating his theological usage of *Logos* in his Christo-ecclesiological framework.

5.1 Ratzinger: The Church— A Story God Himself Has Created

For Ratzinger, the story of the Church is primarily a story about God. In this sense, one cannot give up on the Church, irrespective of the magnitude of the challenges and problems faced today. The most important word about the Church is not what one says, but what God has said through the gift of his Son in the power of the Holy Spirit, granted that the Church is basically what God himself has called into being:

> The word *Ecclesia*, "Church," comes from the Old Testament, where it is the classic expression for the assembly of

> the People of God, the prototype and pattern for which was the assembly at Sinai, the people congregating at the feet of the God who spoke, whose word called people together and united them.[1]

The Church is consequently that community that has responded to the call of the Word of God, the people that could be described as "of God," because having responded to God's summons, they must now live from God and for God. Not only is the nature of this community shaped by the vision flowing from the obedience of faith—the only proper attitude to God's invitation—but the very mission and destiny of this people must be continuously shaped to conform to what God calls it to be, in the certainty of God's revelation as contained in Scripture that has been borne, nurtured, and grown in the living Tradition of the Church. Given this perception, Ratzinger maintains, "The crisis concerning the Church [...] is a crisis about God. It is the result of leaving out what is most essential. What then remains is merely a dispute about power. There is already enough of that elsewhere in the world—we do not need the Church for that."[2] Accordingly, a revival of the sense of Church among Christians and in the wider world must necessarily begin with a rediscovery of the primacy of God. Certainly, prescribing quick fix solutions will not constitute an enduring resolution. Ratzinger adopts a Christo-centric starting point. To Ratzinger, the figure of Jesus vis-à-vis the Church takes on a forceful symbolism in the call of the Twelve, "a symbolic number indicating the new people of God, whose pillars they were destined to be. In them, therefore, in a gesture of Jesus which is both sign and reality, he inaugurates the 'People of God' in a new way, that is, their calling is to be seen theologically as the beginning of all that is 'Church.'"[3] In this light, ecclesiology begins with Christology to the extent that the Church matures in her self-identity through the profession of faith in Jesus as the Christ, a product that Jesus himself brought about thanks to his choice of the Twelve and their association with him through the various stages of his life.

But turning to the question of the Church, what is the Church for Ratzinger? What is his way of seeing the Church and why did he opt for this way of understanding it? When Ratzinger looks at the Church he realizes that it is not the case that the Church has left the world, but that on many counts—such as, on family life; on the level of religious literacy; and on piety and devotion—the world has already left the Church as an institution and for various reasons that must be taken seriously and addressed, such as the participation of Christians in the atrocities of World War II. Already as a young theologian he had written an article, "The New Pagans and the Church," published in 1958 in the journal *Hochland* that caused quite a stir and discomfort within the German Church, owing to Ratzinger's blunt assessment of what he perceived to be the emptiness of external religiosity that was becoming commonplace in Germany and much of Europe. Ratzinger explains that the source of his discernment was the religious instruction classes he was having with the boys and girls as parochial vicar in his first pastoral assignment. He noticed that what he was saying to the children was being contradicted at home by their parents: "But Daddy said you don't need to take it so seriously."[4] Ratzinger reasoned that if such was the state of the transmission of the faith at home, then the post-war German people had already moved away from the Church, even if they were visibly present in the pews. The young Professor Ratzinger wrote in his 1958 lecture:

> The outward shape of the modern Church is determined essentially by the fact that, in a totally new way, she has become the Church of pagans, and is constantly becoming even more so. She is no longer, as she once was, a Church composed of pagans who have become Christians, but a Church of pagans, who still call themselves Christians, but actually have become pagans. Paganism resides today in the Church herself, and precisely that is the characteristic of the Church of our day, and that of the new paganism, so that it is a matter of a paganism in the Church, and of a Church in whose heart paganism is living.[5]

For Ratzinger, what is at stake is the difference between the external and internal life of the Church. Externally, things appear to be running smoothly. There is no cause for alarm. The Christian façade of the contemporary image of the Church has a soothing and reassuring effect. But the internal story of faith, of a living faith, tells another tale, to the extent that the teachings of the Church are largely being ignored, with little or perhaps no bearings in the lives of believers. The central concern is that of unbelief in the hearts of Christians in an increasingly secularized Europe, who, while remaining in the Church, cease believing and living the truths of the Christian faith. And as Ratzinger would later observe in his commentary on Vatican II's Pastoral Constitution on the Church in the Modern World *Gaudium et Spes*, "since the beginning of the modern era there had been increasingly small circles of people ready to bow to the authority of the teaching Church."[6] Even when physically in the Church as members, many are in the Church in body alone, with their hearts far from the Church (Mt 15:8). In other words, though not a state of physical schism, they are mentally ruled by patterns of thought that are foreign, if not explicitly hostile. to Christian dogma.

To Ratzinger, the new pagans, born from the Church, formulate their own subjective autonomous convictions as to what they can and cannot subscribe to, regarding the faith. Ratzinger points out that these new pagans in the Church,

> [...] make a subjective choice from the creed of the Church in order to shape their own world view. And there can be no doubt that most of them, from the Christian point of view, should really no longer be called believers, but that they follow, more or less, a secular philosophy. They do indeed affirm the moral responsibility of man, but it is based on, and limited by, purely rational considerations. The ethics of N. Hartmanns, K. Jaspers, and M. Heidegger, for example, defend the more or less known convictions of many morally upright men, but they are in no sense Christians.[7]

Herein lies the tension that emerges when faith is exclusively identified with the good, so much so that Christianity is reducible to the ethical. Irreligious morality then appears indistinguishable from Christian morality, for the former has all the trappings of the latter, externally Christian, but internally irreligious. To Ratzinger, this state of affairs implies that what was hitherto considered as "cultural Christianity" cannot hold today. Ratzinger argues: "Therefore, the modern man today, when he meets someone else anywhere, can assume with some certainty that he has a baptismal certificate, but not that he has a Christian frame of mind. Therefore, he must presume as the normal state of affairs the lack of faith of his neighbor."[8] In other words, formal membership in the Church says little or nothing about that person's internal adherence to the faith.

According to Ratzinger, the root of this religious externalism with little or no internal adherence is traceable to the eclipse of the conviction of the centrality of religious conversion that marked the initial beginnings of the Church. As Ratzinger points out, "when the Church had her beginning, it rested on the spiritual decision of the individual person to believe, on the act of conversion [...]. There was a fundamental agreement according to which Christians were distinguished from non-Christians, namely, faith in the grace of God which was revealed in Christ."[9] In other words, to be a Christian meant a definitive spiritual choice for Christ, for grace, and was not simply what Ratzinger terms a "political-cultural presupposition."[10] However, the Middle Ages brought with it a significant change, in which the Church became more or less identifiable with the world, so much so that by the twentieth century, specifically in the Western mind, the Church was no longer distinguishable from the world. Ratzinger sees this identification between Church and the world as crucial in explaining the loss of the evangelical and missionary energy of the Church. The Church is now perceived from the prism of social conventions, thoughtless tradition, and empty rituals. And the evidence of this is the lack of consciousness in many in Germany and France (Ratzinger's focus in his lecture), of the sacraments as a grace, according to which the sacraments bring about a religious encounter with God. For Ratzinger, a revival of the Church and her sacramental life calls for a retreat from the romance between Church and world, as understandably painful as this might be on the part of the Church that has grown to be too comfortable with worldliness. He writes:

> In the long run, the Church cannot avoid the need to get rid of, part by part, the appearance of her identify with the world, and once again to become what she is: the community of the faithful. Actually, her missionary power can only increase

> through such external losses. Only when she ceases to be a cheap, foregone conclusion, only when she begins again to show herself as she really is, will she be able to reach the ear of the new pagans with her good news, since until now they have been subject to illusion that they were not real pagans. Certainly, such a withdrawal of external positions will involve a loss of valuable advantages, which doubtless exist because of the contemporary entanglement of the Church with civil society. This has to do with a process which is going to take place either with or without the approval of the Church, and concerning which she must take a stand (the attempt to preserve the Middle Ages is foolish and would be not only tactically, but also factually, wrong).[11]

Is Ratzinger advocating for a ghetto Church? Certainly not, for to Ratzinger the world of faith, whose driving force is the Church, must not be severed from the world of human experience. In fact, faith in Christ is really the center of what it means to be human. Faith, says Ratzinger, "is essentially certainty; it gives men firm ground to stand on."[12] Faith in Jesus Christ is what gives human life meaning and a decisive orientation. But Ratzinger is pragmatic and realistic enough to know, with discernment, that the times will be hard for the Church, due in large part to the pervasive externalism in many a Christian that has plunged the Church into a crisis of faith, especially in the Church's traditional homeland of Europe. In a 1969 radio broadcast, Ratzinger makes a very chilling prediction regarding the Church, that, with hindsight, appears spot on and worth citing at length. Talking about what he saw as the crisis of faith in the Church, Ratzinger said:

> The future of the Church can and will issue from those whose roots are deep and who live from the pure fullness of their faith. It will not issue from those who accommodate themselves merely to the passing moment or from those who merely criticize others and assume that they themselves are infallible measuring rods; nor will it issue from those who take the easier road, who sidestep the passion of faith, declaring false and obsolete,

> tyrannous and legalistic, all that makes demands upon men, that hurts them and compels them to sacrifice themselves. To put this more positively: The future of the Church, once again as always, will be reshaped by saints, by men, that is, whose minds probe deeper than the slogans of the day, who see more than others see, because their lives embrace a wider reality.[13]

This text reveals the personalistic priority of faith in the theological imagination of Ratzinger, in that the saints are the authentic bearers of the gospel of Jesus Christ. From their encounter with Christ, the saints, in patient suffering, purification, and self-denial, in following the path of the Cross, become the guarantors of the fruitfulness of the gospel and by so doing, ensure the continuance of the Church. Clearly, what is worrisome to Ratzinger is a symbiosis that leaves faith without any vitality of its own, essentially diluting or muting the supernatural life of grace that the Church is called to foster in the world. From the ashes of this faithlessness in the Church, Ratzinger prophesizes:

> From the crisis of today the Church of tomorrow will emerge—a Church that has lost much. She will become small and will have to start afresh more or less from the beginning. She will no longer be able to inhabit many of the edifices she built in prosperity. As the number of her adherents diminishes, so it will lose many of her social privileges. In contrast to an earlier age, it will be seen much more as a voluntary society, entered only by free decision. As a small society, it will make much bigger demands on the initiative of her individual members [...]. The Church will be a more spiritual Church, not presuming upon a political mandate, flirting as little with the Left as with the Right. It will be hard going for the Church, for the process of crystallization and clarification will cost her much valuable energy. It will make her poor and cause her to become the Church of the meek. The process will be all the more arduous, for sectarian narrow-mindedness as well as pompous self-will will have to be shed. One may predict that all of this will take time.[14]

Certainly, in hindsight, it is difficult to deny the perceptive nature of this radio broadcast. Much of the Church in the Western world has lived or is living through this period of diminishment, of shedding off the accumulations the Church took upon herself during her days of socio-cultural and political influence. The Church today, especially in the Western world, has become a Church that cannot rely on any political mandate. She is increasingly a Church of the "small" that grows by free attraction, even if many physically within her walls have already made up their minds as to what to believe and what not to believe with respect to the teachings of the Church.

However, when Ratzinger talks about a Church that has lost her socio-political and cultural privileges, it is not with any sense of a utopian nostalgia, but from the perspective of the urgency of the gospel, of the missionary mandate of the Church, for Ratzinger appears to believe that a Church that is at home with the world, a Church that is too comfortable with the world, a kind of chaplain of the zeitgeist, will be a Church suffering from spiritual worldliness that inspires no one. Essentially, Ratzinger is advocating for a de-secularization of the Church wherein primacy is accorded the sacramental life and its relationship to faith; the proclamation of the gospel in ordinary and missionary preaching; and the promotion of an engaging relationship between believing faithful and his or her unbelieving fellow humans. And such a de-secularization is rooted in the conviction that the Church of today is no longer the Church of Christendom, when Western culture helped transmit the faith. The Church of today, more so in the Western hemisphere, is akin to the Church of the apostolic times, when the gospel has to be presented to a culture that is foreign and even hostile to the gospel. Such a de-secularization of the Church must necessarily engage the question of salvation, in which, the "few" of the Church have a role to play in the salvation of the "many" of the non-Church world.[15] Ratzinger does not advocate for a warfare between the Church and the non-Church worlds. Quite the opposite. Ratzinger writes:

> This opposition of Church and non-Church does not mean a state of being next to each other, nor being opposed to each other, but of being for each other, in which both sides retain

> their own necessity, and their own proper function. In the continuation of the mission of Christ, the representation of the many has been committed to the few, who are the Church, and the salvation of both takes place only in their functional coordination, and their common subordination, under the great representation of Jesus Christ, which includes both groups.[16]

This represents a very nuanced perspective on the role that the believing faithful are called to play in the world. There is no lingering triumphalism on the part of the believer. What being a believer entails is a duty for the "many," given that both the believer and the unbeliever are called to salvation in Christ, whose life, death, Resurrection, and the sending of the Spirit are the source of the salvation for the "many," a salvation that cannot be taken for granted because of the true possibility and the danger of rejection, of ending up being lost in the eternity without the love of God, which is hell.[17] To Ratzinger, this intersection of hope for salvation in Christ and the threat of being lost in the eternity of hell where the love of God is absent, is the locus wherein the contemporary Christian is called to live out the Christian calling, for, "the contemporary Christian lives his life for the most part in the midst of the new pagans, which he, in another way, knows are placed in the same situation of hope and threat, because also for them, there is no salvation other than the one in which he believes: Jesus Christ, the Lord."[18] In the final analysis, for both believer and unbeliever, Christ is the hope for salvation, according to Ratzinger. And he shows an admirable and pastoral sensitivity to the status of the unbeliever, to the doubt that might plague the unbeliever. There is absolutely no room for any fideistic triumphalism:

> Faith is always a path. As long as we live we are on the way, and on that account, faith is always under pressure and under threat. And it is healthy that it can never turn into a convenient ideology. That it does not make me hardened and unable to follow the thoughts of my doubting brother and to sympathize with him. Faith can only mature by suffering anew, at

> every stage in life, the oppression and the power of unbelief, by admitting its reality and then finally going through it, so that it again finds the path opening ahead for a while.[19]

What gives energy to this persevering struggle that comes with the maturity of faith is Christian hope in what Jesus has promised, a hope that one must live out in the spirit of the now and the yet-to-come, under the tension of one's concrete situation and what has been promised. Every believer is called to work out the meaning of this hope for his or her life, for as Ratzinger points out, "faith has its own way of life, in which what we believe is gradually substantiated by experience and is shown to be meaningful as a whole."[20] And it is from this spirit of faith and hope that a new Church will emerge from the carcass of a secularized and accommodating cultural Church. Ratzinger declared in his 1969 radio broadcast:

> But when the trial of this sifting is past, a great power will flow from a more spiritualized and simplified Church. Men in a totally planned world will find themselves unspeakably lonely. If they have completely lost sight of God, they will feel the whole horror of their poverty. Then they will discover the little flock of believers as something wholly new. They will discover it as a hope that is meant for them, an answer for which they have always been searching in secret. And so, it seems certain to me that the Church is facing very hard times. The real crisis has scarcely begun. We will have to count on terrific upheavals. But I am equally certain about what will remain at the end: not the Church of the political cult, which is dead already with Goebbels, but the Church of faith. She may well no longer be the dominant social power to the extent that she was until recently; but she will enjoy a fresh blossoming and be seen as man's home, where he will find life and hope beyond death.[21]

From the foregoing text, two insights will shape the emergence of this Church of faith: firstly, the sense of hopelessness that characterizes human life without God—the Augustinian restlessness, on the one hand, and the beauty of the believers who live out the faith, not from abstractions, but in the concrete situations of their lives, on the other hand. Ratzinger writes:

> The gospel is more than (good) "news." It is (glad) "tidings," or a "message" that, as the contemporary philosophy of language puts it, has not only an informative but also a "perfomative" effect, which means that it intends to intervene in the existential situation of the listener and to change it; only when this has happened has the message "arrived" or been received at all.[22]

This performative character of the gospel is its greatest asset, and what will guarantee a future for the faith. Therefore, the beauty of faith will emerge and be attractive to the world thanks to the concrete living of the gospel by believers. Their passion and love for God will provide a new adventure for life, even if that adventure is tedious. The life of the believer will be like Abraham's ascent on Moriah, with all his tension as he reflects on what he perceives to be God's call to sacrifice, the meaning of his life, the heir of the promises, the hope of his present and future, that is, Isaac.[23] The figure of Abraham is therefore put forward by Johannes de Silentio in *Fear and Trembling* as a counterweight to a cultural and bourgeois Christianity that sees faith merely as a mental, notional assent, a system of reflection, a rudimentary phase of intellectual development that must inevitably be transcended, as understood by the Hegelian system.[24] In the epilogue to *Fear and Trembling*, de Silentio writes that "faith is the highest passion in a person."[25] To say that faith is a passion infers that faith is what drives all human action, at least, for de Silentio. It further suggests that it is impossible to quarantine faith to a so-called religious space, leaving us free to attend to our daily cares or what is perceived to be the more important duties. If passion is what drives us to act, it indicates that a rediscovery of the primacy of the religious in human action is indispensable if we are to be truly human and to act as humans. Faith is not just the acceptance of dogmas but is above all, a way of life, what Ratzinger referred to as the performative effect of the gospel.[26] And if faith cannot be simply set aside for the sake of other more "serious" concerns, it is also the case that faith cannot simply be identified with the surrounding culture, irrespective of the length of time that faith, in this instance the Christian faith, might have shared in terms of interaction with any given culture.

The relationship between faith and culture, in the Ratzingerian understanding of things, always demands a movement, what one could refer to as an *exitus*. This *exitus* of the starting point of faith is crucial because though it is helpful to articulate the inner relationality and representationality of faith and culture, one cannot simply speak about a comfortable rapprochement between the two, as close in expression of a worldview as they might be and that we might desire them to be. Ratzinger takes the call of Abraham to leave the land of his kindred (Gen 12:1), which marks the beginning of Israel's faith, to be a significant and normative pedagogy in terms of the relationship between culture and faith: Faith begins with a cultural break. Ratzinger writes: "There will always be such a break with one's own prehistory, such a setting forth, at the beginning of a new moment in the history of faith. Yet this new beginning then proves to be a force for healing, creating a new center with the ability to draw to itself all that is true to the measure of humanity, all that is true to the measure of divinity."[27] Faith, therefore, cannot simply fit perfectly with the cultural ethos or cultural *Weltanschauung*, even if it expresses the culture. Faith always asks for the more, demands a movement which in the final analysis, becomes a healing and liberating experience for culture, for it opens culture up to a new reality coming from revelation. For Ratzinger, the theological fulcrum of a break with culture that returns to heal culture is the Cross: Calvary is a breaking forth from the earth. Jesus is lifted from the earth.[28] But from this lifting forth, from this hill of Calvary, comes a new gravity that heals the world, for Calvary draws a divided world into the unity of love with God's Son: "I, when I am lifted up from the earth, will draw all to myself" (Jn 12:32).

Added to this understanding of faith as a movement from the comfort of culture is another significant realization, namely, that the Church herself has her own culture "with her own many-layered intercultural character that has grown up in the course of her history. Without a certain exodus, a breaking-off with one's life in all its aspects, one cannot become a Christian."[29] Ratzinger's assertion here is that the living tradition of the Church gives the Church her own distinctive culture. In other words, the experiences of faith, hope and love; of worship; of listening to the Scriptures; of discerning the will of God in the midst of the world; of the apostolic witness and the life of the saints; of faith seeking understanding; and finally, of the normative historicity and universality of Jesus of Nazareth have over time built a distinctive Christian culture that shapes the Church from within as a people of God and differentiates her from without, even if the Church lives her life in the midst of the world. Ratzinger declares: "Faith is no private path to God; it leads into the people of God and into its history. God has linked himself to a history, which is now also his history and which we cannot simply erase [...]. We cannot repeat the process of the Incarnation at will, in the sense of repeatedly taking Christ's flesh away from him, so to speak, and offering him some other flesh instead. Christ remains the same, even according to his body. But he is drawing us to him."[30] This implies that catholicity is the first cultural element of the Church, for the people of God who stand before the Lamb are taking from every nation, tribe, people and tongue (Rev 7:9). Hence, faith, understood as a movement from dominant mindset or cultural outlook; and secondly, that entering the Church implies entering a distinctive culture entity with its own history, its own brightness and darkness, eventually points to the ecclesial character of faith, in which one's perception of the self is not only widened to include the other, but more especially, in entering the Church, one takes upon oneself the burden of human ecclesiastical history as well—a history that one might not be prone to readily identify with in every aspect.

And yet, as challenging as the drama of faith could and should be—for Calvary always remains a challenging experience—that is, to continue to believe without societal and even structural support, the hope of faith, the hope in the unseen that gives light to the present and saves the present and future from a repressive nihilism—that hope is what widens the horizon of the believer and could be attractive to the unbeliever who might arrive at the consciousness of the littleness of a life without the great expectations that Christian hope offers. For the believer, this life of faith has as its starting point the "small," "the little."

Taking the metaphor of the mustard seed employed by Christ (Mt 13:31), Ratzinger explains:

> The mustard seed comprises, on the one hand, smallness—wherein I am wretched—but at the same time the potential for growth. In that way there is in this mustard seed a profound depiction of faith. Faith is seen thereby not as the mere acceptance of certain propositions, but is the seed of life within me. I am only a true believer if faith is present within me as a living seed, from which something is growing and which then truly changes my world and, in doing so, brings something new into the world as a whole.[31]

In a post-modern, secularized world, the metaphor of faith as a seed could very well be indicative and depictive of the concrete situation in which the believer finds the self today, that is, to live out the faith "anonymously," with little or no external support from the zeitgeist. And yet, with the conviction that even in this state of hiddenness, the faith is truly alive, truly present, and truly fruitful in the world, and the believer patiently brings forth fruits of faith that are shown in hope and rooted in love. And the Church of faith is the Church of hope, bearing and offering the hope that faith in Jesus Christ offers for and to the world.

To Ratzinger, Catholics today owe it to themselves to confront the question as to why they are unable to proclaim and live out that faith in such a way that they can provide responses to the issues being posed by contemporary men and women? Ratzinger ponders:

> Perhaps our faith had in some ways become too mechanical. Perhaps there was also too much outward show, too little inner reality, in Guardini's terms. Faith has to be rediscovered and relived in every generation. On the other hand, we see how a generation that is no longer aware of the Christian faith and its saving powers turns elsewhere to look for such things in esoteric forms, turning to stones and heaven knows what else for help. That is to say, they look for new forms by which to call on the help of unseen powers, because man feels that

> he could or should have some other help. To that extent, we Catholics, and above all those in positions of responsibility in the Church, must ask ourselves why we have been unable to proclaim our faith in such a way as to offer answers to today's questions. So that people would once again see and feel that there is something in this faith that is just what they are after.[32]

Following this lead, the loss of the sense of faith, for Ratzinger, demands an honest examination of conscience on the part of the Church, especially Church leaders. It is one thing to lament about the decline in the practice of the faith today; but it is another, and perhaps, more crucial, to diagnose the root causes of this precipitous decline. And clearly, according to Ratzinger, Church leaders cannot wash their hands in Pilate's bowl because the witness of their lives is vital to the credibility of the faith, for it is axiomatic that those who preach about the Redeemer, must themselves be a little bit more redeemed. Given this crisis of faith in the Church today, one can draw a similarity to Judah at the time of the Prophet Ezekiel, when the glory of the Lord finally departs from Jerusalem and the Temple:

> The glory of the Lord came out from the Temple threshold and paused over the cherubs. The cherubs spread their wings and rose from the ground to leave, and as I watched the wheels rose with them. They paused at the entrance to the east gate of the Temple of the Lord, and the glory of the God of Israel hovered over them [...]. And the glory of the Lord rose to leave the city and paused on the mountain to the east of the city" (Ez 10:18–19; 11:23).

There is no denying the fact that scandals have always been a part of our history as a Church, but the globalization and flow of information following the culture of the social media have made the damaging actions of Church leaders all the more dramatic and significant. And the question about anger at the Church hierarchy necessitates the question of authority in the Church, especially given that what has scandalized many a Christian has been the abuse of ecclesial authority on the part of the hierarchy. However, while acknowledging the legitimacy of the anger that many have felt and continue to feel regarding the Church, resulting in a mass exodus from the Church in recent years, particularly in his native Germany, Ratzinger still feels that the failures of the Church should not lead to an abandonment of the faith and a walking away from the Church. As the Body of Christ, we enter a new supernatural family when we enter the Church by baptism and the other sacraments of initiation. And while one can exhibit a rightful horror at the mistakes, sins, and even crimes taking place in the bosom of the Church, Ratzinger offers a very simple appeal to the angered and in an ecclesial sense disillusioned:

> Of course, there are things about her, big and little, that are annoying. From the local Church, right up to the Church's overall leadership, within which I now have to work. People are always involved, and this always gives rise to annoyance. But you don't leave your family because you are annoyed; and certainly not if the love that binds you together is stronger, if that is what upholds you in life. And so, it is with the Church. Here too, I know that I am not here on account of this or that: I know that there have been so many mistakes in history, that there may be concrete irritations. But I know also that none of these things can take away the essential quality of the Church. Simply because that comes from a quite different source—and will always reassert itself.[33]

"The essential quality of the Church that comes from a quite different source." This is the germ of the Ratzingerian understanding of how to deal with scandals and frustrations regarding the Church, that is, the reminder that what is essential, when all the human filth has been cleared off, is the supernatural life of faith, hope and love, that comes from "quite a different source," God. And Ratzinger believes that this source is stronger than human sinfulness and human vulnerability, and that this source will outlive the scandal of human sin that is very much present and operative in the life of the Church. In the final analysis, the antidote to ecclesial scandal and sinfulness are the saints, those who live out patiently and perhaps with great suffering, the life of faith, hope and love, those open to God in the simple paths and choices of life. Ratzinger explains the significance of the presence of the simple, humble, believers, thus:

> Of course, the Church needs intellectuals too, absolutely. She needs people who will put their spiritual powers at her disposal. She also needs generous wealthy people, who want to place the powers of wealth at the service of what is good. But she still lives also on the enormous strength of those who are humble believers. In this sense the great host of those who need love and who give love is indeed her true treasure: simple people who are capable of truth because, as the Lord says, they have remained children. Through all the changes of history they have retained their perception of what is essential and have kept alive in the Church the spirit of humility and love.[34]

As it was in the beginnings of the New Testament era, with Mary of Nazareth, Joseph, Elizabeth, Zachariah, John the Baptist, Simeon, and Anna—the poor of the Lord, those who wait for the Lord, so it is even now that the Church will be sustained by humble, believing hearts that stand before God, in patience and suffering, but as well with the joy that comes from above. These are the hearts that will keep the window of the world open to the breeze of God, saving the world from a despairing worldly-centeredness. Through their prayer, faith, and love they reform and heal the Church by bringing God into the world. Above all else, saintliness is the timeless mark of the Church. Saintliness never loses its value, its relevance and its attraction. The saints are the greatest remedy to the plague of ecclesial scandal and sin. And the saints are saints precisely because they love God with their whole being, and live out love. They are the Samaritans of the world. Their hearts are moved with pity at human suffering, not just material suffering, but the greatest suffering that could befall the human being, that is, the absence of the light of God. By being open to God, the saints offer an irreplaceable service to the world, preventing the world from falling into the abyss of the emptiness of unbridled power, pleasure, and wealth. In effect, the life of the saints offers an alternative to the nihilistic spiritual ennui that is characteristic of much of the affluent world. And it certainly is the case that the rediscovery of Christian spirituality as lived out by the saints is absolutely necessary for the healing and revival of the life of faith.

Concerning the exercise of authority or power in the Church, Ratzinger finds a similarity between the hermeneutic of suspicion that often governs the contemporary attitude toward large and powerful state and multinational institutions, on the one hand, and the Church, on the other hand. People tend to be afraid of powerful governments, economic bodies, and political parties that inescapably swallow up the individual. Given this mindset, "in people's perception today the large, organized churches also appear as such instruments of anonymous power and thus not as a hope, but as a danger. It is felt that these churches are part of the establishment and collaborators in the conspiracy of power."[35] To Ratzinger, the anonymity of the ancient, large Churches partly accounts for the attractions felt toward the new "base communities" within the Catholic Church, and likewise the new small churches (largely Evangelical and Protestant), wherein people tend to feel compassion and mutual support, something of the humanness of Jesus. These small ecclesial communities represent hope, in contrast to the powerful threat of the large institutional Church. Ratzinger clearly has a sympathetic reading of these small communities that unassumingly seek to live out the faith with simplicity of heart. Ratzinger observes:

> It is also correct that in the past two decades an excessive amount of institutionalization has come about in the Church, which is alarming. The wish to participate, which is in and of itself justified, has produced ever new organizational bodies, so that those people who simply try to live unpretentiously as Christians in the Church and who would like to find nothing else in her except the communion of Word and sacrament are beginning to feel disqualified. In this situation a Church in the diaspora is probably more fortunate because it does not have as many possibilities for the ostentation we

> observe everywhere in the Western world. Here we are confronted with a tangle of authorities which almost inevitably triggers feelings of their inscrutability and our powerlessness and which can also easily obstruct the view of what is really important. Future reforms should therefore aim not at the creation of yet more institutions, but at their reduction.[36]

To Ratzinger, therefore, living out the faith takes precedence in the life of the Church, for the Church is above all the community of believers in Jesus Christ. However, the preference for a living faith in no way denies the necessity of institutional arrangements. But when institutionalization results in believers abandoning the faith, then something has gone awry. In this light, those charged with authority in the Church have the extra burden of seeing to it that in the exercise of the institutional charism of *exousia* they deploy their authority in a manner that is Christ-like and evangelical, helping in the formation of disciples in mission. Ratzinger notes:

> What makes the Church real is not that there are likeable people in her, which is really always desirable and will certainly always be the case as well. The reality is her *exousia*: she is given the power, the authority to speak words of salvation and to perform deeds of salvation which humans need and can never achieve on their own. No one can usurp the "I" of Christ or the "I" of God. The priest speaks with this "I" when he says: "this is my body" and when he says "I forgive you your sins." It is not the priest who forgives them—that would not count for much—but God who forgives them, and this definitely changes everything. But what a shaking event it is that a human being is permitted to utter the "I" of God! The priest can do it only on the basis of that authority which the Lord has given his Church. Without this authority he is nothing but a social worker.[37]

In other words, friendship with Christ or discipleship, must not be set against the institutional charism, for both are indispensable manifestations of the Church, rooted in the foundationality of the person of Christ.

In this light, authority in the Church is for a salvific purpose, and to the extent that it remains so, that the focus remains Christ's body sacramentally present and God's forgiveness readily available, then the exercise of authority in the Church remains true to the intention of the Church's Divine Founder, Christ Jesus. And to the extent that the holder of ecclesial office recognizes that he is standing in for someone else, that he is making the "I" of his human person to become an "I" of God, that he is an instrument in the hands of God for the sake of the salvation of God's people, then ecclesial office in the Church and the holder of such an office become transparently Christic, a re-presentation of the One who came not to be served but to serve and to lay down his life as a ransom for many (Mt 20:28). In a word, the power structure of the Church or the exercise of authority in the Church must never be governed by a worldly mindset or manner of proceeding, even though the Church lives out her mission in the midst of the world. There is no denying that in her long history, the Church has at different times followed the pattern of worldly power. But such aberrations are just that, that is, anomalies that cannot and must not be allowed to become the norm in any way or form. As Ratzinger reminds his readers:

> Over and again the powerful of the world have offered the Church power, and, along with the power, they have naturally tried to impose the methods of *their* power as well. But it is not the mission of the Church to set up a messianic kingdom in which human power poses and is worshiped as God's power. The power typical of political rule or technical management cannot be and must not be the style of the Church's power. By this statement we are not condemning civil power in general [...]. We are, however, condemning the identification of Church power with civil power and of God's power with civil power, as well as the absolutizing of human power in general that this entails, as if this kind of power could itself be redemption.[38]

In Ratzinger's opinion, therefore, when power is exercised in such a way that it promises to meet all of human needs, this "splendor of power" that sees power as the ability to do what one wants, of having everything at one's disposal and being able to choose the place of honor, is fundamentally, a caricature of power that should have no place in the ecclesial exercise of *exousia*. Returning to the figure of Christ as the paradigm *par excellence* for the exercise of ecclesial power, Ratzinger takes up the post-Resurrection scene of Matthew 28:18, when the Risen Lord says, "All power in heaven and on earth has been given to me." Jesus can say "all power" because Jesus' power includes both heaven and earth. "What he (Jesus) refused to take from the power of the devil," writes Ratzinger, "is now really his, but in a completely different way, since it comes from a different source. He has become the Lord of heaven and earth who now sends his disciples forth as messengers and bearers of his power."[39] According to Ratzinger's position, that it is the Risen One who is speaking in this way is highly significant, for Jesus has passed through death, through the mountain of crucifixion, in which he had relinquished all rights and privileges, letting go of his own will in order to do the will of the Father: "Thy will be done" (Mt 6:10); "Son though he was, he learnt obedience through suffering" (Heb 5:8). The height of Calvary is profoundly different from Satan's height, that position from which Satan had made a proposal to the Lord after Jesus' desert experience (Mt 4:6). As Ratzinger explains, "Satan's heights are the heights of doing things on one's own authority, of uninhibitedly determining oneself in possessing all things and being permitted all things."[40] The Risen Christ can now speak of "all" authority because by doing the will of the Father, he had become truly one with the Father. In this light, "the power he now proclaims from the mountains of exaltation is power coming from the roots of the cross and is thus radically opposed to the unrestrained power of possessing all things, being allowed all things, and being able to do all things."[41]

The implications of this Ratzingerian interpretation of Jesus' *exousia* for the nature and the exercise of ecclesial authority are clear: In the first place, it infers that ecclesial authority or power is a power in obedience. The true form of ecclesial power shows itself in the manner of Christ-like obedience to the Father. The one who exercises power in the Church is called, first and foremost, to the binding of the self to the will of Christ, just as Christ did to the will of the Father. Ecclesial power is the power that comes from a relationship with Christ, who, though equal with God, did not cling to that equality with God, but humbled himself, taking the form of a servant (Phil 2:5–11). Ecclesial power is humble power, a translation of power into humility. At the core of ecclesial power is the will of God, which, to Ratzinger, is "the ordering of the good and the true, love in person. Thus, Jesus' power is power based on love, love becoming powerful. It is power that shows us the way from all that is tangible and visible to the invisible and the truly real of God's powerful love."[42] And by entrusting to the Church the task of showing the way to God's love, Jesus has given his *exousia* to the Church, and the Church participates in the *exousia* of Jesus, and thus, the Church's *exousia*, if it is to be credible, must maintain the essential character of the *exousia* of Jesus, which is not power to subject others to one's beck and call, power of domination, but rather, power of obedience, a power of faith in Jesus, the true measure of power, a power rooted in the truth of the redemption brought about by Jesus, and a power that builds on the love of God which Jesus calls all into, God who is love. Given all that has been said above about ecclesial power, if the sensibilities of contemporary men and women toward ecclesial power is largely that of suspicion and disdain—very much so in the developed world—perhaps it is a summons on the part of ecclesial leadership to an examination of conscience in the light of the model of *exousia* that Christ lived and bequeathed to his Church.

Regarding the nature of the Church, she is first and foremost a sacrament, in that the Church is a sign, and by being a sign the Church is distinguished from other worldly institutions, that is, by her very nature as a sign. In his commentary on the Dogmatic Constitution on the Church *Lumen Gentium*, Ratzinger writes:

> A Church that sees itself sacramentally understands that it partakes of the meaning of a sign, whose responsibility it is to point beyond itself. If the Church is a "sacrament," a sign of God's presence among men, then it does not exist for its own sake. Its responsibility becomes a responsibility of pointing beyond itself. It is like a window which best fulfills its function by allowing one to see greater things through it.[43]

Again, we see Ratzinger returning to the sense of sacramentality, precisely because for Ratzinger, sacramentality indicates that what is taking place in the rites and rituals of the Church is not something contingent on human ingenuity, creativity or willfulness. In other words, sacramentality guarantees that it is God's work, enabling the Church to give what on human power alone, she would not have been able to give. This is the reasoning thanks to which one can understand the declaration in the Dogmatic Constitution on the Church *Lumen Gentium*, that "the Church is in Christ as a sacrament or instrumental sign of intimate union with God and of the unity of all humanity."[44] Chapter two of *Lumen Gentium* further develops this understanding, constructing a very explicit sacramental ecclesiology with each of the seven sacraments building up the Body of Christ, the Church. In this light, the Church is a proto-sacrament in that she understands herself as the Body of Christ that mediates the graces won by Christ for the world, by Christ's life, death, and Resurrection and the sending of the Holy Spirit. As a visible sign of Christ's love for human beings and of their love for him, the Church is indeed the sacrament of Christ.[45] Thus, to Ratzinger, sacramentality properly understood, insulates the Church from secularity, given that the various ministries in the Church are seen as services of God's holy signs.[46] Consequently, the question of the sacramental nature of the Church is tied to the question of God, of the primacy of God in the life of the Church. That is, the Church flows from God and is in the world to bring all of creation back to God. This primacy of God is what *Lumen Gentium* envisaged in its description of the Church as in Christ, a sacrament. And Ratzinger is very keen on articulating this Divine origin, mission, and destiny of the Church, especially when he feels this is being eclipsed by other viewpoints, such as the temptation of a human-produced and anthropocentric Church, largely concerned with the resolution of this-worldly issues.

In the philosophy of religion that emerges from the *Anti-Christ*, the Russian writer Vladimir Soloviev captures this motif of an all too immanent and this-worldly perception of Christianity. The Superman instrumentalizes the Church to serve his vision of universal peace, universal abolition of hunger, and the never-ending enjoyment of miracles. Thanks to fidelity to the person of Christ, Elder John, Pope Peter

II, and Professor Ernst Pauli are capable of discerning that this Superman, this Emperor, and his plan for the "Ecumenical Council of All Christians," is, in fact, the anti-Christ.[47] No one would doubt the goodness of world peace and the food for the world, especially when millions go hungry on a daily basis across the globe. But setting Christ aside for the sake of the necessities of earthly life, for the adoration of human security, welfare, and planning ends up leaving us with mere bodily satisfaction that seldom satisfies the human heart, as persuasively articulated, for example, by Augustine and Blondel. In his treatment of the temptations of Jesus in the first volume of the trilogy *Jesus of Nazareth*, Ratzinger alludes to and concurs with Soloviev's warning against this instrumentalization of Christianity as a socio-political tool whose purpose is to bring about an organized world in which all human aspirations are met, and in the process relegate faith in Christ and the conviction that God can act in history to a secondary position, if not outright rejection.[48] Ratzinger calls our attention to this temptation, which in his reading of things tends to be prevailingly attractive today:

> The tempter is not so crude as to suggest to us directly that we should worship the devil. He merely suggests that we opt for the reasonable decision, that we choose to give priority to a planned and thoroughly organized world, where God may have his place as a private concern but must not interfere in our essential purposes. Soloviev attributes to the Antichrist a book entitled *The Open Way to World Peace and Welfare*. This book becomes something of a new Bible, whose real message is the worship of well-being and rational planning.[49]

Ratzinger is unmistakably weary of this attitude that fashions the Church into one's own socio-political image and likeness, according to relevant social, political, and economic paradigms, irrespective of where one stands in the ecclesial milieu, even with the best of motives. Ratzinger calls attention to the failed attempts at the political instrumentalization of the Church over the centuries, seeing in these attempts the re-proposing of the temptation of Satan to give Christ the kingdoms of the world in all their splendor, if only Christ would worship him:

> The Christian empire attempted at an early stage to use the faith in order to cement political unity. The Kingdom of Christ was now expected to take the form of a political kingdom and its splendor. The powerlessness of faith, the earthly powerlessness of Jesus Christ, was to be given the helping hand of political and military might. This temptation to use power to secure the faith has arisen again and again in varied forms throughout the centuries, and again and again faith has risked being suffocated in the embrace of power. The struggle for the freedom of the Church, the struggle to avoid identifying Jesus' Kingdom with any political structure, is one that has to be fought century after century. For the fusion of faith and political power always comes at a price: faith becomes the servant of power and must bend to its criteria.[50]

At every age, therefore, the Church is faced with the tempting choice of the easy embrace of political structures of power, on the one hand, and the often-times suffering and purifying path of fidelity to Christ, on the other hand. An age cannot presume to make the choice for another. And the question on what path to take before the enticements of political power cannot be ignored nor avoided. It must be faced today, tomorrow, and by every age of Christianity. As Ratzinger points out:

> The Christian empire or the secular power of the papacy is no longer a temptation today, but the interpretation of Christianity as a recipe for progress and the proclamation of universal prosperity as the real goal of all religions, including Christianity—this is the modern form of the same temptation (that Jesus worships Satan in return for power over the kingdoms of the world). It appears in the guise of a question: "What did Jesus bring, then, if he didn't usher in a better world? How can that not be the content of messianic hope?"

In every age, therefore, every Christian must make the discerning decision before the temptation to identify Christianity with the political State, the temptation to embrace the kingdoms of the world in all their splendor, mindful that for the Christian losing one's life, like Christ, is the path to true life and eternal joy, and that no earthly kingdom can be identified with the Kingdom of God, which encompasses the total form of human salvation. Therefore, "earthly kingdoms must remain earthly human kingdoms, and anyone who claims to be able to establish the perfect world is the willing dupe of Satan and plays the world right into his hands."[51] In this light, the content of the Church's message is the hope that Christ brings into the world, the reality that God is no longer distant from the world, but that in Christ, God has entered the world, is close to us and accompanies us through the vicissitudes of life. In Christ, God has fully entered the human condition, understands it from inside, and, in hearts opened to God and from which faith, hope and love lives and flourishes, the Kingdom of God is brought alive in the midst of the world, constantly transforming the world from a valley of dry bones into a garden of love, peace, hope, and justice, challenges notwithstanding.

Consequently, for Ratzinger, while maintaining an attitude of self-criticism of the Church that has steadily developed especially beginning with the Enlightenment, the Church must proceed in a manner in which she is, above all else, faithful to her true identity as the sacrament, a sign of God in the midst of the world, and not primarily an institution whose meaningfulness is contingent on social works and an identification with political structures and programs, which in Ratzinger's opinion, ends up becoming counter-productive regarding the same social aspirations that might have urged the Church to embrace worldly modes of thinking and proceeding. Ratzinger points out:

> It is typical that in the Church today, the more she understands herself first and foremost as an institute for social progress, the more the social vocations dry up—the calls to serve the old, the sick, children, and so forth, vocations that flourished so much when the Church still looked essentially to God. One could say that this is a purely empirical proof of the truth of Jesus' *logion*: "Seek first the kingdom of God and his righteousness, and all the rest will be given you" (Mt 6:33). [...] (The Church) must first do decisively what is her

> very own, she must fulfill the task in which her identity is based: to make God known and to proclaim his Kingdom [...]. The Church must be ready to suffer. She must prepare space for the divine, not through power but through spirit, not through institutional strength but through witness, through love, life and suffering: and in this way she must help society to find its moral identity.[52]

In the dynamic tension between identity and relevance that the Church today faces, Ratzinger clearly weighs in on the side of identity, for he clearly believes that it is only when the Church is faithful to her identity as the people called by God to make God known in the world—only by being faithful to this mission that is simultaneously the identity of the Church—will the Church be capable of living out fruitfully, the social dimension of the Gospel message. In other words, Ratzinger seeks to maintain focus on the sense of *mystery* that is at the heart of the Church. We are not the makers of the Church. The architect of the Church is God himself, and the story of the Church is one which God himself has created, irrespective of the human elements that continue to deface the face of the Church. At the heart of the DNA of the Church is not *manufacture* but *wonder*. Ratzinger writes:

> The maker is the opposite of the wonderer (*ammiratore*). He narrows the scope of reason and thus loses sight of the mystery. The more men themselves decide and do in the Church, the more cramped it becomes for us all. What is great and liberating about the Church is not something self-made but the gift that is given to us all. This gift is not the product of our own will and invention but precedes us and comes to meet us as the incomprehensible reality that is "greater than our heart" (cf. 1 Jn 3:20). The reform that is needed at all times does not consist in constantly remodeling "our" Church according to our taste, or in inventing her ourselves, but in ceaselessly clearing away our subsidiary constructions to let in the pure light that comes from above and is also the dawning of pure freedom.[53]

Basically, two attitudes toward the Church are highlighted and contrasted in this text. On the one hand, the tendency to fashion the Church into one's own image and likeness, shaped by one's own perceptions; and on the other hand, there is the predisposition of the mysterious and the mystical, in which one sees the Church as antecedent to oneself and one's subjective ideas, and strives as much as humanly possible to take a second-place before the mystery of the Church. Certainly, one could argue that there has to be the human genius that works and is operative in the life of the Church, especially in the organizational elements of ecclesial life. Ratzinger would not deny that, as seen in his appreciation of the path of Bonaventure when the latter had to deal with the crisis of the Spiritual Franciscans and their interpretation of Joachim of Fiore. In fact, Ratzinger writes, "there is, of course, a great deal that we ourselves must organize in the Church, because she is deeply immersed in very practical human matters. It is not my intention to support any false supernaturalism."[54] The Church certainly needs the creative ingenuity of her members. Ratzinger is not advocating for an ossified Church. Each generation of believers are called to live out the faith in the new, concrete circumstances in which they live. In fact, Ratzinger clearly articulates this openness of the faith as a living reality by the Church, when he says:

> The Catholic Church knows in faith all that God has said to us in the history of revelation. Our understanding of it, of course—even the understanding of it that the Church enjoys—remains greatly inferior to the magnitude of what God has spoken. On that account there is a development of faith. Each generation, from the point of view of its own circumstances, is able to discover new dimensions of faith that even the Church did not know before. The Lord predicts this in the Gospel of John: "The Holy Spirit will lead you into all truth, so that you will come to know those things which would be too much for now." That means there is always a surplus, something anticipatory in revelation—not only with respect to what any individual may hitherto have understood, but also with respect to what the Church knows. This surplus provides each generation with a new adventure of faith.[55]

Ratzinger's approach to the question of faith is therefore much more dynamic and nuanced. What God has said in history is known in the living Church, guided by the Holy Spirit. And this remains the basis for the life of faith, the life of the Church. However, the burden of understanding and living out this deposit of faith, falls anew on every generation of believers. And this is the realm, that is, of successive generations appropriating, contributing to, and living out the faith, in which one can speak of a development in doctrine that, following another theological mentor of Ratzinger, Cardinal Newman, one can speak of an organic development of doctrine and practice. But the question of the development of doctrine is not tied to an academic exercise, nor is it possible to offer a compelling explanation without a rigorous academic process of reasoning, scrutiny, and judgment. It is basically a communal discernment of the whole Church. A brief presentation of Newman's features for the development of doctrine might be helpful in uncovering Ratzinger's preference for organic development, marked by a hermeneutic of reform, as opposed to a hermeneutic of rupture.

Marking the centenary of the death of Cardinal Newman, on April 28, 1990, in Rome, Ratzinger delivered a keynote address in which he remarked that:

> Newman's teaching on the development of doctrine, which I regard along with his doctrine on conscience, was his decisive contribution to the renewal of theology. With this he had placed the key in our hand to build historical thought into theology, or much more, he taught us to think historically in theology and so to recognize the identity of faith in all developments.[56]

What are the distinctive contributions of Newman to the development of doctrine, and how did he play these insights out in a way that marked a significant contribution to Catholic theology? But more importantly, what is the philosophical basis for the development of doctrine in the Church? In his *An Essay on the Development of Christian Doctrine*, Newman lays the ground rules to justify the idea of the development of doctrine in the Church. He posits that since Christianity imposes an idea of itself on our minds, it is in the nature of ideas to expand to other ideas connected and harmonious, one with the other.[57] The multiplier effect of ideas therefore constitutes a first basis for the development of doctrine in the Church. Secondly, given that Christianity is a universal religion adaptable to all times and places, it is of the essence to "vary in its relations and dealings toward the world around it, that is, it will develop."[58] In this sense, the intrinsic nature of Christianity as an inculturated and Incarnational religion makes room for a development of doctrine. Newman's third argument for the possibility of the development of doctrine is grounded on the nature of Sacred Scripture.[59] Basically, because Scripture does not provide clear answers to questions such as what happens to a Christian who relapses into sin after baptism, or give a clear explanation for purgatory, the development of the episcopacy, *et cetera*, and even if one were to find blueprints for some of these doctrines, the inchoateness in Sacred Scripture favors a development of doctrine over time.

With these presuppositions in mind, Newman goes on to list seven criteria that he called "tests" in the 1845 edition and "notes" in the 1878 edition, which set the stage for the understanding of development of Christian doctrine. These "notes" include the following: Firstly, development and the preservation of the substantial form. The philosophical basis advanced in this argument is that of physical growth, in which, irrespective of later developments, there is a correspondence with the initial being of the organism. Newman maintains, "young birds do not grow into fishes, and small are a baby's limbs, a youth's are larger, yet they are the same."[60] However, this unity or preservation of type does not justify a rejection of considerable differences and alterations in the process of growth and development, for as Newman is quick in pointing out, "great changes in outward appearance and internal harmony occur in the instance of the animal creation itself."[61] Of significant importance here is to distinguish substantial identity from external sameness, in such a manner that the unity of type is consistently preserved, external changes notwithstanding.

The second argument that Newman advances has to do with development and the continuity of principles. Newman argues that doctrines consist in the principles that they embody. He differentiates principles from doctrines by postulating that while principles are abstract and general, doctrines are connected to facts. Also, doctrines can grow and are enlarged, while principles are permanent.[62] This implies that doctrines are developed by the principles at play, and for any development to be faithful it must "retain both doctrine and the principle with which it started."[63] In the Newmanian sense, any discourse of doctrinal development must be grounded on the principles that hitherto defined and shaped the doctrine from the outset. A doctrine rightly develops if it is faithful to its principles. It is a corruption if the doctrine alters its principles.

The third feature has to do with development and the power of assimilation. The philosophical basis for this argument is that development grows by the absorption of external material. As Newman says, "two things cannot become one except there be a power of assimilation in one or the other."[64] Development is a process of incorporation, in which what is new is grafted unto what is old. If the new is incompatible with the old or cannot fit into the old, Newman does not see the possibility of recognizing this as authentic development. The resultant growth or novelty has to be compatible with the tradition. There has to be a unifying power of faithful developments to constitute authentic development.

Advancing the argument for the development of doctrine further, Newman writes that logical consequence is crucial for organic development of doctrine that avoids a rupture. According to Newman, the organization of thought guarantees its intellectual development, in that the reasoning of a doctrine should follow from premises to conclusion. In this way, doctrine grows in the mind by remaining in the mind. This does not imply a rationalism devoid of faith, which Newman defines as "the exercise of reason instead of faith in matters of faith."[65] The kernel of the argument is that the process of the mind goes beyond cold logic, comprising the head and the heart. One is reminded of Pascal's famous declaration, "The heart has its reasons of which reason knows nothing: we know this in countless ways [...]. It is the heart which perceives God and not the reason. That is what faith is: God perceived by the heart, not by reason."[66] Here is a genuine openness to other human motivations that must not be subjected to the workshop of absolute rationalism. In the *Grammar of Assent*, Newman tellingly remarks:

> The heart is commonly reached, not through reason, but through the imagination, by means of direct impressions, by the testimony of facts and events, by history, by description. Persons inflame us, voices melt us, looks subdue us, and deeds inflame us. Many a man will live and die upon a dogma: no man will be a martyr for a conclusion.[67]

One finds here a positive broadening of the horizons that, while admitting the place of reason, opens reason to other critical and profound influences. To return to our theme of logical sequence, true development of doctrine happens when a mature doctrine appears as the logical issue of its original teaching. The fruits of the tree are indicative of the tree.

The next aspect that Newman puts forth has to do with development and the anticipation of the future of that which is being developed. The philosophical principle at play here is that the development of doctrine is the natural consequence of the doctrine from which it proceeds. As Newman maintains, "early or recurring intimations of tendencies which afterwards are fully realized, is a sort of evidence that those later and more systematic fulfillments are only in accordance with the original idea."[68] By implication, one can discern a genuine development of doctrine through the definite anticipation at an early period in the history of the idea to which it belongs. The evidence of this could be found in the evolution of the ideas of mainline Protestantism. The many theories that developed beyond Luther and Calvin, this position seems to suggest, were already present, even if in an embryonic form, in the positions posited *ab initio* by the Reformers. To discern if a genuine development of a given doctrine is possible is to view its anticipated future. A definite indication is a fair presumption of a genuine development of doctrine.

Going further, Newman argues that for there to be a genuine doctrinal development, such a development must reflect a conservative action upon its past. To Newman, a development that contradicts or reverses the course of doctrine that has been developed before it is certainly a corruption of doctrine. It is not a genuine development. Corruption in this sense "is a development in that very stage in which it ceases to illustrate, and begins to disturb, the acquisitions gained in its previous history."[69] A true development therefore conserves antecedent developments, illustrating and corroborating, not obscuring or correcting the body of thought from which it proceeds. In this sense, a true development of Christology, for example, cannot declare that Jesus, the Eternal Word of God, is no longer "true God, true Man," as stated by Chalcedon. Even in an age of religious pluralism, true development cannot reduce Jesus to one messianic figure among others, since his divinity is an essential part of his being. He did not cease to be God's Son by becoming man at the Incarnation. Jesus Christ is the true discriminating point in inter-religious dialogue, the scandal of particularity in an age given over to plurality and diversity, healthy as these might be. In a word, a true development of doctrine conserves what has gone before. It is governed by a hermeneutic of continuity, not one of rupture or discontinuity, Newman would hold.

And finally, for Newman, a true development of doctrine has with it a certain tenacity, a chronic vigor, for as Newman states, "the course of heresies is always short."[70] What readily comes to mind is Gamaliel's intervention before the Sanhedrin: "If this enterprise, this movement of theirs, is of human origin it will break up of its own accord; but if it does in fact come from God you will not only be unable to destroy them, but you might find yourselves fighting against God" (Acts 5:38–39). Newman's argument is that a corruption of doctrine cannot stand out for long. It is of essence transitory in character. One could glean from the history of heresies in the life of the Church a repeated pattern of short life-spans that eventually not only helped the Church in clarifying its understanding of revealed truth, but also provided an opportunity of intense ecclesial discernment. Taken together, these seven points provide the framework for understanding Newman's theory of the development of doctrine, and how that plays out in the life of the faithful in terms that are instinctive, and by which they can judge a development to be in accord with revealed doctrine or contrary to revealed doctrine. Newman sees these seven points as a seamless garment that ensures the process of developing a doctrine within a given context, in order to make that doctrine more accessible and meaningful within that framework or epoch.

As stated above, Ratzinger sees Newman's teaching on the development of doctrine as the keys handed by Newman to the Church that enable the Church to build historical thought into theology, to think historically while thinking theology, and above all, to recognize the identity of faith in historical developments. And for Ratzinger, Newman's theology of the development of doctrine is yet to be fully grasped and utilized by the Church. In other words, its reception by the wider Church is a task in waiting, a future with unimaginable potentials for theology. Ratzinger asserts:

> It seems to me that Newman's starting point, also in modern theology, has not yet been fully evaluated. Fruitful possibilities awaiting development are still hidden in it. At this point I would only like to refer again to the biographical background of this concept. It is known how Newman's insight into the ideas of development influenced his way to Catholicism. But it is not just a matter of an unfolding of ideas. In the concept of development, Newman's own life plays a role. That seems to become visible to me in his well-known words: "[...] to live is to change, and to be perfect is to have changed often."[71]

In other words, doctrinal development for Newman as well as for Ratzinger, was not and is not merely an abstract conceptual framework, but a living, personal reality, in which the believer develops doctrine by converting and allowing the faith to reorient and shape the believer's life. Following Ratzinger's interpretation of Newman, therefore, the heart of doctrinal development is spiritual development. Doctrine and spirituality go together, with spirituality serving as the livewire of doctrine. It is interesting that Ratzinger sees in Newman's idea of development a connection between Augustine and Newman, specifically on the issue of ongoing spiritual conversion.[72] In this sense, even for the Christian, conversion does not bring with it a magical break with the scars of sin and the ongoing battle with sin and temptation. Rather, conversion, as ongoing development, puts the Christian on a lifelong path of inner and outward conformity to the Lord, a spiritual itinerary, an ascent to God. In this regard, Ratzinger writes:

> Conversion is the *iter*—the roadway of a whole lifetime. And faith is always "development," and precisely in this manner

> it is the maturation of the soul to truth, to God, who is more intimate to us than we are to ourselves. In the idea of "development," Newman had written his own experience of a never finished conversion and interpreted for us, not only the way of Christian doctrine, but that of the Christian life. The characteristic of the great Doctor of the Church, it seems to me, is that he teaches not only through his thought and speech but also by his life, because within him, thought and life are interpenetrated and defined. If this is so, then Newman belongs to the great teachers of the Church, because he both touches our hearts and enlightens our thinking.[73]

Given this Ratzingerian reading of Newman, the development of doctrine is a spiritual autobiographical path, for Newman and for every believer. In the final analysis, genuine development of doctrinal truth happens only when the soul is open to the supernatural life of grace in Christ Jesus, in an intense life of holiness. Benedict remarked in his address during the prayer vigil at Hyde Park, Saturday September 18, 2010:

> He (Newman) saw clearly that we do not so much accept the truth in a purely intellectual act, as embrace it in a spiritual dynamic that penetrates to the core of our being. Truth is passed on not merely by formal teaching, important as that is, but also by the witness of lives lived in integrity, fidelity, and holiness; those who live in and by the truth instinctively recognize what is false and, precisely as false, inimical to the beauty and goodness which accompany the splendor of truth, *veritatis splendor*.[74]

For Newman and for Ratzinger, therefore, the kindly light of faith is what leads us not only to grow in our spiritual lives, but likewise to develop intellectually as well. Guided by the kindly light, faith and love intersect in the heart of the believer, finding a home in which they can live and flourish, bringing the believer to that point of abandonment into the hands of God: "I loved to choose and see my path, but now Lead Thou me on!" In faith, the theologian allows the self to be led by that kindly light, and not only by one's own subjective preferences. It is under the kindly light that genuine doctrinal development matures and unfolds.

Turning to Ratzinger's take on Newman and the conscience, which Ratzinger perceives to be integral to Newman's teaching on the development of doctrine, Ratzinger reads Newman's teaching from the perspective that conscience is an antidote to moral relativism. Like John Henry Cardinal Newman, Ratzinger believes that the "way of conscience is everything except a way of self-sufficient subjectivity: it is a way of obedience to objective truth."[75] In the opinion of Ratzinger, the life and work of Newman could be designated as "a single great commentary on the question of conscience."[76] But why is conscience central to Newman? Ratzinger answers that "conscience is central for him because truth stands in the middle. To put it differently, the centrality of the concept of *conscience* for Newman is linked to the prior centrality of the concept of *truth* and can only be understood from this vintage point."[77] It is insufficient to simply follow a clear conscience or, at best, not to act against one. In other words, one could not simply justify one's political actions or compromises on the grounds of following one's conscience, for conscience alone, at least from the Ratzingerian interpretation of Newman, cannot account for the whole reality of human moral action if conscience is severed from objective truth, which finds itself in the searching and listening heart, lived in solidarity with the other, especially with those that will be affected by one's political decisions. As Ratzinger points out, "a man of conscience is one who never acquires tolerance, well-being, success, public standing, and approval on the part of prevailing opinion at the expense of truth. In this regard, Newman is related to Britain's other great witness of conscience, Thomas More, for whom conscience was not at all an expression of subjective stubbornness or obstinate heroism."[78] Conscience demands a higher loyalty to objective truth, as costly as such a loyalty might be, as seen in the life of a statesman like Thomas More. Such is the case because conscience is not intended simply to make us comfortable, but to help us live truthful lives.

It is urgent to remember that conscience cannot be identical to personal wishes and taste. And neither can conscience be reduced to social advantage, to the consensus of the group, much less to the demands of socio-political power.[79] If this is the state of things, then, as Ratzinger points out, "it will not do to identify man's conscience with the self-consciousness of the 'I'—with its subjective certainty about itself and its moral behavior. On the one hand, this consciousness may be a mere reflection of the social surroundings and the opinions in circulation. On the other hand, it might also derive from a lack of self-criticism, a deficiency in listening to the depths of one's own soul."[80] In other words, the subjective judgment of conscience is not necessarily infallible, for conscience is likewise obliged to seek the truth, for the certainty of conscience is not a sufficient criterion for truth. Put differently, the certainty of an erroneous conscience does not make the judgment of such an erroneous conscience right. In the final analysis, conscience must always maintain a relationship with objective truth, which implies that the individual must remain open to reason and to that which does not necessarily conform to one's own preferences and singular comforts.

Similar to Newman, in *True and False Reform in The Church*, the great conciliar French Dominican theologian, Yves Congar, brings forth helpful insights to this question of change and development. Congar argues that while the Church never loses what she once possessed, carrying as it were her youthfulness and immaturity into old age, when the present becomes frozen in the past it blocks the flow of life.[81] The present and future of the Church mean that the Church has to be present to the present and future of the world. Congar singles out two temptations to guard against that provide the motive for why and how the Church needs to be reformed, why and how we must understand and appreciate change and development in the Church, as the Church goes forth in history, in order not to fade into irrelevance. Firstly, the Church must guard against the temptation to Pharisaism, meaning turning the means to an end.[82] The Pharisees started a pious movement of internal resistance to the prevalent watering down of Judaism by Roman presence, but ended up with the lifeless letter of such an observance. The second theological ground for the necessity of openness to change and development in the Church is what Congar describes as the temptation to become a Synagogue. He maintains, "as for the Synagogue of old, *fidelity* is often the reason given for turning away from change."[83] The challenging invitation is to be open to growth and adaptation, conscious all the time of the distinction between what is permanently valuable, such as the sacraments and the essential structure of the Church, and what by its nature can become obsolete, such as even the very formulation of a dogma in language that might not be meaningful to the sensibilities of the post-modern world. It is crucial that the work of the theologian is kept in a healthy balance so that the Church does not become a laboratory for theologians, but a privileged place of genuine faith and spiritual encounter, a theology that is done *sentire cum ecclesia*! The magisterium has a defining and crucial role in this process of development and change, for "if there occur a separation from the bishops who watch over and keep the apostolic tradition alive, it is the bond with Christ which is irreparably compromised."[84]

That said, it is important to highlight that the tradition from the patristic era right up to the Council of Trent could be a necessary corrective to the practice of sometimes excessive heavy-handedness toward theologians, perceived or real, on the part of the magisterium. In Trent, for example, the theologians first took the floor and debated the issue under consideration, while the bishops listened. Thereafter, the bishops were able to make up their minds as pastors of the Church. Without the theologian, the deposit of faith risked becoming ossified, locked in a hovel of crippling irrationalism and paralyzing obscurantism. Without the magisterium, chaos could become the order of the day. The Church needs the two wings of the theologian and the magisterium to fly to the divine heights that faith demands. Sometimes the flight might be rough. But the flight cannot take place with a single wing. And given Ratzinger's long service at the Congregation for the Doctrine of the Faith, the necessity of the work of both theologian and magisterium would be axiomatic to him.

Given all that has been said above regarding doctrinal development, in Newman, and true reform of the Church from the perspective of Congar, when Ratzinger pushes back on the perceived "novelties," it is not a question of him being against the present times for the sake of being against, talk less of Ratzinger's push back being construed as stemming from an obsession with the past. To the specific question of the Church and how the Church must live in the world of today, Ratzinger's bone of contention has to do with the pride of place that is accorded human organizational talents and proclivities in the light of the Divine vision or mission that the Body of Christ is called to be in the midst of the world, namely, to invite all into the spiritual development exemplified in the life of say, Newman and the saints. In other words, there is a dialectical tension between the present and the past, inasmuch as the question remains of how the believer must live today, in the here and now. How do we live the present of the faith, with the consciousness that this faith is that which we have received, that which has come to us from the "outside," from God, and has been transmitted in the living Church of the past to the Church of the present, with the vision of shaping the Church of the present and opening her up with the world to the eschatological Church of the beatific vision, the Church of the blessed at the end of history when history will be handed over to God and God will become all in all (1 Cor 15:28)? For Ratzinger, the *modus operandi* should not be such that rather than conforming ourselves to the Church as revealed in Word and sacraments, that which we have received, that which has been handed to us by the living tradition of the saints, we tend to fashion the faith and the Church into our own image and likeness, into our own "tastes," which ends up leaving us with a "manufactured" faith and a factory-made Church.

Herein lies the distinction that Ratzinger makes between the party of Christ and the Church of Jesus Christ. With the former, what dominates is the human desire to reinvent the Church according to our subjective sensitivities. With the latter, the spirit is one of receptivity, of the consciousness that in dealing with the Church, I am entering into something that is bigger than myself. But what is the central nexus of the latter attitude? Reflecting on the third chapter of Saint Paul's Letter to the Corinthians, which shows the Church in Corinth inundated by divisions and disagreements, Ratzinger writes:

> When I advocate a party, it thereby becomes *my* party, whereas the Church of Jesus Christ is never *my* Church but always *his* Church. Indeed, the essence of conversion lies precisely in the fact that I cease to pursue a party of my own that safeguards my interests and conforms to my taste but that I put myself in his hands and become his, a member of his

> Body, the Church [...]. The Corinthians see in Christianity an interesting religious theory that answers to their taste and their expectations. They choose what suits them, and they select it in the form that pleases them. But when one's own will and desire is the decisive criterion, schism is a foregone conclusion, because there are multiple and opposing varieties of taste.[85]

To Ratzinger, therefore, what can safeguard the Church from degenerating to a party is the spirit of conversion, that is, an attitude that points to human insufficiency without God. The realization here is that Christianity is hard. It is challenging. It is difficult, for it is in the nature of Christianity to ask us to live a different life, a life in which what is decisive is not self-assertion but self-gift. Self-assertion reveals itself in that pick-and-choose mentality, a Christianity of convenience that makes little or no demands on us, for what dominates are our own expedient and fitting preferences. Ratzinger notes in this regard:

> A club, a circle of friends, a party can grow from such an ideological choice, but not a Church that overcomes antitheses between men and unites them in the peace of God. The principle by which a club develops is personal taste; but the principle on which the Church is based is obedience to the call of the Lord as we see it in the Gospel: "He called them, and immediately they left the boat and their father and followed Jesus" (Mt 4:21).[86]

In this consciousness, the purpose of the Church is not to put forth a program that suits oneself, that is convenient for oneself, that works for and makes one comfortable, a club of friends. Undoubtedly not. On the contrary, the Church is there to call a person to a new form of life in Christ Jesus, a form of life that can only come about through conversion, that is, from a focus on the creature to a focus on the Creator. And herein lies the significance of baptism as a doorway into the Church, for baptism marks a new birth, the beginning of the supernatural life, and this supernatural life is the hidden heart of Christian message. Ratzinger affirms:

> The Church cannot act according to the motto: What is going to be possible; what is not? She is not there in order to discover the most acceptable form of compromise, but to hold out to people, without distortion, the whole magnitude of God's Word and his will—even if this speaks against herself and against her own spokesmen.[87]

In other words, the believer is not the sole actor in the Church, visible and important as the believer is to the life of the Church. Ecclesial discernment is therefore not a question of a majority versus a minority, a game of numbers in which the desire is to strive to carry the day. God's Word must not be subjected to the whims and caprices of the recent majority, but must be allowed to challenge and call all to conversion, to the new life offered in Christ thanks to the proclamation of the Gospel and the celebration of the sacraments. Put differently, the Gospel and not the compromising tactics and positions of the latest fashionable sole-actors, is the democratic majority in the life of the Church. Ratzinger cautions against the sole-actors attitude that he senses to be pervasive in the contemporary Church:

> *We* make the Church, we try to improve her and to arrange her like a comfortable house. *We* want to offer programs and ideas that appeal to as many as possible. That God himself becomes active, that *he* acts is something that we no longer take for granted in the modern world. But precisely by making this assumption, we follow in the footsteps of the Corinthians: we confuse the Church with a party and faith with a party program. The circle of what *we* do and are remains closed.[88]

For Ratzinger, two attitudes are at variance in the contemporary Church—namely, the sole-actors attitude, on the one hand, and the mindfulness that God still acts and speaks in history in the Church of today, on the other hand. Regarding the sole-actors attitude, Ratzinger argues that "the more we ourselves do in the Church, the more uninhabitable she becomes, because everything human is limited and is in opposition to other human realities."[89] These two attitudes need not be antithetical, but one must follow the other. That is, while acknowledging one's own existence and perceptions, it is fundamental to recognize that God still speaks and acts today, which demands obedience even when God calls a person to where he readily does not want to go (Jn 21:18). Ratzinger refers to this attitude of obedience to God as the "cruciform character of discipleship," in which "I abandon *my* taste and submit myself to *him*. But it is in this very way that I am set free, because the real slavery is imprisonment in the circle of our own wishes."[90] Ratzinger argues that Jesus Christ himself is the example *par excellence* of this obedience to God. Ratzinger writes:

> Christ is not the founder of a party and not a religious philosopher [...]. He is not someone who thinks up for himself all sorts of ideas and recruits adherents to them. The Letter to the Hebrews characterizes the entrance of Christ into the earthly world with the words of Psalm 40: Sacrifice and oblation you desired not; you have prepared for me a body (Ps 40:7; Heb 10:5). [...] When we say Yes to him, we do not merely choose ideas, but put our life in his hands and become a "new creation" (2 Cor 5:17; Gal 6:15). This is why the Church is not a club, not a party, not even a sort of religious state within the secular state, but a body—Christ's body. And this is why the Church is not of our making but is constructed by the Lord himself when he cleanses us by Word and sacrament and thus makes us his members.[91]

As earlier remarked, this Christological emphasis regarding the nature and mission of the Church has nothing to do with a false sense of supernaturalism. Ratzinger is seeking for the space of God at the heart of the Church, for what truly makes the Church is God, encountered in Jesus in the midst of the Church (Mt 18:20), and in the celebration of the sacraments.

Ratzinger's extended reflection on the pre- and post-conciliar Church led him to coin a description that reveals his deepest ecclesial intuitions, that is, the hermeneutic of continuity and reform, which he opposed to the hermeneutic of rupture.[92] Ratzinger sees the Church as an organism that develops in the various epochs of history, and it is precisely as such, as an organism, that we can discern a true development in the Church, which flows from that which is already there, which has not been invented or created by us, but received from the Lord, in the process of revelation.[93] In other words, the starting point of the Church is not sociology but faith, revelation. The Church is herself the mission of God, the masterful plan to restore all things in Christ (Eph 1:10). In dealing with the Church, therefore, the attitude of mystery and faith takes precedence in that we are encountering an organism that exceeds mere human capacity, a story God himself has created, as Benedict recently described the Church:

> The encounter with God means also, at the same time, that I myself become open, torn from my closed solitude and received into the living community of the Church. That living community is also a mediator of my encounter with God, though that encounter touches my heart in an entirely personal way. Faith comes from hearing (*fides ex auditu*), St. Paul teaches us. Listening, in turn, always implies a partner. Faith is not a product of reflection nor is it even an attempt to penetrate the depths of my own being. Both of these things may be present, but they remain insufficient without the "listening" through which God, from without, from a story He himself created, challenges me.[94]

And still talking about this transcendental and religious nature of the Church, Benedict XVI further insists to Jacques Servais, S.J.:

> The faith community does not create itself. It is not an assembly of men who have some ideas in common and who decide to work for the spread of such ideas. Then everything would be based on its own decision and, in the final analysis, on the majority vote principle, which is, in the end it would be based on human opinion. A Church built in this way cannot be for me the guarantor of eternal life nor require decisions from me

> that make me suffer and are contrary to my desires. No, the Church is not self-made; she was created by God and she is continuously formed by him. This finds expression in the sacraments, above all in that of baptism: I enter into the Church not by a bureaucratic act, but through the sacrament. And this is to say that I am welcomed into a community that did not originate in itself and is projected beyond itself. The ministry that aims to form the spiritual experience of the faithful must proceed from these fundamental givens. It is necessary to abandon the idea of a Church which produces herself and to make clear that the Church becomes a community in the communion of the body of Christ. The Church must introduce the individual Christian into an encounter with Jesus Christ and bring Christians into His presence in the sacrament.[95]

Clearly, notwithstanding the necessity of the human organizational elements of the Church that Ratzinger clearly acknowledges as pointed out above, Ratzinger sees the most important dimension of the Church to be her supernatural origins, that is, a Church that comes about thanks to the explicit will and design of God. This religious sense can definitely not be taken for granted in a post-enlightenment and secularized contemporary world. Trust in the Church, even in the minds of many a good and devout Catholic, has been greatly eroded by scandals that have plagued the Church, as many watched in disbelief the betrayal of the gospel by those who should know better.

Amidst these challenges facing the proclamation of the gospel, Ratzinger argues for what might be described as an "inconvenient Christianity," in which the gospel supposedly comforts the afflicted and afflicts the comfortable. Ratzinger maintains:

> Anyone who wants Christianity to be just a joyful message in which there can be no threat of judgment is distorting it. Faith does not reinforce the pride of a sleeping conscience, the vainglory of people who make their own wishes the norm for their life, and who thus refashion grace so as to devalue

> both God and man, because God can then in any case only approve, and is only allowed to approve, everything. Yet any one of us who is suffering and struggling can be certain that "God is greater than our hearts" (1 Jn 3:20) and that whatever my failures, I may be full of confident trust, because Christ suffered for me, too, and has already paid the price for me.[96]

Naturally, one can discern in this view of a "good Church" a very human-centered perspective, in which the Church is almost something that we ourselves are creating. As noted above, Ratzinger resists this attitude. While public social engagement might bring credibility to the Church before a secular audience, the essential identity of the Church as a mission of God, as a story whose narrator is God himself, demands that at every step on the way, the voice of the story-teller must be given attention; at every instance, it is crucial to allow more room for a discerning silence, so that we can hear the voice of God. Listening has a necessary ecclesial character. Evidently, while not rejecting the essential nature of the social engagement of the Church in bringing about a more just and humane society, Ratzinger is eager that the Church does not lose its transcendental character and mission in the process of carrying out her social doctrine. An anecdote that Ratzinger himself recounts is very telling about this Ratzingerian perspective of the primacy of God in the life of the Church.

Shortly before the German bishops left for the Second Vatican Council, they met to discuss what they would take to the Council as a group. Ratzinger recounted that the members of the German Bishops' Conference were unanimous that the theme of the Council would have to be the Church. After a while, the bishop of Regensburg, Rudolf Graber (1903–1992), took to the floor, and said to his brother bishops: "My dear Brothers, at the Council you must above all talk about God. That is what is most important."[97] The German Bishops present, according to Ratzinger, were most struck by the seriousness of what that colleague from Regensburg said. While the German Bishops' simply could not suggest "God" as the theme of Vatican II, they could not escape the seriousness of the exhortation to "talk about God" by Bishop Graber. This incident never left the young Ratzinger, who would participate in the

Council as a *peritus* of Cardinal Josef Frings, Archbishop of Cologne. According to Ratzinger, Bishop Graber's "talk about God" left an inner unease in Cardinal Frings, as the latter continually asked himself how he could live up to this imperative at the Council.[98] Ratzinger believes that the overarching methodology of the Second Vatican Council in its treatment of the doctrine of the Church was to ground the question of the Church on the question of God: "The Second Vatican Council certainly did intend to subordinate what it said about the Church to what it said about God, and to set it in that context; it intended to propound an ecclesiology that was theo-logical in the proper sense."[99] And this "talk about God" is the central nexus of Ratzinger's perception of the origin, identity, and mission of the Church, a story which God himself has created and is creating. And to talk about God is to talk about love, for God is love (1 Jn 4:7), as Benedict would remind us in his first encyclical.

5.2 *Logos* as Unity of Love: Ratzinger's Engagement with the *Aufklärung*'s Notion of Self-Assertive Love

With his first encyclical *Deus Caritas Est*, Ratzinger sought to place the love of God as front and center of the ecclesial life of the Church. To the many with previously formed negative perceptions about Ratzinger, *Deus Caritas Est* came as a pleasant surprise. But the encyclical itself provides a glimpse into why love has always been central to the theological imagination of Ratzinger. Benedict writes:

> In the critique of Christianity which began with the Enlightenment and grew progressively more radical, this new element was seen as something thoroughly negative. According to Friedrich Nietzsche, Christianity had poisoned *eros*, which for its part, while not completely succumbing, gradually degenerated into vice. Here the German philosopher was expressing a widely-held perception: doesn't the Church, with all her commandments and prohibitions, turn to bitterness the most precious thing in life? Doesn't she blow the whistle just when the joy which is the Creator's gift offers us a happiness which is itself a certain foretaste of the Divine?[100]

In effect, the Church might truly have something to say to contemporary men and women on a whole range of issues, such as on love, on the meaning of life, family, on the just ordering of society, on peace, and on the final destiny of the human being. But perhaps to Ratzinger, Christianity has yet to offer a forceful rebuttal to what appears to him to be a mischaracterization of the Christian understanding of love, by the *Aufklärung*, especially by the extremist voices such as Nietzsche. And if love in all its modes and tenses is the defining heartbeat of everything human, then clearly the Christian faith had the duty to offer anew, the core meaning of Christian love to a skeptical or largely indifferent world. And not only is the question about love concerned with providing a response to the *Aufklärung*, but, more so today, the question of love takes on an urgent necessity when in the name of God, acts of terror are unleashed on large numbers of peoples in almost every corner of the globe. The Christian understanding of love, therefore, can serve as a voice of commonsense in a highly fractured world, both nationally and in the internal coldness in the private lives of many an individual. The task of promoting a culture of love in the contemporary world is certainly an urgent one for Christians, because Christianity understands itself as built upon the foundation of mutual love (Jn 15:35). Discipleship comes about thanks to mutual love.

To Ratzinger, therefore, the question of Christian love is one that is not only central to his theological imagination but has likewise been consistent. Ratzinger himself attests to this when he says to Peter Seewald in *Light of the World*:

> Two themes have always accompanied me in my life, then: on the one hand, the theme of Christ, as the living, present God, the one who loves us and heals us through suffering; and, on the other hand, the theme of love [...] because I knew that love is the key to Christianity, that love is the angle from which it has to be approached.[101]

And as is evident in the corpus of Ratzingerian writings, this angle of love is very much present. But how does Ratzinger do this? How does he keep the twin passions of his theological career, namely Christ and love, so clearly consistently together? Christopher Collins, S. J. provides a plausible response. Collins writes: "With the Logos as the key to his approach, Ratzinger's theology is reasonable, but not abstract. Rather, it is reasonable in a manner that becomes personally attractive when communicated in the context of the biblical narrative as the Logos shows itself as visible, incarnate love in Jesus Christ."[102] This is the basis on which Ratzinger can declare love as the hermeneutical key to understanding Christianity. It is because—as will be seen as this section develops—love, even if it begins with the abstract demarcations of eros, philia and agape[103] as Benedict points out in *Deus Caritas Est*,[104] in the final analysis, love is not an epistemological concept, but an ontological reality that demands a deciding consent before the being of love, Logos as love. And the only explanation for the reality of the Logos as love resides in the very being of God himself as love. Ratzinger rhetorically asks:

> "The Word became flesh." Before this revelation we once more wonder: how can this be? The Word and the flesh are mutually opposed realities; how can the eternal and almighty Word become a frail and mortal being? There is only one answer: Love. Those who love desire to share with the beloved, they want to be one with the beloved, and Sacred Scripture shows us the great love story of God for his people which culminated in Jesus Christ.[105]

In this light, the theological metaphor of love in its incarnate form, has love as its eternal and historical origin. And once again, Ratzinger finds the concept of the *logos* as an entry point for his Christological theology of love.

Returning to the commonplace charge against Christianity by the *post-Aufklärung* mindset that Ratzinger references in *Deus Caritas Est*, one can say that this charge is logically consistent with *Aufklärung* thinking regarding nature, the Sonship of Christ, and their understanding of what essentially comprises personhood. Such is the case because underlining all four aspects is self-assertiveness and the desire for autonomy. Like nature's necessary causality in need of no creator God; like the emptying of any uniqueness of the divine Sonship of Christ which is now interpreted as a functional equivalence of the moral person; and like the unbridled will to power that characterizes the personhood of the *Übermensch*, the principle of self-assertion largely defines the conception of love that is shaped by the spirit of the *Aufklärung*. And it is perhaps not a sheer coincidence that much of this assertiveness has had to do not with love as *philia* or *agape*, but with love as *eros*. In this sense, one could say that the charge by Nietzsche against the Christian understanding of love has become an ideology that cannot account for the communitarian character of how humans must live. Such an ideology fails to explain human beings in their innermost core, which is in their desire to relate, to connect to the other, in a way that he or she finds the self and complements the self without destroying the other.

The contrast could not be more glaring when placed alongside the self-assertiveness, the egocentricity that characterizes the vision of love that emerges from the spirit of the *Aufklärung*. And this sense of self-assertion is not limited to Nietzsche. Even with Kant, the whole ideology of autonomy of the categorical imperative, as discussed above, is built on this understanding of the primacy of the individual reading of things. Judgment for Kant is exclusively a matter of the individual conscience. One cannot therefore expect such individualism not to spill over on the core issue that defines existence which is human love. And with Hegel, the whole *Phenomenology* is essentially the spirit coming into consciousness of itself, as seen above. And one can even go as far back as Descartes' *cogito*, the *magna carta* of individual self-assertiveness. De Gaál offers a comprehensive and trenchant analysis of the philosophical trajectory of this mindset of self-assertiveness that is clearly antithetical to the Christian understanding of love as put forth by Ratzinger. De Gaál writes:

> Friedrich Nietzsche (1844–1900) and Martin Heidegger (1889–976) glorified the project of human self-determination. Rudolf Bultmann (1884–1976)—and other theologians in his wake—claimed to liberate people for a better understanding of the self through a program of demythologization. All these efforts result only in an erosion of the Christian

> message—and *l'ennui* (boredom) is the corresponding reaction on the part of human beings. Apparently, it is useless for Benedict to demonstrate the absurdity of Kant's transcendental aesthetics. The radical otherness of God utterly surprises. Expressed in Augustinian terms: it is divine love that, as it were, enlightens and illuminates people to their actual purpose.[106]

In this sense, the difficulty of the *Aufklärer* lay in their inability to perceive God's will as something other than an extrinsic imposition on human will. Without humanism or personalism, the *Aufklärer* failed to see what Augustine saw, which is, as Benedict rearticulates in *Deus Caritas Est*, that God is more present to me than I am to myself.[107] And this presence of God in the human being is rooted in God's prior love for humanity. Ratzinger declares:

> He (God) loved me first, before I myself could love at all. It was only because he knew me and loved me that I was made. So, I was not thrown into the world by some operation of chance, as Heidegger says, and now have to do my best to swim around in this ocean of life, but I am preceded by a perception of me, an idea and a love of me. They are present in the ground of my being. What is important for all people, what makes their life significant, is the knowledge they are loved. The person in a difficult situation will hold on if he knows, someone is waiting for me, someone wants me and needs me. God is there first and loves me. And that is the trustworthy ground on which my life is standing and on which I myself can construct it.[108]

Without this cognizance and conviction of God's love for me, God appears as an extrinsic authoritarian tyrant that must be resisted, and this largely explains the rejection of God that logically followed the reasoning of some, like Nietzsche. Without the awareness that God loves me, I must put up a fight to overthrow the authoritarian God. Nietzsche clearly saw himself as incarnating this revolt against an authoritarian and an enslaving God whose existence deprives humans of their freedom, in particular, and of course religion, in general. In Nietzsche's own words:

> I know my fate. One day my name will be associated with the memory of something tremendous—a crisis without equal on earth, the most profound collision of conscience, a decision that was conjured up against everything that has been believed, demanded, hallowed so far. I am no man, I am dynamite. Yet for all that, there is nothing in me of a founder of a religion—religions are affairs of the rabble; I find it necessary to wash my hands after I have come into contact with religious people.[109]

Setting aside the polemics and vilifying rhetoric, the position of Nietzsche is crystal clear: He had to reject his religious upbringing in order to be free, in order for him to liberate himself and the world from the obsequiousness that comes with religion. If Nietzsche had lived long enough to see the two world wars that came from the "Christian" heartland of Europe, he might have felt profoundly vindicated and satisfied. But this manner of thinking is clearly not only anthropocentric, but essentially individualistic, because by excluding God from the picture, thinkers such as Voltaire, Sartre, Nietzsche, Feuerbach, Camus, and others reduced the human being to a political program, especially articulated by the French strand of the European Enlightenment movement, with its revolutionary maxim of *liberté, egalité, fraternité*.[110] Such a worldview easily produces a utilitarian perspective of love, an understanding of love that serves me and my interests, an understanding of love that is unable to reach the sublime heights of *agape*. Love is what works for me. Love is the force of my power, what Ratzinger describes as the exercise of brute force, the splendor of power, which "signifies being able to do what you want, enjoying what you want, having everything at your disposal and being able to choose the place of honor."[111] And Ratzinger likewise reads in this utilitarian machinery view of anthropology the basis of a Marxist ethos of life.[112] Quite understandably, then, when Christianity enters the fray with talk about love as self-gift and not self-assertion, love as a paschalizing experience that pulls one away from nihilism to *caritas*, toward the other, Christianity appears to poison the well of the freedom of love as understood by the spirit of the *libertas* of the *Aufklärung*.

And Ratzinger, while refuting the charge that Christianity poisoned *eros*, rightfully remarks:

> Nowadays Christianity of the past is often criticized as having been opposed to the body; and it is quite true that tendencies of this sort have always existed. Yet the contemporary way of exalting the body is deceptive. *Eros*, reduced to pure "sex," has become a commodity, a mere "thing" to be bought and sold, or rather, man himself becomes a commodity. This is hardly man's great "yes" to the body. On the contrary, he now considers his body and his sexuality as the purely material part of himself, to be used and exploited at will. Nor does he see it as an arena for the exercise of his freedom, but as a mere object that he attempts, as he pleases, to make both enjoyable and harmless. Here we are actually dealing with a debasement of the human body: no longer is it integrated into our overall existential freedom; no longer is it a vital expression of our whole being, but it is more or less relegated to the purely biological sphere.[113]

Thus, while respecting and taking care of one's body is a Christian necessity, an exaggerated exaltation of the body risks turning into a hatred of material existence. For Christianity that sees the person as a unity in duality, a duality of spirit and matter that is unity in the person, it is true that *eros* tends to rise "in ecstasy" toward the Divine, to lead us beyond ourselves. But to achieve this rise of *eros* toward the Divine calls for what Benedict characterizes as a path of ascent, renunciation, purification, and healing.[114] And so, the life without inhibitions of pre-Homeric Greece that Nietzsche called for, if anything was at its core a bastardization and debasement of love. It was a divine intoxication, a divine madness, in which at the outburst of perceived love, of *eros*, reason was suspended, and the emotions alone allowed a free hand. And this was how the fertility cults were born. Instead of Christianity destroying *eros* in its pre-Homeric form, *eros* as lived out in Greek tragedy, Christianity saved and redeemed *eros* by opening *eros* up to *agape*. By opening up *eros* to *agape*, *eros* could no longer be overpowered by reason; *eros* could no longer be an intoxication, a madness in which the gods wrestled with humans. Benedict writes:

> The Old Testament firmly opposed this form of religion, which represents a powerful temptation against monotheistic faith, combating it as a perversion of religiosity. But it in no way rejected *eros* as such; rather, it declared war on a warped and destructive form of it, because this counterfeit divinization of *eros* actually strips it of its dignity and dehumanizes it. Indeed, the prostitutes in the temple, who had to bestow this divine intoxication, were not treated as human beings and persons, but simply used as a means of arousing "divine madness": far from being goddesses, they were human persons being exploited. An intoxicated and undisciplined *eros*, then, is not an ascent in "ecstasy" toward the Divine, but a fall, a degradation of man. Evidently, *eros* needs to be disciplined and purified if it is to provide not just fleeting pleasure, but a certain foretaste of the pinnacle of our existence, of that beatitude for which our whole being yearns.[115]

Accordingly, while it is certainly the case that the Church has had sick expressions of *eros* in her long history, these should be understood as distortions that are not representative of the Christian understanding of love, either as *philia*, *eros* or as *agape*, which is the peculiar New Testament understanding of love.

Regarding Benedict's theology of the *logos* as unity of love, the first insight that stands out is its anthropological character, that is, the unity of being regarding love. Benedict writes: "It is neither the spirit alone nor the body alone that loves: it is the human being, the person, a unified creature composed of body and soul, who loves. Only when both dimensions are truly united, does man attain his full stature. Only thus is love—*eros*—able to mature and attain its authentic grandeur."[116] This is all the more so because the human being knows that he or she is a person loved by a creator God. One is grateful for being a person. One is grateful that one is not a non-being. One is grateful that one is body and soul, man and woman, individual and community. This is the sense in which Benedict decries certain pathological ascetical practices that have been present in the Christian experience, which tended to place exclusive emphasis on the spirit over and even against the body. Human bodily existence is not a prison for the soul, but the unity of body and soul, material and spiritual, is what makes for a human being. And the fact that Christian tradition professes the Resurrection of the body attests to the enduring significance of the bodily element in what constitutes the human being. Above all, the event of the Incarnation is the prime exemplar of the value of the body. The fact that the Eternal *Logos* of God takes on human flesh shows that bodily existence is not a curse to be shed, but a gift to be appreciated and attended. The Council of Ephesus (431) was therefore right in asserting the true humanity of Jesus, God's Eternal *Logos* who took flesh in the womb of the Blessed Virgin Mary; hence she deserved the title *Theotokos*.

The second aspect of Benedict's theology of the *Logos* as unitive love is likewise its Christo-centric character. In Christ, God's *eros* for humanity attains the fullness of *agape* by his sacrificial self-giving, to the extent that "everyone is loved by him first and each person who meets him can therefore respond to love and learn love if he or she wishes to do."[117] One is not a Christian because of a religious sense nor because of a theory of an idea of the good or the evil, or of salvation. At the heart of Christianity is an encounter, a person, and the Church is called to become that place of encounter, where all peoples can meet Christ. And the pedagogy of this Christic love resides in the fact that the action of humans is their willingness to receive this love. In other words, God initiates, and humans respond to God's offer of love in Christ Jesus: "For God so loved the world, that He gave his only begotten Son, so that whosoever believes in Him will not perish but will have everlasting life" (Jn 3:16). The very life of the Trinity, as Christian tradition following Augustine has come to understand it, provides a paradigm for this logic of giftedness. The Father gives Himself to the Son in Love and the Son gives Himself to the Father in Love. And this Love between the

Father and Son is the Holy Spirit. In this sense, one can affirm with St. John: "God is Love" (1 Jn 4:8).

A third aspect of Benedict's theology of the *Logos* as love is what Benedict understands to be the redemption of *eros* by *agape*. Benedict's vision is that *eros*, the love that unites a man and a woman, cannot be separated from *agape*, the love that basically seeks the good of the other, the love that is oblative, sacrificial, and altruistic. The great novelty of *Deus Caritas Est* is that *eros* and *agape* cannot be set against each other. As Benedict remarks, "love is a single reality, but with different dimensions; at different times, one or other dimension may emerge more clearly. Yet when the dimensions (*eros* and *agape*) are totally cut off from one another, the result is a caricature or at least an impoverished form of love."[118] This opinion about the unity of love is worked backward from the experience of human love to the mystery of Trinitarian love.

But there is also another challenging insight from *Deus Caritas Est*, as Angelo Scola writes: "The importance of the pope's teaching on the unity of love becomes clear if we keep in mind above all that this unity dispels any kind of suspicion with regard to *eros*: erotic love in its original impulse is willed by God."[119] Consequently, the experience of falling in love (however ambiguous and ambivalent that might be) is the most important natural means with which God has endowed us to learn the way of love. Benedict is hereby claiming that the love between man and woman provides the paradigm of understanding the true meaning of love. Benedict's description of *eros* in this context is inspirational:

> Amid this multiplicity of meanings, however, one in particular stands out: love between man and woman, where body and soul are inseparably joined and human beings glimpse an apparently irresistible promise of happiness. This would seem to be the very epitome of love; all other kinds of love immediately seem to fade in comparison.[120]

Thus, *eros* opens me to the *irresistible promise of happiness* disclosed by the other to me. *Eros* shows itself as desire, as a passion. *Agape* purifies that movement and makes me capable of loving the other for the other's sake. Through *eros* and *agape*, I gain my fulfillment as a human being. As David Schindler rightly points out in his commentary on *Deus Caritas Est*, it is not only *agape* that is good, *eros* is also essentially good, for "taking *eros* to be essentially imperfect love would imply that human nature is essentially imperfect, that is, imperfect precisely as human nature, which is no less difficult to justify within a sound doctrine of creation."[121] *Eros* therefore embraces more than sexuality, which is rather a physical image of *eros*, the physical truth of *eros*.

Furthermore, a fourth feature of Benedict's theology of the *Logos* as unity of love has to do with the question of God, that is, love and the dialectics about how we encounter God. Christianity's uniqueness is not in the sense that it claims that one cannot "see" God (1 Jn 4:20)—a claim already discernible in Israel's faith (Ex 33:20). Christianity's exceptionality lies in the fact that Christian love discovers God in the helpless, the vulnerable, the imperfect, the broken, the materially poor, the wounded, and the excluded. The God of Christianity, the God of Jesus Christ, is radically identified with the broken ones of the world, to the extent that in encountering them in love, one encounters God (Mt 25:35). Certainly, this novelty of Christianity takes on what was best in the Jewish tradition of hospitality as enshrined in the Torah and the common experience of human beings, for if the novelty of Christianity had no continuity at all with what we already are simply as human beings, it would be completely foreign to us.[122] And that which is foreign is usually difficult to comprehend and inspire positive action and engagement.

However, Christianity goes beyond the Torah and common human experience by seeing in those considered excluded from the society the image of its God, of its poor and suffering founder, Jesus Christ. Only in Christianity does one find a God that suffers, a God that is rejected, a God that is weak and vulnerable. Precisely in this way, human nature in all its vulnerability enters into the very being of God and is thus transformed into God's own life and love and sent back into the world to become agents of God's transformative presence. *Caritas*, that is, love that descends into human history therefore becomes the main determinant in answer to the question about the God of Christianity. Rodney Howsare corroborates this reading of things when he writes:

> The human ascent to God, whether through obedience to some law (Judaism or Islam) or through transcending what is finite, material and historical (Buddhism), is replaced in Christianity by God's descent to humanity, a descent which culminates, it should be added, in the folly of the Cross, an affront not only to human reason but to human religiosity as well.[123]

For the Christian, therefore, the question of God is the question about the meaning of love. The Christian can answer to the question about the identity of the Christian God by pointing to the self-emptying of this God in the history of God's dealing with humanity, that culminates in the offering of God's Son on the wood of the Cross, following his identification with sinners, tax collectors, prostitutes, the sick, the poor, the condemned, the weak, and today one could add, the migrants and refugees, the victims of war and terror, those excluded from the blessings of the resources of the earth, the young people from Africa who risk the dangers of the seas and oceans in search of greener economic pastures in the Western world because of the sense of hopelessness in many African countries, still suffering under the weight of Neo-colonialism. Daily, their economic resources are being pillaged by European nations who, though claiming to have granted political independence to these nations, have simply swapped political colonialism with a more insidious economic colonialism. Ratzinger makes a lucid observation about this suffering God who Christianity encounters and comes to know intimately:

> In the figure of Jesus in whom what is said about the Servant of God is fulfilled, [...] God is not loud; he cannot compete with the powers of this world. He is the "poor" God; the God whose only weapons are the humble weapons of love and truth, and who therefore always seems to be the loser. Nonetheless he is the only true saving power in this world. We too experience God's powerlessness; we too seem to see him as the One who always comes off worst. We would prefer him to be stronger, more tangible, more powerful in the

> face of all this world's failures, dangers and menaces. We must learn that it is only in the silent, barely noticeable things that what is great takes place, that man and woman become God's image and the world once more becomes the radiance of God's glory.[124]

The God of Christianity is essentially a God of love and suffering, a God who shows the Christian in the life of Jesus of Nazareth that the measure of true existence and humanity, the measure of true love is to love without measure, in patience, love, and suffering. A God that cannot suffer, a God who does not know what it means to suffer, I believe, cannot be relevant to the millions on the continent of Africa who find themselves helpless in a globalized system that has essentially kept them excluded from the natural resources of their own lands. There are no easy answers to these realities. But perhaps the consciousness that God is not distant from their sufferings, God is not extrinsic to their sufferings, is not nothing. It is something. For where there is God, there is a future, even if in the present all many can do is to hope against hope. It is in this way of hope that the world is transformed from a valley of tears to a garden of paradise.

However, the question of a God who is love in the face of human suffering remains a challenging problem, even for the most reverent believer, as captured by Fyodor Dostoevsky. In the *Brothers Karamazov*, the context of Ivan's practical atheism is the evil nature of the world. It is not so much about the being of God *per se*, but the pervasive nature of evil, the Karamazov, that is rooted in the human heart, that poses a challenge for Ivan. In the depictions of the suffering of children in the *Rebellion*; in the narrative of Richard; and with the story of the Child of Five and the General, Dostoevsky succeeds in painting a sickening picture of humanity, a world that has become hellish thanks to the monstrous actions of humans. Even if one might find some of the narratives perhaps sickening and slightly exaggerated, it is difficult not to find in these incidences humanity's debasement into the abyss of wickedness and cruelty.[125] In the final analysis, Ivan, convinced of the illogicality and the absence of justice before the presence of evil in the world, must reject existence and return the ticket of human existence to God: "And so I hasten to give back my entrance ticket, and if I am an honest man, I am bound to give it back as soon as possible. And that I am doing. It's not God that I don't accept, Alyosha, only I most respectfully return Him the ticket."[126] Ivan despairs of God's good world because evil goes unpunished. Turning to Dostoevsky's *Grand Inquisitor*, the question of evil in the world becomes a question about human freedom and happiness. Following Ivan's dialectics of history, it can either be freedom or happiness, but not both. And for the sake of bread, humans have chosen to give up their freedom, in contrast to the declaration of the One Without Sin, that man does not live by bread alone.[127] The solution to human unhappiness, to the problem of human vileness is to deprive humans of freedom. This is the greatest achievement of the Cardinal Grand Inquisitor which he does not hesitate to flaunt at the Prisoner, the One Without Sin, who, given this context, becomes the merciless one, for daring to give men and women their freedom:

> Nothing is more seductive for man than his freedom of conscience, but nothing is a greater cause of suffering. And behold, instead of giving a firm foundation for setting the conscience of man at rest forever, You chose what was utterly beyond the strength of men, acting as though You did not love them at all—You who came to give Your life for them! Instead of taking possession of men's freedom, You increased it, and burdened the spiritual kingdom of mankind with its sufferings forever.[128]

The Grand Inquisitor is making the case that depriving humans of their freedom especially in exchange for bread is the more merciful line of action. But what justifies this conclusion? The line of reasoning that freedom is the source of evil in the world, that humans cannot proceed in any other way save that of abusing their freedom by meting out evil on others. And this evil in the world brings about profound happiness. With this line of reasoning, therefore, it is only when humans have relinquished their freedom that they can be assured of happiness. Freedom is a curse, and the only way to save humans from the anxiety of conscience, of the primeval mishap of the knowledge of good and evil, is to do precisely what the Inquisitor and his Church have done, which is to deprive humans of conscience—that is, to become the conscience of humans, effectively replacing their consciences. The truly happy person is the one with no freedom and no conscience.

Besides the polemical tone of Ivan's poem, it is difficult to deny that he makes a very strong, consistent, and coherent case against human freedom, to the extent that in the end, even Alyosha the novice monk can notice the satirical paradox: The Grand Inquisitor turns out to be more merciful, compassionate, and understanding of the human predicament than the Prisoner, the One Without Sin, notwithstanding the compassionate looks and actions of the Prisoner. The latter's decision to give freedom to humans ruined the work of creation and redemption by which he shed his blood, and the Inquisitor's Church has salvaged the wreckage caused by the bestowal of this pernicious gift to humanity. If the point of departure is human failings and wickedness, then the jury might likely tilt the verdict in favour of the Inquisitor. But we certainly know that even though evil, which stems from the abuse of human freedom—in the case of moral evil—can be a compelling case against the gift of freedom, it is also the case that human abuse of freedom is not the complete picture. Moreover, if humans must be deprived of freedom in order to be happy, can we legitimately talk about responsibility? The responsibility now falls on the Inquisitor's Church!

But on what basis are these "Church-elect" capable of handling the gift of freedom for the rest of humanity? In the final analysis, the human being that emerges from the world of the Inquisitor is a slave, a robot, with no conscience, no freedom, no will of its own, no sense of moral responsibility. Such anthropology empties humans of their greatness as creatures made in the image and likeness of God, and humans become their own makers. Perhaps it is logically consistent that it turns out that the Cardinal Inquisitor is an atheist who never believed in God, for the human being that emerges from the Inquisitor's handicraft of deprivation of freedom and conscience in order to attain happiness simply ends up becoming a cog in a machine of a determinism that denies the person of the drama of life, of setting out toward the good God as a conscious and free being. Even when factors are put in place that deprive humans of freedom in order for humans to be happy, such a system becomes a caricature, as seen especially in the Marxist system in the many places that it has been tried in world history. Happiness that is coerced is a pseudo-happiness and only enslaves.

Regarding this question of evil in the world, and the tension that evil raises given the Christian conviction of a good God, Ratzinger clearly has a different view from Dostoevsky's Ivan. Christ does not do away with the evil in the world. Christ does not deprive humans of their freedom. Christ's response to human evil is to enter into evil, bearing the full brunt of evil, and yet eventually transforming evil with love. In other words, Christ's sacrificial love is God's response to the question of evil. Ratzinger declares:

> Christ's mercy is not a grace that comes cheap, nor does it imply the trivialization of evil. Christ carries the full weight of evil and all its destructive force in his body and in his soul. He burns and transforms evil in suffering, in the fire of his suffering love. The day of vindication and the year of favor converge in the Paschal Mystery, in the dead and Risen Christ. This is the vengeance of God: he himself suffers for us, in the person of his Son. The more deeply stirred we are by the Lord's mercy, the greater the solidarity we feel with his suffering—and we become willing to complete in our own flesh "what is lacking in the afflictions of Christ" (Col 1: 24).[129]

Consequently, while it is certainly true that innocent suffering poses a real mental and emotional challenge to the assertion of God as love, and in the case of Ratzinger's theology, the *Logos* as unitive love, the transformation of the suffering of Good Friday with the Resurrection is the divine paradigm, in that God allows evil in respect of human freedom, but in allowing evil, God never allows evil to have the last word. God defeats evil by bringing good out of evil, as seen on Easter Sunday, for the Resurrection of Jesus is the supreme vindication of the vision of the good, of love, over the vision of evil and hatred. The Resurrection of Jesus is therefore the historical realization of God's eschatological ultimate triumph of the good in the concrete life of Jesus of Nazareth. Love triumphs. And that is something, as difficult as it might be to comprehend when faced with physical evil in the world.

At this point, one can make the transition in asserting that central to Ratzinger's theology of the *Logos* as unity of love is the question of the doctrine of the Church, that is, ecclesiology, for the Church, as the Body of Christ, is that community which lives from the transformational self-gift of Christ's own life, as encountered in the sacrament of the Eucharist. Ratzinger's encounter with Augustine as seen in chapter one, led him to develop a Eucharistic ecclesiology. The institution of the Eucharist is the event through which Jesus transforms the evil and hatred that will befall him into a gift, a self-gift to the Father for the sake of the world, out of love for the world. As Pope, Benedict XVI penned *Sacramentum Caritatis*, which underscored the fundamental connection between the Eucharist and the Church: the Eucharist builds up the Church, and the Church makes the Eucharist.[130] In other words, the *ecclesia*—that is, the calling together of peoples from all the nations to listen to the memoirs of the apostles and to break Bread—was essential and continues to be essential in bringing about the community called the Church. Ratzinger explains the origins of the Church in Eucharistic terms this way:

> On the night before his Passion, Jesus took another decisive step beyond this: he transformed the Passover of Israel into an entirely new worship, which logically meant a break with the temple community and thereby definitively established a people of the 'New Covenant.'[131]

To Ratzinger, therefore, the institution of the Eucharist is the decisive moment in which Christ brings about the new people from the "old" people, the event in which Christ universalizes the faith of Israel. As Ratzinger argues in *Behold the Pierced One*, this establishment of the Church was not a founding, an abrogation, and much less a replacement. It was a giving of access to the nations to the God of Israel, the Father of Jesus Christ, whose Spirit had guarded revelation throughout history.[132] In other words, the institution of the Eucharist from which the new people of God emerge as the Body of Christ, is a ratification of the historical revelation to Israel. In the Eucharist, the God who had spoken to Israel has now taken up a permanent tent of meeting in the midst, not only of Israel, but of all the nations. This leads Ratzinger to draw this conclusion that might appear startling in its apologetic claim:

> If we grasp this, it becomes clear that Jesus did not need to start by founding a People of God (the "Church"). It was already there. Jesus' task was only to renew this People by deepening its relationship to God and by opening it up for all mankind. Therefore, the question of whether Jesus intended to found a Church is a false question because it is unhistorical. The only proper way to phrase the question would be to ask whether Jesus intended to abolish the People of God or to renew it. The answer to this question, rightly put, is plain: Jesus made the old People of God into a new People by adopting those who believe in him into the community of his own self (of his "Body").[133]

In bringing about the reality of the Church, therefore, Jesus has entered into the existing subject of tradition, that is, Israel, and thanks to his proclamation and his Person, renews and opens the existing tradition by bringing all the nations into the possibility of a personal relationship with his Father, in his body, the Body of Christ. This body is therefore both sacramental, in the Eucharistic species, and also a communion of believers. Ratzinger therefore writes:

> The institution of the Most Holy Eucharist on the evening before the Passion cannot be regarded as some more or less isolated cultic transaction. It is the making of a covenant and, as such, is the concrete foundation of the new people: the people come into being through its covenant relation to God. We could also say that by his Eucharistic action, Jesus draws the disciples into his relationship with God, and therefore, into his mission, which aims to reach "the many," the humanity of all places and of all times. These disciples become a "people" through communion with the Body and Blood of Jesus, which is simultaneously communion with God.[134]

The Old Testament theme of covenant hence takes on a new meaning of covenant with Christ's body. The people of the new covenant take their origin from the Body and Blood of Christ. And it is only because Christ is at the center that this people can be called a people of God, for in Christ, they are taken up into God. As a consequence of this Eucharistic presence that takes up humanity in God making believers a people of God, believers now learn to depend on God and not on themselves, for:

> We can live by God because God now lives for us. We can live by God because God has made himself one of us, because he himself, as it were, has become our bread. We can live by God because he gives himself to us, not only as the Word, but as the Body that is given up for us and is given to us, ever new, in the sacrament.[135]

In the Eucharist, therefore, truly, God is in our midst. He is Immanuel. The Eucharist is therefore the fullest expression of the name Immanuel. God is truly in the midst of humanity. But even more, God feeds humanity in the gathered assembly, the body of Christ as a community of believers, and the Body of Christ as Eucharist received. The Eucharist is therefore, the causal principle of the Church, given that the Church draws her life from the Eucharist, as shown above.

In *Deus Caritas Est*, Benedict XVI taught that *agape* is another name for Eucharist and that in the Eucharist, "God's own *agape* comes to us bodily, in order to continue his work in us and through us [...]. A Eucharist that does not pass over into the concrete practice of love is intrinsically fragmented."[136] Seen from this perspective, the social dimension of Benedict XVI's Eucharistic ecclesiology emerges. If at the center of the institutional narrative stands the self-giving love of Christ, then to receive the Eucharist is to enter into the reality of giftedness, of *caritas*, of giving of the self to the other in concrete acts of love and service. Given this realization, Benedict's Eucharistic ecclesiology of love constitutes the core of his social justice theology.

Granted its summons to service, the Eucharist urges and advocates for justice, peace, and reconciliation in a continent like Africa that has seen and continues to see ethnic and regional conflicts that have claimed and continue to claim the lives of millions. What might it have meant to celebrate the Eucharist in the context of the Rwandan genocide? What can the celebration of the Eucharist say to the armed conflicts currently going on in Nigeria, Cameroon, Chad, the Central African Republic, Somalia, and many other parts of Africa? If the Eucharist comes about from the grain of wheat that falls to the grown and dies, what hopes can it offer to the countless women subjected daily to rape and all forms of sexual violence in the North Kivu region of the Democratic Republic of Congo? To live out the theology of Eucharistic *caritas* in these contexts will definitely call for a rediscovery of the centrality of love and service in the Eucharistic imaginations of many an African. And if Eucharistic faith does not translate into concrete acts of mutual love, service, and peaceful co-existence, not only are such Eucharistic celebrations truncated as Benedict XVI says, but they will in fact be superstitious, empty symbols governed by a magical mindset that begins and ends with what has not become an idolatrous, lifeless devotional object, salt that has lost its saltiness. Benedict XVI called the attention of the Church in Africa to the potentials of the Eucharist to bring about reconciliation in Africa when he writes in *Africae Munus*:

> The table of the Lord gathers together men and women of different origins, cultures, races, languages and ethnic groups. Thanks to the Body and Blood of Christ, they become truly one. In the Eucharistic Christ, they become blood relations and thus true brothers and sisters, thanks to the Word and to the Body and Blood of the same Jesus Christ. This bond of fraternity is stronger than that of human families, than that of our tribes.[137]

In a continent that has seen and continues to witness so much bloodshed based on ethnic and regional lines, this invitation to consider the fact that believers who receive the same Body and Blood are made brothers and sisters, is definitely a necessary and an urgent message in need of attention. A Eucharistic theology of communion is therefore crucial in terms of a spirituality for the African Church. This must be the case, for in its absence, or when the reverse is true, it clearly becomes obvious that Eucharistic celebrations that lead to no individual and societal fruits of justice, peace, reconciliation, and love bear the marks of practical atheism, in which God has ceased to have any real meaning in the lives of people, even if the external trappings of religion are still present. The observation of Rodney Howsare is very expressive here:

> It was obviously not that God had once been alive and had now died, nor was it even that most people had ceased to believe in God; it was that thought and action were not taking place in a world for which the God question made no real difference.[138]

In other words, the celebration of the Eucharist should make a difference in the lives of African Christians. There is therefore no substitute for the social dimension of the Eucharistic ecclesiology of love, for the reason that *caritas*, love, and service are central to Eucharistic faith. In this light, given that the matter of the Eucharist, bread and wine, reflect the fruits of the world, in the light of the doctrine of creation, the world takes on a symbolic meaning in Eucharistic theology. Benedict XVI's Eucharistic theology is therefore essentially a theology of God's love. Hence, the service of charity, the advocacy for social justice is likewise an expression of giftedness, for what has been received as a gift propels us to become gifts to the other in turn.

Given the above insights on Benedict XVI's theology of the *Logos* as unity of love, by which one arrives at Benedict XVI's Eucharistic ecclesiology, one can describe Benedict XVI's Eucharistic theology in one word: Self-gift. And the paradigm of this self-gift is the event of the Incarnation, in which the Father gives his Son into the world out of love for the world (Jn 3:16), and the Son, the incarnate *Logos* of the Father, in turn gives himself as a ransom for the many—"The reason the Father loves me is that I lay down my life and take it up again. No one takes it from me, but I lay it down of my own accord" (Jn 10:17–18). The Church is therefore the place where believers learn to give themselves for one another, in mutual self-gift. Self-gift is that the origin of the Eucharist which comes about as a fruit of Christ's love for us, and self-gift is likewise what sustains the Body of Christ as a community. Without self-gift, there is no Church. Therefore, in response to the self-assertive understanding of love that follows the spirit and logic of the *Aufklärung*, Ratzinger offers self-gift as the true measure and grandeur of love, in such a way that the various forms of love are not set up against each other in a love-warfare, but find a symphonic harmony in the one called into the self-gift of love, after the example of the Incarnate *Logos*, Jesus Christ.

5.3 *Logos* as Word: Ratzinger's Engagement with the *Aufklärung*'s Non-Cultic Rational Faith

The Twelfth Ordinary Assembly of the Synod of Bishops convoked by Benedict XVI from October 5th to 26th in 2008 was centered on the theme: *The Word of God in the Life and Mission of the Church*. In the post-synodal apostolic exhortation *Verbum Domini*, Benedict XVI taught that in the written Word of God, God still speaks and responds to our questions.[139] In other words, *Logos* as the spoken and written Word of God is the basis on which the dialogue between humans and God is established. To cite Vatican II: "The unseen God, from the fullness of his love, addresses men and women as his friends, and lives among them in order to invite and receive them into his company."[140] To Ratzinger, this sense of dialogue between creatures and the Creator has profound implications regarding the truths of God and the truths about human beings because, "The Eternal *Logos* does not concretely become bread for man until he has taken flesh and speaks to us in human words."[141]

In this sense, we are no longer groping in uncertainty about what God expects of us as creatures. We know God's will because God has used human language, human speech, to communicate with us. As *Dei Verbum* taught, "the words of God, expressed in human language, are in every way like human speech, just as the Word of the eternal Father, when he took on himself the weak flesh of human beings, became like them."[142] In this light, Scripture is the book of the Church, for it is the Church that receives the spoken Word, understands it, lives it, and has the duty to transmit it through the authentic interpretation of the Magisterium of the Church, which is received and celebrated in the womb of the Church's liturgy.

Thus, the metaphor of the *logos* serves as the entry point into Ratzinger's liturgical theology, for it is the Word of God that calls the people into a community, gathered around the name of Christ. In his exegesis of Acts 2:42: "They (the early Christians) devoted themselves to the Apostles' teaching and to fellowship, to the breaking of bread and to prayer," Ratzinger points out that it is the word of Scripture that stands in-between teaching and breaking of bread. It is this word that brings both sides together, that brings about both aspects, the teaching ministry and the fellowship of the breaking of bread, two aspects that are essential to the foundational nature of the Church.[143] And what animates Scripture by bringing it alive, and the teaching of the apostles with inspiration, and the breaking of bread that makes Christ's sacrificial memorial present, is the Holy Spirit that breathes life into all, giving life to all and making God's power operative in all. As Benedict says, "there can be no authentic understanding of Christian revelation apart from the activity of the Paraclete. This is due to the fact that God's self-communication always involves the relationship of the Son and the Holy Spirit, whom Irenaeus of Lyons refers to as *the two hands of the Father*."[144] Thus, the "Spirit of Truth" (Jn 14:16) is indispensable in the understanding of the words of the Lord Jesus Christ.

However, Ratzinger makes a distinction between the Word of God, God's *Logos*, the incarnate Second Person of the Trinity, and the Word of God as Scripture, the Word of God as written, as a text:

> As the Prologue of John clearly shows us, the *Logos* refers in the first place to the Eternal Word, the only Son, begotten of the Father before all ages and consubstantial with him: the Word was with God, and the Word was God. But this same Word, Saint John tells us, "became flesh" (Jn 1:14); hence Jesus Christ, born of the Virgin Mary, is truly the Word of God who has become consubstantial with us. Thus, the expression "Word of God" here refers to the person of Jesus Christ, the eternal Son of the Father, made man.[145]

This analogy of "Word of God" is theologically significant, for it points to the fact that the real center of Christianity is not the written text, but the living Christ whose Spirit animates the hearts and lives of believers.

This is the sense in which one could say that Christianity is not "a religion of the book," not only for the simple reason that the community of believers predated the canon of Scripture and in fact, determined the canon, but more importantly, because the event of the Incarnation forever places a human being, of flesh and blood, at the center of the Christian religious experience. This Christology of the Word is captured in this text from the Letter to the Hebrews: "In many and various ways God spoke of old to our fathers by the prophets; but in these last days he has spoken to us by a Son, whom he appointed the heir of all things, through whom also he created the world" (Heb 1:1–2). As Benedict comments, here, that is, in the Incarnation of the Word, "the Word finds expression not primarily in discourse, concepts or rules. Here we are set before the very person of Jesus. His unique and singular history is the definitive word which God speaks to humanity."[146] Hence, the event of the Incarnation explains in large measure why Christianity cannot be an ethical choice, but an experiential encounter with a person, Jesus Christ.

Given this distinction between the Incarnate *Logos*, Jesus Christ, and the written word of Scripture, when Acts 2:42 talks about the believers as devoting themselves to the teachings of the apostles, the referent is the Word of God as Scripture, the written word, the text, the memoirs of the apostles, the writings the apostles left behind. This implies, as Ratzinger points out, that the New Testament is the Church's book, that it presupposes the Church as its subject.[147] In other words, the Bible grew from the Church, and the unity of the Bible is a fruit of the Church's faith that brings together the diverse elements of Scripture into a symphonic unity, over a long period of time along which the canon of Scripture developed.

In this light, therefore, *Logos* as Word essentially has two significations. Firstly, it points to the person of Jesus, the Eternal Word of the Father. And secondly, it points to the written Scriptures that are the voice of the Incarnate Word. The Dogmatic Constitution on Divine Revelation *Dei Verbum*, provides a lucid explanation of how these two aspects of the *Logos* as Word are expressive of each other:

> In Sacred Scripture, therefore, while the truth and holiness of God always remains intact, the marvelous "condescension" of eternal wisdom is clearly shown, "that they may

> learn the gentle kindness of God, which words cannot express, and how far He has gone in adapting His language with thoughtful concern for our weak human nature." For the words of God, expressed in human language, have been made like human discourse, just as the Word of the eternal Father, when He took to Himself the flesh of human weakness, was in every way made like men.[148]

In this sense, word is not only speech that is written, but simultaneously a person that utters the spoken word.

A further aspect in Ratzinger's theology of the *Logos* as Word has to do with the broad question of the interpretation of Scripture. For the specific purposes of the question of this work, which is that of understanding Ratzinger in the context of the *Aufklärung*, as must have become obvious at this point, I will highlight what Ratzinger calls the "*danger of dualism and a secularized hermeneutic*."[149] Ratzinger maintains that to distinguish two levels of approach to the Bible does not imply that these levels ought to be separated or opposed. Neither do they imply a simple juxtaposition of things. In other words, the work of exegesis which spells out the different layers of tradition in the coming-to-be of the texts must not lead to a severing of the relationship between exegesis and theology, between exegesis and dogma, which reflects on the faith of the Church.[150] Here again, one returns to the limitations of the historical-critical method earlier pointed out, in the consideration of the *Gestalt* of Jesus. Ratzinger thus calls for a hermeneutic of faith to counteract the secularized hermeneutic. Ratzinger argues that this secularized hermeneutic is:

> Ultimately based on the conviction that the Divine does not intervene in human history. According to this hermeneutic, whenever a divine element seems present, it has to be explained in some other way, reducing everything to the human element. This leads to interpretations that deny the historicity of the divine elements.[151]

In my judgment, this description of the secularized hermeneutics fits very well the reinterpretations of the figure of Christ, the New Testament, and the sacramental life of the Christian Church, specifically, the Catholic Church, that emerged from Kant, Hegel, and other *Aufklärung* figures. As seen in the earlier sections of this chapter, the ethical and rational reductionism of the person of Christ and the New Testament witness to Christ that came with the *Aufklärung*, essentially leaves us with a human, moral Christ, not a Christ to whom one can pray to and worship. As Ratzinger points out:

> Such a position can only prove harmful to the life of the Church, casting doubt over fundamental mysteries of *Christianity* and their historicity—as, for example, the institution of the Eucharist and the Resurrection of Christ. A philosophical hermeneutic is thus imposed, one which denies the possibility that the Divine can enter and be present within history. The adoption of this hermeneutic within theological studies inevitably introduces a sharp dichotomy between an exegesis limited solely to the first level and a theology tending toward a spiritualization of the meaning of the Scriptures, one which would fail to respect the historical character of revelation.[152]

In other words, and as previously highlighted, a philosophical hermeneutic alone, even when one presumes its best of intentions, cannot adequately covey the fullest and deepest contents of the historical revelation of God in Christ Jesus, and the witness of the New Testament to this revelation. Perhaps the difficulty might lie in the fact that the postulates of pure reason that guided, say, Kant, Hegel, Feuerbach, and other *Aufklärung* figures, succumbed to the tendency of an unwarranted amplification of the concept of rational faith. They ended up promising more than they could deliver, for human reason alone cannot fully explain the contents and significance of divine revelation.

That said, it is important to note that the high point of Ratzinger's theology of the *Logos* as Word centers on the liturgy, particularly the Eucharistic prayer, that is, the institutional narrative. In the preceding section, the connection between Eucharist and the founding of the Church was considered. At this point, the consideration will focus on the how the word, spoken, brings about the Eucharist as a sacrifice that replaces the animal sacrifices that preceded it, in the evolution of Israel's faith and the pagan sacrifices of the nations. Essentially, this keeps in mind all that has been said above about the relationship between the Eucharist and the Church. What is distinct here is the relationship between the Eucharist and the Word, the form of speech that comes about thanks to the Incarnation of the *Logos* as Word that is spoken, one might say *Logos* as speech.

In this light, reflecting on Jesus' Eucharistic discourse in the sixth chapter of the Gospel of John, Ratzinger writes:

> In the discourse at Capernaum, John's Prologue is brought to a deeper level. There, God's *Logos* became flesh, but here this flesh becomes "bread" given for the life of the world (cf. Jn 6:51), with an allusion to Jesus' self-gift in the mystery of the cross, confirmed by the words about his blood being given as drink (cf. Jn 6:53). The mystery of the Eucharist reveals the true manna, the true bread of heaven: it is God's *Logos* made flesh, who gave himself up for us in the paschal mystery.[153]

Logos as Word, that is, as Person, and *Logos* as Word, that is, as speech, find a meeting point in bringing about the self-gift of the Eucharist. As the *Logos*, Jesus gives of himself to us in the Eucharist. And speaking *in persona Christi*, the word uttered by the priest brings about the presence of the *Logos*, the person of the *Logos* under the form of bread and wine. As Ratzinger points out, "it is clear that in the liturgy of the *Logos*, of the Eternal Word, the word and thus the human voice have an essential role to play."[154] The human word therefore takes on a divine efficacy in the Eucharistic prayer, in that the human being can speak with God, can address God in very personal and relational terms.

This human communication with God is possible because God himself is speech, word. God's nature is to speak, to hear, and to reply. And as Ratzinger points out, "only because there is already speech, '*logos*' in God, can there be speech, '*Logos*' of God. Philosophically we could put it like this: The *Logos* in God is the ontological foundation for prayer."[155] This implies that prayer is possible because speech belongs to the nature of God. Only because God *is* speech, can the human being speak to God in return. And only because of this ontological character of speech can humans enter into prayer. This speech between God and humans makes them partners in dialogue. It establishes a relationship between God and human beings.

In addition, for Ratzinger, human beings are capable of dialoguing with God, of entering into communication with God, because God has drawn humans into this internal speech with God, which comes about thanks to the event of the Incarnation of the *Logos*. In this context, the Incarnation is the definitive mode of divine-human communication. Ratzinger explains:

> He who is speech, Word, *Logos*, in God and to God, participates in human speech. This has a reciprocal effect, involving man in God's own internal speech. Or we could say that man is able to participate in the dialogue within God himself because God has first shared in human speech and has thus brought the two into communication with one another. The Incarnation of the *Logos* brings eternity into time and time into eternity.[156]

In this light, the word or the speech between human beings and God is grounded primarily in the very being of God, in that it is God who speaks to humans, and humans—in Christ, with Christ and through Christ—speak to God in return. One could say that in Christ, the human word has definitively responded to the word first spoken by the Father.

This is the context in which one can understand the theological unicity and significance of the *oratio*, the Eucharistic prayer, during which in the name of the whole Church the priest speaks through Christ to the Father in the power of the Holy Spirit. To Ratzinger, the *oratio* is the true liturgical act that forms the core of the Eucharistic celebration.[157] The *oratio* is the essence and center of the liturgy. To call the liturgy *oratio* is simultaneously a refutation of false worship and a declaration for true, authentic worship. Ratzinger writes:

> The sacrificial animals and all those things that you had and have, and which ultimately satisfy no one, are now abolished.

> In their place has come the Sacrifice of the Word. We are the spiritual religion, in which in truth a Word-based worship takes place. Goats and cattle are no longer slaughtered. Instead, the word summing up our existence is addressed to God and identified with *the* Word, the Word of God, who draws us into true worship.[158]

In other words, the *oratio*, the word, has now ushered in a sacrifice that is spiritual, a sacrifice that reflects a most profound level of interaction between God and human beings. This liberates humans from the debasement of animal sacrifices. Most importantly, however, because of the word, humans are no longer left to their own devices in the worship of God. Speaking the word, humans enter into the Word of God, the Eternal *Logos*, and now address the Father with the Word of the Son.

For Ratzinger, this word, the *oratio*, is not just word as utterance, as speech, but is primarily an action as well. It is an *actio* in which the human action, that is, the person of the priest who speaks in the name of the community to the Father, cedes place to the divine *actio*, for in speaking to the Father, the priest speaks with the word of the Father's Divine Son. As Ratzinger explains:

> In this *oratio* the priest speaks with the I of the Lord—"This is my Body," "This is my Blood." He knows that he is not now speaking from his own resources but in virtue of the Sacrament that he has received, he has become the voice of Someone Else, who is now speaking and acting. This action of God, which takes place through human speech, is the real "action" for which all of creation is in expectation.[159]

Given this perspective, therefore, one might say that what is distinctive about Christian worship is that it is God himself in the sacramental configuration of the presence of His Son in the priest, who does what is essential in the worship of God. God himself does what is essential because in the event of the Incarnation, God has become a human being. God has a body and the believer is a part of this mystical body of God. And becoming a member of this body is not only a gift but also a duty, for it implies that humans "must still pray for it to become our sacrifice, that we ourselves, as we said, may be transformed into the *logos (ogisiert)*, conformed to the *Logos*, and so be made the true Body of Christ."[160] Thus, the *actio* in which the believer is taken up into the Body of Christ is such that in responding to the Lord's invitation, it becomes clear, in the final analysis, that the believer is participating in something that only the Lord can do. That is the quintessence of the meeting of the human and divine word, in the Incarnate and Risen Christ.

Given the above considerations of the *Logos* as Word that opens the theology of worship, it can be stated that the Christological reading of worship, of the cult, provides a framework thanks to which one sees both the life of Christ and the life of the believer as an *oratio* and an *actio*. The life of the believer is an offering to God in Christ, and the liturgy is the space for that worship. However, in this new dispensation, animal sacrifices have lost their efficacy to the *oratio rationabilis*, to the Word, the *Logos*, who having become a man in Jesus of Nazareth makes it possible for the believer to speak to the Father in the name of the Son. The worship of God is therefore not something peripheral, that which might be attended to after all other important concerns have been dealt with. The worship of God is central because the sacrifice of Christ, the penultimate sacrifice of the Cross, indicates that sense of *actio* and *ratio* that becomes the pattern of all human speech and action before God.

Certainly, this Ratzingerian position builds on Justin's *logikē thusia*, *oratio rationabilis*—that is, Justin's understanding of sacrifice as spiritual in which all animal sacrifices terminate with the Eucharist, as seen in chapter three. In *The Spirit of the Liturgy*, following a presentation of the historical trajectory of the critique of the externalism and syncretism of the cult in the pre-exilic and exilic periods of Israel's history as it opens up toward the figure of Christ, Ratzinger maintains that the concept of *logikē latreia* (*thusia*)—that is, worship and sacrifice understood as worship with spirit and mind as noted by Paul in Romans 12:1—constitutes the definitive Christian response to the crisis of the cult of the ancient world.[161] Ratzinger makes this conclusion:

> The sacrifice is the "word," the word of prayer, which goes up from man to God, embodying the whole of man's existence

> and enabling him to become "Word" (*Logos*) in himself. It is man, conforming himself to *logos* and becoming *logos* through faith, who is the true sacrifice, the true glory of God in the world. Israel's experience of suffering during the Exile and the Hellenistic period first brought the word of prayer into prominence as the equivalent of exterior sacrifice. Now, through the Word, *Logos*, the whole philosophy of *logos* in the Greek world is incorporated into the concept. The Greek mind elevates it eventually to the idea of a mystical union with the *logos*, the very meaning of all things.[162]

In the concept of the *Logos*, Word, therefore, the worship of God has found its fullest and most sublime form and expression. Worship is the human being, the *logos* in humans, humans who themselves have become *logoi*, offering their very selves to God in prayer. To worship therefore becomes self-offering. Nothing, no other animal sacrifice, can replace the self-offering, the spiritual offering of humans made in speech, in the *logos*, *oratio*, to God. True worship is therefore a spiritual worship, a worship that engages the spirit of humans from the inside, a spiritual worship that conforms to the nature of God who is spirit, and those who worship must worship in spirit and in truth (Jn 4:24). Worship is therefore, the lifting of the human being in prayer to God. Prayer is the Christian sacrifice. Worship is no longer the sacrifice of animals, but the offering of the self to God, the self which is all that is. In the final analysis, as Ratzinger will have it, true worship happens thanks to the synthesis of three *logoi*, that is, "the *logos* of creation, the *logos* in man, and the true and Eternal *Logos* made flesh, the Son."[163] With the Word, the *Logos*, by which humans can utter the *oratio*, or prayer, worship finally attains its fullest form. Prayer is the sacrifice *par excellence*, the worship and sacrifice with mind and spirit in which nothing is substituted or replaced in the human offering to God. Humans offer their very selves, a spiritual offering to God. The *oratio* therefore goes beyond the cult to a fuller experience of God, a vision of glory of God.

With this understanding, the *oratio*, prayer in other words, the Christian cult can be described as a school of humanization, for as Ratzinger says, "worship, that is, the right kind of cult, of relationship with God, is essential for the right kind of human existence in the world."[164] In other words, a right relationship with God in worship is a guarantor for a right ordering of human affairs. Worship is therefore not superfluous. The cult is not something that must be set aside so that humans can attend to more pressing concerns. As Ratzinger argues, "a life no longer opened up to heaven, would be empty, a leaden life. That is why there are really no societies altogether lacking in cult. Even the decidedly atheistic, materialistic systems create their own forms of cult."[165] In the spirit of thc Ratzingerian reading of things, such societies strive in vain to conceal the nothingness that follows their rejection of right worship, which is the ordering of their relationship with God.

Granted this consciousness, therefore, one cannot be indifferent to the largely suspicious attitude of the *Aufklärung* toward the Christian cult, viewed as superfluous and essentially superstitious, a "fetish-faith," to cite Kant:

> Praying conceived as an inner ritual service to God and hence as a means of grace, is a superstitious delusion (a fetish-making); for it only is the declaring of a wish to a being who has no need of any declaration regarding the inner disposition of the wisher, through which nothing is therefore accomplished nor is any of the duties incumbent on us as commands of God discharged; hence God is not really served.[166]

To Kant, therefore, the cult is irrelevant because all that mattered is the disposition of the heart, that is, the attention one pays to the moral law within us. In effect, the cult is a distraction because the human being in the *oratio*, is according to Kant seeking to work externally upon God by using words. But the real work, the real *actio*, should be the focus on the self, the work on the internal disposition of the self.[167] And this does not require words. If the cult is to have any value at all, it is simply that it is a moral solemnity. It is not a means of grace. It will simply be a space that embraces the moral concerns of all human beings.[168] And having characterized Christian cult as unnecessary, a distraction lacking in any religious efficacy, Kant makes this conclusion about the Eucharist:

> But to boast that God has attached special graces to the celebration of this solemn ritual, and to incorporate among the articles of faith the proposition that the ritual, though a purely ecclesiastical action, is in addition a *means of grace*—this is a delusion of religion which cannot but work counter to the spirit of religion—*Priestcraft* would thus be, in general, the dominion which the clergy has usurped over the mind by pretending to have exclusive possession of the means of grace.[169]

The Eucharist is delusional because Kant does not see any direct influence that the Eucharist can bring on the moral law within humans. It is delusional because it is an external action, and only the moral law within is of any value to Kant.

And where Kant goes, Hegel follows. In Hegel's interpretation of the encounter between Jesus and the Samaritan woman (Jn 4:1–42), a text that otherwise might provide a rich source for liturgical theology, Hegel has Jesus say to the Samaritan woman:

> Believe me, woman, Jesus answered, a time is coming when you will no longer celebrate divine service, whether on Garizim or in Jerusalem—a time when nobody will any longer suppose that divine service is limited to prescribed rituals or to a specific place. The time will come—indeed it is already upon us—when those who truly revere God will worship the universal father in the true spirit of religion. These alone are pleasing to him; their worship of God is authentic, being animated solely by the spirit of reason and its flower, the moral law.[170]

Similar to Kant, Hegel clearly displays a judgment of irrelevancy regarding the cult. Worship is reduced to reason and the moral law. In a sense, the human being is a God unto itself. Any talk of worship that points the human being to an external God possesses no value. And further developing his anthropocentric liturgical philosophical theology, Hegel again writes: "So, do not let yourselves be deceived by mere pious words; not everyone who cries out to God, who offers him prayers and sacrifices, is a member of his kingdom, but only he who does God's will, which is disclosed to men in the law of his own reason."[171] In other words, a good life, an ethical life, replaces the cult for these *Aufklärung* thinkers.

To Ratzinger, therefore, the *Aufklärung* sought to provide for a radically different Church along the lines of liturgy, the cult, and Christian devotional life. And even when orthodox Christianity did not fully embrace the positions of the *Aufklärer*, Ratzinger believes that their thoughts impacted the devotional and cultic life of the German Church. Ratzinger writes:

> The Enlightenment had its liturgical movement, the aim of which was to simplify the liturgy and restore it to its original basic structure. Excesses in the cult of relics and of saints were to be removed, and, above all, the vernacular, with congregational singing and participation, was to be introduced.[172]

In this text, Ratzinger identifies liturgy, biblical hermeneutics, and the sacramental life of the Church in their traditional forms as being reinterpreted by the *Aufklärung* currents. For a Church man with Ratzinger's ecclesial and intellectual temperament who holds that the cult is primary to Christian living as shown above in his theology of the *Logos* as Word, Ratzinger clearly feels ill at ease with the liturgical theology that emerged from the *Aufklärung*. Ratzinger believes that:

> The rationalism of the Enlightenment had tried to reduce religion to one or two universally self-evident propositions. Behind the positive religions it wanted to reconstruct a religion of pure reason, which would unite all men. This artificial edifice, a religion synthetically manufactured in reflection, had vanished like a soap bubble at the impact of Kant's critique.[173]

Here, Ratzinger is not taking issue with enlightened reason *per se*, but the manner in which the *Aufklärung* was interpreting reason and reason's morality, especially in the light of the Christian cult. In the sense of the cultic theology of the *Aufklärung*, the believer eventually becomes a mere subject of morality. This eschews the transcendental dimension of the life of the believer, whose only God becomes the self, and whose only task is to live according to the moral law found within the self. But the worship of a God who is utterly different from me and yet, has taken me into God's self as seen in the liturgical interpretation of the Incarnation above, does not detract the believer from the dignity of self-worth, from obeying the voice of conscience or the moral law within it. If anything, for Ratzinger, and very much for the Christian faith, the one who worships God rises with courage to face not only the moral law within the individual, but the vicissitudes, uncertainties, and challenges without, under Kant's starry skies. And while this does not eschew morality, it definitely widens the basis from which one looks at morality, in this sense, from a humanistic and communal point of view. And Christian worship, understood as *logikē latreia* (*thusia)*, that is, the *Logos*-filled liturgy, is the deepest enlightenment possible, the reason being that, as already indicated above, it is the worship and sacrifice with spirit and mind.

In fact, it is precisely this dimension of communal faith that is lacking in much of the *Aufklärung*, for while the ecclesiology of the *Logos* as love and the *Logos* as Word helps bring about the Church, or more precisely, explains the origins of the Church as shown above—at least from the Ratzingerian perspective—the *Aufklärung* leaves the individual almost in isolation. The individual is either standing alone with a moral law within (Kant); or standing alone on a plane of unbridled self-assertiveness or narcissism (Nietzsche); or essentially gets trapped in a cyclic process of psychologizing in which the spirit of the individual that is also present is divinized, and in the process, creates a God within (Hegel).

In summary, this chapter set out to study Ratzinger's appropriation of the central metaphor of *Logos*, or Reason, and his application of *Logos* to the ecclesiological motifs or aspects of his theology. Given the framework of the *Aufklärung,* which also had reason as its central metaphor, the chapter opened up a space for an interaction between Ratzinger and the *Aufklärer* around the theological themes of the centrality of love and the worship of God based on the principle of the spoken word, that is, *Logos* as Word. Love and Word are seen to be foundational in understanding Ratzinger's ecclesiology, as argued above. Granted that the overriding framework from chapter two through chapter five has been that of a dialogue, a conversation between philosophy and theology, between the God of faith and the God of the philosophers, the aim of chapter five was to place the positions of Ratzinger and the *Aufklärung* on an interactive, conversational stage, so that both sides would emerge clearly in their respective positions regarding the questions of love and worship, and what that says about Ratzinger's ecclesiology. I believe that this corresponds to Benedict's initiative of the Court of the Gentiles, which, as Pope he saw as the needed space to foster a dialogue between the Christian faith and the heirs of the secular *Aufklärung*. And herein lies the contributions of not only chapter five but chapter four as well. That is, Ratzinger and *Aufklärer* do not just talk past each other but can talk to each other by speaking on some common areas, such as on the identity of Jesus as Son, or on the meaning of love as the strongest human emotion. And even when it might appear that they are talking past each other, the fact that they can talk, that Ratzinger can converse with Hegel on the identity of Jesus, is no small achievement, on both philosophical and theological grounds.

Certainly, as seen in chapter one, Ratzinger is a firm believer that Jesus Christ is not only the end of history (Augustine), but Jesus is also the center of history (Bonaventure). It therefore should come as no surprise that the positions espoused by Ratzinger when placed in conversation with those put forth by, say, Kant, Hegel, or Nietzsche, reflect the convictions of a pious soul, a humble and firm believer for whom reason is not just an autonomous entity, but one that is, at some point, subservient to faith. As is likely to be the case, not everyone agrees with the Ratzingerian rational-faith hermeneutics. Chapter six will shed light on some of these critical voices, on both sides of the debate.

Notes — Chapter Five

1 Joseph Ratzinger, *Pilgrim Fellowship of Faith: The Church as Communion*, trans. Henry Taylor (San Francisco: Ignatius Press, 2005), 105.

2 Ratzinger, *Pilgrim Fellowship of Faith*, 129.

3 Joseph Ratzinger, *Behold the Pierced One: An Approach to a Spiritual*

Christology, trans. Graham Harrison (San Francisco: Ignatius Press, 1986), 18.

4 Benedict XVI, *Last Testament in His Own Words with Peter Seewald*, trans. Philip Jacobs (New York: Bloomsbury, 2016), 88.

5 Joseph Ratzinger, "The New Pagans and the Church," trans. Fr. Kenneth Baker, S. J., Homiletic & Pastoral Review, https://www.hprweb.com/2017/01/the-new-pagans-and-the-church/. Accessed July 8, 2020, # 1.

6 Joseph Ratzinger, *Theological Highlights of Vatican II*, trans. Henry Traub, S.J, Gerard C. Thormann, & Werner Barzel (Mahwah, NJ: Paulist Press, 2009), 224.

7 Ratzinger, "The New Pagans and the Church," # 3.

8 Ratzinger, "The New Pagans and the Church," # 3.

9 Ratzinger, "The New Pagans and the Church," # 4.

10 Ratzinger, "The New Pagans and the Church," # 5.

11 Ratzinger, "The New Pagans and the Church," # 9.

12 Ratzinger, *Theological Highlights of Vatican II*, 223.

13 Joseph Ratzinger, *Faith and the Future* (San Francisco: Ignatius Press, 2009), 114.

14 Ratzinger, *Faith and the Future*, 116–117.

15 Ratzinger, "The New Pagans and the Church," # 12–18.

16 Ratzinger, "The New Pagans and the Church," # 18.

17 Ratzinger, "The New Pagans and the Church," # 17.

18 Ratzinger, "The New Pagans and the Church," # 20.

19 Joseph Ratzinger, *God and the World A Conversation with Peter Seewald*, trans. Henry Taylor (San Francisco: Ignatius Press, 2002), 36.

20 Ratzinger, *God and the World*, 48.

21 Ratzinger, *Faith and the Future*, 118.

22 Joseph Ratzinger, *Handing on the Faith in an Age of Disbelief*, trans. Michael J. Miller (San Francisco: Ignatius Press, 2006), 69.

23 Søren Kierkegaard, *Fear and Trembling*, ed. & trans. Howard V. Hong and Edna H (Princeton, NJ: Princeton University Press, 1983), iii 61–iii 67.

24 Ronald M. Green, "'Developing' Fear and Trembling," in *The Cambridge Companion to Kierkegaard*, eds. Alastair Hannay and Gordon D. Marino (Cambridge, UK: Cambridge University Press, 1999), 259.

25 Kierkegaard, *Fear and Trembling*, iii, 167.

26 Ratzinger, *Handing on the Faith in an Age of Disbelief*, 69.

27 Joseph Ratzinger, *Truth and Tolerance Christian Belief and World Religions*, trans. Henry Taylor (San Francisco: Ignatius Press, 2004), 70.

28 Ratzinger, *Truth and Tolerance*, 71.

29 Ratzinger, *Truth and Tolerance*, 71.

30 Ratzinger, *Truth and Tolerance*, 71.

31 Ratzinger, *God and the World*, 46.
32 Ratzinger, *God and the World*, 57.
33 Ratzinger, *God and the World*, 66.
34 Ratzinger, *God and the World*, 71.
35 Joseph Ratzinger, *A New Song for the Lord Faith in Christ and Liturgy Today*, trans. Martha M. Matesich (New York: The Crossroad Publishing Company, 1996), 64–65.
36 Ratzinger, *A New Song for the Lord*, 65–66.
37 Ratzinger, *A New Song for the Lord*, 66–67.
38 Ratzinger, *A New Song for the Lord*, 48–49.
39 Ratzinger, *A New Song for the Lord*, 49.
40 Ratzinger, *A New Song for the Lord*, 50.
41 Ratzinger, *A New Song for the Lord*, 51.
42 Ratzinger, *A New Song for the Lord*, 52.
43 Ratzinger, *Theological Highlights of Vatican II*, 78–79.
44 Norman Tanner, S. J., *Vatican II The Essential Texts*, Dogmatic Constitution on the Church *Lumen Gentium* (New York: Image Books, 2012), 1.
45 Edward Schillebeeckx, *Christ the Sacrament of the Encounter with God* (London: Sheed & Ward Press, 1977), 66.
46 Ratzinger, *Theological Highlights of Vatican II*, 79.
47 Vladimir Sergaevitch Soloview, *A Story of Anti-Christ* (Middletown, DE: Kassock Bros. Publishing Co. 2012), 14–33.
48 Joseph Ratzinger/Benedict XVI, *Jesus of Nazareth, From the Baptism in the Jordan to the Transfiguration*, trans. Adrian Walker (New York: The Doubleday Broadway Publishing Group, 2007), 35.
49 Ratzinger/Benedict XVI, *Jesus of Nazareth*, 41.
50 Ratzinger/Benedict XVI, *Jesus of Nazareth*, 39–40.
51 Ratzinger/Benedict XVI, *Jesus of Nazareth*, 44.
52 Joseph Ratzinger, *A Turning Point for Europe? The Church in the Modern World: Assessment and Forecast*, trans. Brian McNeil, C.R.V. (San Francisco: Ignatius Press, 1994), 177–179.
53 Joseph Ratzinger, *Called to Communion: Understanding the Church Today*, trans. Adrian Walker (San Francisco: Ignatius Press, 1996), 140.
54 Ratzinger, *Called to Communion*, 162.
55 Ratzinger, *God and the World*, 38.
56 Ratzinger, Joseph, "Centenary of the Death of Card. John Henry Newman" accessed July 28 2020, at http//www.vatican.va, 1990.
57 John Henry Newman, *An Essay on the Development of Christian Doctrine* (Indiana: University of Notre Dame Press, 1960), 55.
58 Newman, *Development*, 58.
59 Newman, *Development*, 60.
60 Newman, *Development*, 172.

61 Newman, *Development*, 173.
62 Newman, *Development*, 178.
63 Newman, *Development*, 181.
64 Newman, *Development*, 185.
65 Newman, *Development*, 191.
66 Blaise Pascal, *Pensées*, trans. A. J. Krailsheimer (Suffolk: Penguin Books, 1995), II, 423–424.
67 John Henry Newman, *An Essay in Aid of a Grammar of* Assent (Indiana: Notre Dame Press, 1979), 89.
68 Newman, *Development*, 196.
69 Newman, *Development*, 199.
70 Newman, *Development*, 204.
71 Joseph, "Centenary of the Death of Card. John Henry Newman" accessed July 28 2020, at http//www.vatican.va, 1990.
72 Joseph, "Centenary of the Death of Card. John Henry Newman" accessed July 28 2020, at http//www.vatican.va, 1990.
73 Joseph, "Centenary of the Death of Card. John Henry Newman" accessed July 28 2020, at http//www.vatican.va, 1990.
74 Ratzinger, "Centenary of the Death of Card. John Henry Newman" accessed July 28 2020, at http//www.vatican.va, 1990.
75 Ratzinger, "Centenary of the Death of Card. John Henry Newman" accessed July 28 2020, at http//www.vatican.va, 1990.
76 Joseph Ratzinger, *On Conscience* (San Francisco: Ignatius Press, 2007), 23.
77 Ratzinger, *On Conscience*, 24.
78 Ratzinger, *On Conscience*, 26.
79 Ratzinger, *On Conscience*, 26.
80 Ratzinger, *On Conscience*, 20.
81 Yves Congar, *True and False Reform in the Church* (Liturgical Press, Minnesota, 2011), 149.
82 Congar, *True and False Reform*, 140.
83 Congar, *True and False Reform*, 149.
84 Congregation for the Doctrine of the Faith, Instruction on the Ecclesial Vocation of the Theologian, *Donum Veritatis*, accessed July 29 2020, at http//www.vatican.va, 1990, 38.
85 Ratzinger, *Called to Communion*, 158–159.
86 Ratzinger, *Called to Communion*, 159.
87 Ratzinger, *God and the World*, 65.
88 Ratzinger, *Called to Communion*, 160.
89 Ratzinger, *Called to Communion*, 162.
90 Ratzinger, *Called to Communion*, 160–161.
91 Ratzinger, *Called to Communion*, 161–162.

92 Benedict XVI, "Address of His Holiness Benedict XVI to the Roman Curia Offering them his Christmas Greetings," Thursday December 22, 2005, accessed July 9, 2018 at www.vatican.va.
93 Benedict XVI, "Farewell Address to the Eminent Cardinals Present in Rome at the Clementine Hall," February 28, 2013, accessed July 9, 2018, at www.vatican.va.
94 Benedict XVI, "Interview by Fr. Jacques Servais, S.J.," 1–2.
95 Benedict XVI, "Interview by Fr. Jacques Servais, S.J.," 2.
96 Ratzinger, *Pilgrim Fellowship of Faith*, 111.
97 Ratzinger, *Pilgrim Fellowship of Faith*, 124.
98 Ratzinger, *Pilgrim Fellowship of Faith*, 124.
99 Ratzinger, *Pilgrim Fellowship of Faith*, 125.
100 Benedict XVI, "Encyclical Letter *Deus Caritas Est:* On the Meaning of Christian Love," (December 25, 2005) 3, accessed October 9, 2018 at www.vatican.va.
101 Benedict XVI, *Light of the World: The Pope, the Church, and the Signs of the Times*, trans. Michael J. Miller and Adrian J. Walker (San Francisco: Ignatius Press, 2010), 102.
102 Collins, *The Word Made Love*, 20.
103 The expression "unity of love" is intended to capture these three facets of love, that is, the sexual love of desire, the brotherly or sisterly love of friendship, and the service or *caritas* love of *agape*.
104 Benedict XVI, *Deus Caritas Est*, 3.
105 Benedict XVI, "*Urbi et Orbi* Christmas Message, 2010," accessed February 2, 2019, at www.vatican.va
106 Emery de Gaál, *O Lord, I Seek Your Countenance: Explorations and Discoveries in Pope Benedict XVI's Theology* (Steubenville, OH: Emmaus Academic, 2018), 12.
107 Benedict XVI, *Deus Caritas Est*, 17.
108 Ratzinger, *God and the World*, 26–27.
109 Friedrich Nietzsche, *Ecce Homo*, "Why I Am a Destiny," trans. Walter Kaufmann (New York, Vintage Books, 1989), 1.
110 Joseph Ratzinger, *The Meaning of Christian Brotherhood* (San Francisco: Ignatius Press, 1993), 15.
111 Joseph Ratzinger, *A New Song for the Lord: Faith in Christ and Liturgy Today*, trans. Martha M. Matesich (New York: Crossroad Publishing, 1986), 48.
112 Ratzinger, *The Meaning of Christian Brotherhood*, 16–17.
113 Benedict XVI, *Deus Caritas Est*, 5.
114 Benedict XVI, *Deus Caritas Est*, 5.
115 Benedict XVI, *Deus Caritas Est*, 4.
116 Benedict XVI, *Deus Caritas Est*, 7.

117 Angelo Cardinal Scola, "The Unity of Love and the Face of Man: An Invitation to Read Deus Caritas Est," *Communio: International Catholic Review*, 33, 2006, 319.
118 Benedict XVI, *Deus Caritas Est*, 8.
119 Scola, "The Unity of Love and the Face of Man," 326.
120 Benedict XVI, *Deus Caritas Est*, 2.
121 David Schindler, "The Redemption of Eros" *Communio: International Catholic Review*, 33, 2006, 381.
122 Schindler, "The Redemption of Eros," 377.
123 Rodney Howsare, "Why Begin with Love? Eros, Agape and the Problem of Secularism," *Communio: International Catholic Review* 33, (2006), 432.
124 Joseph Ratzinger, *Many Religions–One Covenant*, trans. Graham Harrison (San Francisco: Ignatius Press, 1999), 82–83.
125 Fyodor Dostoyevsky, *The Gospel in Dostoyevsky*, "The Rebellion" from *The Brothers Karamazov*, trans. Constance Garnett (Farmington PA: The Plough Publishing House, 1998), 43–57.
126 Dostoyevsky, *The Gospel in Dostoyevsky*, 55.
127 Dostoyevsky, *The Gospel in Dostoyevsky*, 26–27.
128 Dostoyevsky, *The Gospel in Dostoyevsky*, 29.
129 Joseph Ratzinger, Mass 'Pro Eligendo Romano Pontifice': Homily of His Eminence Card. Joseph Ratzinger, Dean of the College of Cardinals" (Vatican City, Monday April 18, 2005). Accessed July 20 2020, at www.vatican.va.
130 Benedict XVI, "Post-Synodal Apostolic Exhortation Sacramentum Caritatis: On the Eucharist as the Source and Summit of the Church's Life and Mission, 2007, 14, at www.vatican.va, accessed January 30, 2019.
131 Ratzinger, *Called to Communion, 26.*
132 Ratzinger, *Behold the Pierced One*, 29.
133 Ratzinger, *Behold the Pierced One*, 29–30.
134 Ratzinger, *Called to Communion*, 28–29.
135 Joseph Ratzinger, *Many Religions–One Covenant: Israel, the Church and the World*, trans. Graham Harrison (San Francisco: Ignatius Press, 1999), 84.
136 Benedict XVI, *Deus Caritas Est*, 14.
137 Benedict XVI, "Post-Synodal Apostolic Exhortation On the Church in Africa in Service to Reconciliation, Justice and Peace *Africae Munus*" (Vatican City: Libreria Editrice Vaticana, 2011), 152.
138 Howsare, "Why Begin with Love?" 428.
139 Benedict XVI, Post-Synodal Apostolic Exhortation *Verbum Domini*, on the Word of God in the Life and Mission of the Church (Vatican City: Libreria Editrice Vaticana, 2010), 4.
140 Second Vatican Council, *Dei Verbum*, 2.

141 Ratzinger/Benedict XVI, *Jesus of Nazareth*, vol. I, 156.
142 Second Vatican Council, *Dei Verbum*, 13.
143 Ratzinger, *Behold the Pierced One*, 76–77.
144 Benedict XVI, *Verbum Domini*, 15.
145 Benedict XVI, *Verbum Domini*, 7.
146 Benedict XVI, *Verbum Domini*, 28.
147 Ratzinger, *Behold the Pierced One*, 30.
148 Second Vatican Council, *Dei Verbum*, 13.
149 Benedict XVI, *Verbum Domini*, 35.
150 Benedict XVI, *Verbum Domini*, 35.
151 Benedict XVI, *Verbum Domini*, 35.
152 Benedict XVI, *Verbum Domini*, 35.
153 Benedict XVI, *Verbum Domini*, 54.
154 Joseph Ratzinger, *The Spirit of the Liturgy*, trans. John Saward (San Francisco: Ignatius Press, 2000), 207.
155 Joseph Ratzinger, *The Feast of Faith: Approaches to a Theology of the Liturgy*, trans. Graham Harrison (San Francisco: Ignatius Press, 1986), 25.
156 Ratzinger, *The Feast of Faith*, 26.
157 Ratzinger, *The Spirit of the Liturgy*, 172.
158 Ratzinger, *The Spirit of the Liturgy*, 172.
159 Ratzinger, *The Spirit of the Liturgy*, 172–173.
160 Ratzinger, *The Spirit of the Liturgy*, 173.
161 Ratzinger, *The Spirit of the Liturgy*, 45–46.
162 Ratzinger, *The Spirit of the Liturgy*, 46.
163 Ratzinger, *The Spirit of the Liturgy*, 50.
164 Ratzinger, *The Spirit of the Liturgy*, 21.
165 Ratzinger, *The Spirit of the Liturgy*, 21.
166 Immanuel Kant, *Religion within the Boundaries of Mere Reason*, trans. Allen Wood and George di Giovanni (Chelsea MI: Sheridan Books, 2016), 6:195.
167 Kant, *Religion*, 6:195.
168 Kant, *Religion*, 6:196–198.
169 Kant, *Religion*, 6:200.
170 G.W.F. Hegel, ed. and trans. Peter Fuss and John Dobbins, *Three Essays, 1793–1795: The Tübingen Essay, Berne Fragments and The Life of Jesus* (South Bend, IN: University of Notre Dame Press, 2004), 81.
171 Hegel, *Life of Jesus*, 87.
172 Ratzinger, *Faith and the Future*, 105–106.
173 Ratzinger, *Faith and the Future*, 63–64.

Chapter Six: *Ratzinger: Beyond the* Aufklärung *Historical Scientificity of Reason—Interacting with Critical Voices*

At this point, it is clear that faith and reason, or the dialogue between the God of faith and the God of the philosophers, constitute a central concern in terms of how Ratzinger thinks about the figure of Christ and the Church. Faith and reason constitute an indispensable framework if one is to properly understand much of Ratzinger's theological positions, as seen in the metaphors he makes regarding *Logos* as creative Reason, Son, Person, unity of love, and Word. In other words, one gains a more profound grasp of the conclusions espoused by Ratzinger when read in the context of the philosophical postulates of the modern and post-modern Western philosophical tradition, which are heavily shaped by the eighteenth century *Aufklärung* movement that swept across much of Western Europe. Thus, Ratzinger's theology has a contextual character, if by context one implies not just sociological trends, which Ratzinger clearly has little esteem for due to what he perceives to be their transitory nature, but, and more pointedly, context as reflected in the critical thinking of the times or the age. In a word, context here indicates thought patterns.

What stands out thus far is the realization that the concerns one finds in the philosophical theology of some of the *Aufklärer* are similar to what one finds in the systematic or dogmatic theology of Ratzinger. In effect, and taking into consideration the points treated in chapter three, it is plausible to make the assertion that much of Ratzinger's theology is an engagement with what he considers to be interpretations and reinterpretations of Christian orthodox truth claims by the *Aufklärung*, in a spirit of rational and critical thinking, in which reason is declared the primary and exclusive basis of engagement with the truth claims of Christianity. Given that many of these "new" readings of Christ and the New Testament are decisively at variance with the classical truth claims of Christianity in many areas, it turns out that Ratzinger appears to be on the defensive, an impression that one might get from reading the preceding chapter, especially on the question of the *Gestalt* of Christ.

However, such a conclusion fails to do justice to the wider picture, which is that of a genuine engagement on the part of Ratzinger, with these *Aufklärung* positions on Christ. As is evident from the reading of chapters two and three, Ratzinger adopts a respectful and open attitude toward the claims of the *Aufklärung* regarding Christ and the Church, in that he is interested in hearing what they have to say. He is eager to listen to their perspectives, as seen in his autobiographical recollections in chapter one. That said, and as seen in chapter three, Ratzinger is prepared to challenge the *Aufklärung* positions by inviting them to what one might call an intellectual conversion, that is, going beyond the limits of mere reason, beyond the postulates of scientific rationality.

This entails, as one sees in the multiple appropriations of the metaphor of *logos*, adopting a worldview in which transcendental or religious truths are no longer eschewed simply because they do not fit into the narrative of pure or mere reason. Such must be the case because mere reason or mere rationality cannot explain the whole of human reality, even if the *Aufklärung* sought to portray reason as the ground of all things, as seen in chapter three. For example, even if reason can explain the processes, reason cannot account for why humans exist in the first place, that is, why there are beings instead of nothing. Reason cannot explain the mission of humans in the world, that is, the purpose of human life, even if it can explain the choices humans make in terms of practical arrangements and options. Furthermore, reason *qua* reason cannot explain what happens to the human being, when biological life is over. Reason cannot go beyond the grave. If reason must be consistent with its inner logic of *Aufklärung* scientism, reason must stop when biological life ceases. And over and above all, reason *qua* reason cannot fully explain the two most profound emotions and realities of the human heart—namely, love and suffering. The scientific nature of reason that emerged in the *Aufklärung* is one that identified reason with science and, hence, with mathematics. To be rational implied being mathematical. And love and suffering transcend mathematics. Love and suffering are the two realities that explain the human life, for no human being can escape these two realities. Therefore, an understanding of rational scientism that understands and limits reason to the laboratory of science, excludes reason from the possibility of entering into the dialogue of the human heart, where the human being finds his or her most profound meaning.

Little wonder, therefore, that in calling forth reason and the *Aufklärung* to what one might describe as an intellectual conversion, Ratzinger essentially presents the postulates of faith as an intellectual culture, as seen in his multiple appropriations of the Greek concept of *logos*, as seen in chapter three. In his homily in Washington National Cathedral during his Apostolic Visit to the United States, April 17, 2008, Benedict talked about the necessity of this intellectual conversion of reason and the challenge rational scientism poses to the faith. Benedict said, *inter alia*:

> The challenges confronting us require a comprehensive and sound instruction in the truths of the faith. But they also call for cultivating a mindset, an intellectual "culture," which is genuinely Catholic, confident in the profound harmony of faith and reason and prepared to bring the richness of faith's vision to bear on the urgent issues which affect the future of American society.[1]

But what explains this Ratzingerian call for a new intellectual conversion that sees faith as an intellectual culture? It is precisely because Benedict believes that truth and virtue, truth and morality, constitute a single whole, a synthesis of reality that must not and cannot be fractured. In other words, Benedict adheres to the scholastic tradition that saw truth, beauty, and goodness as one, as a unity, as constitutive of a single reality or expression of reality. And conscious of a world in which these are not too evident today, in his homily at St. Patrick's Cathedral, New York, April 19, 2008, Benedict asked rhetorically: "Is not this ongoing 'intellectual' conversion as necessary as 'moral' conversion for our own growth in faith, our discernment of the signs of the times, and our personal contribution to the Church's life and mission?"[2] In a word, the truths arrived at by reason cannot be such that they are contrary to moral truths, to the truths of the grammar of creation and natural law. If it is the case that reason turns a blind eye to moral truths, then reason is logically severed from freedom, for what is the purpose of the truths of reason if they cannot set one free, and how can they set one free if they are unable to adhere to the moral law or if they, for the sake of reason's autonomy, develop a cynical or skeptical attitude toward the moral law, and not only that, but also to the postulates of faith? It is, therefore, a correct interpretation of Ratzinger to hold reason, morality, faith, and truth in an organic whole. Such a unity deters a fragmentizing of the human person.

At this point, and given all that has been said above, the sense of the unfolding of revelation in the context of the vicissitudes of history constitutes a central concern for Ratzinger. Such is the case because ideas do not operate in a vacuum but are born from contextual and cultural positions that demand a reasonable response, inspired by the dynamics of faith. But what might constitute the deeper, theological warrants through which one might explain this sense of the historical in Ratzinger vis-à-vis the concerns of reason, faith, and morality? To Ratzinger, the answer to the question lies in the space of God in history, that is, the space that society is willing to concede to God in its sociocultural imaginations.

Along this line of history and the dialogue between faith and reason, reason and revelation, that imposes itself on the theologian, Vincent Twomey offers an incisive perspective worth citing here at length because of the light it sheds on Ratzinger's consciousness of the necessity of paying attention to history and the philosophies of history:

> His [Ratzinger's] theology is marked, first of all, by attention to the whole history of human questioning (philosophy) up to and including those questions articulated or implied by the situation in which we find ourselves today. Second, this theology is characterized by attention to the answers—often partial and inadequate ones—given in the course of history by

> great thinkers of mankind, theologians and otherwise. Third, and most important, his theology is given its definitive form by its attempt to hear and interpret God's revelation of himself in Jesus Christ, that is, his design for mankind entrusted to the Church and testified to by Scripture read in the light of the history of dogma. I have just mentioned the word "history" three times. This is no accident. One of Ratzinger's basic methodological principles—following the examples of Plato, Aristotle, Augustine, and Aquinas—is that no serious philosophical or theological question can ever be adequately posed or answered, however tentatively, if the philosopher or theologian does not listen to the objections to it; and this implies being at least to some degree aware of the history of the question (and of the prior attempts made to answer it).[3]

One can translate this reading of Ratzinger by Twomey this way: Theology for Ratzinger is a historical reading of the questions of history; a historical reading of the answers and partial answers offered; and a historical offering of solutions based on the historical event of Jesus of Nazareth. And one can say that Ratzinger does not shy away from questions because, as Twomey again puts it, "all of Ratzinger's writings betray the courage to face any question or objection because of the confidence he has in the truth revealed in Jesus Christ and handed on by the Church's apostolic tradition."[4] The certainty of truth as incarnated in Jesus and transmitted through the apostolic tradition remains a hermeneutical framework for Ratzinger.

What emerges from this Christological attitude of certainty on Ratzinger's part is a characteristically diachronic texture of theology. As Twomey points out, Ratzinger's theology has always been influenced by the whole sweep of theological and philosophical history, and not primarily by the intellectual assumptions in vogue today.[5] This is the perspective from which one can understand Ratzinger's penchant for reading the Second Vatican Council in light of the hermeneutic of continuity and reform as opposed to an absolute watershed with little relation to the past. In effect, Ratzinger's historical reading of theology seeks to reconcile the diachronic with the synchronic movements of faith and reason, of the God of faith and the God of philosophers, as seen in the primacy and urgency that Ratzinger himself gave to this theme in his inaugural lecture.

Nonetheless, assuming all that has been said thus far in the preceding chapters and up to this point, it must be stated that this Ratzingerian reading of history with the eyes of faith is certainly fraught with difficulties. And this is the point at which Ratzinger's critics often accuse him of either wanting to turn back the hands of history, the gains of history, or worse still, to ignore them in his theological positions and conclusions. At this point, it is not a matter of offering a defense of Ratzinger, but of asking the question that Ratzinger raises in the face of such criticisms that have never slackened in their passion and fervor. I think that at the root of the criticism levied against Ratzinger stands this question of how the theologian must read the rational, autonomous developments of history, and to what extent the theologian must allow these new claims and positions to influence, renew, and shape the postulates of Christian faith.

Hence, this is needlessly going into the rabbit hole of ecclesial politics and politicking. It is reasonable to stay within the theological question which is essentially this: Given that the *Aufklärung*, as Ratzinger himself says above, marked a watershed moment in the evolutionary process of human thought—and given its radical redefinitions of many truth claims of Christian orthodoxy—how must one interpret history? How must one interpret theological history? In a word, how must one interpret philosophical theology as seen say in Kant, Hegel, and other *Aufklärung* figures? What is history? Are there limits to the human rationality of the historical, especially when it concerns the question of God, Christ, the Church and the life of faith?

I think Hans Küng articulates the perspective of some regarding Ratzinger's reception of the gains of the *Aufklärung*, in a somewhat dramatic and memorable fashion. Küng will therefore serve as the representative of the critical voices regarding Ratzinger's Augustinian, Bonaventurian, and *Aufklärung* conclusions, hoping that taken together, one can better assess and understand Ratzinger in terms of his point of departure and his theological destiny or goal, a spectrum that cannot be set aside even when considering Ratzinger's theological critics.

Definitely, given his long and public presence in the theological world, Ratzinger has certainly garnered more critical voices overtime. But confronting criticism regarding Ratzinger on issues like liberation theology, ecumenism, inter-religious dialogue, liturgy, and other positions that Ratzinger has held will definitely be too broad for the space of this work. Küng has been selected for the reason that his criticism of Ratzinger speaks directly to the issue of the Ratzinger's willingness or unwillingness to accept the fruits of the *Aufklärung* pertaining to the *Gestalt* of Christ and the question of the Church.

6.1 A Critical Voice: Ratzinger's Devotion to an *Anti-Aufklärung* "Old Fashioned Bavarian God."

James Corkery, S. J. points out that, especially in the 1980s when Ratzinger as Prefect of the Congregation for the Doctrine of the Faith was dealing with the issues ranging from liberation theology and moral theology to Christology and inter-religious dialogue, many theologians who dissented from what Corkery calls "certain non-infallible teachings of the magisterium"[6] read things regarding the Church and the science of theology very differently from how Ratzinger saw them. Especially after the publication of the famous *The Ratzinger Report* in 1985, there were many loud voices that disagreed with what was perceived to be a bleak, pessimistic, and dualistic characterization of the Church by Ratzinger, on the part of theologians, journalists, and historians of the ecclesial Anglo-sphere such as Nicholas Lash, Eamon Duffy, Richard McCormick, David Gibson, among others.[7] Sampling these less-than-flattering views of those who saw the reality of the Church as it emerges from their lived experiences and interpreted such different from Ratzinger's, Corkery concludes that:

> Thus, it is not unreasonable to say that theologians were discouraged by the pessimistic views that were emerging from Ratzinger in the 1980s, particularly as these views appeared to envisage a more constricting relationship of the magisterium to theologians, above all in the area of moral theology.[8]

With no intent of downplaying the voices of the critics of Ratzinger, I tend to think that what most serves the purpose of this work is the criticism that is specifically related to the *Aufklärung*, that is, to the question of how much space mere rationality has to be accorded in the Christological and Ecclesiological portraits thus far considered, especially in chapters four and five. In other words, the goal is not to study each individual objection made against Ratzinger. That will be too broad for this work.

But as Corkery points out,[9] Ratzinger's fundamental attitude toward theological criticism appears to be captured in his conviction as articulated in *The Ratzinger Report*:

> In a world in which, at bottom, many believers are gripped by skepticism, the conviction of the Church that there is *one* truth, and that this one truth can as such be recognized, expressed, and also clearly defined within certain bonds, appears scandalous. It is also experienced as offensive by many Catholics who have lost sight of the essence of the Church. The Church is, however, not only a human organization; she also has a deposit to defend that does not belong to her, the proclamation and transmission of which is guaranteed through a teaching office that brings it close to men of all times in a fitting manner.[10]

To Ratzinger, therefore, defending the deposit of faith against what he perceived to have been the relativizing tendencies of some theologians, was essentially an ecclesial service of correcting what he saw as a misconception of the nature and function of the Church. Such a misconception, Ratzinger points out, manifests itself in an insidious way in what appears to be a parallel magisterium of theologians:

> Today we do not encounter this aforementioned "obstinate denial" and this "obstinate doubt" openly. It is to be expected from the outset that they nevertheless exist in a multi-layered intellectual age like ours, only they do not wish to appear as such. Today one frequently opposes one's own theological

> hypotheses to the Magisterium by asserting that the teaching office does not express the faith of the Church but only "the archaic Roman theology." It is contended that it is not the Congregation but they, the "heretics," who represent the "authentic" meaning of the transmitted faith. Where a still stronger ecclesiastical bond exists, we encounter similar but essentially related phenomena: I wonder at the adroitness of theologians who manage to represent the exact opposite of what is written in clear documents of the Magisterium in order afterward to set forth this inversion with skilled dialectical devices as the "true" meaning of the documents in question.[11]

Clearly, the Ratzinger in *The Ratzinger Report* displays a great unease with what he sees as the corrosive influence of theological dissent, and he is not shy to say so even in the face of very critical reactions. Ratzinger sees much of dissent as being influenced by what he famously described as the dictatorship of relativism, his central concern being its inability to recognize anything as definitive and beyond one's own subjective desires.[12] Definitely, not everyone saw things the way Ratzinger saw them, in terms of the definitive nature of the truth claims of Christian dogma.

Hans Küng, Ratzinger's erstwhile colleague at the University of Tübingen, writing in the first volume of his own *Memoirs*, maintains that what can be described as a confidence in the revealed truths in Jesus Christ as transmitted by the Church, resulted in a kind of pious instinct that inhibited Ratzinger's theology. Wondering rhetorically "how so gifted, friendly, open a theologian as Joseph Ratzinger can undergo such a change: from progressive Tübingen theologian to Roman Grand Inquisitor,"[13] Küng makes the conclusion that "even in Tübingen my colleague, who for all his friendliness always seems distant and cool, had kept something like an unenlightened 'devotional corner' in his Bavarian heart."[14] I think that for Küng, it was near impossible to truly consider Ratzinger as a dialogue partner for the reason that his theological method already shielded Ratzinger from breaking new grounds, of letting the force of the argument lead him on. Commenting on Hermann

Haring's work on Ratzinger, Küng further explains his reading of Ratzinger:

> In an acute analysis of more than 200 pages, Professor Hermann Häring, my assistant in Tübingen at the time, shows how from the beginning "Theology and Ideology in Joseph Ratzinger" (2002) have been interwoven. He simply didn't put certain questions to himself; he always had a skeptical attitude toward modern exegesis (i.e. historical critical) and was open to historical arguments only to a limited degree.[15]

Given the clear interactions with modern philosophy by Ratzinger as seen in the preceding chapters, it certainly comes across as ludicrous for Ratzinger's theological thought to be characterized in any way, shape, or form as "ideological," and even less as displaying a "skeptical attitude." And for good reasons. Firstly, an attentive study of Ratzinger's theology demonstrates a profound spirit of self-effacement, in which Ratzinger allows himself to be taken over by the thought of the Fathers. There is no evidence that Ratzinger ever sought to create a "theological system" of his own. From Augustine and Bonaventure, Ratzinger emerges as a theologian deeply rooted in the spirit of *sentire cum ecclesia*. A thoughtful and an objective study of Ratzinger shows no iota of an agenda-driven activistic theologizing. In fact, the evidence weighs heavily on the opposite side. When Ratzinger decries the "party of Christ" in preference for the "Church of Jesus Christ," for example, it is as a consequence of his profound dislike for a theology that is driven by any ideology, be it to the left or to the right (whatever those shibboleths meant and continue to mean today). Ratzinger's theological instincts display an attitude of thoughtful and overwhelming receptivity, of trusting that the faith of the Church and the truths of faith that one receives precedes one's subjective preferences. That is not ideological. If anything, it shows that feature of *humilitas* that is so characteristic of the shy Bavarian theologian.

Furthermore, the robust and broad engagement that Ratzinger has with modern philosophy as demonstrated in this work does not portray a man with a skeptical temperament toward modern thought and modern exegesis, which found its most articulate form and expression in the historical-critical method. As demonstrated in this work, Ratzinger is a theologian who takes modern thought seriously and is very much willing to play on the field of modern philosophical and exegetical thought. Ratzinger is not skeptical about the historical method, if by historical critical method one means the gains that biblical scholarship has achieved through the study of the various literary genres and textual criticisms; linguistic constructions; history of texts; a cross cultural and intra-textual and inter-textual exegesis; ecumenical insights and interpretations; and of course, the sociological and philosophical currents brought to bear on the texts of Sacred Scripture. Ratzinger is very explicit about his appreciation of all that the contemporary biblical movement has achieved. And he says as much in the preface to the first volume of his trilogy on Jesus. The historical-critical method is a useful exegetical tool because Christianity is a historical religion. It was at the fullness of time (Gal 4:4) that the Son of God entered history. Hence, there is a theological necessity for a historical-critical method, and that this method found a home in biblical scholarship, both Catholic and Protestant, is welcomed by Ratzinger.

However, what Ratzinger dared to do, to the angst of Küng et al., was to challenge the reigning "orthodoxy" of the self-sufficiency of the historical-critical method of biblical scholarship that, its helpful aspects regarding the understanding and the interpretation of the bible notwithstanding, had become, especially in the liberal Protestant strand of it, a tool that sought to cast skepticism over the historical reliability and veracity of not only the gospel narratives, but, and more worrisomely, the figure of Jesus Christ. In other words, Ratzinger, while acknowledging the gains of the historical-critical method, does not shy away from pointing to the limits of the historical-critical method. A method is just that, a method, a tool, an instrument, and hence cannot become the *regula fidei*. In other words, the historical-critical method could not become an end in itself. To Ratzinger, the fruits of the method have been reaped, and it was now time to move beyond the method to what ultimately and truly matters, namely, the encounter between the believer and Jesus Christ. An excessive focus on the method overlooks the fact that as a historical method—and if it is to be true to itself, it studies the text as *history*, from the perspective of the past. Without the balancing act of faith, of believing with the community of the Church from whom the Scriptures emerged, and without paying attention to the living experience of the saints, then we are left with two lamentable consequences, perhaps unintended: firstly, the figure of Jesus easily becomes something of the past. We are struck with the Jesus of first-century Palestine. And because we are preoccupied with the historical, the Jesus who is present today in the midst of the believing community of the Church, is easily eclipsed. The Jesus present today in the heart of the Church becomes inaccessible or his countenance, blurred, for what tends to preoccupy are the minute historical details which are heaped, one against the other, as they struggle for scholarly attention amid the remoteness of two millennia.

But more importantly, at least from the Ratzingerian perspective, the Bible easily becomes a tool for the experts only, with competing exegeses that often reflect preferred positions of the exegetes. Vladimir Soloviev's *The Anti-Christ* is a chilling reminder of the real possibility and disastrous consequences of a scholarly exegesis without a believing heart. With his doctorate in biblical exegesis from the University of Tübingen, the anti-Christ employs his knowledge of the sacred Word with one intent, that is, to empty the sacred text of its meaning, of its call to all for conversion to God. Hence, we use our learning and knowledge of the Scriptures to water down the seriousness of God's Word, all in a bid to make the Bible more attuned to the sensibilities of contemporary society. The Bible is then made to appear in the form of our own image and likeness. When Ratzinger resists this form of scholarship, he is doing so because the Bible, for Ratzinger, cannot be a book of the experts, but a living Word, a gospel, the good news for all, accessible to all, meant for the nourishment of the life of faith for all. Such must be the case because from the perspective of the grand scheme of things, it tends to be the simple souls that are open to revelation, that allow God's Word to influence them and take root in their lives: "At that time Jesus exclaimed, 'I bless you, Father, Lord of heaven and of earth, for hiding these things from the learned and the clever and revealing them to mere children. Yes, Father, for that is what it pleased you to do'" (Mt 11:25–26). From this perspective, therefore, it is not so much a matter of a skeptical attitude toward modern exegesis as Küng will have us believe regarding the Ratzingerian position. It is, for Ratzinger, the necessity of defending the faith of the simple believer against a scholarly approach to the bible largely guided by a this-worldly hermeneutic that barely recognizes the supernatural quality of the written text.

In *Benedict XVI: An Intimate Portrait* by Peter Seewald, one finds a further explication of Küng's critical apprehension of Ratzinger:

> There is a break in his (Ratzinger's) biography, no question. This change is of course only contingent. I believe there must still have been, somewhere in his heart, an unenlightened shrine to an old-fashioned God. I should say that in my case there is no belief on which I have not actually cast the light of reason. But somewhere or other, he (Ratzinger) still has his Bavarian shrine to an old-fashioned God, where reason ceases.[16]

It is not difficult to imagine what Küng implies by "in my case there is no belief on which I have not actually cast the light of reason." Küng's history of dissent from settled Church teaching is well documented. However, facts, they say, are stubborn, and from the look of things, one is left wondering what evangelical fruits have emerged from Küng's baptizing of Kantian and Hegelian rationalism? The fatal misstep for Küng is not that he submits the deposit of faith to reason, but that he believes that his subjective reasoning in the light of the new positivistic understanding of reason should correct the faith. In other words, while the Catholic tradition even before Anselm had proceeded along the lines of faith seeking understanding, for Küng and his allies, it is understanding seeking faith, and once faith does not square with the subjective understanding, then faith requires a make-over. From this perspective, therefore, even the rapport between faith and reason that has marked Catholic thought is jettisoned in the name of the *Aufklärung*, for reason must reign supreme. There is little or no room for the "darkness of faith," for the plunging of myself into the reality of the great unknown, of allowing myself to be pulled into that vastness that precedes me, that zone of insecurity within which I am not in charge of things, but a small one in the arms of a great God whom I cannot fully understand, even with the most endowed of human intellects. Rather than reason ceasing before an old-fashioned God, Ratzinger simply recognizes what the book of Job so aptly demonstrated, when God responds to Job's making the case of his innocence before God, which one could translate in this instance to be thus: Where was the human intellect when God created the heavens and the earth, and all contained therein? Ratzinger will be the first to defend the "light of reason" that Küng talks about. We have seen much of that in his engagements with the *Aufklärung* thought in the preceding chapters. And even his inaugural lecture demonstrates Ratzinger's love for reason. But even human reason is not entirely a "light," for rationality suffers the same fate of brokenness that marks the human condition from the time of Adam and Eve. In other words, just as human nature suffers from a weakened will, so too humans suffer from a defective intellect, and that explains why the good (that is, the object of the will), and truth (that is, the object of the intellect), continue to be a struggle for every human being. And recognizing the limits of reason does not amount to a negation of reason, much less a cessation of reason. It simply means that faith is likewise a legitimate source of knowledge that can and should challenge the positions of mere reason *à la* Küng, even when the latter continues to characterize Ratzinger as anti-*Aufklärung*, as Patrick G. McGlinchey summarizes:

> Küng indicates that Ratzinger was consistently reluctant to allow the claims of reason (at least when defined by the standards of the Enlightenment) to limit or determine the content of revelation. Küng's words may be somewhat disparaging of Ratzinger, not to say repetitive, but they confirm that he (Küng) had always suspected that some form of "superstition" had inhibited Ratzinger from accepting the hegemony of rationalism.[17]

Certainly, the reality regarding faith and its relationship with the rationalism of the *Aufklärung* that Küng accuses Ratzinger of being unwilling to embrace is much more complex than Küng might be willing to concede. And even with this, it clearly emerges that pure reason is unable to account for the whole picture of the symphony of faith. While it is true that the common ground for the *Aufklärer* is a scientific understanding of reason, it is also the case that across the broad, one notices, as seen in chapter three, an unwillingness or inability to move from a pure rational faith to a faith that is both rational, but religiously experiential. In addition, it is not clear what openness to the *Aufklärung* might constitute for Küng, in terms of a concrete manifestation of such an openness. In other words, at what point can one say that one has heard or appreciated the gains of the *Aufklärung*? When one starts rejecting the orthodox truths of Christian dogma? Greek philosophy taught the world the principle of non-contradiction as belonging to the nature of rationality. If it turns out that following Küng's understanding of the "light of reason" one is led into dissenting from Christological and Ecclesiological truths of the faith, or more broadly, from settled Church dogma and discipline, then non-contradiction demands that one position has to be repudiated for the other to stand true. And it is certainly not what has been believed *semper*, *ubique*, *et ab omnibus* (Vincent of Lèrins), that should be jettisoned in fidelity to the principle of non-contradiction.

Nonetheless, if chapters two to five bear any indications, they testify to the fact that Ratzinger clearly takes the dialectical tension between faith and reason seriously, and definitely not from a somewhat naïve perspective, as Küng might have us believe. As McGlinchey points out, for Ratzinger, "the fusion of revelation and reason properly understood was justified in that Christianity was the true philosophy and Christ the *Logos* personified."[18] Even Ratzinger's inaugural lecture at the University of Bonn, in which he argued for a reconciliation between the God of philosophy, the One, with the God of faith, of Abraham, Isaac, and Jacob, sheds light on why Ratzinger's theological instincts would have deterred him from pitting the faith against reason in such a way that faith appears unable to hold its grounds on its own inner consistency and according to its own terms, and thus, appearing irrational or contra reason or unenlightened, as Küng seems to be suggesting. If anything, Ratzinger's desire, as he himself expresses it in his address to the Bundestag, is to help "reason to rediscover its true greatness, without being sidetracked into irrationality."[19] As already pointed out, Benedict sees the positivistic understanding of reason as limited and limiting in its interpretation of the full breadth of all that comprises the human condition.

"Where positivist reason considers itself the only sufficient culture and banishes all other cultural realities to the state of subcultures," declared Benedict XVI at the Bundestag, "it diminishes man, indeed it threatens his humanity."[20] Reason must pay attention to data and the wisdom that comes from empirical data. But the mathematization of the character and nature of reason, when taken in an exclusive manner, misses out on realities and experiences of the human being that transcend attempts at mathematization and that cannot even be submitted to such mathematical interpretations. This is the context from which Benedict XVI is arguing for the legitimacy of the meta-mathematical and the non-positivistic experiences and realities of human life to be considered legitimate sources of knowledge as well. As Benedict XVI pointed out in his Bundestag address:

> In its self-proclaimed exclusivity, the positivist reason which recognizes nothing beyond mere functionality resembles a concrete bunker with no windows, in which we ourselves provide lighting and atmospheric conditions, being no longer willing to obtain either from God's wide world. And yet we cannot hide from ourselves the fact that even in this artificial world, we are still covertly drawing upon God's raw materials, which we refashion into our own products. The windows must be flung open again, we must see the wide world, the sky and the earth once more and learn to make proper use of all this.[21]

The image of a *concrete bunker with no windows* is certainly catchy and mentally stimulating. The issue is not with the bunker, but the lack or absence of windows, which leaves us with only one logical conclusion, namely, suffocation. And this is definitely a dire warning: If we were to continue on the path of a positivistic reason that admits of no other legitimate sources of knowledge and human experiences, then we might end up suffocating ourselves out of human existence. A form of reason that is entirely calculative and calculated leaves no fresh air in the room of human existence. There is no space for the new, for the breadth that comes with the reasonableness of faith, to the experience of faith that lies beyond positivistic reason. As Marta Cartabia and Andrea Simoncini point out in their commentary on the above cited text from Ratzinger's Bundestag lecture, "It is finally time, once again, to deal with reality as a whole, without assuming that the only way to effectively understand it is to reduce it into preconceived frameworks."[22] To open reality beyond "preconceived frameworks" makes room for the dynamism that characterizes religious experience, Christian experience, at the root of which is the abandoning of the self into the providential hands of a good God, who faith tells me, knows me, cares about me, and wants my true good and happiness. Hence, rather than pursuing a path of unenlightened faith as Küng would have us believe about Ratzinger, the exact opposite is the case: Ratzinger sees faith and reason as traditional allies, to the extent that reason understands that there are things beyond its grasp, that someone outside has to help lift reason out of the concrete bunker with no windows that the *Aufklärung* and its bent on *mere reason* have placed reason into. In this vein, Ratzinger writes:

> By no means the least important practical function of faith is to offer healing for the reason as reason, not to overpower it or to remain outside it, but in fact to bring it to itself again. Faith, as a historical instrument, can set reason itself free again, so that—now that faith has set it on the right path again—reason can once more see properly for itself. We have to strive toward such a renewed process of dialogue between faith and philosophy, for each has need of the other. Without faith, philosophy cannot be whole, but faith without reason cannot be human.[23]

Therefore, rather than obscuring reason, faith actually liberates reason from the bunker of finitude and positivistic restrictions that have been placed on reason by the spirit of the *Aufklärung*. And faith is capable of carrying out the task of this liberation of reason because, for the Christian, faith is, above all, not about moral postulates and rational ideas, but an encounter with a person, for as Benedict XVI points out in *Deus Caritas Est*, "being Christian is not the result of an ethical choice or a lofty idea, but the encounter with an event, a person, which gives life a new horizon and a decisive direction."[24] Hence, the source of faith is a real encounter with a person, the Infinite God in Jesus of Nazareth, an experience out of whose abundance the preconceived nature of positivistic reason is broken through and opened up to the infinity and limitlessness of the experience of faith. In this light, "the world of reason and the world of faith—the world of secular rationality and the world of religious belief—need one another and should not be afraid to enter into a profound and ongoing dialogue, for the good of our civilization. Religion, in other words, is not a problem for legislators to solve, but a vital contributor to the national conversation."[25] In Ratzinger's opinion, therefore, faith and reason are bound together by a deep mutual friendship that eschews any form of subjugation. Cartabia and Simonicini comment, "as with true friendships, encounter is fundamental: that moment in which something unexpected occurs and leaves the other changed; in which new, previously ignored perspectives open up, and different personalities become attuned in a way that a person becomes aware of the richness of his/her own identity, but also aware of his/her need of the other, without whom such an awareness would be impossible."[26] From this perspective, reason and faith need each other in facing the challenges of the contemporary world. And even in the contemporary secular world that tends to place pride in positivistic reason as the only sure and steady source of knowledge, faith still has a chance because as Ratzinger points out, faith corresponds to the nature of the human being:

> For man is more generously proportioned than the way Kant and the various post-Kantian philosophies see him or will allow him to be. Kant himself ought to have found a place for this. Somehow or other, among his postulates. The longing for the infinite is alive and unquenchable within man. None of the attempted answers will do; only the God who himself became finite in order to tear open our finitude and lead us out into the wide spaces of his infinity, only he corresponds to the question of our being. That is why, even today, Christian faith will come to man again. It is our task to serve this faith with humble courage, with all the strength of our heart and of our mind.[27]

In other words, reducing the human being and human experiences to the postulates of mere rationality diminishes the human being, for in the final analysis human nature is such that it continues to remain open to the infinite, for as Augustine declares in book one of his *Confessions*, God has created us for himself, and our hearts are restless until they rest in God. Reason alone will never satisfy and account for what it means to be human. And faith alone will miss out on the element of rationality which is divinely endowed in humans. And Ratzinger is eager to keep the dialogue between the two, for both are needed in meeting today's challenges of living in pluralistic, secular societies; for together, both provide a much more comprehensive account of human nature and human experiences in the world.

Still within this context of the Küng-Ratzinger controversy on the place of reason vis-à-vis faith and revelation, one finds an interesting contribution from Thomas Aquinas. The Angelic Doctor raises the question why, besides philosophy, should any other science such as theology be required? Opposing the position of the self-sufficiency of reason in light of the attainment of truth, Aquinas argues that it was necessary for human salvation that besides philosophy built up by human reason, there should be a knowledge revealed by God—that is, theology—for the human being is directed to God as to an end that surpasses the grasp of human reason. Given that the end must first be known by people who are to direct their thoughts and actions to that end, Aquinas maintains that it was therefore necessary for the salvation of humans that certain truths that exceed human reason be made known to humans by divine revelation.[28] Secondly, Aquinas points out that even regarding the truths about God that are accessible by human reason, it was necessary that humans should be taught by a divine revelation, because the truth about God discoverable solely by reason would only be known by a few, after a long while and with an admixture of errors.[29] It was therefore necessary that humans be taught, for the sake of their salvation, those divine truths by divine revelation that exceeds human reason.

Given these Thomistic insights, the burden of proof is no longer on Ratzinger and Küng's characterization of Ratzinger's theological method as a Bavarian shrine paying allegiance to an old-fashioned God before whom reason ceases. Quite the contrary, what one finds in Ratzinger is the willingness to concede what Pascal so forcefully realized, that the heart has its reasons that reason itself does not have.[30] Isn't it telling that from this realization of the limits of reason, Pascal is able to encounter the illuming experience of the God of Abraham, Isaac, and Jacob, the God of fire and not of the philosophers?[31] In a word, what Ratzinger is unwilling to do is to transform Christian faith into a thing of the "rational experts" only. In this sense, Ratzinger certainly believes what Pascal believes, that the organ of "seeing" God, of religious experience, transcends the mind and is best captured by the human heart.[32] Within the mind of his "Bavarian Shrine"—to employ Küng's image—Ratzinger certainly recognizes, with Anselm of Canterbury, that God is that which nothing greater is able to be thought,[33] for human reason, in spite of its grandeur, has its limits. Rather than accusing Ratzinger of rejecting the gains of the *Aufklärung*, I am rather inclined to see in Ratzinger this methodology of Anselm: "For I do not seek to understand so that I may believe, but I believe so that I may understand. For I believe this also: that unless I will have believed, I will not understand."[34] Little wonder that in the opening chapter of his *Introduction to Christianity*, Ratzinger gives this Anselmian formulation a warm and laudable reception.[35] Faith is therefore understood by Ratzinger as standing firm and understanding. To paraphrase Pascal, faith has its own rationality that reason itself does not have, and this rationality is evident most of all in the lives of the saints of the Church.

Overall, Ratzinger's conservatism on the question of the truths of dogma could boil down to the following reasons, as enunciated by Corkery. Firstly, that the God of philosophy and the God of theology are one. Corkery sees this as a "facial feature" of Ratzinger's theology.[36] As shown in chapter two of this work, which studied the inaugural lecture, Ratzinger sides with Aquinas against Brunner. For Aquinas, the Christian understanding of God complements and elevates but does not destroy the philosophical idea of God. For the Protestant Brunner, the personal God who has a name, who has revealed himself in the tetragrammaton, is opposed to the non-personal God of philosophy. As seen in both the inaugural lecture and the further development of the same theme in the *Introduction to Christianity*, for Ratzinger the God of Abraham, Isaac, and Jacob, the One God of the Bible, is the same One, the Absolute

Being, the *Logos*, of Greek philosophy. As Corkery points out, "this 'facial feature' constitutes a principle that expresses the radical monotheism of the Bible and ensures, thereby, that Christianity's claim to truth stands and that the Christian faith tradition cannot be relegated to the status of one tradition among many."[37] In other words, Ratzinger's conservative attitude to truth—if one might describe it this way—is shaped by his conviction of preventing Christianity from losing its characteristic uniqueness.

A second reason that explains Ratzinger's conservative attitude toward truth claims of Christian dogma is what Corkery describes as "showing a contempt for God."[38] In other words, to give up on the possibility of the objective truths of the faith is tantamount to a rejection of the possibility that God can and actually does give us the gift of truth, that God can actually make himself known to humans.[39] In this sense, it is not arrogant to be definitive about the truth. On the contrary, it takes an attitude of humility to be able to receive truth from God, for God has done the unimaginable by becoming human, true God and true Man, in the historical Jesus of Nazareth.[40] And as Ratzinger compellingly asserts in *The Nature and Mission of Theology*:

> To remove from faith its claim to truth, to stated, understandable truth, is an example of that false modesty which is diametrically opposed to humility because it refuses to accept the *condition humaine*; it is a renunciation of that dignity of being a man which makes human suffering bearable and endows it with greatness.[41]

In a word, for Ratzinger, accepting the definitive nature of the truth claims of Christianity is not a sign of arrogance or theological or religious intolerance. Quite the contrary, it is a manifestation of humility before God who has revealed himself at the fullness of time in Christ Jesus (Gal. 4:4), who is the way, the truth, and the life (Jn 14:6).

In standing for the objective character of truth claims, Ratzinger is not indifferent to the theological and philosophical principle that speaks of the limits of the finite mind to comprehend infinity, which brings about the relevance of the principle of analogy.[42] As Ratzinger maintains:

> True, faith does not remove the essential limitation of man in his relation to the truth: it does not, in other words, eliminate the law of analogy. Nevertheless, analogy is not the same as metaphor. Analogy can always be broadened and deepened, but, within the boundaries of man's possibilities, it declares the very truth.[43]

In this sense, to reject theological relativism while insisting on the definitive and objective character of dogma is not a denial of human finitude before an infinite God. It is to recognize that, because of the Incarnation, God has accepted to limit God's self so that humans can know God with certainty. And in a cited remark made by Ratzinger in an interview with Alfred Läpple in the magazine *30 Days*, cited by Tracey Rowland in *Ratzinger's Faith*, Ratzinger is quoted as saying, "God is not recognized because He is a *summum bonum* that is able to be grasped and demonstrated with exact formulas, but because He is a You who comes forward and gets Himself recognized [...]. An abstraction didn't need a mother."[44] In other words, the principle of the Incarnation is what explains Ratzinger's conservatism to the definitive character of the truth claims of the Christian faith.

6.2 Understanding the Ratzingerian Claim of the Insufficiency of *Aufklärung*'s "Mere Rationality"

In his Christmas message of 2006, Benedict XVI unambiguously stated that, "without the light of Christ, the light of reason is not sufficient to enlighten humanity and the world."[45] In other words, faith has a wider space for operating than reason regarding the core issues that concern human beings, such as the question of origin and destiny of human beings, the question of suffering and love. Commenting on the above cited text by Benedict, James Schall, S.J., maintains that Benedict believes that the "depths of reason are discovered more under the stimulus of revelation than by science or human reflection, however legitimate and valuable these are."[46] In this sense, reason can get to a better realization of its potentials if it opens itself to faith, to revelation. Tracey Rowland cautions and comments:

> It would also be wrong to regard Ratzinger as fundamentally hostile to either philosophy or science (though he may be hostile to many projects which market themselves as a scientific theology). His basic principle is that reason needs to be informed by faith and that cultures and cultural practices need to be judged with reference to Revelation, but this does not mean that he sees no value in philosophy or science. The point is that alone, cut off from Revelation, not only do they fail to save us, but they have a tendency to turn into oppressive ideologies.[47]

Certainly, others for whom the *Aufklärung* constitutes the summit of human rational achievement will disagree with Ratzinger. But what should inform one's evaluation of Ratzinger's position are the reasons he gives for adopting the conclusion of the guiding role of revelation regarding philosophy. And this has as much to do, firstly, with the inherent contradictions of the various schools as thought. We see demonstrated in the history of philosophy, beginning from the question of the origin of all things that concerned the pre-Socratics; the conflicting positions between Plato and Aristotle on cosmology and ethics; and in modern philosophy, the differing takes on the questions of morality, politics, epistemology and metaphysics. Secondly, as Rowland points out, the tendency of turning one's rational positions into ideologies that justify one's conclusions, even if oppressive to others. There is the willfulness that comes with a fixated rationality that manifests itself in a supra-rational conception of reason, transforming reason into a voluntaristic utilitarian tool by which the strong impose their will on the weak.

A third factor would be the honest acknowledgment of the developments that flowed from *mere reason*, especially in the latter part of the twentieth century—that is, a rationality that tied itself to technological advancement and decidedly against any moral foundations. As Ratzinger points out, "for in the last analysis, even the atomic bomb is a product of reason; in the last analysis, the breeding and selection of human beings is something thought up by reason."[48] Serious questions emerge from this technological application of reason severed from morality. The production and usage of the nuclear bomb raises the questions of the limits beyond which the human mind should not go, even with the intent of defeating an enemy at war, given the scale or magnitude of human and environmental suffering left in the wake of the usage of such dreadful weapons. What does it say about human dignity and human rights as inalienable rights bestowed by the Creator, if the human being is now a product of a laboratory, manufactured in the name of freedom and in the name of science, and no longer a gift from a Creator? These are questions that cannot be ignored as we face the consequences of the application of mere reason, or in this case, reason within the boundaries of technology and science. And because these questions touch on anthropology, on the meaning of the human being, his origins, his nature, his purpose and the fulfilment of that purpose, religion cannot ignore these questions, religions cannot be sidelined. Faith must engage and speak with reason and vice versa, for as Ratzinger points out, the *Aufklärung* understanding of reason, of philosophy and the role that philosophy is called to play, is limited and limiting. Ratzinger points out:

> Above all, however, we must affirm that this Enlightenment philosophy, with its related culture, is incomplete. It consciously cuts off its own historical roots, depriving itself of the powerful sources from which it sprang. It detaches itself from what we might call the basic memory of mankind, without which reason loses its orientation, for now the guiding principle is that man's capability determines what he does [...]. The radical detachment of the Enlightenment philosophy from its roots ultimately leads it to dispense with man.[49]

And understanding Ratzinger, an openness to faith provides the unique opportunity of reconnecting the gains of the *Aufklärung* to its roots. It also implies that without the roots faith provides the gains of the *Aufklärung*, such as the articulation of human dignity, human rights, and freedom of thought and expression, might end up being steps that mutilate and even annihilate the human person, for one ends up with reason *qua* reason, with no inspiration from the breadth of faith, which has been fundamental to human self-understanding of human nature, identity and mission, down the ages. As Ratzinger further points out:

> This philosophy (that is, the *Aufklärung*), expresses not the complete reason of man, but only one part of it. And this mutilation of reason means that we cannot consider it to be rational at all. Hence, it is incomplete and can recover its health only through reestablishing contact with its roots. A tree without roots dries up.[50]

Again, Ratzinger is in no way denying the gains of the *Aufklärung*. He is just making a reasonable observation that *Aufklärung* philosophy, left to itself, cannot stand on its own, cannot explain the whole phenomenon of human existence, in its complexities, joys, pains, anxieties, and hopes. A culture of reason *qua* reason misses out and severs the link with other cultures that open reason beyond itself, that keeps faith and reason in a healthy and enriching equilibrium, and is willing for one's horizon to be widened by the boundlessness that comes with faith and the religious experience. In this light, a radical emancipation of the human intellect from faith does not serve the human being. If anything, it ends up leaving reason without roots, according to Ratzinger. What then emerges as the new normal is a relativism that becomes dogmatism, as each one argues for the superiority of one's subjective thought.

For Ratzinger, therefore, the distinction between the faith and reason, between the God of faith and the God of the philosophers, need not have such accents of differentiation, because the net result would be a psycho-social schizophrenia, in which the individual person is torn between the energies of faith and reason that otherwise might have afforded an inspiring life synthesis. Even reason detached from faith cannot account for the ethical foundations of society and could end up being very destructive, Ratzinger argues:

> If we have noted the urgent question of whether religion is truly a positive force, so we must now doubt the reliability of reason. For in the last analysis, even the atomic bomb is a product of reason; in the last analysis, the breeding and selection of human beings is something thought up by reason. Does this then mean that it is reason that ought to be placed under guardianship? But by whom or by what? Or should

> perhaps religion and reason restrict each other and remind each other where their limits are, thereby encouraging a positive path?[51]

This text, as much as texts elsewhere in Ratzinger, reflects a clear call for a mutual relationship of correction and support between faith and reason. It seems to be in the nature of the human being to seek unity, to understand the whole picture, to seek commonality, since, as Thomas Aquinas observes in the *Summa Theologica*, all persons have the same last end.[52] This appears to be the case, so much so that even for a philosopher like Heidegger inclined to drawing a strict line between philosophy and theology, faith and reason, one still finds expressions that reflect a desire for a rapprochement between faith and reason. Ratzinger appears to believe that the inner structure of reason challenges the subject to truth and the adherence to it. Reason therefore becomes a constraint on freedom understood as license because reason demands to know the truth or falsity of a given proposition.

The rejection or suspicion of the objectively reasonable is at bottom a suspicion of the possibility of knowing the truth. It demands a subjective adherence, given that while the object of the intellect is truth, truth is not truth for truth's sake, but is meant to open the will toward that which is good, or the proper object of the will. Only in this sense of the true and the good can we understand Ratzinger's bold denunciation of what he coined as the dictatorship of relativism in his homily "Pro Eligendo Romano Pontifice."[53] This was not a denunciation of worldliness as much as an invitation to regain confidence in truth and in reason's capacity to know the truth and the will's possibility of submitting to the truth. In contrast to contemporary skepticism regarding human capacity to know and assent to truth, Ratzinger continues to believe the contrary. His reasoning seems to be that if the human mind cannot know truth, then the very act of creation is delusionary, for why would God create an intellect only to render the object of that intellect, which is truth, an impossible dream, a Sisyphean Myth, in which we roll the stone up the hill only for it to roll back down? Ratzinger sees in this rejection of truth and reason a rejection of the human being, an abandonment-philosophy, or an embrace of a philosophy that is closed and cut off.

This is the context from which one can understand Heidegger's famous "*Nur ein Gott kann uns noch retten*"—the "only a god can save us now" passage, a confession he made in his *Der Spiegel* interview shortly before his death in 1976:

> Philosophy cannot produce an immediate effect which would change the present state of the world. This is not only true for philosophy, but for all specifically human endeavors. Only a God can save us now. The only possibility remaining to us in thought and in poetry is to remain available for the manifestation of this God or for the absence of this God in our decline.[54]

But what kind of God are we talking about here, when the adherents of secular *Aufklärung* such as Heidegger talk about God? One cannot be presumptuous on this question, for while certainly for Heidegger the God he meant was not the God of theodicy and of metaphysicians; for Kant, this God was anthropological, the human conscience; while for Hegel, this God was sociological, the spirit of the community; and for Feuerbach, this God was psychological, the projection of the human mind.

And I think this is where the problem resides, for in advancing a rapprochement between the God of faith and the God of philosophers in order to build a bridge with the *Aufklärung*, Ratzinger is willing to concede a large space to reason. Ratzinger appears, in my opinion, to be too enthusiastic and trusting that reason, if and when it follows its own logical coherence, might one day find itself in the sanctuary of God. Reason, with a reasonable openness, might be able to burn incense and dance, to paraphrase Heidegger. But reason can only achieve this profundity of religious expression if reason opens itself up to the possibility and necessity of seeing reality, not just with the eyes of the rational, but with the eyes of love. Without *logos* understood and encountered as love, reason risks remaining at the level of abstractions and syllogisms. This understanding of reason in no way implies a withdrawal from the dialogue with the heirs of the *Aufklärung*, namely, the contemporary secularists whose *Weltanschauung* today is largely shaped by the outlook of autonomous reason. On the contrary, Ratzinger sees the reality of the ongoing effects of the *Aufklärung* as an indispensable opportunity for what Ratzinger calls "the great task that awaits Christians today,"[55] which he describes this way:

> We must help reason to function in a comprehensive manner, not only in the spheres of technology and the material development of the world, but above all with regard to the capacity to perceive truth, the capacity to recognize the good, since the good is the precondition of law and thus also the presupposition of peace in the world. Our task as Christians today is to contribute our concept of God to the debate about man.[56]

In this sense, within a context marked by what Ratzinger calls a scientism of reason which as seen in chapters four and five, tends to limit reason to the empirically verifiable, Christianity owes it to the contemporary secularist world to show that reason can be greater than what it is thought to be. In other words, reason can encounter the transcendentals, such as goodness, beauty, and unity, provided it allows itself to be touched by that which reason in and by itself cannot bring about—namely, reason's seeing of things with what Ratzinger characterizes as "the heart which sees."[57] Ratzinger's theological commentary on the twenty-fifth anniversary of Pius XII's encyclical on the devotion to the Sacred Heart, *Haurietis Aquas* as published in *Behold The Pierced One*, offers a trenchant picture of this Ratzingerian position of seeing reality with the eyes of the heart, the eyes of love. Ratzinger gleans a wide range of images from the Fathers, which includes some of the following: Gregory the Great's *Amor ipse notitia est* (*Love Itself Is Knowledge*); Hugh of St. Victor's *Intrat dilectio et appropinquate, ubi scientia foris est* (*Love Enters and Comes Closer where Knowledge Has Been Left Outside*); or Richard of St. Victor's formulation, *Amor oculus est et amare videre est* (*Love Is the Eye and to Love Is to See*).[58] To Ratzinger, these utterances of the Fathers—and other examples abound—might be considered as a spiritual exegesis of this text from the Letter to the Ephesians, which Pius XII himself cites in his encyclical on the Sacred Heart:

> For this reason I bow my knees before the Father, from whom every family in heaven and on earth is named, that according to the riches of his glory he may grant you to be strengthened with might through his Spirit in the inner man, and that Christ may dwell in your hearts through faith; that you, being rooted and grounded in love, may have power to comprehend with all the saints what is the breadth and length and height and depth, and to know the love of Christ which surpasses knowledge, that you may be filled with all the fullness of God (Eph 3:14–19).

Employing this text in buttressing his position of seeing with the eyes of love and not only with reason, Ratzinger maintains: "This passage had led theologians to stress that reason had its limits. This is the origin, in the latter tradition, of the *ignote cognoscere*, knowing in unknowing, which leads to the concept of *docta ignorantia*. Thus, the mysticism of darkness comes about where love alone is able to see."[59] In other words, the heart, or love, has the capability of seeing when mere rationality cannot see. And one finds this position of the centrality of love in Augustine, Bonaventure, and Pascal, as shown in chapter one, which together with other Fathers, such as Hugh of St. Victor and Gregory the Great, largely influenced Ratzinger. And as Millare observes, this primacy of love is a central element in the Christology, theological anthropology, liturgical theology, and finally eschatology of Ratzinger.[60] And Ratzinger is always eager to keep love and *logos* together, in a mutually enriching relationship: "The primacy of the *logos* and the primacy of love proved to be identical. The *logos* was seen to be not merely a mathematical reason at the basis of all things, but a creative love taken to the point of becoming sympathy, suffering with the creature."[61] As seen in chapter five, this identification and transformation of *logos* into love that comes about in the Incarnation, makes possible a relationship of mutual enrichment between faith and reason, between the God of philosophy and the God of theology, even if the former undergoes a transformation at some point when it encounters the relationality of the latter, who is not only the philosophical One, but also Person, Love.

Ratzinger maintains that such a relationship between Athens and

Jerusalem frees both reason and faith from the tempting pathologies that affect both religion and reason.[62] Ratzinger warns reason against cutting itself from the insights of great religious traditions of the world, and he warns religion against severing itself from the sterilizing influence of reason.[63] And, while Ratzinger acknowledges that this worldview of a relationship between faith and reason is one largely marked by the two forces of Christian faith and Western secular rationality, he likewise cautions against what he calls a "false Eurocentrism."[64] Ratzinger writes:

> These two (that is, the Christian faith and Western secular rationality) determine the situation of the world to an extent not matched by another cultural force; but this does not mean that one could dismiss the other cultures as a kind of *quantité négligeable*. For a Western hubris of that kind, there would be a high price to pay—and, indeed, we are already paying a part of it. It is important that both great components of the Western culture learn to listen and accept a genuine relatedness to these other cultures, too. It is important to include the other cultures in the attempt at a polyphonic relatedness, in which they themselves are receptive to the essential complementarity of reason and faith, so that a universal process of purifications (in the plural!) can proceed. Ultimately, the essential values and norms that are in some way known or sensed by all men will take on a new brightness in such a process, so that that which holds the world together can once again become an effective force in mankind.[65]

It is noteworthy that Ratzinger does not only maintain the inner necessity of the rapport between the dialogue that must go on between faith and reason, but that, while acknowledging the European character of the same, Ratzinger consciously points and pushes toward the direction of openness to other cultures. Not only is this indicative of Ratzinger's perception that faith can engage reason in a universalist cross-cultural context, but even more, that Europe itself, the land of the historical Enlightenment, must rediscover the ground of reason by overcoming a paralyzing skepticism regarding the question of truth. I believe this to have been a central invitation that Ratzinger made at Regensburg, which unfortunately was lost in the politicization that followed the lecture. To put it differently, reason cannot surrender before the mystery of the truth claims of faith, but must allow itself to enter into the experiences of faith that, as has been repeatedly pointed out, is broader than reason. As Ratzinger says: "In the beginning was not the 'deed' but Father, the Word; this is mightier than the deed. Doing does not create meaning; rather, meaning creates doing [...]. This means that Christian faith essentially and originally has to do with the truth."[66] Therefore, for Ratzinger, it appears that to hold on to what he perceives to be the truth claims of Christianity in the face of *Aufklärung* positions that fundamentally differ with the dogmas of Christians, might be construed as a service to truth.

In the light of the tension between Christian truth claims and the dissents thereof, Christianity has a crucial role to play by pointing out that reason is not just mere rationality, but in the encounter in the embodiment of the philosophical concept of *logos* in the Christological interpretations of this same *logos*, reason when it opens itself up finds a more humanizing and life-affirming position in the *Logos*-Christological and the *Logos*-ecclesiological positions that have been treated in chapters four and five of this work. It is therefore not a question of an irrational devotion to an old-fashioned God. Rather, the challenge is for reason, for the *Aufklärung*, to open up to seeing reality with the aid of the eyes of revelation—that is, with the eyes of faith and love, which as Paul says in his Letter to the Ephesians surpasses all knowledge (Eph 4:19).

Notes — Chapter Six

1 Benedict XVI, *Pope Benedict in America: The Full Texts of Papal Talks Given During His Apostolic Visit to the United States* (San Francisco: Ignatius Press, 2008), 66.

2 Benedict XVI, *Pope Benedict in America*, 117.

3 Vincent Twomey S.V.D., *Pope Benedict XVI, The Conscience of Our Age: A Theological Portrait* (San Francisco: Ignatius Press, 2007), 39.

4 Twomey, *Pope Benedict XVI*, 40.

5 Twomey, *Pope Benedict XVI*, 39.

6 James Corkery, S.J., *Joseph Ratzinger's Theological Ideas: Wise Cautions and Legitimate Hopes* (Dublin: Dominican Publications, 2009), 83.

7 Corkery, *Joseph Ratzinger's Theological Ideas*, 82.
8 Corkery, *Joseph Ratzinger's Theological Ideas*, 82.
9 Corkery, *Joseph Ratzinger's Theological Ideas*, 83.
10 Joseph Ratzinger, *The Ratzinger Report: An Exclusive Interview on the State of the Church – Joseph Cardinal Ratzinger with Vittorio Messori*, trans. Salvator Attanasio and Graham Harrison (San Francisco: Ignatius Press, 1985), 24.
11 Ratzinger, *The Ratzinger Report*, 26.
12 Joseph Ratzinger, "Mass 'Pro Eligendo Romano Pontifice': Homily of His Eminence Card. Joseph Ratzinger, Dean of the College of Cardinals" (Vatican City, Monday April 18, 2005), # 2, accessed March 17, 2019 at www.vatican.va.
13 Hans Küng, *My Struggle for Freedom: Memoirs*, trans. John Bowden (Grand Rapids MI: Eerdmans Publishers, 2003), 457.
14 Küng, *My Struggle for Freedom*, 457.
15 Küng, *My Struggle for Freedom*, 458.
16 Peter Seewald, *Benedict XVI: An Intimate Portrait* (San Francisco: Ignatius Press, 2008), 109.
17 Patrick G. McGlinchey, *Ratzinger's Augustinianism and Evangelicalism* (Bletchley, Milton Keynes: Paternoster Lightning Source, 2017), 28.
18 McGlinchey, *Ratzinger's Augustinianism and Evangelicalism*, 29.
19 Benedict XVI, Address to the Bundestag: "The Listening Heart: Reflections on the Foundations of Law," September 22 2011, at www.vatican.va, accessed August 20, 2020.
20 Benedict XVI, Address to the Bundestag.
21 Benedict XVI, Address to the Bundestag.
22 Marta Cartabia & Andrea Simoncini, (eds.), *Pope Benedict XVI's Legal Thought A Dialogue on the Foundation of Law* (New York: Cambridge University Press, 2015), 20.
23 Joseph Ratzinger, *Truth and Tolerance: Christian Belief and World Religions*, trans. Henry Taylor (San Francisco: Ignatius Press, 2004), 136.
24 Benedict XVI, Encyclical Letter on Christian Love *Deus Caritas Est* (December 25, 2005), 1, accessed August 20 2020 at www.vatican.va.
25 Benedict XVI, Meeting with the Representatives of British Society at Westminster Hall, Westminster, September 17, 2010.
26 Cartabia & Simoncini, (eds.), *Pope Benedict XVI's Legal Thought*, 29.
27 Ratzinger, *Truth and Tolerance*, 137.
28 Thomas Aquinas, *Summa Theologiae*, I, q. I, art. 1. trans. Laurence Shapcote, O.P. (Lander, Wyoming: The Aquinas Institute, 2012).
29 Aquinas, *Summa Theologiae*, I, q. I, art. 1.
30 Blaise Pascal, *Pensées*, trans. A. J. Krailsheimer (Suffolk: Penguin Books, 1995), 127.

31 Pascal, *Pensées*, 285.
32 Pascal, *Pensées*, 127.
33 Anselm of Canterbury, *Proslogion*, trans. Matthew D. Walz (South Bend, Indiana: St. Augustine's Press, 2013), 2.
34 Anselm, *Proslogion*, 1.
35 Ratzinger, *Introduction*, 75.
36 Corkery, *Joseph Ratzinger's Theological Ideas*, 30.
37 Corkery, *Joseph Ratzinger's Theological Ideas*, 95.
38 Corkery, *Joseph Ratzinger's Theological Ideas*, 95.
39 Corkery, *Joseph Ratzinger's Theological Ideas*, 95.
40 Corkery, *Joseph Ratzinger's Theological Ideas*, 95.
41 Joseph Ratzinger, *The Nature and Mission of Theology: Approaches to Understanding its Role in the Light of Present Controversy*, trans. Adrian Walker (San Francisco: Ignatius Press, 1995), 92.
42 Corkery, *Joseph Ratzinger's Theological Ideas*, 96.
43 Ratzinger, *The Nature and Mission of Theology*, 56.
44 Tracey Rowland, *Ratzinger's Faith: The Theology of Pope Benedict XVI* (New York: Oxford University Press, 2008), 2–3.
45 Benedict XVI, Christmas Message, *L'Osservatore Romano*, (Vatican City: Vatican City Press, January 4, 2006).
46 James V. Schall, S.J., "On Reading the Pope: Part II," January 20, 2006, http://www.ignatiusinsight.com/features2006/schallreadingbenxvi2jan06.asp, Accessed October 26, 2018.
47 Tracey Rowland, *Ratzinger's Faith: The Theology of Pope Benedict XVI* (New York: Oxford University Press, 2008), 14.
48 Joseph Ratzinger/Benedict XVI, *Western Culture Today and Tomorrow*, trans. Michael J. Miller (San Francisco: Ignatius Press, 2019), 93.
49 Joseph Ratzinger, *Christianity and the Crisis of Cultures*, trans. Brian McNeil (San Francisco: Ignatius Press, 2006), 41–42.
50 Ratzinger, *Christianity and the Crisis of Cultures*, 43.
51 Jürgen Habermas and Joseph Ratzinger, *The Dialectic of Secularization: On Reason and Religion*, trans. Brain McNeil, C.R.V. (San Francisco: Ignatius Press, 2006), 65–66.
52 Thomas Aquinas, *Summa Theologiae*, Ia-IIae, q. 1, art. 7. trans. Laurence Shapcote, O.P. (Lander, Wyoming: The Aquinas Institute, 2012).
53 Joseph Ratzinger, Homily at Liturgy "Pro Eligendo Romano Pontifice," (April 18, 2005): www.vatican.va, accessed April 25, 2018.
54 Martin Heidegger, "Only a God," *Der Spiegel,* 31 May 1976, in Richard Kearney, *Strangers, Gods and Monsters, Interpreting Otherness* (London: Routledge Taylor & Francis Group, 2002), 215.
55 Joseph Ratzinger, *Values in a Time of Upheaval*, trans. Brian McNeil (San Francisco: Ignatius Press, 2006), 112.

56 Ratzinger, *Values in a Time of Upheaval*, 112.
57 Pope Benedict XVI, *Deus Caritas Est*, 31.
58 Joseph Ratzinger, *Behold The Pierced One: An Approach to a Spiritual Christology*, trans. Graham Harrison (San Francisco: Ignatius Press, 1986), 55.
59 Ratzinger, *Behold The Pierced One*, 55.
60 Roland Millare, "The Wedding Feast of the Lamb Has Begun: The Relationship Between Eschatology and the Liturgy in the Logoscentric Theology of Joseph Ratzinger" (STD Dissertation, University of St. Mary of the Lake, Mundelein, IL, 2018), 61.
61 Ratzinger, *Truth and Tolerance*, 182.
62 Jürgen Habermas and Joseph Ratzinger, *The Dialectics of Secularization: On Reason and Religion*, trans. Brian McNeil (San Francisco: Ignatius Press, 2006), 77.
63 Habermas and Ratzinger, *The Dialectics of Secularization*, 78.
64 Habermas and Ratzinger, *The Dialectics of Secularization*, 79.
65 Habermas and Ratzinger, *The Dialectics of Secularization*, 79–80.
66 Joseph Ratzinger, *Dogma and Preaching: Applying Christian Doctrine to a Daily Life*, trans. Michael J. Miller (San Francisco: Ignatius Press, 2011), 94.

Conclusion: *Ratzinger and the Philosophical Hermeneutics to Faith—The Task for Today*

This work set out to examine the assertion that a proper hermeneutical framework for understanding the Christological and Ecclesiological assertions of Joseph Ratzinger/Benedict XVI is the eighteenth-century movement called the *Aufklärung,* or the German Enlightenment. This assertion is based on the fact that, in his formative years, Ratzinger displayed a penchant for a harmony between faith and reason, between theology and philosophy, as evident in his acute interest in the thoughts and positions of modern philosophy. More especially, Ratzinger's inaugural lecture, which often defines the intellectual temperament and character of a scholar, clearly indicated Ratzinger's resolve to always seek a harmony of the insights from faith and reason, searching for an inner affinity between the God of faith and the God of the philosophers. Given that theology is *theo-logos*, the study or reasoning about God, it clearly became evident for Ratzinger that *logos*, reason, had to be the path thanks to which he would have to engage the concerns of faith that stood out for him.

The choice for *logos*, for reason, clearly did not emerge from out of the blue, from nowhere. As seen in this work, especially in chapter two, which dealt with the Inaugural Lecture, the choice of the Fathers to embrace Greek philosophy in place of pagan myths, marked for Ratzinger a decisive point of inculturation of the Christian faith, from which there is no turning back. That explains why Ratzinger has always come out strongly against what he sees as attempts at dehellenization, as seen in his Regensburg Address, treated in this work as well. The choice for *logos*, for reason, therefore, places Ratzinger squarely in the thought-context of the eighteen-century *Aufklärung* movement, which, following its motto of *sapere aude* (dare to use your reason), saw reason as everything and everything as reason. As seen throughout chapters two to five, the *Aufklärung* brought about an understanding of reality under the name of reason that not only absolutized science, but eventually led to what Ratzinger characterized as scientism, that is, reducing all of reality to the laws of Newtonian physics, in effect, to the rules of laboratory experiment.

Given this newfound understanding of science, of nature, and of reason by the *Aufklärer*, it was only a matter of time for Christian dogma to be also called into question, following these new principles of scientism. In Descartes, Kant, Hegel, Nietzsche, Feuerbach, Heidegger, and others, there emerged a consistent attempt to reinterpret Christological and ecclesiological dogma or truth claims of orthodox Christianity. As seen in this work, especially in chapters four and five, Christ is reduced to a moral exemplar, and the Church a sociological community of remembrance and comfort that, in misunderstanding the primary mission of Christ, has gotten stuck in all forms of religious superstitions. The *Aufklärer*, therefore, saw themselves as heralds of liberation, as persons who, as it were, having stepped outside Plato's Cave and seen reality in the light of the sun in the light of reason, felt it their duty to return to the Cave of traditional Christianity and liberate it from the shackles of irrational superstition.

As seen in the text, while Ratzinger clearly has a profound attraction for the position of applying reason to the truth claims of faith, he definitely does not subscribe to the conclusions of the *Aufklärer*. The *Gestalt* of Christ is much more than a moral ethicist for Ratzinger. From a Christological perspective, therefore, Christ is creative Reason, Son, and Person. And as shown in the chapter four, Ratzinger employs the concept of rationality, of *logos* in reasserting these postulates of faith, convinced that both pure and practical reason might lead to these. From an ecclesiological perspective, owing to the Christ-event the Church emerges as a community that is much more than horizontal. In other words, the nature of the Church, the inner logic of the Church, runs from a vertical beam, that is, from Christ the *Logos* as unity of love and from Christ the *Logos* as Word. These foundations do not eschew the horizontal dimension of the

Church, but rather ground the horizontal dimension on the firmer grounds of what Ratzinger considers to be the vertical.

A tension therefore arises at this point, for how far can reason go? How far can reason as pure reason get along? How far can the journey continue between the God of the philosophers and the God of faith, of Abraham, Isaac, and Jacob? Is there a point at which reason must begin to open itself to the wider logic of the transcendent? These questions are helpful because they serve to provide an answer to the cynical "what next?" that might be asked following the dialogue between faith and reason. While this might appear as a disingenuous strategy for conversion, it still remains true that if one is to be consistent with Ratzinger's pastoral heart and mind, one cannot avoid the logical next step that Ratzinger's ultimate desire is to invite the rationalist, the secular heirs of the *Aufklärung,* and all persons into a friendship with Christ, the Incarnate *Logos*.

Accordingly, Ratzinger does not seek to be either a philosopher or a theologian, if by these we mean their academic and professional descriptions. At heart stands a pastor's heart, the heart and person of a believer, in that for Ratzinger it is always and ever faith seeking understanding. Ratzinger is not interested in looking at ideas and theories as ends in themselves. His goal is to first of all—as shown in chapter five in the treatment of the theological appropriation of *Logos* as Son in the context of the *Aufklärung's* reinterpretation of the concept of Divine Sonship—to come to know the figure or person of Jesus Christ, and from that starting point to engage the prevalent philosophical and theological ideas. And his argument for a mutually enriching dialogue between faith and reason is ultimately geared toward this evangelical intention of bringing men and women into friendship with the God of Jesus Christ. In a sense, one can describe Ratzinger as a commonsense, pastoral, down-to-earth, critical thinker, and theologian, with the singular goal of paying attention to ideas that were circulating in Germany and Europe during his theological career, with the intention of responding to them from a faith perspective.

Furthermore, Ratzinger's insistence on friendship with Christ as the decisive hermeneutical framework, as seen particularly in chapter four, likewise implies that Ratzinger is convinced of the insufficiency of the positions espoused by the *Aufklärung* in terms of arriving at the center of who Jesus of Nazareth is, and what the Church is, as a community gathered by the Holy Spirit in the name of the Risen Christ as a spiritual offering to the Father. In other words, even if one finds Hegel's *The Life of Jesus* to be a work of great literary and philosophical value, Hegel's inability to lead the reader to a discovery of that which is most essential—that is, the identity of Jesus as the unique Divine Son of God, a discovery that can only elicit the reaction of adoration—is indicative of the limits of these *Aufklärer* attempts and undertakings. In other words, while reason can shed light on the moral demands and ethical contours of historical revelation, such as the definitive revelation of God in Jesus of Nazareth, it is in the nature of reason, without going against reason, to need divine help as a complementary and widening succor. And this is the crucial role that faith is called to play. As Ratzinger shows in the inaugural lecture as treated in chapter two, the gains of philosophical reasoning that arrived at the concept of the philosophical One of Greek monotheism, clearly provide a point of convergence between the God of philosophy and the God of theology. But as seen in the same chapter, Ratzinger does not hesitate to move the ball beyond mere rapprochement to a transformation of the God of philosophy, a transformation of reason, which happens when the concept of relationality is introduced into the hermeneutical dialectic of faith and reason, of philosophy and theology.

This is the perspective from which Ratzinger argues that philosophy has to open itself to faith. It has to ask the hard questions, the searching questions, and what is applicable to philosophy in terms of a spirit of questioning and searching should also be applied to theology as well, for a faith that is blind and irrational is not a helpful faith. It appears to be, either by instinct or by temperament, that Ratzinger always feels that a process of reflection on issues of the present always holds the potential for a deepening of meaning, of comprehension and apprehension, which will ultimately lead to a friendship with Jesus Christ. In other words, one's faith must not shy away from current problems because faith is life with Jesus Christ, who as the Incarnate Son of God, brings God's help into all the challenges of life. God is with us, Immanuel. Hence, humans are not abandoned to face life's challenges without any external help.

There is, therefore, a sense of openness to deepening one's comprehension of theological formulations from the perspective of one's living context. For Ratzinger, faith does not imply simply a repetition of theological formulas. Ratzinger genuinely seeks to engage the *Zeitgeist* with the person of Christ, trusting that reason will ultimately find its grandeur, its loftiness, its most sublime aspirations in Christ, the Wisdom of God, the *Logos*, Reason, whose Incarnation as the "abbreviated" God has made it possible for finite intellect to comprehend infinitude. That said, what might be distinctive about Ratzinger, perhaps as opposed to his critics, is that Ratzinger's intellectual temperament always had the conviction that in the figure of Jesus of Nazareth, God has definitively communicated the possibilities and expanse of knowledge of which the human mind can come to a full realization, without shrinking the prerogatives of reason. In other words, there is what one can describe as a modesty or *humilitas* of the human intellect in the pursuit of truth or knowledge because Ratzinger turns out not to read truth simply as an abstraction. This is a conclusion arrived at through a process of rational deduction or induction, but over and above all, as a rational experience of what is fundamentally a religious phenomenon. Put more pointedly, revelation offers a liberating light for reason, and not the other way around, for whilst following Aquinas, the human quest for truth can end in admixtures of truth and errors, yet revelation because it is God communicating God's self to creation cannot proceed in such a way that God can communicate error. It is the human reception of revelation that can slide into error, not revelation itself.

While the itches of the mind certainly deserve to be attended to, when all else is said and done the ultimate challenge is to make the leap to faith, to walk through the door of mere rationality into the light of absolute reason, whose breadth, depth, and length no eye has seen nor ear heard, nor can the mind of the human being conceive what God has prepared for those who love him (1 Cor 2:9). Through reason, through Descartes, Kant, Hegel, Nietzsche, and others, the intellectual and the searching academician can walk through the door of reason into the door of faith—the *porta fidei*, which, for Ratzinger, is certainly not a replacement theory, but a broadening experience, in which the contours of reason are rather thrown wider in the meeting of Christ, the *Logos*, the Reason of God.

At this point, perhaps in a kind of speculative theological excursion, the rationalist intellectual who is a seeker must go beyond Christology and ecclesiology, beyond theological formulas and creedal statements, beyond Nicaea, Ephesus and Chalcedon, to Capernaum, and there, like Simon, allow the mind and heart to utter the profession of the unlettered, unsophisticated Fisherman of Galilee: *Domine, ad quem ibimus? Verba vitae aeternae habes* (Jn 6:68). And if Capernaum is not sufficient, then the searching intellectual, the *Aufklärer*, the enlightened one, might again allow the self to be led by this unlettered and humanly unenlightened fisherman to Caesarea Philippi, where he might this time accept that given that the intellect can only go so far, help from above is needed, thanks to which one can confess with the mind and heart: *Tu es Christus, Filius Dei vivi* (Mt 16:16). In Capernaum, *verba*, word, leads the wondering intellectual to the object of the mind—namely, truth. In Caesarea Philippi, *Filius*, Son, brings the intellect, or the mind, into friendship, into a personal relationship.

And this explains why Ratzinger's Christological and ecclesiological path is best described as a philosophical hermeneutic to faith, unfolding in an ongoing dialectic between faith and reason, in which philosophy continuously opens up to theology and theology continuously opens up to philosophy. Ratzinger begins from Capernaum and Caesarea Philippi, moves on to Athens and then brings Athens along to Capernaum and Caesarea Philippi, where Athens finds its fullest potentials explored, broadened, challenged, and fully utilized. For faith in Christ, friendship with Christ, embodied in the encounter between Christ and Peter at Caesarea Philippi, brings about a reliable form of knowing, of cognition, and of living. To Ratzinger, therefore, it is not a question of denying the gains of the *Aufklärung* and the *Aufklärer*, what would amount to a kind of *Ausklärung*—a dis-enlightenment, but of taking the *Aufklärer* seriously on their own home front, that is, on the grounds of rationality, in a spirit of receptivity to what the "Kingdom of Thought"—to use a Hegelian phrase—could bring about, while at the same time being willing to challenge the Kingdom of Thought to free itself from a sectarianism of the mind and engage that which is not only produced by the Kingdom of Thought, but that which is likewise shown to the Kingdom of Thought from the outside, an "outside" that is an invitation into friendship with Jesus of Nazareth. In a word, the Kingdom of Thought and the Kingdom of the Son of God go together, and when all else fails or suffers limitations owing to human finitude and the state of naturalness, the light of faith and glory that comes from the Kingdom of the Son is sufficient to continue to lift the human spirit to the sublime heights of truth, of life, of beauty, of goodness, and to enduring meaning with God, the ultimate desire of the human spirit.

Afterword: *Joseph Ratzinger, Theological Reformer* by George Weigel

At the end of Father Maurice Agbaw-Ebai's scholarly exploration of Joseph Ratzinger's theological response to the Enlightenment, it may be useful for someone who has known Pope Emeritus Benedict XVI for over three decades to reflect in a more personal key on the man and his position in the flow of modern Catholic theology. That position remains too often misunderstood, and sometimes deliberately misinterpreted, throughout the world Church. And to misunderstand, or misinterpret, Ratzinger is to misunderstand or misinterpret both the modern history of theology and the Second Vatican Council.

I doubt that the Pope Emeritus is much bothered by the fact that his work is so often misrepresented. He knows the truth of who he is and what he has tried to do for Christ and the Church with his scholarship. Moreover, he has long measured himself in a life of prayer that leaves the final and authoritative judgment to God. Having had calumny visited upon him for more than half a century—especially the cruel calumny of being pilloried as the *Panzerkardinal* or, worse, "God's Rottweiler"—he long ago, I suspect, became impervious to slander. A gentle and kindly man, he may have felt a measure of compassion for the small-minded people who continually told untruths about him and his theology. But he long understood that he had better things to do than fret about his detractors: midgets tossing pebbles at a serene giant.

His friends and admirers find it hard to take such a benign view of the situation, however, because the trashing of Joseph Ratzinger that began shortly after Vatican II and that continued well into his tenth decade is agenda-driven and aimed at shoring up the crumbling foundations of the Catholic Lite project. That salvage operation requires his detractors to claim that Ratzinger/Benedict XVI betrayed Vatican II, or never understood Vatican II, or was (and is) deeply opposed to Vatican II. This is nonsense. And while often perpetrated by those who claim competence as scholars of contemporary Catholic affairs, such misrepresentations of Ratzinger's thinking betray a sorry ignorance of what happened in Catholic theology in the decades prior to the Council, and what actually happened in Rome during Vatican II's final two years.

In the years immediately before the Council, Ratzinger, then a very young man, was a significant figure among the theological proponents of a *Ressourcement* in Catholic theology: a "return to the sources" of the Church's doctrinal mind in Holy Scripture, the Fathers of the Church, and the great medieval commentators on the Catholic tradition. The *Ressourcement* theologians knew that the Church's situation in the mid-20th century posed new challenges for evangelization and mission. The world had been through the upheavals of the scientific and industrial revolutions, the overthrow of the old regimes, the rise of new forms of tyranny, and two sanguinary world wars; in the worlds of culture, philosophy had decayed into subjectivism even as the rise of the avant-garde signaled a new irrationality in the arts. In a disenchanted and cynical world, skeptical about the truth of anything, the syllogisms of scholastic theology were no longer apologetically effective. What was required, the *Ressourcement* theologians believed, was a new encounter with Jesus Christ, the incarnate Son of God who reveals both the face of the Father of mercies and the full truth about our humanity and its noble destiny. That encounter could be facilitated by a Christocentric approach to theology that drew from the fonts of Christian wisdom: the Bible; the great patristic authors of both western and eastern theology; and medieval giants like Thomas Aquinas and Ratzinger's beloved Bonaventure.

The theological program of *Ressourcement* paralleled Pope John XXIII's intention for Vatican II. Pope John wanted the Council to be a new experience of Pentecost, from which the Church would enter its third millennium with new evangelical fervor. Evangelization in late modernity would require both a comprehensive grasp of the truths of

Catholic faith and a way of proposing and explaining those views that met the challenges of a post-Enlightenment world. The young theologian Joseph Ratzinger couldn't have agreed more. And in league with other reformist theologians, he set to work as a peritus or theological adviser at the Council to realize Pope John's intention through an aggiornamento, or updating, of the Church's self-understanding and its presentation of the settled truths of the faith, which always radiate from the Church's living center, Jesus Christ.

This approach met with considerable success in the first two sessions of the Council. But as I wrote in *The Irony of Modern Catholic History*, a fissure in the ranks of the reformist theologians at Vatican II began to open up during the Council's third session, held in the fall of 1964. A new theological journal, *Concilium*, was being planned by some of the Council's influential theological advisers (many of whom had been heavily censored in the pre-Vatican II years). A towering figure among them, the French Jesuit Henri de Lubac, began to worry that Concilium would take the reformist project in a deconstructive direction: one that would do serious damage to what John XXIII, in his opening address to the Council, called "the sacred deposit of Christian doctrine," which Pope John urged "be more effectively defended and presented." That this damage would be done in the name of meeting the challenge posed by the various European Enlightenments only made the matter more serious. For as de Lubac understood it, the reformist program at Vatican II should seek the conversion of the post-Enlightenment world through a re-presentation of the truth of God and humanity revealed in Christ; it should take from the various Enlightenments what was useful in that work of evangelization; but it should not surrender Catholic truth claims to Enlightenment modes of thought, as if Kant, Hume, Hegel, and Heidegger were infallible.

The first several issues of the new journal intensified de Lubac's concerns. So, in May 1965, this most venerable member of *Concilium*'s editorial committee quietly withdrew from the *Concilium* project while continuing his work at the Council itself. As Vatican II drew to a close, others, including Joseph Ratzinger, would join de Lubac in expressing serious reservations about the tack being taken by their onetime theological allies. And those concerns did not lessen over time.

The result was what I have come to call "The War of the Conciliar Succession": the war to define what Vatican II was and what Vatican II intended for the Catholic future. This war was *not* a struggle between "traditionalists" and "progressives." It was a bitterly fought contest *within* the camp of Vatican II theological reformers. It continues into the third decade of the twenty-first century, and the question that so concerned Henri de Lubac remains entirely pertinent more than a half-century later: Would an interpretation of the Council that effectively set the Catholic Church against "the sacred deposit of Christian doctrine" end up betraying the Gospel and emptying it of its power, all in the name of responding to the post-Enlightenment world?

Joseph Ratzinger joined Henri de Lubac and other dissident conciliar reformers in launching another theological journal, *Communio*, which he and his colleagues hoped would advance an interpretation of Vatican II that was in continuity with the Church's settled doctrine even as it developed the Church's understanding of that doctrine to meet Enlightenment challenges. *Communio*, now published in fourteen language editions, has been a creative force in Catholic intellectual life for decades. Like Ratzinger, *Communio* is not against Vatican II; it has challenged what its authors contend is a wrong-headed interpretation of Vatican II and a wrong-headed approach to the intellectual challenges posed by Enlightenment thought.

The bottom line in the War of the Conciliar Succession is the reality of divine revelation: Does God's revelation in Scripture and Tradition include truths that are binding over the centuries, irrespective of cultural circumstances? Or do history and culture judge revelation, which the Church is then authorized to improve, so to speak, in light of "the signs of the times"? Those who stand with the reality of revelation (which was robustly affirmed by Vatican II) are by no means "fundamentalists," despite what their opponents charge. They are creative theologians who believe in the development of doctrine, but who also understand, with Chesterton, that "an open mind, like an open mouth, should close on something." Among those creative theologians, Joseph Ratzinger has no peer, not least because of the depth of his understanding of the Enlightenment challenge.

In the War of the Conciliar Succession, there are true reformers, and then there are the forces of deconstruction. Joseph Ratzinger is emphatically a true Catholic reformer. To argue otherwise suggests ignorance, malice, or both. Father Agbaw-Ebai's fine book should help the world Church understand that, and thus the world Church owes him a vote of thanks for this work.

GEORGE WEIGEL is Distinguished Senior Fellow of Washington's Ethics and Public Policy Center, where he holds the William E. Simon Chair in Catholic Studies. His twenty-seven books include his two-volume biography of Pope St. John Paul II, *Witness to Hope* and *The End and the Beginning*, and a memoir, *Lessons in Hope: My Unexpected Life with St. John Paul II.*

Bibliography

Primary Sources

Benedict XVI. Address to the Roman Curia Offering them his Christmas Greetings (22 December, 2005). At The Holy See: http//www.vatican.va.

_____. Address to the Bundestag: "The Listening Heart: Reflections on the Foundations of Law." (September 22 2011). At the Holy See: http// www.vatican.va.

_____. Apostolic Letter for the Induction of the Year of Faith *Porta Fidei,* October 1, 2011. Nairobi: Pauline Publications Africa, 2012.

_____. Christmas Message, (December 25, 2005). At The Holy See: http//www.vatican.va.

_____. *Church Fathers: From Clement of Rome to Augustine*. San Francisco: Ignatius Press, 2008.

_____. *Doctors of the Church: Wednesday General Audiences from June 20, 2007–April 6, 2011*. Huntington, IN: Our Sunday Visitor, 2001.

_____. Encyclical Letter on Christian Love *Deus Caritas Est* (December 25, 2005) at The Holy See: http//www.vatican.va.

_____. Farewell Address to the Eminent Cardinals Present in Rome at the Clementine Hall (February 28, 2013). At The Holy See: http//www.vatican.va.

_____. Homily for the Beginning of the Petrine Ministry of the Bishop of Rome (April 24, 2005). At The Holy See: http//www.vatican.va.

_____. Interview by Jacques Servais (October 2015), www.catholicworldreport-text of-benedict-xvis-recent-rare-and-lengthy-interview.

_____. *Last Testament in His Own Words with Peter Seewald*. Translated by Philip Jacobs. New York: Bloomsbury, 2016.

_____. *Light of the World: The Pope, the Church, and the Signs of the Times*. Translated by Michael J. Miller and Adrian J. Walker. San Francisco: Ignatius Press, 2010.

_____. "Mass of the Inauguration of the Pontificate of Pope Benedict XVI: Homily of Pope Benedict XVI." In *First Messages of His Holiness Benedict XVI*. Nairobi: Paulines Publications Africa, 2005.

_____. Message for the Celebration of the World Day of Peace *The Human Person, The Heart of Peace* (1 January 2007), at The Holy See: http//www.vatican.va.

_____. Message for the Celebration of the World Day of Peace *If you want to Cultivate Peace, Protect Creation* (1 January 2010), at The Holy See http//www.vatican.va.

_____. Meeting with the Representatives of British Society at Westminster Hall, Westminster, September 17 2010.

_____. *Pope Benedict in America: The Full Texts of Papal Talks Given During His Apostolic Visit to the United States*. San Francisco: Ignatius Press, 2008.

_____. Post-Synodal Apostolic Exhortation on the Church in Africa in Service to Reconciliation, Justice and Peace *Africae Munus*. Vatican City: Libreria Editrice Vaticana, 2011.

_____. Post-Synodal Apostolic Exhortation on the Eucharist as the Source and Summit of the Church's Life and Mission *Sacramentum Caritatis* (22 February 2007), at The Holy See http//www.vatican.va.

_____. Post-Synodal Apostolic Exhortation *Verbum Domini*, on the Word of God in the Life and Mission of the Church. Vatican City: Libreria Editrice Vaticana, 2010.

_____. "Prayer Vigil on the Eve of the Beatification of John Henry Cardinal Newman, Address of the Holy Father," accessed July 29 2020 at http//www.vatican.va, 2010.

_____. Solemnity of the Nativity of the Lord Midnight Mass Homily (24 December 2006), at The Holy See: http//www.vatican.va.

_____. *The Regensburg Lecture*. South Bend, IN: St. Augustine's Press, 2007.

Ratzinger, Joseph. *A New Song for the Lord: Faith in Christ and Liturgy Today*. Translated by Martha M. Matesich. New York: Crossroad Publishing, 1986.

_____. *Being Christian*. Translated by David Walls. Chicago: Franciscan Herald Press, 1970.

_____. *Behold the Pierced One: An Approach to a Spiritual Christology*. Translated by Graham Harrison. San Francisco: Ignatius Press, 1986.

_____. "Centenary of the Death of Cardinal John Henry Newman." Accessed at The Holy See: http//www.vatican.va, 1990.

_____. "Christ, Faith and the Challenge of Cultures." Accessed at The Holy See: http//www.vatican.va. 1993.

_____. *Called to Communion: Understanding the Church Today*. Translated by Adrian Walker. San Francisco: Ignatius Press, 1996.

_____. *Christianity and the Crisis of Cultures*. Translated by Brian McNeil. San Francisco: Ignatius Press, 2006.

_____. *Church, Ecumenism and Politics: New Endeavors in Ecclesiology*. San Francisco: Ignatius Press, 2008.

_____. *Der Gott des Glaubens und der Gott der Philosophen*. Bonn: Johannes-Verlag Leutesdorf, 2005.

_____. *Dogma and Preaching: Applying Christian Doctrine to Daily Life*. Edited by Michael J. Miller. Translated by Michael J. Miller and Matthew O'Connell. San Francisco: Ignatius Press, 2011.

_____. *Europe: Today and Tomorrow*. Translated by Michael J. Miller. San Francisco: Ignatius Press, 2007.

_____. *Faith and the Future*. San Francisco: Ignatius Press, 2009.

_____. *God and the World A Conversation with Peter Seewald*. Translated by Henry Taylor. San Francisco: Ignatius Press, 2002.

_____. *Handing on the Faith in an Age of Disbelief*. Translated by Michael J. Miller. San Francisco: Ignatius Press, 2006.

_____. *The Feast of Faith: Approaches to a Theology of the Liturgy*. Translated by Graham Harrison. San Francisco: Ignatius Press, 1986.

_____. *"In the Beginning…": A Catholic Understanding of the Story of Creation and the Fall*. Translated by Boniface Ramsey. Grand Rapids, MI: William B. Eerdmans Publishing Company, 1995.

_____. *Introduction to Christianity*. Translated by Michael J. Miller. San Francisco: Ignatius Press, 2004.

_____. *Jesus of Nazareth: From the Baptism in the Jordan to the Transfiguration*. Translated by Adrian J. Walker. New York: The Doubleday Broadway Publishing Group, 2007.

_____. *Jesus of Nazareth, The Infancy Narratives*. Translated by Philip J. Whitmore. New York: Image Books, 2012.

_____. *Many Religions—One Covenant*. Translated by Graham Harrison. San Francisco: Ignatius Press, 1999.

_____. Mass 'Pro Eligendo Romano Pontifice': Homily of His Eminence Card. Joseph Ratzinger, Dean of the College of Cardinals." Vatican City, Monday April 18, 2005), accessed at www.vatican.va.

_____. *The Meaning of Christian Brotherhood*. San Francisco: Ignatius Press, 1993.

_____. *Milestones: Memoirs 1972—1977*. San Francisco: Ignatius Press, 1998.

_____. *The Nature and Mission of Theology: Approaches to Understanding its Role in the Light of Present Controversy*. Translated by Adrian Walker. San Francisco: Ignatius Press, 1995.

_____. *On Conscience*. San Francisco: Ignatius Press, 2007.

_____. *Pilgrim Fellowship of Faith: The Church as Communion*. Translated by Henry Taylor. San Francisco: Ignatius Press, 2005.

_____. Presentation on the Occasion of the Centenary of the Death of Cardinal John Henry Newman, (28 April, 1990). At the Holy See: http//www.vatican.va.

_____. *Principles of Catholic Theology: Building Stones for a Fundamental Theology*. San Francisco: Ignatius Press, 1989.

_____. *The Ratzinger Report: An Exclusive Interview on the State of the*

Church—Joseph Cardinal Ratzinger with Vittorio Messori. Translated by Salvator Attanasio and Graham Harrison. San Francisco: Ignatius Press, 1985.

_____. *Salt of the Earth, The Church at the End of the Millennium*. Translated by Adrian Walker. San Francisco: Ignatius Press, 1997.

_____. *The Spirit of the Liturgy*. Translated by John Saward. San Francisco: Ignatius Press, 2000.

_____. *Theological Highlights of Vatican II*. Translated by Henry Traub, S.J, Gerard C. Thormann, & Werner Barzel. Mahwah, NJ: Paulist Press, 2009.

_____. *The Theology of History in St. Bonaventure*. Translated by Zachary Hayes, O.F.M. Chicago: Franciscan Herald Press, 1971.

_____. *A Turning Point for Europe? The Church in the Modern World: Assessment and Forecast*. Translated by Brian McNeil, C.R.V. San Francisco: Ignatius Press, 1994.

_____. *Truth and Tolerance: Christian Belief and World Religions*. Translated by Henry Taylor. San Francisco: Ignatius Press, 2004.

_____. "The New Pagans and the Church." Translated by Fr. Kenneth Baker, S. J. Homiletic & Pastoral Review. https://wwwhprweb.com/2017/01/thenewpagansandthe-church/. 2017.

_____. *Values in a Time of Upheaval*. Translated by Brian McNeil. San Francisco: Ignatius Press, 2006.

_____. *Western Culture Today and Tomorrow*. Translated by Michael J. Miller. San Francisco: Ignatius Press, 2019.

_____. *Volk und Haus Gottes in Augustine Lehre von der Kirche*. St. Ottilien: EOS-Verlag, 1954.

Secondary Sources

Anselm of Canterbury, *Proslogion*. Translated by Matthew D. Walz. South Bend, IN: St. Augustine's Press, 2013.

Aquinas, Thomas. *Summa Theologiae, Prima Pars*, 1–49. Translated by Laurence Shapcote, O.P. Lander, Wyoming: The Aquinas Institute, 2012.

_____. *Summa Theologiae, Prima Secundae*, 1–70. Translated by Laurence Shapcote, O.P. Lander, Wyoming: The Aquinas Institute, 2012.

_____. *Summa Theologiae, Secunda Secundae*, 1–91. Translated by Laurence Shapcote, O.P. Lander, Wyoming: The Aquinas Institute, 2012.

Augustine of Hippo. *Against Cresconius the Grammarian*. Translated by Allan Fitzgerald. Grand Rapids: Eerdmans Publishing, 1999.

_____. *The City of God*. Translated by Gerald G. Walsh, S.J., Demetrius B. Zema, S. J., Grace Monahan, O.S.U. and Daniel J. Honan. New York: Image Books, 1958.

_____. *Confessions*. Translated by F. J. Sheed. Cambridge: Hackett Publishing Company Inc, 2006.

_____. *Enarrationes in Psalmos*. Translated by Maria Boulding, OSB. Vienna: Austrian Academy of Sciences Press, 2004.

_____. *The Trinity*. Translated by Edmund Hill, O.P. New York: New City Press, 2012.

Bardazzi, Marco. *In the Vineyard of the Lord, The Life, Faith, and Teachings of Joseph Ratzinger/Benedict XVI*. New York: Rizzoli International Publications Inc. 2005.

Balz, Horst Robert and Schneider, Gerhard. *Exegetical Dictionary of the New Testament*. Grand Rapids, Michigan: William B. Eerdmans, 1990.

Beiser, C. Frederick, ed. *The Cambridge Companion to Hegel*. New York: Cambridge University Press, 1993.

Blondel, Maurice, *L'Action (1893)*. Translated by Oliva Blanchette. South Bend, IN: Notre Dame Press, 2007.

Boyd, R. Ian. *Dogmatics Among the Ruins: German Expressionism and the Enlightenment as Contexts for Karl Barth's Theological Development*. Bern: Peter Lang, 2004.

Brann, Eva. *The Logos of Heraclitus*. Philadelphia, PA: Paul Dry Books Inc. 2011.

Buber, Martin. *I and Thou*. Translated by Walter Kaufmann. New York: Touchstone, 1970.

_____. *Eclipse of God*. Translated by Leora Batnitzky. Princeton, NJ: Princeton University Press, 2016.

Bunson, Matthew. Editor. *Encyclopedia of Catholic History*. Huntington, IN: Our Sunday Visitor, Inc. 1995.

Cameron, Peter John. *Benedictus: Day by Day with Pope Benedict XVI*. New York City: Magnificat, 2006.

Cartabia, Marta, & Simoncini, Andrea. Editors. *Pope Benedict XVI's Legal Thought A Dialogue on the Foundation of Law*. New York: Cambridge University Press, 2015.

Caputo, John, ed. *The Religious* Blackwell Readings in Continental Philosophy. Malden, MA: Blackwell Publishers, 2002.

Cassirer, Ernst. *The Philosophy of the Enlightenment*. Princeton, NJ: Princeton University Press, 2009.

Cavadini, John. Editor. *Explorations in the Theology of Benedict XVI*. South Bend, IN: University of Notre Dame Press, 2012.

Chadwick, Henry. Editor. *Lessing's Theological Writings*. Redwood City, CA: Stanford University Press, 1956.

Collins, Christopher. *The Word Made Love: The Dialogical Theology of Joseph Ratzinger*. Collegeville, MN: Liturgical Press, 2013.

Congar, Yves. *True and False Reform in the Church*. Liturgical Press, Minnesota, 2011.

Congdon, William. *The Sabbath of History: With Meditations on Holy Week by Joseph Ratzinger*. New Haven, CT: Knights of Columbus Museum, 2012.

Congregation for the Doctrine of the Faith, Instruction on the Ecclesial Vocation of the Theologian, *Donum Veritatis*, at The Holy See: http//www.vatican.va, 1990.

Corkery, James. *Joseph Ratzinger's Theological Ideas: Wise Cautions & Legitimate Hopes*. Dublin: Dominican Publications, 2009.

Cottingham, John. Editor. *The Cambridge Companion to Descartes*. New York: Cambridge University Press, 2005.

De Gaál, Emery, *O Lord, I Seek Your Countenance: Explorations and*

Discoveries in Pope Benedict XVI's Theology. Steubenville, OH: Emmaus Academic, 2018.

________. *The Theology of Pope Benedict XVI, The Christocentric Shift*, New York, Palgrave Macmillan, 2010.

Descartes, Rene, *Meditations on First Philosophy*. Translated by Donald A. Cress. Indianapolis, IN: Hackett Publishing Company, Inc., 1993.

Dostoyevsky, Fyodor. *The Gospel in Dostoyevsky*. Translated by Constance Garnett. Farmington PA: The Plough Publishing House, 1998.

Gardiner, Patrick. *Kierkegaard: A Very Short Introduction*. New York: Oxford University Press, 2002.

Gerson, P. Lloyd. Editor. *The Cambridge Companion to Plotinus*. New York: Cambridge University Press, 1999.

Guerriero, Elio. *Benedict XVI His Life and Thought*. Translated by William J. Melcher. San Francisco: Ignatius Press, 2018.

Guyer, Paul. Editor. *The Cambridge Companion to Kant*. New York: Cambridge University Press, 2008.

Habermas, Jürgen and Ratzinger, Joseph. *The Dialectic of Secularization: On Reason and Religion*. Translated by Brain McNeil. San Francisco: Ignatius Press, 2006.

Hahn, W. Scott, *Covenant and Communion: The Biblical Theology of Pope Benedict XVI*. Grand Rapids, MI: Brazos Press, 2009.

Hannay, Alastair and Marino, Gordon. Editors. *The Cambridge Companion to Kierkegaard*. Cambridge: Cambridge University Press, 1999.

Hegel, Georg. W. F. *Lectures on the Philosophy of Religion, Volume 1: Introduction and the Concept of Religion*. Edited by P.C. Hodgson et al. Berkeley, CA: University of California Press, 1984.

_____. *Faith & Knowledge, or the Reflective Philosophy of Subjectivity in the Complete Range of its Forms as Kantian, Jacobian, and Fichtean Philosophy*. Translated and Edited by Walter Cerf & H.S. Harris. New York: State University of New York Press, 1977.

_____. *Three Essays, 1793—1795: The Tübingen Essay, Berne Fragments and The Life of Jesus*. Translated and Edited by Peter Fuss and John Dobbins. South Bend, IN: University of Notre Dame Press, 2004.

_____. *Lectures on the Philosophy of Religion, Vol. III The Consummate Religion*. Edited by Peter C. Hodgson. Translated by R. F. Brown, P. C. Hodgson and J. M. Stewart with the assistance of H. S. Harris. Oxford: Clarendon Press, 2007.

_____. *Lectures on the Proofs of the Existence of God*. Edited and Translated by Peter C. Hodgson. New York: Oxford University Press, 2011.

Heim, Maximilian Heinrich. *Joseph Ratzinger: Life in the Church and Living Theology: Fundamentals of Ecclesiology with Reference to Lumen Gentium*. Translated by Michael J. Miller. San Francisco: Ignatius Press, 2007.

Hemming, Lawrence Paul. *Benedict XVI: Fellow Worker for the Truth: An Introduction to his Life and Thought*. London: Burns & Oates, 2005.

Hilary, Arthur, Armstrong. *An Introduction to Ancient Philosophy*. London: Methuen & Co Limited, 1968.

Hodgson, Peter "Hegel's Approach to Religion: The Dialectic of Speculation and Phenomenology." In *The Journal of Religion*, Vol. 64, No. 2. Oxford: Oxford University Press, April 1984.

Horkheimer, Max and Adorno, W. Theodor,*Dialectic of Enlightenment: Philosophical Fragments*. Stanford, CA: Stanford University Press, 2002.

Howsare, Rodney. "Why Begin with Love? *Eros, Agape* and the Problem of Secularism." *Communio* 33, (Fall 2016): 423–448. https://www.communio-icr.com/files/HowsareDCEFormat.pdf.

Hünermann, Peter et al., eds. "The Council of Chalcedon," in Henrich *Denzinger*. San Francisco: Ignatius Press, 2012.

Irenaeus of Lyons. *Against Heresies*. Washington, D.C.: Ex Fontibus Co., 2016.

John Paul II. Encyclical Letter on the Relationship between Faith and Reason *Fides et Ratio* (14 September 1998), at The Holy See, http.www.vatican.va.

Kant, Immanuel. *Groundwork of the Metaphysics of Moral*. Translated and Edited by Mary Gregor. New York: Cambridge University Press, 2012.

_____. *Practical Philosophy:* "An Answer to the question: What is the Enlightenment?" Translated by Mary J. Gregor. New York: Cambridge University Press, 2016.

_____. *Religion within the Boundaries of Mere Reason and Other Writing*. Translated and Edited by Allen Wood and George di Giovanni. Chelsea Michigan: Sheridan Books, Inc. 2016.

Kearney, Richard. *Poetics of Modernity Toward a Hermeneutic Imagination: Philosophy and Literary Theory*. New York: Humanity Books, 1995.

_____. Editor. *Strangers, Gods and Monsters, Interpreting Otherness*. London: Routledge Taylor & Francis Group, 2002.

Kreeft, Peter. *Socrates' Children The 100 Greatest Philosophers Volume IV: Contemporary Philosophers*. South Bend, IN: St. Augustine's Press, 2019.

Kierkegaard, Søren. *Either/Or. Either/Or*, Part 1. Edited and Translated by Howard V. Hong and Edna H. Hong. Princeton, NJ: Princeton University Press, 1982.

_____. *Fear and Trembling*. Edited and Translated by Howard V. Hong and Edna H. Princeton, NJ: Princeton University Press, 1983.

Komonchak, Joseph, Collins, Mary, and Lane, A. Dermot. *The New Dictionary of Theology*. Collegeville, Minnesota: The Liturgical Press, 2000.

Küng, Hans. *My Struggle for Freedom: Memoirs*. Grand Rapids, MI: Eerdmans Publishers, 2003.

Lauer, Quentin, S.J. *Hegel's Concept of God*. Albany: State University of New York Press, 1982.

Lonergan, Bernard. *Method in Theology*. Toronto: University of Toronto Press, 2003.

Long, A. A., *The Cambridge Companion to Early Greek Philosophy*. New York: Cambridge University Press, 2011.

Mansfield, Stephen. *Pope Benedict XVI His Life and Mission*. New York: Penguin Group USA Inc., 2005.

McGinn, Bernard, Translator. *Apocalyptic Spirituality: Treatises and*

Letters of Lactantius, Adso of Montier-en-der, Joachim of Fiore, the Franciscan Spirituals, Savonarola. New York: Paulist Press, 1979.

Martin, Nicholas. "*Aufklärung und kein Ende*: The Place of Enlightenment in Friedrich Nietzsche's Thought," *German Life and Letters* 61, no. 1 (January 2008): 79–97. Malden, MA: Blackwell Publishing Ltd, 2008.

Markie, Peter. "The Cogito and its importance," in John Cottingham, Editor. *The Cambridge Companion to Descartes*. New York: Cambridge University Press, 2005.

McCaughey, Mary. *The Church as Hermeneutical Community and the Place of Embodied Faith in Joseph Ratzinger and Lewis S. Mudge*. Bern: International Academic Publishers, 2015.

McGlinchey, Patrick. *Ratzinger's Augustinianism and Evangelicalism*. Bletchley, Milton Keynes: Paternoster Lightning Source, 2017.

McGrath, E. Alister. *The Making of Modern German Christology: From the Enlightenment to Pannenberg*. New York: Basil Blackwell Inc. 1953.

Millare, Roland. "The Wedding Feast of the Lamb Has Begun: The Relationship Between Eschatology and the Liturgy in the Logoscentric Theology of Joseph Ratzinger." STD Dissertation, Mundelein, IL: University of St. Mary of the Lake, 2018.

Mofor, Christian. *Plotinus and African Concepts of Evil: Perspectives in Multi-Cultural Philosophy*. Bern: Peter Lang, 2008.

Müller, Gerhard Ludwig. *Der Glaube ist einfach*. Regensburg: Friedrich Pustet, Verlag, 2007.

Newman, John Henry. *An Essay on the Development of Christian Doctrine*. Indiana: University of Notre Dame Press, 1960.

_____. *An Essay in Aid of a Grammar of* Assent. Indiana: Notre Dame Press, 1979.

Nichols, Aidan. *The Thought of Benedict XVI*. New York: Burns & Oates Press, 2005.

Nietzsche, Friedrich. *On the Genealogy of Morals*. Translated by Walter Kaufmann. New York: Vintage Books, 1967.

_____. *The Will to Power*. Translated by Walter Kaufmann and R. J. Hollingdale. New York: Vintage Books, 1968.

_____. *Ecce Homo*. Translated by Walter Kaufmann. New York, Vintage Books, 1989.

Origen of Alexandria. *On First Principles*. Translated by G.W. Butterworth. South Bend, IN: Ave Maria Press, 2013.

Pascal, Blaise. *Pensées*. Translated by A. J. Krailsheimer. Suffolk: Penguin Books, 1995.

Philo. Volume I: *On the Creation and on the Allegorical Interpretation of Genesis*. Translated by F. H. Colson and G. H. Whitaker. Cambridge MA: Harvard University Press, 1929.

Plotinus. *Enneads I*. Translated by A. H. Armstrong. Cambridge, MA: Harvard University Press, 1989.

_____. *Enneads, III*. Translated by A. H. Armstrong. Cambridge, MA: Harvard University Press, 1993.

Printy, Michael. *Enlightenment and the Creation of German Catholicism*. Cambridge: Cambridge University Press, 2009.

Pursell, Brennan. *Benedict of Bavaria: An Intimate Portrait of the Pope and his Homeland*. New Haven, CT: Circle Press, 2008.

Quasten, Johannes. *Patrology* Vol. I. Westminster, MD: Christian Classics Inc. 1993.

Ratzinger, Georg. *My Brother, The Pope*. Translated by Michael J. Miller. San Francisco: Ignatius Press, 2011.

Ricoeur, Paul. *Freud and Philosophy: An Essay on Interpretation*. Translated by Denis Savage. New Haven, CT: Yale University Press, 1970.

Rowland, Tracey. *Ratzinger's Faith: The Theology of Pope Benedict XVI*. New York: Oxford University Press, 2008.

Schall, James. "On Reading the Pope: Part II," (20, January 2006), http://www.ignatiusinsight.com/features2006/schallreadingbenxvi2jan06.asp.

Schillebeeckx, Edward. *Christ the Sacrament of the Encounter with God*. London: Sheed & Ward Press, 1977.

Schofield, Malcolm and Nussbaum, Martha. Editors. *Language & Logos: Studies in Ancient Greek Philosophy*. New York: Cambridge University Press, 2006.

Schindler, David. "The Redemption of Eros." *Communio* 33, (Fall 2016): 375–399. https://www.communio-icr.com/files/schindlerdc33-3.pdf.

Scola, Angelo. "The Unity of Love and the Face of Man: An Invitation to Read *Deus Caritas Est.Communio*33. (Fall2016):316–345. https://www.communioicr.com/files/scola33-3.pdf.

Seewald, Peter. *Benedict XVI: An Intimate Portrait*. San Francisco: Ignatius Press, 2008.

Soloview, Vladimir Sergaevitch. *A Story of Anti-Christ*. Middletown, DE: Kassock Bros. Publishing Co. 2012.

Spinoza, Baruch. *Tractatus Theologico-Politicus* 4, in *Works*, Vol. 1. Translated by R. H. M. Elwes. New York: Rowman & Littlefield Publishers Inc., 1951.

Schweitzer, Albert. *The Quest of the Historical Jesus*. Minneapolis, MN: Fortress Press, 2001.

Tanner, Norman, S.J. Editor. *Vatican Council II: The Essential Texts*. New York: Image Books, 2012.

Taylor, Charles. *A Secular World*. Cambridge, MA: Harvard University Press, 2007.

Till, Nicholas. *Mozart and the Enlightenment*. London: Faber and Faber, 1992.

Tracey, Rowland. *Benedict XVI: A Guide for the Perplexed*. London: T & T Clark, 2010.

Twomey, Vincent. *Pope Benedict XVI, The Conscience of Our Age: A Theological Portrait*. San Francisco: Ignatius Press, 2007.

Wilcox, Joel. *The Origins of Epistemology in Early Greek Philosophy: A Study of Psyche and Logos in Heraclitus*. New York: Edwin Mellen Press, 1994.